MACMILLAN NETWORK ARCHITECTURE AND DEVELOPMENT

Designing Addressing Architectures for Routing and Switching

Howard C. Berkowitz

MACMILLAN
TECHNICAL
PUBLISHING
U·S·A

International Standard Book Number: 1-57870-059-0

Library of Congress Catalog Card Number: 98-84330

2002   01   00   99   4   3   2   1

Interpretation of the printing code: The rightmost double-digit number is the year of the book's printing; the rightmost single-digit, the number of the book's printing. For example, the printing code 99-1 shows that the first printing of the book occurred in 1999.

Composed in XXX and MCPdigital by Macmillan Computer Publishing

Printed in the United States of America

Trademark Acknowledgments

All terms mentioned in this book that are known to be trademarks or service marks have been appropriately capitalized. Macmillan Technical Publishing cannot attest to the accuracy of this information. Use of a term in this book should not be regarded as affecting the validity of any trademark or service mark.

Warning and Disclaimer

This book is designed to provide information about network addressing. Every effort has been made to make this book as complete and as accurate as possible, but no warranty or fitness is implied.

The information is provided on an as-is basis. The author and Macmillan Technical Publishing shall have neither liability nor responsibility to any person or entity with respect to any loss or damages arising from the information contained in this book or from the use of the discs or programs that may accompany it.

Feedback Information

At Macmillan Technical Publishing, our goal is to create in-depth technical books of the highest quality and value. Each book is crafted with care and precision, undergoing rigorous development that involves the unique expertise of members from the professional technical community.

Readers' feedback is a natural continuation of this process. If you have any comments regarding how we could improve the quality of this book, or otherwise alter it to better suit your needs, you can contact us at softwareengineering@mcp.com. Please make sure to include the book title and ISBN in your message.

We greatly appreciate your assistance.

Vice President
Don Fowley

Associate Publisher
Jim LeValley

Executive Editor
Ann Trump Daniel

Managing Editor
Caroline Roop

Development Editor
Kitty Wilson Jarrett

Project Editor
Theresa Mathias

Copy Editor
Kelli M. Brooks

Indexer
Bront Davis

Acquisitions Coordinator
Amy Lewis

Manufacturing Coordinator
Brook Farling

Book Designer
Gary Adair

Cover Designer
Sandra Schroeder

Proofreader
Megan Wade

Production
Liz Johnston
Brad Lenser
Jeannette McKay
Louis Porter, Jr.

About the Author

Howard C. Berkowitz is an independent consultant in network architecture, working with network operators and internetworking product vendors in defining strategies. He is a Certified Cisco Systems Instructor for Internetwork Design and has developed advanced routing seminars for several organizations.

As an active participant in the Internet Engineering Task Force, he is the author or coauthor of several RFCs in addressing, and his current IETF work includes documents on multihoming and on OSPF network deployment. He has given tutorials on these areas at the North American Network Operators' Group and various industry shows.

His professional experience includes work as a network management product architect and developer of protocol test systems. He has designed network architecture for large users, including the Library of Congress.

Dedications

To Harvey Deitel, who mentored me in the craft of writing books.

To my feline assistants, Clifford and the late Chatterley, who kept up my spirits while writing.

Acknowledgments

I'd like to thank my colleagues in the PIER Working Group for stimulating comments that spawned the idea for this book: Jim Bound, Paul Ferguson, Geert Jan de Groot, Roger Fajman, Matt Holdrege, Dorian Kim, Walt Lazear, Eliot Lear, Will Leland, and Bill Manning. Dave Crocker's RFC 1775, "To be 'on' the Internet," was also a stimulus to my thinking.

Peer reviewers contributed enormously to the book. Thanks to Peter Welcher, Lou Breit, Clare Gough, Kim Hubbard, and Bill McInerney.

My students in Cisco Internetwork Design classes helped me formulate the questions to ask in defining requirements and address plans. Ideas also sprang from my participation in revising that course, and I thank Priscilla Oppenheimer, Peter Welcher, and Kip Peterson for thought-provoking discussions.

Mariatu Kamara helped keep my home life and office sane.

About the Technical Reviewers

Louis Breit, Peter J. Welcher, Clare Gough, and Kim Hubbard contributed their considerable practical, hands-on expertise to the entire development process for *Designing Addressing Architectures for Routing and Switching*. As the book was being written, these folks reviewed all the material for technical content, organization, and flow. Their feedback was critical to ensuring that *Designing Addressing Architectures for Routing and Switching* fits our reader's need for the highest-quality technical information.

Cover Photograph: The Brooklyn Bridge

For more than half a century, New Yorkers had been asking for a bridge across the East River. After much political and technical debate, in January 1870 the New York Bridge Company began construction of the Brooklyn Bridge. Thirteen years and many fatalities and injuries later, the suspension bridge connecting Brooklyn and Manhattan was complete. A brilliant feat of 19th-century engineering, the 1,595-foot-long bridge was 50% longer than any bridge built to that point and was the first bridge to use steel cable wires and pneumatic caissons.

A distinctive feature of the Brooklyn Bridge is the broad promenade above the roadway, which John Roebling, the bridge's engineering designer, accurately predicted "in a crowded commercial city will be of incalculable value." Roebling was also justified in his statement that "as a work of art, and a successful specimen of advanced bridge engineering, this structure will forever testify to the energy, enterprise, and wealth of that community which shall secure its erection."

Contents at a Glance

Table of Contents

Preface

Several years ago, I did a major renovation of my house, an experience that gave me a new perspective on networking. I knew a good deal about specific skills such as plumbing and carpentry, but I had to develop some additional skills: the "big picture" view of the architect, and the ability of the general contractor to integrate the many skilled tasks.

Turning to my own profession, I realized that there was a shortage of these skills in networking. Books tend to be either on the order of a low-level configuration cookbook or at an academic level of interest to protocol implementers. There is a shortage of information on how to deploy substantial networks.

The "standards track" of the Internet Engineering Task Force (IETF) work emphasizes protocol definition and implementation. Deployment issues, such as global Internet addressing, tend to be considered on an ad hoc basis. Inter-provider work in the general Internet is discussed in operational groups, such as the North American Network Operators' Group (NANOG), but NANOG does not produce documentation beyond its meeting minutes and mailing list.

In 1996 and 1997, I was an active participant in an ad hoc IETF working group in the Operations Area, Procedures for Internet/Enterprise Renumbering (PIER). As part of this effort, I co-authored a document, RFC 2071, on why you might need to renumber your IP address space. I wrote a more lengthy document, RFC 2072, on how to renumber routers as part of a renumbering project.

While writing these, I realized that although the IETF was providing guidance on how to renumber an existing network, there was no real document on how to set up the numbering plan for a new network, or how to manage the address space and related mechanisms in an operational network. This book is intended to fill that gap.

—Howard C. Berkowitz, August 1998

Introduction

Readers who will get the most from this book are not beginners in networking, but have had some basic experience in operating networks and are ready to go to the next professional step.

I assume that you, the reader, have already been exposed to IP addressing. If you are like most people, however, you learned a rote approach to the problem of addressing and may not have a real sense of how addresses are used in complex systems. You know the basic layout of an IP address and a subnet mask, but are less familiar with determining the address space requirement for networks of substantial size, designing internal and external address plans, and obtaining globally routable address space. You have done basic routing with RIP or more complex protocols.

The Organization of This Book

This book is arranged in five major parts, which reflect my approach to the design, followed by the building or rebuilding of a real-world network.

Addresses exist to help computers move data. Other than in research networks, however, there is little need to move data unless real-world applications call for them. So your first task is to understand the requirements.

Part I, "Why Address?" begins with requirements analysis. Chapter 2, "Principles Underlying Addressing," reviews key terminology and principles underlying network design and then moves to defining addressing requirements at the user-visible edge of the network. These requirements are best stated in terms of names of application-visible endpoints and the flow among them, which is the theme of Chapter 3, "Application Topology: Naming Endpoints."

Naming is a recurring theme, which complements addressing. I do not believe any serious network can be designed without considering naming, yet most introductory networking presentations ignore or minimize naming. Overemphasizing pure addresses leads to building inflexible networks.

Now you know who will live in the house. The next step is selecting the technologies that will be used to build the house. In Part II, "Foundations of Network Addressing," we examine the specific technologies that use addresses. The addressing discussion begins at the lowest level, the transmission system. Intelligent transmission systems, including Frame Relay and Asynchronous Transfer Mode (ATM), do not neatly fit the layering conventions of the OSI reference model. Little-known extensions to the OSI model, as well as work in the IEEE LAN and ISDN WAN architectures, extend the addressing model to fit current technology. Chapter 4, "Transmission System Identifiers and Logical Address Mapping: A View from the Bottom," establishes the transmission context for medium-independent logical addressing, where IP addresses operate.

IP addressing itself is the focus of Chapter 5, "Classical IP Addressing: An Evolution," and Chapter 6, "Internet Failing: Details at 11." IP addressing has evolved from the original ARPAnet work, which did not foresee the incredible growth of the Internet and of private networks that use IP. The original design of IP addressing is not adequate to deal with the networks of today and tomorrow. Chapter 5 describes basic IP addressing, limitations of the basic model in dealing with modern networks, and workarounds to these limitations appropriate for private networks.

Chapter 6 presents the limits to addressing and routing growth that, at times, have threatened Internet growth. This chapter then explains various architectural strategies that extend the basic IP model, making it scalable to the everincreasing demands of the Internet and of private networks connected to it. Such strategies include Classless Inter-Domain Routing (CIDR), Variable Length Subnet Masking (VLSM), RFC 1918 private address space, and network address translation (NAT).

Modern networks need to operate reliably and have protection against inadvertent and deliberate threats. Chapter 7, "Addressing, Security, and Network Management," examines the role of address-based mechanisms in ensuring network integrity. This chapter is written from an unusual but useful perspective: Security is the broad context of ensuring users can use the resources they need, and traditional network management is a subset of the process of security. Network management deals with configuration, performance, and nonmalicious fault management. Budgeting and planning for security and network management should be done in an integrated way.

After you have selected the technologies on which you can build your architecture, your next task is to prepare the working plans from which the new network is to be built. This is the thrust of Part III, "Drawing the Addressing Architecture," which covers defining what is already there and drawing the overall plan to include both old and new. Chapter 8, "The Existing IP and Non-IP Address Structure: Preparing for Remodeling," considers both existing (and potentially limited) IP usage and handling non-IP protocols within an IP backbone.

Chapter 9, "The Address Plan," guides you in developing a scalable IP addressing structure for your network. It goes beyond your internal requirements and explains how to obtain globally routable address space to meet Internet connectivity requirements. This chapter goes into the complex administrative requirements involved in justifying, obtaining, and operating global address space.

It is now time to build. With the addressing plan in hand, you can now move to configuring the names and addresses into the devices of your network. The chapters of Part IV, "Implementing Network Addressing," provide a structure for building the interrelated configurations of directory services, end hosts, hubs, switches, and routers. Real-world configuration examples illustrate concepts without overwhelming the reader with the arcane details of vendor command languages and menu systems. We wrap up Part IV with selective mechanisms that complement basic addressing, such as tunneling, filters, and bandwidth management.

The thrust of this discussion is to unify and strengthen ideas that really are common to multiple devices, but are all too often treated separately. Layer 2 switching, for example, is presented in a consistent manner that avoids increasingly artificial distinctions among WAN, LAN, and ATM forwarding.

Finally, Part V, "Integration and the Future," helps you plan for managing your addressing mechanisms in the near term, reducing operational support to the necessary minimum. It then discusses strategic issues in planning addressing structures for the future, including multicast addressing and IP Version 6.

PART I

Why Address?

CHAPTER 1

What Is the Problem You Are Trying to Solve?

Any sufficiently advanced technology is indistinguishable from magic.

—Arthur C. Clarke

What is the answer? ...In that case, then what is the question?

—Gertrude Stein

Start at the beginning, go to the end, then stop.

—Lewis Carroll

Networking is like building, or often remodeling, a house. Although nothing happens until the detailed building plans are drawn, before those plans can be prepared, the architect has to know the purpose of the building.

A truly outstanding design for a bank is unlikely to do well as a summer vacation cottage. A wonderfully designed retirement home will fall short as a police station.

Before the detailed design of a network or a physical building can be done, the architect must determine the requirements for the project: Who will use it and what do they expect from it? In preparing the plans, there is definitely room for choosing styles that are known to work based on experience. Professional judgment is also needed to select those new features that make the difference between success and failure in a specific project.

Networking is broader than data alone. Its roots are in voice, and the current trend in networking is to integrate voice and data applications. So it is good to review the better experiences from voice as prerequisites to analyzing the requirements for data networks. There is a tremendous amount of operational experience in telephony that should not be discarded.

Why Consider Addressing?

Look at your telephone. Has its number or area code changed recently? Have you had to learn new area codes to call friends and business associates? Telephone numbers are the first network addresses most people encounter, because the telephone and telegraph network is the oldest of all our forms of electrical communications.

These addresses evolved over time. Different countries have different national conventions for the structure of telephone numbers. The United States and Canada, for example, use the following structure: a three-digit area code (which is omitted for local calls), a three-digit exchange code, and a four-digit line code.

Note

The system of area codes and exchanges is formally called the North American Numbering Plan (NANP).

I still remember my home number while in high school: Redwood 1-3294. It was in area code 201, but that wasn't too important because I had to go through the long-distance operator to call outside my local calling area.

"Redwood?" people today ask. For many years, the telephone system attempted to have mnemonic, pronounceable names for exchanges. Today, Redwood would be 736.

Eventually, North American telephone companies ran out of reasonably pronounceable exchange names. (999, I suppose, could have been called Wyvern 9, but not everyone is familiar with the wyvern, a kind of dragon.)

To make more telephone numbers available, area codes were established for dialing outside the immediate area. This switch did incur costs, including those for creating scripts in autodialers and making changes in business cards, letterheads, and so on. For some time, there was an attempt to reserve exchanges with certain numerals ([2–9], [0–1], [1–9]) for long distance and special service codes. With this system, the exchange number could not contain a 0 or 1 as its second digit. Telephone switching systems assumed that if a 0 or 1 was in the second position, the call was long distance, and the leading three digits should be interpreted as an area code.

This convention significantly restricted the number of available area codes. The convention that long-distance calls would start with 1, regardless of the area code, made many more area codes available. If the called number started with 1, the next three digits could be interpreted as an area code. If the called number did not start with 1, the next three digits could be interpreted as an exchange code within the caller's area code.

Other conventions still applied. Exchange codes ending in 11 did not require a line number, and were reserved for special services, such as directory service (411) and public emergency (911).

> **Note**
>
> *Emergency codes are not standardized worldwide. Australia uses 000, and the United Kingdom uses 999. There are many other variations.*
>
> *There is a lesson here: Don't assume that the American way is the way the rest of the world does addressing. The Internet is based on global conventions rather than those of any given country. Problems arise when eager U.S. lawyers attempt to impose U.S. law on a global system.*

In the early history of the United States, whenever a pioneer became tired of neighbors, it was easy to move westward and find a new place to live. Eventually, however, the westward expansion stopped at the Pacific Ocean. Land was no longer an infinite resource.

Telephone numbers have suffered from the same limits to growth. A heavy user of communications technology may have an individual office telephone number on the public network, an intercom number, a home telephone, a shared facsimile number, an internal network address, an electronic mail address, and a shared voicemail center telephone number. Some people add a pager, a car phone, a home facsimile, and other devices. This sort of requirement has led to the explosion in area codes.

As telecommunications demands increased, it was easy to add new area codes—until area codes became a scarce resource. As you will see in Chapter 6, "Internet Failing: Details at 11," Internet addresses were first assigned as if they were an infinite resource. The successes of the telephone network and the Internet created their own problems.

> **Note**
>
> *When I first came to the Washington, D.C., area, I had one telephone number and worked in a conventional office. Now I'm a telecommuter and my house has four analog telephone lines (telecommuting voice, dedicated data, fax/data, and personal voice), an Integrated Services Digital Network (ISDN) line, and a cellular telephone number. I have much more capability, but I need more telephone numbers.*

The shortage is not as much in phone numbers as in area codes and exchanges inside area codes. An individual phone number might be available in a lightly populated area such as the state of Idaho, but that telephone number is not available for use in Manhattan. And the same telephone number can no longer be unique in area codes 202, 703, and 301. Figure 1.1 shows the various ways codes have evolved.

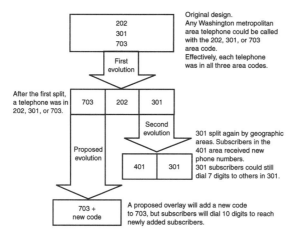

FIGURE 1.1. *Originally, each telephone number was in a single area code, and that area code had clear geographic boundaries. Some special cases emerged, such as the Washington, D.C., area, where a telephone number was reserved in multiple area codes. Newer models include area code splits, where geographic boundaries remain meaningful, and area code overlay.*

Area codes originally covered a single geographic area, but as demand for telephone numbers increased, area codes either split into smaller geographic coverage areas or used an overlay model in which the same geographic area had multiple area codes.

Both overlay and split models have advantages and disadvantages. Overlay models may introduce the inconvenience of dialing a 10-digit number to reach someone across the street; but if the newly overlaid numbers are given to new subscribers, the conversion costs for existing subscribers are minimized.

Although there is unfortunately no standardization as to whether area codes split or use an overlay model, the basis of telephone number assignment is geographical. Internet address allocation began with an organizational basis for assignment and has migrated toward a connectivity provider basis. Some proposals for addressing with the new Internet Protocol version 6 (IPv6), discussed in Chapter 15, "Your Addressing Strategy: Integration for the Present and Planning for the Future," describe alternatives that are very loosely geographically based. The actual basis of allocation is the exchange, which has a loose correspondence to the local phone company as an access to long-distance providers.

Continued demand for more numbers is leading to an overlay model, where a single geographic area may have more than one area code, with new subscribers assigned to the new code. This does make more numbers available, but it eventually means you may need to dial 10, not 7, digits to reach your next-door neighbor.

Periodic renumbering is an unfortunate reality of participation in large public networks. In telephone networks, area code exhaustion forces some existing users to dial 10 digits rather than 7 (in the overlay model) or change their documents to reflect a new area code (in the split model). In the Internet, there are practical operational requirements that tend to force renumbering when a user organization changes its Internet service provider.

Simply saying, "I don't want to renumber," may result in connectivity failures. Various proposals—often originated by lawyers rather than engineers—to have "portable telephone numbers" or equivalent Internet addresses have not yet proven reliable in real-world operations.

One of the major themes of this book is to teach methods—not to avoid renumbering in data networks, but to make the inevitable renumberings as painless as possible.

> **Note**
>
> When I first came to the Washington, D.C., area, the 202 area code for Washington, D.C., proper was interchangeable with the 703 area code for suburban Virginia and the 301 area code for suburban Maryland. I could call a Maryland number from Virginia without prefixing it with 301. Now, I need to dial the 10-digit number, because having the same number effectively taken in area codes 202, 301, and 703 was too wasteful.

The Importance of Addressing in Network Design

The Internet suffers from shortages of computer "telephone numbers," called Internet Protocol (IP) addresses. As in the shortage of area codes, IP address shortages are more of prefixes—the equivalents of country and area codes—than individual line numbers. The idea of a prefix, as the part of an IP address that tells how to reach a given host inside a routing system, is further discussed in Chapter 5, "Classical IP Addressing: An Evolution." Even a small business needs to comply with the rules of global Internet addressing if it is to be connected to the Internet.

What if you are designing networks for an organization that does not plan to connect to the Internet? Why should you play by its rules? Chapter 6 deals with routing issues of the current IP version 4 (IPv4) addressing structure. Chapter 7, " Addressing, Security, and Network Management," examines scaling issues affected by security and network management. Chapter 9, "The Address Plan," discusses building a specific address plan whether you connect to the Internet or not.

Another relevant addressing analogy can be drawn to the plan of streets in a city. In new developments, streets are named by housing developers. The developer who names the streets in a large complex may not be concerned with the level of detail involved with numbering individual houses on the street.

And so it is with enterprise addressing plans. Even when there is no external connectivity, if the organization grows, no single person can be responsible for specifying every "house number" in a large network. There needs to be an overall structure for naming streets and then delegating house numbering to local crews. Enterprises need to have a consistent structure for naming the "streets" that form the communications infrastructure, while individual local area network (LAN) and host administrators take responsibility for numbering computers on the various networks.

Even if an enterprise does not connect to the general Internet, the trend of industry and government is to have different enterprises connect electronically. For example, within a set of banks, each bank might be individually administered and, for security reasons, might choose not to be on the Internet; however, the set may have private interconnections for electronic funds transfer. In the absence of an overall addressing plan, there is a danger of duplication if each bank randomly chooses its own addresses.

Developing a Strategy

In normal human communications, people deal with other people, and organizations, by name. A *name* is who you are, and an *address* represents where you are.

Although computer networks have a charm and beauty of their own, these attributes are unlikely to be seen unless the network serves some purpose. Purposes derive from the users and the computer applications they address. When you first start defining user requirements, do this by name rather than address. The addresses are absolutely necessary for the computers to know, but names are more appropriate for defining application data flow. Addresses of various sorts define the internal topology of the network. The topology by which edge users and applications relate to one another is more naturally described with names.

Note

A worthwhile distinction in network design is between edge functions and backbone functions. Edge devices include all user client and server hosts and their directly attached interconnection devices. Backbone devices provide connectivity among edge nodes. You need to be clear where the edge ends and the backbone starts, because this is often the point at which organizational responsibility ends. Backbone functions often are outsourced.

The separation of responsibility between edge and backbone lies in an interconnection device, such as a router or switch. Both the edge and backbone may contain other interconnection devices, such as wiring hubs in the edge network or large ATM switches in the backbone.

This book begins a systematic approach to defining topologies in an enterprise network. After formalizing the definition of some terminology, Chapter 2, "Principles Underlying Addressing," begins with application topology, the description of the network as users see it. Application topology will first be described with names, and then these names will be mapped to application addresses. The mechanisms of address mapping at the application level are introduced in Chapter 3, "Application Topology: Naming Endpoints." The book then progresses to various logical and physical topologies. An iterative approach is used, refining earlier topologies based on newer information learned at the Open Systems Interconnection (OSI) physical through network, and possibly transport, layers.

Network architects experienced with conventional router networks might question this early emphasis on application flow. As we will explore in detail, new information-forwarding techniques—including LAN switches, Asynchronous Transfer Mode (ATM) switches, and an emerging category of OSI Layer 2/ Layer 3 switches—are best deployed with a knowledge of traffic patterns. These new devices tend to be more specialized than routers in the type of traffic they best handle and more efficient than routers at handling certain types of traffic that require a specific quality of service or other special handling. Routers complement them and are more general in their approach, and quality of service mechanisms indeed are evolving. The overall naming and addressing plan has to reflect the needs of both routers and switches.

Note

OSI layering is used because it is generally familiar. Nevertheless, the OSI model was developed primarily to describe edge-to-edge, application-to-application user communications. Although network architectures are indeed layered, models such as those of IP, ATM, ISDN, IEEE LANs, and so on do not use strict OSI layering. As you read this book, do not try to force OSI layering on every architectural feature; it will not always fit and may simply be confusing.

A Design Methodology

The design methodology we will use has several major phases. Boundaries between phases may not be clear, and information learned in the later phases is apt to refine information collected and decisions made in earlier phases. One of the fine arts of network design, largely taught by experience, is when to stop a phase and go on to the next.

Often, even more experience is needed to know when the results of an earlier phase are simply too flawed to build upon. In such a case, you need to go back, refine the information in the earlier phase, and redo the subsequent phases of design. This is apt to ruin an overly optimistic schedule, and you should plan on a certain amount of going back to refine.

I use an informal six-phase design approach:

1. Determination of top management goals, expectations, budget, and fears

2. Application topology analysis and design

3. Internal topology analysis and design

4. Infrastructure analysis and design (security, network management, and so on)

5. Hardware/software selection and circuit provisioning

6. Deployment planning

High-level requirements analysis, the focus of the remainder of this chapter, deals with the overall business requirements and constraints on the overall enterprise network. An assortment of identifiers tie the users to the underlying requirements, and the grand plan of identifiers is discussed in Chapter 2.

Application topology describes the network as seen by its users, remembering that users do not see an integrated enterprise communications utility. Chapter 3 deals with this topic. Ideally, users are not aware of network communications at all. Rather than the details of connectivity, they see a certain set of services they can use, and the network simply becomes the underlying magical miracle.

Until the user-visible requirements are identified, there is little point in going into internal network design, as discussed in Part II, "Foundations of Network Addressing." People procure routers and other networking devices because they perceive a need in their existing network. They recognize that their existing technology is inadequate and accept that they will need to change. The methodology described here is intended both for new router customers and for users whose router networks "just grew" and who have run into scaling problems.

Beginning network designers start creating networks by drawing routers, hosts, and other "boxes," and drawing lines between them. More experienced network designers begin with a map of interuser flow patterns, deferring hardware specification to a second step. Flows can be any sets of cooperating endpoints, which can be clients and servers, or peer-to-peer partners.

The most experienced designers know that executive management concerns about what the network will do for them must be considered. Managing user/client expectations is one of the most important parts of successful network design. You need to understand top management expectations early in the development cycle. Some of those expectations might be unrealistic, and you will need to educate and negotiate early. A top manager might say he or she never wants users to be aware of a system failure, but he or she might be surprised by the additional expense that would be incurred by a fully redundant network. An acceptable tradeoff might be a service that slows down, but does not stop completely, after a relatively unlikely event.

Internetworking design need not begin with a major management analysis, but nontechnical management factors must be considered. Some managers want the latest in technology whether it is applicable to their problem or not. Other managers want to be extremely conservative in adopting new technology, even though the new technology may be of demonstrated reliability.

Security is an especially difficult area for balancing expectations and implementation realities. The more secure a system, the more inconvenient it will be to use. Users often bypass security features they regard as inconvenient, unless upper management strongly pushes the use of security features.

Use a doctrine derived from that of Willie Sutton, the infamous bank robber. Sutton responded to the query, "Why do I rob banks?" with the answer, "Because that's where the money is." In our case, the question is, "Why do I have internetworks?" and the answer is, "To help information flow among users." Remember who is paying for the network!

Executive Expectations, Spoken and Unspoken

As you deal with executives, it's worth understanding their backgrounds, which may in turn lead to understanding their expectations. Computer communications began in the 1960s, first using direct, limited-range connections between computers and terminals. Use of modems over the telephony network offered wider access to computers. With modems, computers now used a network more widespread and more appropriate to interactive communications than the telegraphy network.

As telecommunications have developed, so have the computers using telecommunications networks for distributed processing. A large part of the development of distributed processing has come from organizational needs and perceived needs, not directly from technological change. Technological change has enabled new organizational strategies.

Beginning with the centrally directed mainframe organization, teleprocessing organization has evolved through several political generations: from mainframe dictatorship to departmental computing, to office automation anarchy, and to federation through networking.

The Mainframe Culture

Just as transatlantic cables are an expensive and critical resource, so were the early computers. Large computer mainframes offered interactive timesharing. To maximize their utilization, access to mainframes was centrally managed. Mainframe vendors and the customer's experts on the mainframe dictated the nature of this access. Access was not designed to meet user needs, real or perceived.

Users would be told, for example, which terminals they would be allowed to use, with no exceptions. The user interface to the computer was a command language sensitive to the efficiency of the computer, not of the human user. This was economically sensible at the time because computer time was more expensive than programmer time.

In the beginning, mainframe managers had total control of interactive and remote batch processing. As shown in Figure 1.2, the mainframe was at the center of the network. Political scientists describe this philosophy as similar to the way kings ruled by divine right.

These local manager priests of computing power were the interpreters of doctrines of computing as decreed by the high priesthood of computer vendors. There were no generally agreed-to standards for computer communications, only the proprietary specifications of vendors.

Note

The traditional strength of the mainframe culture is that it provides reliable, predictable computing services. Its traditional weakness is lack of flexibility. The traditional fear of the mainframe culture is loss of control.

When you obtain the requirements of a manager who grew up with the mainframe culture, be sure you have a clear idea of the expected performance of the network. Also, be sure you have a clear idea of who the manager expects will control the operational network.

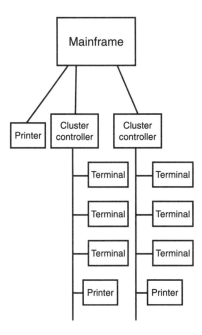

FIGURE 1.2. *Centralized computing: A central mainframe owns all resources.*

There were at least two reasons for the lack of general standards. First, the technology was in its infancy, and there were not yet generally accepted methods for all functions. Second, many vendors, for commercial reasons, really did not want well-understood interconnection strategies. It was a commercial reality that after a vendor had sold a computer to a customer, that customer was inhibited from going to another vendor's product by the extremely high costs of converting from one vendor-specific technology to another. If computers complied with the same interface standards, it would be much easier for the customer to oust one vendor and replace it with another.

The Departmental Computing Culture

Contrary to some public opinion, the Magna Carta did not grant freedom to the people, but merely gave "departmental authority" to the king's barons. When authority passed to the barons of computing (that is, the various large departments of organizations), those barons procured mainframes or smaller departmental minicomputers in accordance with their departmental visions of computing, shown in Figure 1.3. Such visions were not necessarily compatible with the visions of peer departments or with the actual and perceived needs of users in the department. Brick walls of incompatible, vendor-specific networking technologies tended to separate these departments.

Each of these departmental technologies had its own, separately managed, addressing system. Conflict arose only when peer systems were interconnected using a common addressing method.

Note

The strength of departmental computing is its responsiveness to the needs of its department. Its weaknesses include poorer operational support tools than are available on mainframes and the tendency for different departmental systems to be separately procured and incompatible.

When determining executive attitudes and dealing with executives whose experience is with departmental computing, be sure you understand who is responsible for the functions in each department. Determine if there is a single architectural point of contact for defining the interactions among departments. Identify known incompatibilities.

Be sure your eventual design shows a decentralized approach for responding to routine changes. At the same time, make an effort to educate top management that some level of overall architecture is necessary to facilitate communications among departments. Emphasize that security and Internet connectivity usually should be centrally controlled.

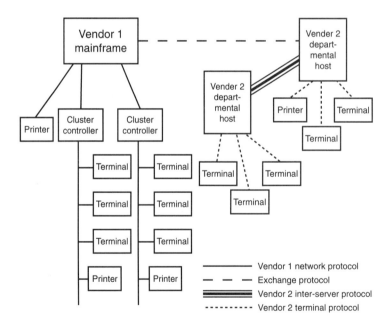

FIGURE 1.3. *Departmental computing involves separately administered computing systems, often without unifying technical architecture.*

Figure 1.3 shows the proliferation of protocols necessary for machines to talk to one another in a departmental computing environment where each department's vendors specified its own protocols. Each vendor had at least one major protocol, such as IBM System Network Architecture (SNA). Some, such as Digital Equipment Corporation, had multiple specialized protocols, such as DECnet and LAT. It was sometimes necessary to have exchange protocols that did nothing but link pairs of vendor computers. Exchange protocols sometimes were defined by pairs of vendors, but neutral, standards-based protocols (such as the IP family) emerged.

At the Versailles Conference deciding the new political order after World War I, the French diplomat Clemenceau is quoted as saying (in French, of course), "Must every little language have its own country?" Organizational diplomats can also cry in pain over the proliferation of incompatible departmental computers. Although these solutions might be more attuned to the needs of individual departments, they failed to meet general organizational goals and were a major obstacle to general reorganizations.

Users requiring access to different departmental computers often required separate terminals on their desks. At this stage of network development, integration of voice and data services was a dream, if it had become that specific.

My Early Experience with Accessing Multiple Computers

In 1972 or so, I was excited by my first experience with intelligent network switching. Rather than having three separate terminals on my desk, I was able to have a single physical terminal switch among three dedicated lines, with a mere twist of a knob on a mechanical switch (see Figure 1.4).

It seemed exciting at the time. But the tradition of separate devices continued.

Perhaps the most ironic example of incompatible computing in my experience came when I worked at the Corporation for Open Systems, a research center for interoperable OSI and ISDN protocols. Our receptionists did additional data entry functions, so they needed keyboards at their desks. The reception desk—the first look at the vendor-independent future—sported a Sun UNIX workstation for the engineering network, a Wang terminal for the office automation system, a PC for finance, and a Macintosh for graphics.

Many executives used to departmental computing see no incongruity in this scene. I regard it more as a gathering of lemmings, preparing to drown themselves in a sea of incompatibility.

You need to educate executives of this mindset that multivendor interoperability is quite practical given reasonable adherence to a common architecture. You also need to be ready to provide ways to connect islands of vendor-specific communications through the ocean of your backbone.

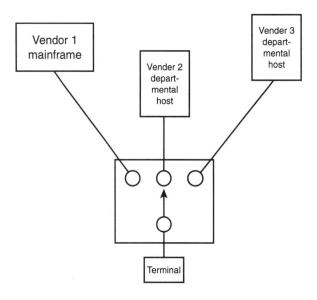

FIGURE 1.4. *The high technology of a three-way mechanical switch.*

Another characteristic of this period was that end users—those who used a computer to help them in their main work—were unhappy. They were unhappy with centralized computer services because of their lack of flexibility. They were unhappy with departmental computers because they did need access to data other than their department's. Above all, they wanted a sense of being in control. It appeared that the personal computer, which appeared to transfer power into the hands of the user and not require programmers, was the answer.

The Desktop Culture

Political revolutionaries, as well as communications revolutionaries, desire to transfer power. In the practice of revolution, however, power does not always transfer to those without it; it may stay within the revolutionary leadership.

The Cultural Revolution of the People's Republic of China, among other revolutions, is an example of an effort to impose political correctness, or something believed to be the correct solution to all problems by the leadership, on a varied set of problems. Where the little red book, *The Thoughts of Chairman Mao Tse-Tung,* was the tool of the cultural revolution, many user organizations felt the personal computer was the tool of the user independence movement. Many of those organizations learned that user independence was a mixed blessing.

With the availability of personal computers, users rebelled against what they perceived as the fascism of the centralized computer center priesthood. Personal computers could respond to the needs of the immediate user. With the advent of LAN technology in the mid-1970s, it became possible to build simple user-controlled networks, as shown in Figure 1.5.

Users were not always aware of the operational impacts of their quick implementations. Popular user solutions emphasized plug-and-play technologies requiring minimum user involvement in network management. Plug and Play, in small networks, avoided complex addressing planning. AppleTalk still has very effective plug-and-play in small networks, and autoconfiguration methods are prominent in the emerging IP version 6.

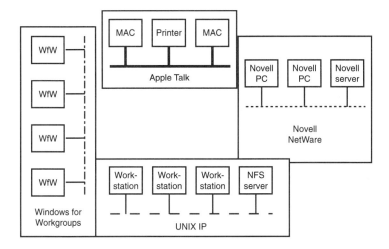

FIGURE 1.5. *Desktop computing offered flexibility, but it also turned the administration of mission-critical resources over to end users untrained in system support. The differing networks could not intercommunicate; they were sealed from one another.*

Some simple and reliable solutions for small networks achieved simplification by restricting the number of computer addresses that could be interconnected. Other simplifications reduced speed compared with that of high-capacity networks. Such restrictions mean that a personal computer network solution might not easily scale to a large network. Techniques that wasted bandwidth, such as the broadcasting in NetBIOS and earlier Novell LANs, worked acceptably with 200 devices but not with 20,000. Unfortunately, many upper managers did not realize that the smaller solutions could not grow to large scale without reengineering.

Many solutions were first deployed using early Microsoft or Novell workgroup operating systems. The networking protocols of such operating systems assumed all hosts were connected to a common LAN. On this LAN, bandwidth was effectively unlimited, and it was convenient to use broadcasts to let clients and servers find one another.

Broadcast-intensive protocols, however, do not scale well over slower wide area links. After an application originally deployed with personal computers grew to multiple sites interconnected with WAN links, severe scalability problems arose.

Note

Personal computing's strength is its responsiveness and potential for low cost. Its weaknesses lie in the lack of troubleshooting skills of end users and the capability to scale personal computer–based systems to large numbers of users or large amounts of data.

I remember well, when doing user support, explaining to an end user how to fix his problem. My last instruction was, "Restore your files from your last backup."

He responded, "What's a backup?" Mainframe staffs might have been bureaucratic, but they were used to the idea of preparing for recovery from system failures. End users tended not to think about failures until they experienced them.

Some users continued using centralized solutions; some kept their local solutions. Virtually all approaches were incompatible. This resulted in a chaotic period analogous to that which took place in China, when Mao encouraged "a hundred flowers [to] bloom" with new ideas on revolution.

Networks, as shown in Figure 1.6, were out of control. Reliability dropped horribly, in part because there were so many protocols in use, the support staff could not maintain a high skill level in all of them.

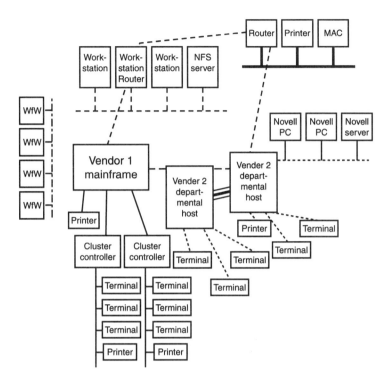

FIGURE 1.6. *Anarchy in computing: design as if by a committee of cats. Departmental, mainframe, and desktop computing mixed chaotically in many organizations. The need for generally accepted protocols became more and more apparent.*

This seeming freedom caused even greater incompatibilities. It became apparent to the industry in general that some level of standardization was necessary in the interfaces between different computers. In other words, while the individual computers could continue to have unique capabilities, the physical and logical "plugs" between them had to follow some common standards. This means that end users would not see changes in the services they now use, but a more efficient infrastructure would support these services.

Open Systems

The inadequacy of vendor-specific definitions led to the open systems movement. There is not a single pure definition of open system, but an open system specification will include a freely available set of well-defined interfaces to the technology being defined. In the purest definition of open systems, the interfaces and functions they access have been defined by a public consensus process.

Different organizations develop this consensus with different levels of formality. The Internet Engineering Task Force (IETF) has a pragmatic approach of "rough consensus and running code," and "letting the market decide," among alternatives. Other standards bodies operating at a governmental level—such as the International Organization for Standardization (ISO) or the International Telecommunications Union (ITU)—have a more formal, slower process. The slower and more formal process of the formal standards bodies led in part to the OSI protocols being largely superceded by the IP protocols. Another practical factor was that free or low-cost IP implementations were available from subsidized research, while vendors tried to recover development costs of OSI products, making them quite expensive.

Superceded may be charitable; the OSI protocol suite never really became common in commercial products. Besides the slow process of standardization, high cost and failures of different vendor products to work with one another were critical factors.

From personal experience, the design approach for OSI protocols was to have extensive discussions among vendors about what the protocol should do, followed by developing a paper specification. During the development process, there was no requirement to implement even prototype code and test it. The lack of real-world input led to a huge number of features creeping into the protocols. Many of these features were optional, so different implementations easily could select a different, incompatible set of options.

Public-domain implementations of IP protocols were available, but OSI implementations were funded by individual vendors. Those vendors wanted to recover their development costs, so OSI code often cost tens or hundreds of thousands of dollars, while IP code came bundled with UNIX.

The OSI architecture, as opposed to most of the OSI protocols, has survived, but has evolved. In Chapter 4, "Transmission System Identifiers and Logical Address Mapping: A View from the Bottom," you will see how the original separation of the lowest OSI layers has evolved into a structure with additional sublayers and new boundaries.

Features of some OSI protocols, such as the X.500 directory service, autoconfiguration methods at the network layer, and so on, have been incorporated into evolving IP protocols.

In networking practice, the IP suite (widely called TCP/IP) is the clear open standard approach. Proprietary networking solutions, such as those of Microsoft, Novell, Digital, and so on, have recently tended to migrate to IP strategies at the internetworking level. These vendors still have proprietary software mechanisms for the end hosts (for example, clients and servers).

OSI begins with a Reference Model, which is a systematic approach to talking about networking [ISO 1984]. Although the OSI protocols themselves have not gained wide usage, it is still perfectly meaningful to use OSI terminology to talk precisely about other communications architectures. Dominant protocols such as the TCP/IP suite, as well as major proprietary protocols, draw significantly from OSI formal description methods.

The OSI architecture was developed in the late 1970s; the core reference model was published in 1984. Formal network architecture continued to evolve. OSI working groups themselves developed refinements, and major architectural improvements in the architecture came from telecommunications and LAN standards bodies. The refinements, discussed further in Chapter 4, include better handling of management methods and appropriate sublayering to deal with hardware independence in transmission technologies.

ISDN was developed for telecommunications; its architectural model is richer than OSI's and is much better at integrating management functions. ISDN's methods of describing management can be used with the OSI and IP models. It contains features that complement OSI architecture, especially the separation of control and management protocols from user information transfer. This separation allows much better specification of functions such as routing information exchange.

Other important work comes from the Institute of Electrical and Electronic Engineers' Project 802 on LANs, especially in the idea of sublayering the OSI layers to deal with hardware realities. As a practical set of protocols, OSI did not meet its early promise. There was a perceived war between OSI and the IP suite, and the latter dominates today's marketplace. It's perhaps too strong a statement to say IP won; rather, the fighting stopped and the two camps allied with one another. Many current Internet protocols contain features born in OSI work.

Even proprietary software from Microsoft, Novell, Banyan, and Apple increasingly uses IP as the lower-level communications suites. Proprietary lower-level protocols are gradually being replaced by IP.

Although each of these protocol families has its own addressing structure, the world is becoming IP-centric. Proprietary protocol addressing will persist at the edge of a primarily IP backbone. New hybrid switching techniques involve both IP and Layer 2 addressing, but are complementary to IP. Your network design should be based on IP, with other protocols treated as special cases.

We often speak of *legacy* protocols as ones that are not the primary mechanism for new applications, but must be supported in the new environment because the older applications are essential and cannot easily be changed.

Most vendors of proprietary or legacy protocols appear to be placing their software development budget into application-oriented services that run over the network. If you use a proprietary operating system, understand your vendor's strategic networking direction. Microsoft originally used the broadcast-intensive NetBIOS upper layer protocols over nonroutable lower layers as its default, but newer Windows versions default to IP stacks. The NetBIOS application interface has been retained, but its broadcast functions are being replaced with IP-based services that do not use broadcasts. NetBIOS simply does not scale to large network size.

NetBIOS, in its original form, had two problems that limited scalability. NetBIOS itself is an upper layer protocol, specifically at the OSI session layer. Early NetBIOS implementations make extensive use of broadcasts for clients and servers to find one another. Broadcasts do not scale well to WANs, or to large LANs.

NetBIOS upper layer information was most often transported directly over the data link layer. This transport mechanism, called NetBEUI or NetBIOS Frame Format (NBF), could not pass directly through routers. It was limited to the size of pure bridged networks at Layer 2, or required software translation to let it work with routed networks.

Microsoft has been evolving NetBIOS to use a directory function, including the IP Domain Name Service, at the upper layers, avoiding the need for broadcasts. At the lower layers, NetBIOS is encapsulated in TCP and is routable over IP networks.

Novell also is moving to IP, and Banyan is adopting a similar strategy.

Note

It makes little sense for Novell, locked in life-or-death competition with Microsoft, to expend resources enhancing the IPX protocol suite when IP will adequately serve the functions of IPX. By deemphasizing IPX, Novell frees development resources to concentrate on its application services, where it has strong competitive products.

The proprietary architecture with the most independent viability is IBM's, due to the tight coupling between mainframes and the underlying Systems Network Architecture (SNA) communications. Even IBM, however, has recognized IP compatibility and includes IP support in many of its formerly proprietary products.

C H A P T E R 1 WHAT IS THE PROBLEM YOU ARE TRYING TO SOLVE?

27

Network as Utility

From the extremes of centralized mainframes and wildly undisciplined departmental computing, a common network evolved as the unifying political and technical solution. Users and centralized computer departments could continue to use their preferred technologies because all implementations could effectively connect to a shared network. Such shared networks, at first, unified computer networking within organizations such as businesses and government organizations. The term *enterprise network* has come into use as a generic description of an organization-wide network; it applies to business, government, and utility networks.

Enterprise networks require a degree of standardization in the interfaces between communicating components. Because the initial enterprise networks were within single organizations, a high-level decision maker could dictate the standard interconnection architecture to be used. In practice, within a single organization, this architecture could often be vendor specific, such as IBM Corporation's Systems Network Architecture, Digital Equipment Corporation's Digital Network Architecture, and so on. Most components from these major vendors followed the vendor architecture, and many third-party vendors built independently manufactured devices that followed these vendor rules.

In enterprise networks, a central authority has to set the overall addressing policy, although its administration can be delegated.

Current practice, however, emphasizes using open specifications to interconnect different vendors' systems. From a networking standpoint, IP is the real-world standard for linking multivendor systems. IBM's Advanced Peer-to-Peer Networking (APPN) is probably the only serious contender for enterprise networks, but is not widely used. APPN appeals to some existing IBM shops but is unlikely to grow other than in existing IBM shops.

In an enterprise network, shown in Figure 1.7, the network is operated independently of the hosts, but the network manager provides services to hosts. Think of the telephone network, in which the telephone service provider is not responsible for the content of conversations.

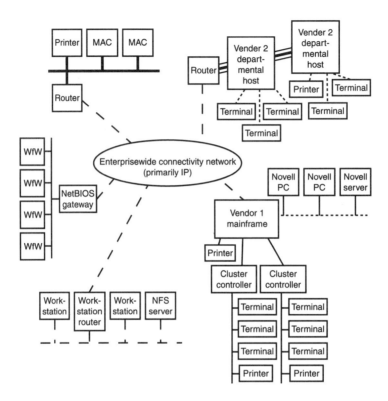

FIGURE 1.7. *An enterprise network. IP provides most connectivity, although some Layer 2 techniques, such as ATM, complement IP.*

The logical next step is to combine both computer and noncomputer (for example, voice and images) services in the enterprise network.

Note

The industry has gone back and forth between integrating voice and data and separating these services. They were separated either by buying them from different carriers, some specializing in voice and some in data, or by the user buying dedicated circuits and multiplexing separate voice and data channels onto them. Today's trend is to integrate them, especially using frame relay and ATM.

The trend toward integration follows a period when data and nondata services were procured separately. That period, in turn, followed a period in which users consolidated bandwidth onto which they multiplexed data and digitized voice. Both in high fashion and in networking, styles come and go.

Large commercial and government organizations often build a backbone network among their major facilities, using transmission technologies that support both voice and data services. These technologies for managing quality of service and prioritizing real-time traffic such as voice include frame relay, ATM, and, in early deployment, voice and video over IP. Such a network allows access to all computer services in the organization.

Interenterprise Networks: Extranets and Internet Commerce

As organizations develop enterprise networks, opportunities arise for interconnecting enterprise networks. Manufacturers commonly set up automated parts-ordering services for their assembly facilities to order parts from suppliers. Financial organizations interconnect their networks for funds transfers. Even individuals have needs for access to multiple networks, such as their employers' corporate networks, cable television networks, the public telephone network, and electronic tax filing networks. Mobile (that is, cellular) telephones, pagers, and facsimile systems also are accessed as specialized networks, usually more associated with telephone than data services.

A consequence of this wide range of network needs is frequent splitting of telephone area codes to provide additional telephone numbers for the increasing range of services. In several metropolitan areas, there are more network addresses than people.

Networks of all types are becoming more pervasive. *Universal networking* leads to yet another model of communications and organization: the strategic interconnection of the separately managed networks of multiple organizations. Such interconnection is selective, and usually private, as opposed to the public information sharing model of the Internet. Interenterprise networks link multiple independently operated enterprise networks. Linking networks with different organizational policies introduces a wide range of privacy, financial, and security challenges. The desirability of such internetworking, however, is such that these challenges must be met. Linked networks tend to reduce cost while providing more flexibility to the organization.

There is no generally accepted term for a set of interconnected private networks, such as a credit card authorization system serving multiple banks. The function sometimes is called interenterprising, or the set is interenterprising. Other terms have been used, including extranet and multinet. (Extranet is used here.)

Given that the constituent networks of an interenterprise environment are owned and operated by different organizations, it cannot be assumed that each network will be built from a single vendor's components. Vendor-specific definitions of the interfaces between networks, computers, and users are clearly inadequate for interenterprise networks because there will be no consensus on which vendor's definition to use. Business process functions, such as just-in-time ordering to minimize inventory, are impossible without reliable, secure extranets.

The Internet

As networking becomes a more fundamental way to do business, it becomes necessary to interconnect networks managed by different organizations, organizations that do not always trust one another. On a worldwide basis, however, it is increasingly necessary to interconnect networks operated by different organizations. A network comprising interconnected networks is often called an *internet*. Note the lowercase *i*. (The extranets described in the previous section are examples of such lowercase internets.)

When participating in the Internet, you must follow global addressing conventions as well as those conventions appropriate to your enterprise network.

> ### Note
>
> *A generic lowercase* internet *is a set of interconnected networks. Some people say it can use any protocol, but the most common usage is that the set of networks use the IP protocols—although the term* internet *implies nothing about administrative relationships.*
>
> *The uppercase* Internet *is the set of interconnected IP networks that cooperate in the global Internet routing structure. The* Internet *refers to a specific set of interconnected networks that generally use the Internet Protocol Suite. (More precise definitions are developed in subsequent chapters.) Networks connected to the Internet need not be full, integrated service enterprise networks, but can simply link related functions (for example, research, funds transfer) of different organizations.*
>
> *An* intranet *uses IP protocols, and indeed typically uses Internet-oriented applications like Web browsers (as opposed to more corporate-oriented applications like cc:Mail). The general implication of* intranet *is that it either does not connect to the general Internet at all or is isolated behind a firewall.*
>
> *An extranet is a set of interconnected IP networks under different administrative authorities (although with some overall coordinating body) that does not connect to the general Internet. It may be huge, such as military or interbank networks, but the lack of connection to the general Internet is usually quite deliberate (most often for security reasons).*

Basic IP addressing is discussed in Chapter 5 with the underlying transmission media considerations in Chapter 4. Chapter 6 is most definitive about the overall Internet structure of interconnection, but Chapter 3 deals with the naming (as opposed to addressing) structure of the Internet. Chapter 5 deals with the basic structure of IP addresses, and Chapter 9 with Internetwide address management.

Network technology differs among organizations. Some organizations emphasize LAN technology; some packet switching; some integrate voice and data; some separate them into different networks.

Perhaps above all, different organizations use different computing and communications architectures. Some internets are intended as general purpose highways for messages in the formats of multiple architectures; some accept traffic in the format of only a single architecture.

C H A P T E R 1 What Is the Problem You Are Trying to Solve?

31

There are many ways to use the Internet:

- For electronic commerce, offering products and services

- As an information resource for your own staff

- As a generalized communications structure for messages and, increasingly, voice and images

- To provide technical support for your customers

- For secured links to strategic business partners, tunneling through the Internet

- To enable workforce distribution with mobile users and telecommuters

- To link campuses in your organization via secure tunnels in virtual private networks operated by ISPs (these may be separate from the general Internet)

Integrated Service and Multimedia Networking

Interenterprise networks are in wide use, generally for data. There are fundamental differences in the way data and nondata communications need to be handled, but the current thrust of networking finds ways to integrate them.

At a fairly basic level, it is necessary to reduce all types of communications—whether voice, data, or image—to common bit formats for transmission. Samuel F. B. Morse was more right than he realized in 1845, when the telegraph was introduced as the first—and first digital—form of electrical communications.

Remember that there is a distinction between the integration of the communications transmission system and the integration of applications that use more than one type of communications in an integrated way. There are several kinds of integrated applications:

- *Integrated voice/data*—Applications that use computers to control the coordinated use of telephone switching and terminal-oriented data display.

- *Multimedia*—Terminal inputs affect the order in which more than one type of information (for example, sound, moving pictures, characters) is presented to the user. In multimedia, the user still has a clear sense of controlling a computer.

- *Virtual reality*—An interactive process between the user and computer-generated system, with multiple types of information flowing in both directions.

Even though images and data are converted to common bits, there are special transmission requirements for signals that people will directly see and hear. Although computers can resequence out-of-order messages, sound and sight become completely confused if out of order. Humans are also less tolerant of variable transmission delay than are computers.

ISDN prescribes the basic unified architecture. Its introduction has been delayed as much for legal and financial reasons as for technical ones. One technical reason that has limited the introduction of integrated services is high-speed switching. The cell relay and ATM techniques seem to be adequate solutions to these needs.

Another technical issue is transmission capacity. Although a voice channel commonly is converted to a 64Kbps bit stream, a broadcast-quality video channel can require up to 90Mbps. Such channels can be compressed into slower data streams. High-resolution services have greater needs. Nevertheless, the bandwidth requirements of voice are perhaps three orders of magnitude greater than those of typical terminal interaction, and the bandwidth requirements of broadcast-quality video are three orders of magnitude greater than those of voice.

Lower-quality video can be perfectly adequate for many business videoconferencing or remote education applications. The first digital transmission systems were cost-justified in the context of a video experiment called Picturephone.

AT&T introduced Picturephone in the early 1960s. It was advertised as a less-than-broadcast-quality interactive telephone system that would be used in the home as well as business.

Picturephone came along before its time. The lack of computing power in the user terminals necessitated prohibitively expensive transmission lines. The privacy aspects of Picturephone had not been thought out. Optical rather than electronic transmission technologies appear adequate to support these speeds. There are, however, great concerns about the cost to replace existing telephone cabling.

Social as well as technical factors will affect these new applications. Assume that you have a home videophone. Would you want to have to get dressed to answer the telephone?

Failed Leading-Edge Applications

Many of what appear to be leading-edge applications have been tried in the past. They may have failed due to a lack of an enabling technology that is available today. They may not have become widely deployed due to social, political, or legal considerations, but may be ready for deployment in a changed environment.

In 1970, I worked on medical applications that interviewed patients in ordinary language and produced a medical history report in medical language. I would have called it an expert system today, but the medical group in which I worked did not know that term. So it is in many medical applications, where applications work before the formal information technology terminology is defined.

An experimental installation at Boston's Logan Airport combined a one-way television link from the remote location to a physician at Massachusetts General Hospital, a two-way voice link, and an additional voice-quality link for sending analog electrocardiograms. The video link allowed the physician to see the patient and examine rashes, something that needs color and high resolution to diagnose. The physician talked with the patient and nurse over the voice link. This was an early example of a *telepresence* application, where the physician and patient share the same virtual reality of being physically together.

Medical telepresence applications work, as demonstrated by the Logan Airport system. At the time, there were technological limitations in getting the necessary bandwidth into remote areas that needed the specialized medical services. Today, telepresence consultation is becoming much more common. Military medical facilities use it routinely, and it is being explored as a cost-effective way to bring specialized medical services to remote areas served by managed care programs.

The Reverse Executive Summary: Discovering Executive Fears and Expectations

Consultant reports traditionally begin with an executive summary, giving a brief discussion of the report for people who are too busy to read the detailed contents. It is my contention that network designs should begin with acquiring a reverse executive summary, which identifies the issues of most concern to upper managers.

These concerns are not necessarily quantifiable. One of the more critical elements is understanding the attitudes of top management. Some top managers are risk averse, which, in design terms, translates into emphasizing well-proven technologies, even those that have less cost-effectiveness or flexibility than newer but shakier methods. Such managers may demand that the network be built around the exact needs of the legacy protocol, in its exact present form, rather than in a form that meets legacy needs but efficiently shares bandwidth.

Risk avoidance can be a rational strategy when the cost of a risk factor happening—if a technology containing that risk were adopted—could jeopardize the mission. You need to understand top managers' attitudes about risk, quantifying it if at all possible. How much risk is the manager willing to take for a cost reduction or better performance?

Other managers are early adopters. They want to use the latest technology, with the intention of gaining strategic advantage. As a responsible network designer, you will sometimes have to restrain managers, diplomatically, when they are interested in a technology that really is inappropriate to the design goals. Advanced technologies often seem "ready for prime time" in the trade press or at industry shows, but may not be of real production quality.

Business politics often play a large role. Although the greatest operational efficiencies usually are gained by unified design of a single enterprise utility, internal politics often dictate that certain organizations want to control all resources associated with them, or want special treatment in the network. Are there politics in your (or your client's) organization? What are the financial implications of budget and revenue generated by the network?

What growth will come in the distribution of workers? Will applications themselves have significant changes in volume of traffic or quality of service requirements?

Do you need to connect to other organizations or to the general Internet? If you do need such connectivity, with what degree of security and reliability?

Money: The Ultimate Decision Factor

A crucial factor for the network designer can be understanding the way in which top management looks at the cost of the enterprise network. If minimal acquisition cost, rather than life cycle cost, is a major driving factor, this needs to be reflected in the design. The designer may need to design a flexible naming and addressing plan that accommodates future enhancements but minimizes the initial implementation cost.

See Chapter 9 and Chapter 15 for a discussion of flexible, scalable strategies.

Other naming and addressing strategies may be more appropriate when the overall design is being judged on life cycle cost.

What have these things to do with addressing? The most basic consideration is that addresses, and to a lesser extent names, change through the life of a system. Extra effort at the beginning of system design, effort that makes the system "renumbering friendly," will have an effect on initial cost. Several studies have shown that there are two major cost elements over the life cycle of most enterprise networks:

- *WAN line costs*—Often 75% or more of the total cost.

- *Support cost*—Support takes 75% of the 25% remaining total cost.

Readdressing, which might be needed due to reorganization or workforce relocation, can be a major part of the support cost. Renumbering-friendly practices tend, in any case, to be good network design practices, but they increase the initial cost.

Another major factor in enterprise network costing lies in the extent to which the enterprise will be visible on the Internet and, to a lesser extent, to business partners. Under the present strategies, there are no direct charges for globally unique network address space, but this may change in time. There certainly are administrative and flexibility costs associated with having address space that is visible on the Internet.

Rekhter and Li observed in RFC 1518 that the economic value of having globally visible Internet addresses is intimately tied to making information available to outside Internet users. If the Internet cannot provide outside connectivity due to scaling issues discussed in Chapter 6, then Internet-unique addresses lose their economic value.

What does this mean? Upper managers must bear in mind that there is a direct economic benefit associated with addressing plans that support the growth of the Internet. Some of these measures, without question, will inconvenience the enterprise. At present, if it is our desire to keep the Internet running, there are no general alternatives to these measures. These measures are likely to require periodic internal renumbering.

A reasonable parallel exists in the changing area codes in the NANP. As described earlier in the chapter, it might become necessary to dial 10, rather than 7, digits to reach even a local destination.

While businesses grumble about the costs associated with area code changes, there is general acceptance that a telephone number must change when the subscriber moves to a new geographic area. If I moved to Silicon Valley, in area code 408, I certainly would not expect to keep the low-order seven digits of my telephone number.

Yet many Internet users have made the assumption that they "own" their Internet addresses, and the Internet as a whole must permit them to move those addresses wherever they want, without any loss of connectivity. This indeed was a practical assumption in the early Internet, when the scaling issues discussed in Chapter 6 had not yet emerged.

We won't go into the technical details at this time, but please accept that universal address portability is no longer compatible with continued growth of the Internet. There are ways to have location-independent identifiers, but they use names, not addresses.

Attitudes toward growth and scalability must be understood and placed in the context of finance.

Topological Growth

Growth in general is a critical issue. Will growth be in terms of geographic locations, in numbers of users at a slower-growing number of sites, or minimal?

Even before we get into the mechanics of addressing, consider this basic problem: Each unique transmission medium, in general, needs a unique address. Think of this address as a street name, which has subordinate building numbers.

Whenever a new site is added, even a small one, it will need at least two "street" addresses: the street that connect it to other sites (that is, the WAN media) and the street for its local devices. It isn't hard to see that the more sites, the more higher-level (with respect to host) addresses will be needed.

When Internet connectivity is required, globally unique addresses are needed. An organization now needs to justify its requests for address space. Authorities that control address allocation may very well demand that the enterprise prove that it has exhausted its current allocation, that efficient policies are used to manage the existing and planned space, and that the growth estimates for new addresses are realistic. Address authorities may want auditable documentation of the business patterns involved.

There may be fundamental changes in topology due to changes in the places work is done. What types of users, and how many of them, will be mobile (for example, sales and service personnel)? A mobile user constantly changes location.

In telecommuting, designated workers work all or part of the time at their homes or specialized telecommuting centers. How will the home users connect? Typical home users will need voice, data, and probably facsimile communications; a single phone line will not suffice.

Are mergers and acquisitions in the future? This will drive needs for globally unique addresses or choices to use address-translating gateways.

Application Growth

The nature of applications, including both bandwidth and connectivity, affects growth. A system currently adequate for simple terminal–to–central-host connectivity for text data does not work for videoconferencing among many parties.

You should also consider several software factors before selecting the communications infrastructure because applications and supporting software really determine the amount and characteristics of data to be transmitted.

Pay close attention to the application architecture. The user interface defines the type of data to be handled. Slightly lower-level application services define caching, compression, and so on. End-to-end quality of service is a transport layer function, and congestion control and router-level resource management is a network layer function.

Application architecture affects both the design of the actual application and the selection and tuning of the end-to-end transport and applications software that runs on end hosts. Even though an application needs to send large volumes of data, it may be better to improve the end systems than the "pipes" between them.

Compression: An Example of Tradeoffs

Much application data contains redundancies, and thus is a candidate for compression. In virtually every case, more effective compression is available on the host system than in communications devices such as routers. This isn't because host designers are smarter than router designers, but the host software designers can know more about the data characteristics.

Compression is an especially good candidate for a host-based solution because there is special knowledge available to the host that cannot be available to the internetwork.

End system compression itself involves tradeoffs. Compression is CPU intensive. If the end systems have fast processors, software compression may be effective. Older end systems may need add-on compression cards, which may not have as wide a range of available algorithms.

The processing power needed to handle a single workstation's compression may be moderate and within the capabilities of the workstation. Nevertheless, older workstations may not have the power to do complex compression and might lack the hardware slots to plug in a special-purpose compression board.

Even if it is not feasible to put compression in each workstation, before committing to router-based compression, consider linking the clients to a new server. Such a server would do application-level compression, then transfer files to the router. Essentially, it is a compression proxy and might add other proxy services such as firewalling.

Router-based compression might be appropriate and might be aided by plug-in compression hardware. Compression algorithms appropriate for full motion video of reasonable quality is not the same algorithm that's best for high-resolution medical graphics, which in turn isn't the same algorithm that's best for digitized voice. Each of these algorithms is best for a particular application and can be coded into the application. Router-based compression, however, usually can't know the details of the data being compressed and has to use a more general algorithm.

In general, there may be more CPU resources available when you consider the set of hosts, each doing the compression for its own application traffic. This is not an absolute rule and can be a challenge for system designers. Hosts might be old and underpowered or not have the slot available to plug in a specialized compression board. It might be too expensive to add compression hardware or software to each of a large number of end hosts.

Even if the end host is not the place to do compression, that place may not be the router. It might be appropriate to put in a server responsible for doing application compression on behalf of all the end hosts and let this server send to the router.

More Tradeoffs: Should a Feature Be on Routers or Hosts?

More complex issues arise when a given function can be done with equivalent resources on either internetwork devices or on hosts. When analyzing tradeoffs in such complex situations, always remember to include not just the hardware and software component cost, but also the personnel costs of making changes.

Let's consider a generic example of trading off the costs between doing things on a host and doing things in networking devices such as routers. Figure 1.8 shows a system of remote sites and a server farm interconnected by routers. Assume the host software is fairly old and produces more overhead traffic than is feasible if the network is to scale to a larger size.

Either the host software can be upgraded so that it does not produce the overhead traffic or the routers can add features that filter or otherwise reduce this overhead. Remember that the routers need to be there for connectivity; it is not a choice to have or not have the routers.

This sort of choice comes up very frequently when dealing with workgroup protocols. You might face it on Microsoft machines that could either use NetBIOS with broadcasts at the upper layer and nonroutable NetBEUI at the lower layer, or NetBIOS over TCP (NBT) that uses a directory at the upper layer at IP at the lower layer. Alternatively, you might face it with Novell machines, with NetWare 3.1.2 that uses Service Advertisement Protocol (SAP) broadcasts at the upper layer, or with NetWare 4.x that uses the broadcast-free NetWare Directory Service.

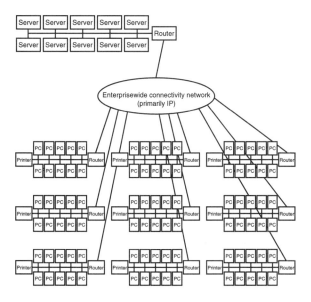

FIGURE 1.8.   *A representative network with nine workgroups and a server farm, all linked by routers. One computer in each workgroup is a print server.*

Some hosts allow remote administration; others do not. Assume that fully burdened network administrator time costs $25 per hour. If it takes 30 minutes per host to install new host software, there will be a $1,250 cost to install software.

A representative upgrade price for 100 workstations, which moves them to a software version that does not do broadcasts, is between $1,800 and $2,000. These prices are intended to give an order of magnitude for comparison. This does not consider personnel costs or the possible need to upgrade computer resources to run the new software.

Assume that routers already are in place. Most commercial routers can prevent local broadcast traffic (for example, from local print servers) from propagating beyond the workgroup LAN. They also can include static definitions of paths to central servers, reducing or removing the need for transmitting server location broadcasts for these servers.

The workgroup software vendors generally assumed that all devices were LAN connected and bandwidth was essentially free. This is not a reasonable assumption in larger wide area networks. The vendors made a simplifying assumption that it didn't hurt to have all devices know the location of all servers.

But if some of the servers are printers intended for use only on their own LAN, there is no application-level reason for them to be visible to clients on other LANs. Filtering out the addresses of servers before they reach the WAN, where bandwidth is definitely not free, is one way to reduce WAN costs.

Note

The means by which the print servers are remotely administered, if they need remote administration, need to be considered if printer announcements are filtered. There are ways to do this and still limit traffic, but such a discussion is beyond the scope of this book.

If there were no other reasons to migrate the old software to the new and the existing routers can be configured in 30 minutes each to control SAPs, the cost of controlling SAPs would be $125. This contrasts strongly with $3,070 for the upgrade cost and installation time.

However, the new software provides other services beyond broadcast control; it might have to allow better centralized administration, Internet connectivity software, and so on. If these capabilities are needed, then it is worthwhile to do the upgrade.

When you go deeper into the design of your network, you will constantly need to make tradeoffs about the level of addressing detail that must be visible everywhere in your network. This application-level example introduces that need, in posing the question "Do local print servers need to be visible every-where?" SAPs and NetBIOS broadcasts are means by which hosts learn the addresses of other hosts. Address learning mechanisms are a major source of overhead in large networks and need to be planned thoroughly if the networks are to scale well.

External Connectivity: Growth and Policies

There are many reasons an organization needs to connect to other organiza-tions. Such connectivity may or may not involve the public Internet. Several basic types include the following:

- The organization needs to make applications available on the public Internet. Arbitrary public users will access the enterprise's servers to obtain information, place orders, and so on.

- The enterprise's own personnel need access to arbitrary Internet resources.

- Internet services are used to interconnect sites within the enterprise. These communications should not be accessible from the general Internet.

- The enterprise connects with business partners, either over the Internet or private communications facilities. Again, these communications should be secured from unauthorized access.

For any of these connectivity types, upper management will need to define policies for availability, performance, and security. Controlled point-to-point connectivity with specific vendors is a very different problem from general Internet connectivity.

External connectivity can have a wide range of requirements for address space, depending on the number of points of communication with the outside and the security desired for this communication. If the connectivity involves any Internet access, then the parts of the organization that touch the Internet have to follow the addressing rules of the global Internet.

It may be desirable to have most internal computers hidden from the general Internet, with only the addresses of the firewall visible to the outside. Alternatively, it may be an organization's policy to use globally unique addresses for all its computers.

The First Approach to the Requirements Analysis

While talking with executives, get an initial impression of what they consider to be the existing critical applications and desired new strategic applications. Executives may have expectations different from the real technical requirements, but executive management still needs to be satisfied with the eventual network. As you do subsequent phases of requirements analysis, it's important to recognize conflicts between executive expectations and application- or network-level technical requirements. When you recognize such conflicts, you need to resolve them before the network requirements are finalized. If the budget is too small to meet the necessary requirements, there needs to be reconciliation. If executives want a very high level of security, but the planned network technology is inherently insecure, you need to educate executives on what is realistic and either have them accept reduced security or increase resources to allow security to be enhanced.

At this point, you are asking about applications less to get a full inventory, but to identify those that are most important in executive minds. Chapter 3 presents how to do a much more detailed application inventory.

New applications affect the design. These will be especially important when they involve new connectivity needs (for example, groupware or fault-tolerant servers using multicasting), new bandwidth requirements (for example, image traffic), or a combination of the two (for example, videoconferencing).

Will the distribution of the workforce change through telecommuting? Are mergers and acquisitions in the future? These answers will drive needs for globally unique addresses, or choices to use devices that translate between local and global addresses.

Begin by identifying the major applications as seen by upper management. Figure 1.9 shows an example of such an identification brainstorming session. Do this in brainstorming mode, getting things identified without worrying if this is the right mixture.

Tip

I do application brainstorming as a fast and informal interview process with upper managers. An excellent way to do this is using large flip chart easels. As the facilitator, I encourage people to throw out ideas, and I write them in large letters with a marker. As sheets fill up, I have an assistant tape them to the wall.

During this brainstorming phase, I do not reject any ideas and stop criticism in the group. I constantly emphasize that the purpose of the exercise is to get all ideas on paper.

After discussion of major application slows, change quickly to discussing major user types. Only after both are written down, discuss the lists with the group, identifying which applications are subsets of others and generally organizing the charts.

Save the charts. You will organize them even further, adding technical and workload factors, when you discuss them with information technology staff. Methods for this discussion are in Chapter 3.

Email

Payroll

Ordering

Shipping

Sales
   Sales catalog
   Order entry   Accounts payable

FIGURE 1.9. *Encourage executives to throw out names of applications. Breadth of coverage is most important; don't worry about one application being a subtask of another.*

After you have is a basic list of applications, identify the major groups/types of users using the template in Figure 1.10.

General employee

Finance
                 Executive

Inside sales

Shipping

Outside sales

Accounts payable
   Engineering

FIGURE 1.10. *Ask the executives to name representative kinds or groups of users. It's quite all right if some of the same names will recur both in the user and application lists.*

These bullets will form the starting point for more formal application analysis by technical staff using methods described in Chapter 3.

Looking Ahead

Chapter 3 links these users and services to characterize application flow requirements. Chapter 2 defines some terminology and approaches that will be used in Chapter 3.

CHAPTER 2

Principles Underlying Addressing

*Great fleas have little fleas upon their back to bite 'em/And little fleas have
lesser fleas, and so on ad infinitum.*

—Augustus de Morgan

I yam what I yam.

—Popeye

*If all your aircraft navigational systems fail, one last resort is to fly to ground
level and follow a railroad. The US Navy is not responsible for what happens
if the tracks enter a tunnel.*

*—Anonymous flight instructor,
Pensacola Naval Air Station.*

When the United States entered World War II, Winston S. Churchill began to
speak of the Grand Alliance, the group of allies that only together could beat
the Axis Powers. No one nation could do that on its own.

And so it is with network design. No one type of abstraction or component can
solve all network computing problems. The application layer is proper to
describe end-to-end traffic characteristics, but does not have the proper semantics to deal with the issues of media sharing. We need names as well as
addresses at various layers. Application gateways, protocol tunneling/
translation units, routers, bridges/switches, hubs/repeaters, and transmission

medium level switches all have distinct and useful roles. They are tools in your toolbox. Think of this chapter as having a similar function to the chapter of a carpentry or home repair book that reviews how to identify different kinds of saws and hammers.

Note

Switch *is one of the most overloaded terms in networking. In general, it is an interconnection device operating at OSI Layer 1 or 2. But LAN switches, circuit switches, frame switches, and cell switches are quite different devices. Pay attention to the context in which* switch *is used.*

Novice network designers tend to focus on addressing as the piece of network design that must happen first, and, after this is done, everything else will fall into place. Addressing is part of a larger context. Many organizations confuse the roles of routing and addressing, thinking they "just need advice on their addressing plans." In reality, they need coordinated advice on the three related technologies: routing, addressing, and naming. Some addressing methods only work with specific routing techniques, the use of appropriate naming tools can vastly simplify addressing, and so on.

Logical addressing is conceptually independent of the underlying transmission system. If an address is truly logical, it can be moved from a LAN to a modem connection without significant difficulty. In early development of the Internet Protocol suite architecture, the layer that interconnected intermediate and end hosts, in a medium-independent manner, was first called the *internetworking layer*. As usage of the term evolved, it came to be called the *Internet layer*. This layer is equivalent to the OSI network layer or OSI Layer 3. In all these, there is a basic protocol that carries user and most management data through the network layer. In the Internet Protocol suite, this is the *Internet Protocol* (IP). Source and destination addresses in IP packets are generically *network* or *logical* addresses, and specifically *IP addresses*.

As opposed to the formalism with which the OSI reference model [ISO 7498] was developed, there is no generally accepted protocol reference model for the Internet Protocol suite. Many consider the definitive reference to be a set of t-shirts often seen at the Internet Engineering Task Force meetings:

- "IP over everything"

- "Be conservative in what you send, be liberal in what they receive."

- "We don't believe in kings, presidents, or voting. We believe in rough consensus and running code."

Let's deal with that broader context, beginning with some informal definitions. Names identify *who* you are, whereas *addresses* define where you can be reached. Because identity does not change, addresses need to change with changes in your position. This chapter discusses the relationships between several key kinds of identifiers. Although it gives examples of identifiers, the focus of this chapter is to give a high-level review of the relationships among them, with the details of identifiers to follow.

Names are subtly different than other kinds of identifiers. Names are conceptually portable, associated with the person or computer rather than its location. In practice, names need to be translated to an internal, computer-friendly identifier before they can be used for transferring data. But because the names of humans or computers at the edge of the network are the best representation of the users that justify the network, good practice employs names as endpoint identifiers.

Treating names as identifiers, or more correctly placeholders that will translate into identifiers, we come up with several families of identifiers:

- *Names*—Human friendly, location independent, and unique within a naming domain. Commonly have aliases. May have hierarchical structure (for example, DNS subdomains).

  During actual network operation, names map to some other type of identifier. This mapping may be hard-coded, but is generally done by *directory services*. Further architectural characteristics of names are discussed in Chapter 3, "Application Topology: Naming Endpoints," while deployment characteristics of a representative directory service, the Internet Domain Name System, are discussed in Chapter 10, "Addressing and Name Services."

- *Logical addresses*—Router friendly, media independent, but dependent on logical topology, unique within routing domain. Always hierarchical, with at least two hierarchical levels encoded in address and possibly with additional levels available from context (for example, assignment to OSPF area). IP logical addresses are discussed in Chapter 5, "Classical IP Addressing: An Evolution," with refinements of them extending through the next several chapters.

  Logical addresses map to specific transmission system addresses in actual operation. Such mapping is the forte of *address resolution protocols*, discussed in Chapter 4, "Transmission System Identifiers and Logical Address Mapping: A View from the Bottom."

- *Transport identifiers*—These denote the origin and destination of end-to-end flows. In practice, this means the user process (for example, a window) and the application host server process that handles user requests. Although research efforts continue to look into a general location-independent endpoint identifier, today's reality is that location identifiers tend to be two-part or more. Typically, the endpoint identifier is a combination of a logical address with a port number known to the application program.

- *Transmission system addresses*—Hardware friendly, medium/transmission system dependent, unique within transmission system context (for example, MAC address on medium, telephone number within telephone system). Generally nonhierarchical in connectionless transmission systems (for example, MAC addresses) but hierarchical in switched systems (for example, X.25, ISDN, ATM). Especially in switched transmission systems, might include persistent address/physical endpoint identifier and transient address/connection identifier. The mapping between logical addresses and transmission system addresses, in practice, does not necessarily map cleanly to the OSI layers. A subsequent refinement of the OSI reference model [ISO 8646], discussed in Chapter 4, made the mapping much more clear.

The preceding identifiers generally are associated with specific points, or possibly groups of points. Another type of identifier deals with paths among points:

- *Route*—In general, a sequence of addresses defining a path between two or more endpoints. Also used to refer to the next hop logical address a specific router will use to forward a data unit along the route.

- *Connection*—A semi-permanent or permanent route among two or more endpoints, to which resources along the path are dedicated. There is an implication these resources are not available for the use of other connections.

- *Flow*—A one-directional association between a source endpoint and one or more destination endpoints. The emphasis is on the end-to-end connectivity, as distinct from the hop-by-hop aspect of a route. Flows usually are associated with performance requirements and an expected workload.

Before we get into these identifiers, we should put names into context and then review some general descriptive terminology referring to the way the identified objects relate to one another.

Names Versus Addresses

End users view networks as providing communications between computers and between computers and workstations. Network designers, however, tend to view them from the standpoint of the paths traversed by data.

Before an application can do useful work, it must know how to reach its peer at a desired location. It can be preconfigured with the name and address of the application, or it must be able to call upon a service that helps it find its peer.

Names are more human friendly than computer friendly. They are generally location independent and hierarchical. Among the most basic errors is assuming that organizational structure should be part of the address design. It is a given in modern corporate life that organizational structures will change constantly, either to improve efficiency or to simply gyrate in the manner well described by Dilbert. It is safest to put organizational information into names, not addresses.

Terms for these views, or, more correctly, the services that make the views possible, are *upper layer* and *lower layer*. Upper-layer services are provided between pairs (or multiples) of users and operate on units of data that are meaningful to users or user applications. Lower-layer services concentrate on moving data through one or more real networks and are more concerned with the movement of data in units most convenient for the communications resources. The OSI transport layer, realized in the Internet as the Transmission Control Protocol (TCP) or User Datagram Protocol (UDP) in the end-to-end layer, provides the glue between upper- and lower-layer views. In TCP and UDP, the transport service identifiers are called *ports*. In TCP/IP, an endpoint identifier is an IP address further qualified with a port.

Transport Identifiers and Ports

The idea of a port can be confusing, but a mundane example illustrates it well. Think of dialing a company's switchboard at 555-1234 and asking for the mail room. The telephone operator knows that the mail room is actually extension 25.

There are many mail rooms and many extension numbers in the world, but there is only one mail room and one extension 25 at logical address 555-1234. Borrowing from a convention actually used in Integrated Service Digital Network (ISDN) addressing, you could write the destination of your call as 555-1234:25. In ISDN, the number after the colon is a subaddress. In IP, it would be the TCP or UDP port number.

In the Internet Protocol suite, there are *well-known ports* for standard services. Port 25, for example, is the Simple Mail Transfer Protocol (SMTP) protocol. So to reach the SMTP server at address 192.168.1.1, you would need to reach the combination of address and port 192.168.1.1:25. To go to the Hypertext Transfer Protocol (HTTP) Web server at the same IP address, you would go to 192.168.1.1:80.

So think of ports as the "extension numbers" that further qualify the "telephone numbers" of network addresses. The list of well-known ports is in the Internet Assigned Numbers document, currently RFC 1700.

The terms port and socket often are used interchangeably. Some protocols, such as Novell, do use the term socket as its transport identifier. I try to discourage using these terms interchangeably, because UNIX and other operating systems do distinguish between ports and sockets.

In UNIX, a socket is a destination for interprocess communications on a single computer. Some sockets are network sockets, which are the endpoints associated with specific port numbers. Other sockets are simply other processes on the same computer and do not involve any network communications.

Because the upper layers service true application programs, and true application programs are created to do useful things for people, it seems reasonable that the upper layers are more oriented to service people than are network components. Communications among upper-layer entities tend to be defined more in relation to people-oriented names than machine-oriented addresses.

The difference between naming and addressing is the difference between the orientations of the upper and lower layers, shown in Figure 2.1. The transport layer maps between those orientations: flow among people and applications programs, and flow among network components.

Upper-layer services are application oriented, while lower-layer services are transmission oriented.

In voice communications, many services of the upper layers are provided by natural language and conversational custom. Between computers, however, these services must be realized with explicit protocols.

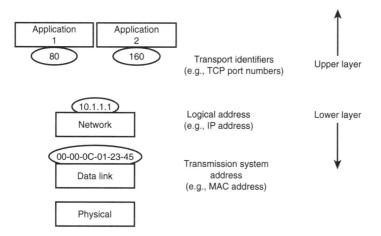

FIGURE 2.1. *The processes implementing upper and lower layer services are shown in rectangles. The identifiers of these processes are in ovals.*

Names

A *name* is something that belongs to a user (or some equivalent information resource such as a specific file) independently of where it is located; an address changes when something is moved. As an example of a name, consider the addressee name on a letter. The postal service normally carries the envelope to the address specified on the label, but first examines it to see if a change of address exists for that name at that address. If such a change exists, the letter carrier ignores the old address and uses the new address. Where a name specifies what something is, an *address* specifies where it is.

Without delving too deeply into the philosophy of personal identity, your name is normally considered your unique identifier of you as a person. Your address, however, is the identifier of where you are. You have a home address, but you also might have any number of temporary addresses, such as an office, a vacation home, a hotel, and so on. If you keep a name-based directory advised of your address, then the name service has the potential to route information to you without the sender knowing your current address.

We refer to a *distinguished name* as one that is unique within the overall upper layer system and to a relative distinguished name as one that is unique only within a subcontext of the upper layer system. In Internet Domain Name System conventions, detailed in Chapter 3, a fully distinguished name would be `sara.smith.red.house`. A *relative distinguished name* is unique within a specific context, such as "Sara Smith in the red house," as opposed to "Sara Smith in the blue house." In DNS conventions, `sara.smith` is relative to a specific name. As long as a name is unique within a context, it can be translated to a unique address. Names that are not unique, however, cannot be resolved into an address without further information.

Aliases

Even a distinguished name may have *aliases*, and the aliases may or may not be unique. An alias is a name that maps to the same address as another name.

> **Note**
>
> As an example, my feline literary assistant, Clifford, is uniquely described in the local context by being called "the huge black cat with the white tail tip." This description is not his name. He also frequently has the alias "the demented cat," but this is an alias that applies at random times to most cats. In a human analogy, George Washington will always be George Washington, but the alias "President of the United States" no longer applies to him.

Administering names and addresses are separate, yet interacting, processes. Some applications hard-code addresses rather than names, a practice done in the name of efficiency, but that should be condemned for inflexibility. Storing the address avoids the need for a name translation, but prevents the correct address from being found if the named person or resource moves to another address.

There is nothing wrong with caching an address retrieved from a name translation and using it in the short term. The directory service may even return a lifetime with the translation, a period of time over which the name to address mapping can be assumed stable. But assuming the name-to-address relationships never change is wrong.

> **Note**
>
> I routinely suffer from confusion between naming and addressing by the U.S. postal service. I live on what the local postmaster terms a "permanent temporary route" at 5012 South 25th Street. Permanent temporary routes are always served by temporary mail carriers, or carriers in training. The postal service uses the meaning of "route" here that refers to a final destination rather than a next hop.

As explained by the postmaster, when a carrier is not permanently assigned, the postal service directs that carrier to sort and deliver mail to specific addresses. A permanent carrier, however, is allowed to become familiar with the names of occupants in the various houses on the route. In other words, the permanent carrier knows names and maps them to addresses. The temporary carriers only can work with addresses.

Because it is easy to mis-sort material for South 24th Street into South 25th Street, and there is no cross-checking to name by the carriers in training, mail frequently is misrouted.

This leads to confusion even on the street, due to the various types of naming used. Both a former member of my household and a neighbor have the same first name. If the postal carrier were to try to deliver mail to this first name alone, with only the street name, there would be ambiguity. This name is unique only within the context of a house number. It is a relative distinguished name.

Name-to-Address Mapping

Names map to logical addresses associated with end devices such as work-stations and servers. Transport-level identifiers supplement those endpoint addresses. Think of the endpoint address as the address of a computer, but the transport identifier (for example, a TCP port number) as the sub-address of a specific piece of software that runs on that computer. Refer to the discussion in the earlier section "Transport Identifiers and Ports."

On the other hand, electricity flows to houses at specific addresses, not, in the eyes of the power company, to individual users at that address. Even if individuals at a power address do not owe money to the power company, electricity to all will stop if a bill owed by one individual is not paid and if all the residents are served by a single administratively controlled power service. This address orientation is a technical necessity, as the electrical power system's configuration must be controlled for safety and performance; it must be oriented to physical locations defined by addresses.

Transmission System Addresses

In the power company example, the transmission system address is the end-point of the company's service to a subscriber: a specific cable from a distribution point to a house. In telephone practice, the physical transmission endpoint is a pair of wires associated with a specific telephone number.

Reflect a bit on telephone service. From the data network perspective, you dial a phone number and run a data link protocol, such as the Point-to-Point Protocol (PPP) over it. From your perspective, the telephone number is a transmission system address.

From the perspective of the telephone company, the telephone number is a logical address. I live in an area where squirrels occasionally regard telephone cables as a delicacy. There is an eight-pair cable from the closest telephone pole into my house. Let's say a squirrel nibbled on this cable and bit through the first pair before my vigilant cat scared him off. My business line was provided through this pair.

My business line telephone number would still remain 998-5819, even if the telephone repair technician moved its service from the broken pair 1 to the spare pair 7.

You will find that real-world transmission systems, especially in WANs, tend to have multiple levels of addressing. The highest level is seen by a data user as the transmission system address, but those responsible for the transmission system will see additional levels corresponding to internal paths in the transmission system, or to physical media. If you are responsible, for example, for an Asynchronous Transfer Mode (ATM) network below your IP network, you need to be concerned with switch-to-switch addresses.

In a routable system, names are mapped to logical addresses. Nonroutable architectures, such as NetBIOS, map them directly to transmission system addresses. Transmission system addresses are usually tied to specific hardware and thus do not have the generality of network addresses.

In LANs, the MAC address is the basic transmission system address, yet you might be very concerned with knowing the physical port number on a LAN switch into which a server is plugged. Telephone companies use the useful term *provisioning* to describe how a circuit is set up. This setup involves assigning a wire pair at the subscriber location, deciding which pair in a main cable to splice it to, and selecting the punch-down position in the central office on which the cable terminates. There can be multiple addresses, at multiple levels, in a transmission system.

Functions for mapping between names and addresses generically are called *directory services*. In the Internet, the main such service is the Domain Name Service (DNS). DNS is a widely deployed directory system that emphasizes name-to-address mapping. It has a distributed directory model, and operations are performed with a client/server paradigm.

In workgroup architectures such as Novell NetWare and Banyan VINES, which emphasize a client/server processing model, application servers actively advertise their existence. Directory services do exist (for example, the NetWare bindery and VINES StreetTalk), but clients often have services offered to them rather than needing to search for them.

In NetBIOS and AppleTalk, clients search for servers. Novell NetWare has a separate protocol, GetNearestServer, which clients use to ask a synchronized local server about the location of the nearest server of a desired type.

A directory service, at its most basic level, accepts a name and returns an address. More sophisticated capabilities include reverse or inverse lookup, where an address is accepted and a name returned. Reverse lookup becomes more complex when aliases are in use, because more than one name can be associated with the same address.

Topological Concepts

A network with one component is a rather useless thing. Networking, whether the technical definition we are discussing here or the exchange of business cards at a cocktail party, is about relationships.

Before we get into specific terminology, consider the general ways in which components can relate. Network components may have one-to-one, one-to-many, many-to-one, and many-to-many relationships. In a simple view of network topology, all of these relationships can be drawn with lines directly connecting network components. In the real world, the components in the drawing may themselves be collections of components and links between them. Real networks of any complexity have relaying devices (for example, routers and switches) whose job it is to interconnect other components, not perform direct services for end users.

Topology Terminology

The term *topology* originally came from formal mathematics, where it is used to describe the study of the shapes or forms of things. In networking, it is used in a broader sense, to describe the interconnections of the network. Careful use of topological terms avoids confusion in talking about network layout.

In mathematics, graphs are generalized structures for describing the relationships of elements of a set, elements which have some relationship or ordering among them. Their basic principles are shown in Figure 2.2. Somewhat more formally, a directed graph (or *digraph,* or, as used here, a *graph*) is a set of "things," or *nodes,* and a set of *arcs* (also called links, pointers, or lines), which define whether a relationship between two nodes exists (that is, if the arc exists between nodes a and b, then a points to b).

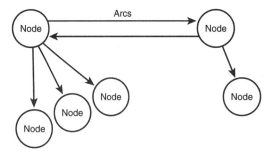

FIGURE 2.2.   *"Things" and the connections between them are called graphs in topology. All graphs are built from nodes and arcs.*

There is an underlying assumption that identifiers are permanent, or at least long-term, while locators are transient. In the networking literature, permanent identifiers often are called *persistent*. Whatever it is called, it has generally been understood that locators can change, as, for example, when a telephone associated with one number is moved to another pair of wires.

New technologies make this transience much worse. In cellular telephony, the transmission system address—a radio frequency and possibly digital codes— constantly changes as you move out of one cell and into another. The cellular network has to keep track of these changes to maintain the call.

Many data networks historically assigned a network address to a specific user machine and used this as a weak security measure to identify that machine. When users are mobile, even calling in from hotels rather than moving constantly, the most useful address to locate them is the address of the remote access server interface to which they have dialed, not the actual address of their laptop.

Arcs, unless otherwise specified, are one-directional. A graph in which all arcs are one-directional is called a *directed graph*. A two-way interconnection between two nodes requires two arcs. This actually allows much more precise definitions, as well as more complex configurations such as broadcasts and one-way flows.

Simple topologies, such as point-to-point and stars shown in Figure 2.3, are easy to understand. Real networks are rarely that simple, and you need more sophisticated terminology to describe their interactions.

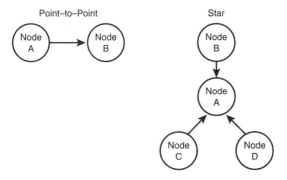

FIGURE 2.3. *The most basic relationship is point-to-point. A simple star is the next refinement, with one intermediate hop between all endpoints.*

Adjacency, Connectivity, and Hops

Adjacency and connectivity, illustrated in Figure 2.4, are terms from mathematical graph theory, which are extremely useful in discussing network topology. More common terms are that adjacent things are *neighbors*, while connectable things are reachable through a network. *Connectable* is a synonym for *reachable*; it can be achieved either with connection-oriented or connectionless protocols. There are multiple meanings of *connection* in networking, and we are only using the topological meaning here!

You can have logical connectivity between endpoints even if you don't have physical connectivity. For this to happen, the underlying transmission system has to be able to reach each successive link on the path between source and destination. Technologies such as dynamic routing might make the path change over time, but there always must be a set of reachable links for logical connectivity to exist.

Formally, two things (nodes, in graph-theoretic terms) have adjacency when information can be exchanged between them without the intervention of intermediaries: Persons A and B standing next to each other are adjacent in the context of conversation. In other words, an arc directly connects them in a graph.

Two things have connectivity when they can exchange information, but not necessarily directly. Intermediary things (for example, the telephone network) might be needed to carry out the information exchange. Not long ago, I had a landscaper build a gravel walk in my garden. I was concerned with having three tons of gravel piled in my yard, but not with the specific number of wheelbarrow loads needed to spread the gravel from the pile. The garden path is the layer while the wheelbarrow loads formed the (N-1) layer.

From the mathematical standpoint, more than one arc may be involved in the path between the nodes. Look at Figure 2.4, where the layer (N-1) links support the logical flow at layer.

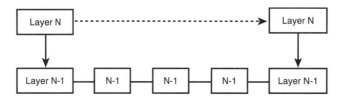

FIGURE 2.4. *Information flow between two endpoints at a higher layer might actually happen over multiple links at a lower layer.*

When we discuss the actual services and protocols used in communications, we will see that some deal with adjacent nodes and others deal with connectable end nodes. We can now refine our definition of cluster to a set of nodes that has connectivity with one another.

From the topological standpoint, any two nodes that are adjacent are also connected, but not all connected nodes are adjacent. The term *hop* is often used to describe the degree of closeness of two nodes, but the definition of a single hop is not consistent. In routing, the number of hops is the number of intermediate nodes that connect two end nodes.

In other discussions, the number of hops might be the number of media or links between two end nodes. Putting the latter definition in graph-theoretic terms, it is the number of arcs between the nodes. Some definitions even consider a hop either an arc or a node, and the hop count in such cases is the sum of intermediate arcs and nodes (see Figure 2.5).

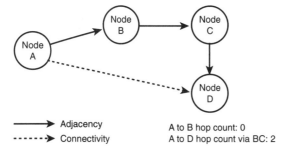

FIGURE 2.5. *All nodes here have connectivity but are adjacent to no more than two other nodes.*

The most general abstraction is full mesh, shown in Figure 2.6. All stations have many-to-many connectivity to one another. This might be a valid model for application connectivity, but simply does not scale well at the levels actually concerned with moving bytes. The need for all workstations to know the name and location of all other workstations would present, as the number of users grew, an overwhelming maintenance and performance penalty. Applications can have full-mesh connectivity even though there is not physical or routing-level full connectivity. Traffic among application endpoints is carried by communications facilities at the layer below the application. The application topology maps on top of the underlying network topology.

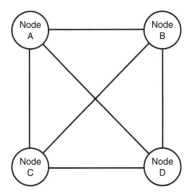

FIGURE 2.6. *In a full mesh, every node connects directly to every other node.*

Backbone or hierarchical models are a key to scaling, even for applications. Consider a typical email application, in which local groups of workstations know how to reach other workstations in their group. When they want to send a message to a destination outside the local group, they do not send it directly, but instead send it to a backbone network that interconnects all local groups. The backbone knows how to reach each local group.

It is worth noting that a given station might belong to several different topological relationships. Tightly controlled hierarchies often are most reliable for the infrastructure task of maintaining the network itself, while more meshed structures are a better fit for the user view for interapplication communications. Even at the application level, there often is a hierarchy not visible to the end user. A local workstation, for example, might interact with a local server. The local server interacts with other servers only when it needs to, on behalf of a number of local workstations. The network is more scalable when every workstation does not need to communicate *directly* with every server.

One-to-One and One-to-Many Relationships

The simplest one-to-one network topology is a direct, or *one-to-one*, connection between two entities. Both users in a pure one-to-one relationship are zero hops from each other.

We can still speak of a one-to-one relationship at layer N if there is a relaying device between the two nodes. The relaying device, however, needs to be transparent at layer N for the relationship to be one-to-one. As shown in Figure 2.4, the relaying device needs to operate at layer (N-1) to be transparent.

Arcs of graphs are also called *lines*. Several simple topologies can be created with direct lines between nodes. When speaking in terms of graphs, do not confuse the abstraction of a line with a physical, one-to-one transmission facility such as a telephone line. In practical terms, however, a persistent one-to-one relationship is nicely illustrated by a cable, while a telephone call is a good example of a transient one-to-one relationship.

One-to-one relationships, in a very trivial way, illustrate *any-to-any connectivity*. To consider more complex relationships such as hierarchies, you will want to generalize the idea of a one-to-one topology to a one-to-many topology.

Any-to-Any Relationships

When all nodes in a graph are directly connected, a *mesh* is formed. A mesh is a many-to-many topology.

In actuality, a mesh is made up of multiple one-to-many relationships. Each of the N nodes needs (N-1) arcs to all other nodes.

In a full mesh, all nodes are zero hops from one another (refer to Figure 2.6). This might be the view of connectivity from the application perspective, although there might be multiple hops in the underlying lower-layer connectivity network. Application connectivity is discussed further in Chapter 3.

Hierarchies

Star topologies can be considered an extension of the one-to-one. In a star, each user connects directly to a central point or hub; each star user (other than the hub) is one hop from each other user. Depending on the direction of flow, stars can be many-to-one or one-to-many.

> ### Note
>
> *The topological relationships described simply show topology. In practice, it can be quite useful to consider the number of devices involved. Many-to-few relationships characterize the interaction among a large number of client workstations and a small, but greater than one, number of cooperative or fault-tolerant servers.*

Few-to-few relationships characterize small full mesh groups, perhaps among a subset of users on a single LAN that are using a collaborative application or are in a videoconference.

In large networks, any-to-any connectivity tends not to be scalable at the logical or transmission layers.

There are several ways to talk about stars. A star in which all non-hub nodes connect through the hub is the simplest possible *hierarchy*. It is a one-to-many topology.

Note

Stars are the archetype of centralized mainframe processing environments. The mainframe at the root of the star controls all resources.

As described in Chapter 1, "What Is the Problem You Are Trying to Solve?" executives whose careers began with mainframes often have a mental picture of centralized control and administration. This is opposite to people whose experience began with workgroup LANs, where there is no central point of control.

The two administrative models—totally centralized and totally distributed—each have strengths and limitations. A scalable network tends to have aspects of both in a hierarchical design. The overall structure of the hierarchy is defined centrally, but aspects of administration are distributed into branches of the tree.

Hierarchical structures are found in all but the very simplest networks. In the real world, a given node may belong to multiple hierarchies, but the hierarchical model still is a very basic way of organizing network structure.

In a simple hierarchical network, all nodes have connectivity, but connectivity is achieved through a variable number of intermediate nodes, the number often different between different pairs of nodes. Topologically, hierarchies are trees, in which there is a single root node to which all other nodes are either adjacent or connected indirectly through other nodes.

If there is a single root, there is a single point of failure. More complex hierarchies can be defined that have redundancy at key points, but that is beyond the scope of this chapter.

Domains, shown in Figure 2.7, define contexts in which some attribute, such as node naming, is controlled by a single authority. Information related to domain attributes flows both inside the domain and among domains (that is, intradomain and interdomain). Domains can contain subdomains.

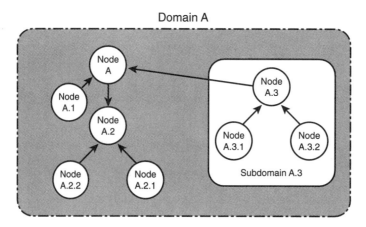

FIGURE 2.7. *Hierarchies can be divided into domains for administration.*

Hierarchies have many applications in networking. They provide structures in which the assignment of node identifiers can be delegated. They can be used to localize the effect of changes to one subdomain. As long as other subdomains reach the changed subdomain through the subdomain root, the change can be kept from them.

Some level of hierarchical organization is found in all but the most trivial real networks. The address structure represents the logical network topology, and usually the physical topology as well.

Hierarchical definition is recursive in that sets of contiguous addresses can be aggregated into a single piece of information.

Hierarchical organization has long been necessary in the world's largest network, the telephone system. In the early days of the Internet, hierarchical organization was not strictly necessary, simply because of the small scale of the early experimental networks. This is still the model that underlies many workgroup or desktop network architectures, such as early Novell or Apple systems. Desktop architectures tend to optimize their protocols for a specific environment and do best in that environment. (Best has to be interpreted; it can mean speed or cost.)

Hierarchy in Telephone Numbering

In the telephone numbering plan, for example, country numbers are unique on a worldwide basis defined in the International Telecommunications Union. The national (or national *Registered Private Operating Agency* (RPOA)) numbering plan for each network is defined individually, but national numbers are always prefixed with country codes when used internationally. In North America, three-digit centrally assigned area codes are the next hierarchical level to the numbering plan, whereas in the United Kingdom, city codes with a variable number of digits form the top level in that national network.

Switches exist at given levels of the hierarchy. An international switch, for example, has tables that define how to reach other international switches, but not low-level exchange switches.

As shown by the telephone numbering plans, hierarchies might have hierarchies within them, under the control of different high-level roots, such as country codes under the CCITT root and area codes under the North American numbering plan, which defines area codes and exchanges as Numbering Plan Areas (NPA). The NPA is part of a global numbering system with w subscribers.

If flat (that is, non-hierarchical) addressing were used to look up p worldwide telephone numbers, telephone switches would have an address lookup requirement on the order of O. Clearly, this is beyond any cost-effective technology available. By breaking the system down into

N	National network prefixes
A	Regional/area code prefixes
E	Exchange/local prefixes
L	Line numbers

The worst case workload is $O(N+A+E+L)$. This drastic improvement is possible because the various parts of the address are not random, but provide topological information. Each element points either to a local table, or gives a path to another switch that has the local information.

If the parts of the address point to real switching systems, they have to be assigned in a manner consistent with the real topology. If a subscriber moves to a new location served by a new switch, rational hierarchical addressing requires that the subscriber's number change to reflect the new topology.

Regulatory agencies in the United States and Canada, in the interest of enhancing competition, are pressing for subscriber telephone number portability. In this model, one's telephone number is associated with the subscriber, rather than the subscriber's location. Although this will make it easier for a telephone subscriber to change telephone companies, because the various address parts are associated with switches run by specific companies, number portability might place an enormous additional load on the telephone system. The true operational and cost implications of this are unknown.

The reality is that switches have to use hierarchical addressing. In address portability, the subscriber telephone number has to be looked up in a database and converted to a logical address that the switching system actually can use to define a path for the call. The telephone number has taken on the attributes of a name and has to be translated to a real telephone number.

A similar problem exists in the Internet. Historically, Internet Protocol addresses were assigned to specific organizations. If the organization changed its connectivity, the original routing tables were sufficiently small to keep track of paths to each endpoint. With the explosive growth of the Internet, this is no longer feasible. Just as telephone subscribers historically did not expect to be able to keep their telephone numbers when moving to a new area code, it is a reasonable operational requirement to expect that an Internet user would change his logical address, but not his name, when moving to a new geographical location or changing service providers.

The distinction between names, which do not have topological significance, and logical addresses, which do, is critical. Names tend to be *persistent*. Their lifetime is longer than that of IP addresses. Name-to-address translations can be done at the start of an attempt to access a given resource, and an address relevant at that moment can be returned by the directory service. Hard-coding addresses may cause the access attempt to fail or reach the wrong resource if the resource has been readdressed.

Administering Hierarchical Models

In any system where globally unique identifiers are needed, some organization must be responsible for the administrative process of assigning identifiers without duplication. In sufficiently large organizations, one person or team cannot cope with the workload of assignment, and a practical necessity is *delegating* the workload to lower elements in the organizational hierarchy.

Chapter 6, "Internet Failing: Details at 11," discusses administrative models involved in IP address assignment. IP addresses, as with names in the DNS, need worldwide uniqueness when used in the Internet. Even when used solely within a private network, duplication must be avoided with administrative mechanisms.

A top-level body, the Internet Assigned Numbers Authority (IANA), "owns" the potential IP address space. At the time of this writing, in mid-1998, IANA is undergoing significant organizational changes, but its function will continue, perhaps under a new name. It is typical of such bodies that they rarely, if ever, deal directly with user organizations, but delegate to regional authorities. In the case of IP, regional authorities, generally at a continental level, do the detailed management of the address space. The major authorities are the following:

- American Registry for Internet Numbers (ARIN), formerly the InterNIC. Primary responsibility: North America.

- Rèseaux IP Europèens (RIPE). Primary responsibility: Europe.

- Asia-Pacific Network Information Center. Primary responsibility: Asia and Pacific Rim.

Originally, DNS names were also under the IANA umbrella. Name registration is a more complex problem than address registration, because it includes such issues as intellectual property rights to trademarks. Name registration also is perceived as a profit-making business and is complicated by competitive issues. In contrast, address registration bodies are, at the present time, not-for-profit organizations funded by user and membership fees.

Pathologies of Hierarchical Models

A tree, or a hierarchical network, can become *partitioned*, with loss of connectivity between domains. Picture an army that operates under rigid central control. All communications between the eastern and western divisions must go through general headquarters. If the link to general headquarters is lost, the two divisions cannot execute any coordinated operations. They are partitioned from one another.

If control is so rigid that each division can take no action in its own area until ordered by general headquarters, all activity stops. If some authority is delegated, each division can do things in its own area, but no farther.

Depending on the application of the network, the partitions of the network may still be able to operate with the loss of some functionality. If, however, the network cannot operate at all if partitioned, a true tree organization might be inappropriate. Rather, some sort of mesh topology, with multiple paths to the critical network elements, might be more appropriate. Such multiple paths provide redundancy for critical communications.

It might be possible to repair partitions with nonhierarchical *backdoor routes*, the E-F path in Figure 2.8. Tradeoffs must be carefully considered before using backdoor routes that break a hierarchical model. Such routes might appear to add robustness, but think about how they can complicate debugging and capacity planning. Good design often involves increasing the reliability and redundancy of links to a higher hierarchical level, rather than using back doors.

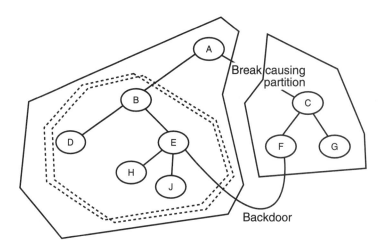

FIGURE 2.8. *Although total connectivity is lost as a result of the break between A and C, local connectivity still exists in two partitions—one rooted in B and one rooted in C.*

Although backdoor routes rarely add real robustness, they can be appropriate as a means of handling special traffic flows. If there were heavy traffic between two edge sites, it might make sense to provide a direct connection between the two. To keep troubleshooting as easy as possible, only the routers in the direct path between the two edge sites should know about the special-case path; it should not be injected into the general routing system.

All-hierarchical and all-peer network topologies are nice theoretically, but are impractical to implement. It is difficult to manage totally distributed peer-to-peer networks, and tree networks are inflexible for configuration and often have performance limitations. Although many network architectures originally were defined emphasizing peer-to-peer or hierarchical organizations, most have evolved to a hybrid of meshed subdomains linked into a hierarchy.

Generic Network Addresses

The term *endpoint identifier* tends to be associated with computers on the edge of the underlying backbone network, or with individual software processes running in these computers. Endpoint identifiers usually are a combination of a generic network address and a port number. Generic network addresses are a more general idea, and they also identify the internal interfaces inside the backbone. An architectural extension of the OSI reference model, ISO 9575, extends the OSI model to include intermediate systems as well as end systems. An intermediate system is OSI terminology for a router. IP router functions are discussed in RFC 1812. Both architectural documents describe network layer forwarding as done among generic network addresses, with ports being considered only at the endpoints.

In the earlier section "Transport Identifiers and Ports," a port was described as the supplementary information that lets you find an endpoint at an IP address. Figure 2.9 shows the path of IP addresses between a client and server via several routers. The router interfaces all have IP addresses, but they are not endpoints. Traditional routers forward on destination IP address and do not consider port numbers.

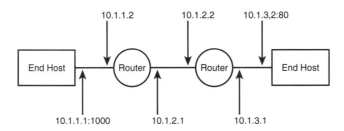

FIGURE 2.9. *Every interface on the path has an IP address, but only the endpoints have port numbers.*

Because there are different levels of abstraction with which we look at data transmission, hardware, and logical software at a minimum, we have several types of point addresses. These types are generally associated with layers of the OSI reference model.

Note

Take care in calling something a Layer 3 or Layer 2 address. When you deal with the details of modern transmission systems and indeed of routing systems, you will find that they are indeed layered, but their layers might not correspond neatly to OSI layers. In general, there are important sublayers of the OSI reference model at OSI Layers 3 and below. For example, the IEEE LAN model splits OSI Layer 2 into Logical Link Control (LLC) and Media Access Control (MAC) sublayers.

Transmission System Identifiers

Transmission system identifiers are used by the actual hardware that transmits the bits. Such identifiers might be physically bound to a specific device, such as a *medium access control* (MAC) identifier on a local area network, or might be software-defined inside the transmission system, such as a telephone number.

The reason for this is that the process of mapping between logical and transmission system addresses is as important as name-to-logical address mapping and deserves detailed discussion. Defining the transmission system address first helps this process.

A simple model of the transmission system might describe it as a wire; but that would be far too simple. Transmission systems might have considerable intelligence. A basic topology splits them into several attributes:

- Topologies, including one-to-one, point-to-multipoint, mesh/broadcast

- Connection modes

- Addressing

Logical Addresses

The IP is our archetype of a logical, or network-layer, protocol. Logical addresses are the basis on which routing operates. The structure of IPv4 addresses will be discussed in Chapter 5; the structure of non-IP addresses in Chapter 6; and the structure of IPv6 addresses in Chapter 15, "Your Addressing Strategy: Integration for the Present and Planning for the Future." Briefly, they are the following:

- *IP Version 4 (IPv4)*—32 bit. The split between prefix and host part varies.

- *IP Version 6 (IPv6)*—128 bit. The split between prefix and host part varies.

- *IPX/Novell*—80 bit total split into 32-bit prefix and 48-bit node. In recent routing systems, prefixes can be aggregated.

- *AppleTalk*—16-bit network, 8-bit host.

- *DECnet*—6-bit area, 10-bit host.

- *Banyan VINES*—32-bit prefix and 16-bit element.

Media can have no prefix, one prefix, or multiple address prefixes. Using Virtual LAN (VLAN) technology, a given logical prefix can split across several physical media. In Figure 2.10, the multiple physical media are linked by *trunk* media invisible to the logical level.

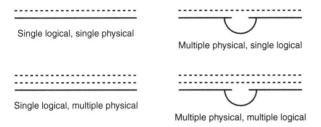

FIGURE 2.10. *The solid lines are physical media, and the dotted lines are logical networks. VLAN trunks are special physical media which, when used with LAN switches not shown in this drawing, link multiple physical media.*

Endpoint Identifiers

Endpoint identifiers denote the origin and destination of flows. In practice, the origin is the user process (for example, a window), and the destination is the application host server process that handles user requests. Although research efforts continue to look into a general location-independent endpoint identifier, today's reality is that location identifiers tend to have two or more parts. At the level of data flow, they are seen as an ordered pair of a logical address and a transport protocol identifier. In various protocol families, these include the following:

- *IP*—IP address

  Protocol identifier denoting TCP, UDP, or other transport protocol

  Transport protocol ID (16-bit port number in TCP and UDP)

- *IPX*—IPX address

  Socket number (16 bit)

- *AppleTalk*—DDP address

  Socket number (8 bit)

The idea of an endpoint identifier remains valid in nonroutable protocols as well. As we will see in later chapters, this is the basis for tunneling nonroutable protocols through a routed network. The endpoint identifier of the nonroutable protocol is passed to software above the transport level of a routable protocol, and the endpoint identifier of the encapsulating gateway is used to deliver traffic to a peer encapsulating gateway.

Examples of nonroutable endpoint identifiers include the following:

- SNA over LLC2

- NetBIOS over LLC2

- LAT over LLC1

Note

At this point, alert readers are likely to be thinking I've contradicted myself. In Chapter 1, I harped on the point that logical addresses should not reflect the application topology. Yet, here I am describing application flow in terms of logical addresses.

Butler Lampson, a distinguished computer science academic, said, "There is no problem in computer science that does not yield to a sufficient level of indirection." This is a saying that often guides me when I am looking for the answer to a tough design problem.

Indirection, in this context, is the process by which one identifier points you to another identifier, which might in turn point to another. There is no question that this sort of identifier chaining adds overhead and complexity, but it also adds great flexibility. Think of the ability to receive email sent to your name, even though you might be at your office, at your home, or dialed in from a hotel.

We want to define the application topology in terms of endpoint identifiers. These identifiers indirectly refer to logical addresses, but the endpoint identifiers are considered long term or permanent. These endpoint identifiers are mapped by architecture-specific mechanisms to logical addresses. This mapping, however, can change based on changes in network configuration, or even workload.

Path Identifiers

Connection-oriented communications follow a telephony model, where there is a distinct call setup phase that leads to the allocation of resources in the transmission system. User information flows over these resources. *Connectionless* communications follow the postal model, where each "envelope" of information is self-contained with complete source and destination addresses.

A third model is evolving, the *flow* model. Flow models have awareness that a relationship exists between a source and destination, but do not necessarily allocate specific resources to service them.

In their first data communications education, most readers probably learned that communications mechanisms fall into two categories: connection oriented and connectionless. Connection-oriented communications are modeled after the telephone system: They have a setup and teardown phase in addition to user information transfer, they commit network resources whether the resources are actually used or not, and they are highly predictable in operation. This predictability enhances network operators' ability to predict capacity needs. The continued relationship between sender and receiver also enhances the ability to do explicit flow and error control.

A machine that forwards connectionless communications can be simpler and faster than an intermediate node in a connection-oriented communications system, because the connectionless machine need not keep track of the state of connections through it. It uses a simple model of "see the packet, forward the packet, forget the packet."

Any communications process has at least two points: an origin and one or more destinations. This is true of both connectionless and connection-oriented communications. In connectionless communications, the intermediate nodes do not maintain state, and there is only the most rudimentary concept of state in the end systems. Connection-oriented communications explicitly maintain state and generally reserve resources to support them. The resources reserved might be no more than a connection identifier, but it also can be an allocation of bandwidth or a physical path. Flow-oriented communications maintain state but need not reserve resources.

Connections

Overhead functions are involved in setting up a connection, but after the connection is established, the transient identifier can be used as a shorthand reference to the connection by switches that have to route traffic belonging to the connection. Transient identifiers tend to be significantly smaller than a pair of endpoint identifiers (plus any optional connection information that may be needed).

Over a sufficiently long connection time, there can be bandwidth savings through the need to include only a small transient identifier in each unit of information, compared with full addresses needed in connectionless units.

If the duration of association between source and destination is short, the overhead of connection setup might not be worth amortizing over a short lifetime. Connectionless models can be lower in overhead for query/response and similar sorts of information transfer.

Connectionless switching devices also tend to be faster in forwarding traffic than connection-oriented devices, because connectionless devices (for example, LAN switches and routers) do not have the overhead of tracking connections.

Unfortunately, although connectionless devices can be faster and simpler, their performance is less predictable than that of devices that control resource allocation. Various hybrid schemes are used to improve performance while simultaneously making performance predictable and manageable. These schemes include flow-based communications and cell relaying. In the latter, exemplified by Asynchronous Transfer Mode (ATM), which is connection-oriented, the units of information transferred are highly optimized for efficient hardware switches.

Chapter 4 discusses in more detail the tradeoffs in transmission technology. The intention here is to make clear that transmission systems have their own addressing independent of names and logical addressing, and connection-oriented transmission systems have two kinds of identifiers: transient and persistent.

A confusing reality is that a given address might appear to be a transmission system, hardware-oriented address from one level of abstraction, but in fact is a logical address within the transmission system. Telephone numbers are a good example of this dual definition. They are logical from the perspective of the telephone system, whose hardware addresses are of lines and switches. From the perspective of the OSI network layer, they represent physical addresses.

Routes

Routes are sequences of addresses. There might be more than one route that leads to the same destination. There might be preferences among routes. As Robert Frost wrote, "Two roads diverged in a wood, and I /Took the one less traveled by,/And that has made all the difference." Frost's criterion, apparently, was to take the less congested path.

In general, routes are sequences of logical addresses. The term *route* is also used to refer to sequences of transmission system addresses, as in *source route bridging*.

There are really two contexts for routes. The first is the end-to-end, complete sequence of addresses from a source to a destination.

The second is the usage of the term *route* on a specific router. Also known as an entry in a routing table, it consists of the following:

- A prefix

- Optional supplementary information about the prefix

- A next hop logical address of an interface either on a router one hop closer to the destination or on the destination medium

- A transmission system address for the next hop logical address

- Transmission-specific information necessary to transfer data

The usual case is the address of the router that advertises a route is the address that should be used to reach the next hop. There might be exceptions to this in complex routing systems beyond the scope of this text, such as Border Gateway Protocol (BGP) connectivity at inter-carrier exchange points.

Flows

As with the real world in general, simple categorizations are suspect. As data rates grow increasingly faster, a new model, the flow model, has emerged. The original motivation for flows was in research on gigabit-rate communications, but it has evolved to include effective use as a method of describing end-to-end requirements and enforcing these requirements in real systems.

Abstractly, a flow is an association between a source and one or more destinations. As shown in Figure 2.11, an association from a source to a single destination is called a *point-to-point flow*, while a flow from a source to multiple destinations is called a *point-to-multipoint flow*. Flows differ from connections in that establishing a flow does not necessarily reserve resources.

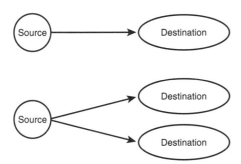

FIGURE 2.11. *To have interactive communications, it is necessary to have at least two flows, one in each direction. It is often convenient to model host processing as an additional flow when monitoring response time.*

The use of flows to describe application requirements is detailed in Chapter 3. Explicit flow-aware protocols are evolving, and IPv6 has a flow identifier in its header, discussed in Chapter 15.

Note

The book Enterprise Routing and Switching *(also from Macmillan Technical Publishing) contains further discussion of protocols that use flow information to provide communications with a specified quality of service.*

At the present time, consider flows as an application analysis technique. Flow identifiers are generally internal to routers.

Network Interconnection Devices

A variety of things interconnect entities at the various layers of architectural model hierarchy, and interconnections inside and among layers can create mazes. Terminology might differ in the several architectural models in use, including OSI, the IP protocol architecture, the telephony models associated with ISDN and ATM, the IEEE 802 LAN model, and so on. Architectural understanding is the voice in these mazes and will lead you out of chaos.

The generic term for an interconnection device is *relay*. Relays interconnect two or more entities that use a particular protocol. They can cooperate with other relays to form a system of relays for building complex information highways. All relays share one property: They interconnect two communications subsystems.

In practice, a relay is a box containing the following:

- Some number of input ports

- Some number of output ports

- Hardware or software logic to handle protocol behavior at the input and output ports

- Hardware or software logic to determine the destination port for traffic arriving on incoming ports

These are the fundamental aspects. Other issues that refine the relay structure include the following several choices:

- How does the relay find the destination of a PDU to be forwarded?

- How does the relay assure that its forwarding rules continue to match reality?

- When the relay tries to forward a PDU out an interface (or medium) that is busy transmitting another PDU, what happens?

- Will the relay accept new traffic when it is busy processing other traffic? How does it reject excess traffic (if it does)?

There are operational and economic aspects of specific implementations, as follows:

- If the destination in the PDU is logical, not physical, how does the relay select the physical interface on which to forward the PDU?

- How quickly can these decisions be made?

- How important is it for devices in the relaying environment to recognize, without human intervention, their place in the map?

- How much overhead is necessary for the relay to keep track of the map?

Formally, relays are defined at the physical, data link, network, transport, and application layers [ISO 10000].

Relays connect two peer entities at the same layer. There are names for the types of relays used at each layer. Some meaningful types of relays do not fit neatly into OSI layers, but their names are still relevant.

Repeaters connect entities at the physical layer. They are primarily concerned with extending cable lengths or otherwise managing wiring.

MAC bridges connect LAN MAC-entities at Layer 2 of the OSI model. WAN switches for frame relay, X.25, and arguably ATM also operate at this layer.

Routers (or intermediate systems, in formal OSI terminology) connect network entities.

Transport relays interconnect entities at the transport layer. The most common realization of a transport layer is as tunneling software, which carries a payload in one protocol over a delivery network.

Application relays interconnect application entities. There are two main types of application relays: pure application relays that pass along application information based on protocol header information and application gateways, which manipulate the contents of application data. Think of the first as a post office and the second as one that opens the mail and forwards a translation in another language.

Practical networks are apt to contain different types of relays at different layers.

As we have seen, the basic model of a relay is a two-port device. A relay of any level of complexity, however, can be generalized from a set of two-port relays. Most relays select among different possible destinations for the information they are relaying.

Selection decisions usually are based on some sort of topological map of the context in which relaying is done. These maps tend to be based on a hierarchical organization, much as different rules are used to select neighborhood driving routes versus freeway routes.

Circuit Switches and Repeaters

Circuit switches, repeaters, and hubs interconnect physical layer devices. They transfer electrical or optical signals peculiar to the transmission system among physical layer interfaces.

The first relays in telecommunications were *telephone switchboards* and *switches*. (In today's terminology, they are called *circuit switches*.) These devices relayed voice information between telephones, which first was represented with analog tones and more recently as bit streams.

From the perspective of the telephone user, a telephone can potentially connect to any other phone. The set of all potentially reachable phones can be called the cluster of controllers and treated topologically as a single entity. Elements of a cluster share the ability to communicate with one another. We will refine that definition as we continue.

Without getting into the details of telephone technology, look at the complexity of identifier and locator relationships in a telephone. The telephone number is persistent. The mapping of telephone numbers to a specific wire is considered transient and can change without changing the telephone number. In practice, the assignments of wires to telephones does not change on a routine basis.

Real telephones do not actually call one another. Instead, they call the telephone switch, which in turn connects them either to the destination telephone or to another switch.

For two phones to communicate, even though they are served by a single switch, the communication is mediated through the switch.

Cellular phones, however, enter into a constantly changing relationship to entry points into the telephone networks; these entry points change based on the geographic position of the car (that is, in which cell of the cellular network is it?). Transient identifiers change on a near-real-time basis.

Bridges and Layer 2 Switches

Traditionally, packet switching devices that make decisions based on data link information have been called *bridges*. The various media interconnected by pure bridges typically are assigned to a single prefix. See Chapter 12, "Addressing in Hubs and Switches," and Chapter 13, "Addressing in Routers," for more complex relationships between prefixes and media.

The terms *switch* and *LAN switch* have come into vogue to describe devices that are fundamentally optimized bridges.

Just as a highway has local optimizations—carpool lanes, high speed lanes, emergency shoulders, and so on—there might be local optimizations implemented by lower-layer devices, such as LAN switches. Switches are invisible to routing, but insert "passing lanes" into media.

Routers

IP routers make decisions on next-hop forwarding by stripping the data link header from a received packet, examining at least the destination IP header field, and selecting an output interface. The packet is re-encapsulated into the data link format—OSI Layer 2—appropriate to the output interface transmission type.

Multiprotocol routers strip the data link header, determine which protocol family to which the packet belongs, and send it to a routing function that does family-specific forwarding. Completely separate handling is called *ships-in-the-night routing*, in contrast with *integrated routing*, which uses a common mechanism to pass routing tables among different routing processes.

There really is no single thing called routing, but rather a router is a device with several major functions, as follows:

- *Path determination*—The identification of potential paths to a destination and selecting the best of these paths if more than one potential path exists. This process can be partially or fully static, or can involve dynamic path protocols that take seconds to minutes to "draw the map."

  The output of this process, which usually changes over time, is a set of one or more tables that specifies the output path to be taken from individual forwarding engines toward the destination.

  Path determination can apply at Layer 3 or Layer 2. In other words, it can define paths based on logical address or MAC address.

  Label switching inserts a special field, optimized for cache lookup, that can map to a route, a flow, an aggregated route, or an aggregated flow.

- *Forwarding*—The near-real-time forwarding of incoming data units (frames or packets) arriving at one port of the forwarding engine to one or more output ports of the engine. If the unit of information forwarded internally to the engine is a Layer 3 packet, Layer 2 information must be stripped on input and reapplied at output.

It is the job of the output part of the forwarding mechanism to know how to encapsulate logical information into the proper output framing. In other words, the forwarding mechanism is concerned with mapping logical addresses at the network layer—OSI Layer 3—to next-medium addresses at the data link layer—OSI Layer 2.

- A third component can be important, especially when non-broadcast multi-access (NBMA) or demand media (for example, dialup) are involved. Special issues become involved because these break the fundamental model of an IP subnet: All devices in a subnet, in principle, have Layer 2 connectivity with one another. This is not the case, however, in such things as partial-mesh frame relay or subnets internal to a dialup server.

Routers traditionally have been the main internetworking devices involved in routing. They still are, although the forwarding engine might be offloaded onto other processors. Functional components of a router are shown in Figure 2.12.

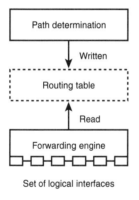

FIGURE 2.12. *Routers have several architectural components, including path determination and forwarding.*

Depending on the architecture, routers can be treated as collections of interface addresses with no unique identifier, as single addresses with no interface addresses, or both. As we will see in Chapter 12, this can lead to interesting configuration issues.

Routers need to be able to cope with unlikely combinations of addressing errors. RFC 1812 suggests [router] software should be written to deal with every conceivable error, no matter how unlikely. Eventually a packet will come in with that particular combination of errors and attributes, and unless the software is prepared, chaos can ensue. It is best to assume that the network is filled with malevolent entities that will send packets designed to have the worst possible effect. This assumption will lead to suitably protective design. The most serious problems in the Internet have been caused by unforeseen mechanisms triggered by low probability events; mere human malice would never have taken so devious a course! [RFC 1812]

Transport and Tunnels

Relaying at the transport layer is done less as a means of moving data through complex topologies and more as a means of handling architectural incompatibilities. Because a transport implementation can appear to be an end system to any architecture, it can "lie" to a network and hide the existence of a dissimilar network on its "other side."

The term *transport relay* is indeed used in formal literature, but in routine practice, transport relays are referred to as tunnels. The usage is a bit confusing, as there are both true transport-layer tunnels (for example, DLSw+ for carrying SNA and NetBIOS traffic over full TCP/IP stacks), as well as network layer tunnels (for example, Generic Route Encapsulation using a thin shim layer over IP).

Tunnels, shown in Figure 2.13, allow PDUs of a foreign "payload" protocol to be carried over a "delivery" network of a different architecture. To understand tunnels, think of a sensitive letter that is sealed in a double envelope. The inner envelope is marked "for the addressee only." The outer envelope, which gives the necessary information to deliver it to the building where the addressee works, provides the delivery protocol mechanism. The inner envelope is the payload protocol, meaningful only at the endpoints of the tunnel between the sender's and receiver's buildings.

Tunnels, as discussed in Chapter 5, also can be used to heal various addressing problems in networks of a common protocol but inconsistent addressing spaces.

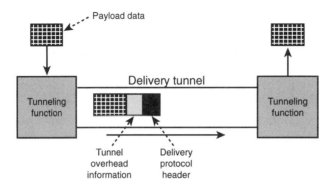

FIGURE 2.13. *Transport-level tunneling.*

Application Relays

Relaying functions also can be designed at the application layer. Their model tends to be one of exchanges among equals. There are two main places to do this: One above the application service access point and the other between application layer entities.

Other application level relaying is relevant to the basic application service. In messaging, for example, messages are destined to people with names, not nodes with addresses. Application layer functionality is needed to translate names to addresses, forward email, and so on.

Application relays are joined together into application transfer systems. Such relays exchange application-level records of the same application layer protocol. In the IP world, there are several well-known applications such as `sendmail` for exchanging mail records in the RFC 822 format. Internet mail systems also interact with DNS, as discussed in Chapter 11, "Addressing in End Hosts."

Application gateways, above the application service interface, are an architecturally clean way to mix multiple application architecture stacks. Application gateways convert application-level protocols, do processing as required, and then forward the application message. Commercial email systems normally have gateways from proprietary mail protocols (for example, cc:Mail, PROFS) to Internet-standard SMTP. The two application-associated methods are shown in Figure 2.14.

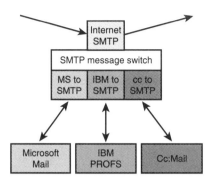

FIGURE 2.14. *Relays handle application protocols directly, while gateways process application data above the application service interface.*

Looking Ahead

This chapter gives a broad overview of the types of identifiers used for addresses and address-associated things, such as names. The next chapter, Chapter 3, emphasizes endpoint naming.

Chapter 4 deals with the lowest level of addressing, the transmission system.

Logical addressing builds from there with Chapter 5, dealing with traditional IP addressing, and Chapter 6, dealing with more modern methods.

CHAPTER 3

Application Topology: Naming Endpoints

Good name in man and woman, dear my lord/Is the immediate jewel of their souls./Who filches from me my purse/Steals trash/Tis something, nothing/But he who steals from me my good name/ Robs me of whatnot enriches him/And makes me poor indeed.

—*William Shakespeare*

Though from another place I take my name, a house of ancient fame.

—*Edmund Spencer*

What's in a name? that which we call a rose/by any other name would smell as sweet.

—*William Shakespeare*

Fundamental to network design is knowing the end-to-end requirements that will be placed on it. At the level of knowing these requirements, the underlying connectivity network should comply with Clarke's Second Law: "Any sufficiently advanced technology is indistinguishable from magic."

When thinking about the internetworking environment, all too often the emphasis is on where things are (that is, their addresses), rather than who they are (that is, their names). Which is more important: you or your location? Names can be as important as addresses in setting up an effective internetworking environment. Remember that a viable network design has routing, naming, and addressing components.

Novice, and unfortunately not-so-novice, network designers often design their address structure to reflect their organizational structure. Unless you work for an organization that never reorganizes, this sooner or later leads to an obsolete addressing structure. Address structures should reflect logical topology of the internetwork, not the organizational structure. In some firms, of course, there is no stable organization, so trying to reflect it with addressing is especially futile. The address structure tends to reflect physical locations and the connections among them. As the organization changes, you can remap changed names to the underlying addresses.

A given server can be accessed by many user clients. If that host moves and the clients have been accessing the host using IP addresses, each user needs to learn the new address. If, however, the users access the server by name rather than address, equipment moves can be fairly transparent to the users. A database entry that maps the host name to the new IP address is the only thing that needs to change.

The proper way to describe the organization, from the perspective of application topology, is with names, not addresses. Names can be translated to addresses, but the mechanics of such translation can be made invisible to end users.

In discussing application topology, you should be concerned with one-to-one or one-to-many communications among endpoint identifiers. The actual application communications are described using a valuable new idea, the flow. But before you can learn about flow among endpoints, you need to explore the conventions used to refer to endpoints.

As mentioned in Chapter 2, "Principles Underlying Addressing," the idea of a general endpoint identifier is still evolving. The discussion of application topology will begin by discussing names, which in practice are the basis of most endpoint identification conventions.

Note

Names are a practical way to refer to endpoints. In practice, the internal network uses the combination of an IP address and a TCP or UDP port number (T/U port) as a real-time endpoint identifier.

Names are human friendly, at least in comparison with numeric addresses. They are human friendly ways to refer to logical, and sometimes physical, addresses. One of the attractions of having applications refer to endpoints by name is that addressing in the infrastructure can change, transparently, the mapping of a given name to an internal address.

Such indirection is quite useful for allowing network elements to move without needing to make changes at large numbers of end hosts. Dynamic name mapping can help balance load among multiple servers or otherwise help tune performance, without end user or application participation in such tuning.

Defining Your Endpoints

It's probably best to begin informally in a brainstorming mode. Chapter 1, "What Is the Problem You Are Trying to Solve?" discussed doing this with executives, but that brainstorming effort was intended more to identify the critical issues in executive minds than to come up with an exhaustive inventory.

In the procedure described in this section, I suggest jumping back and forth between a user perspective and a server perspective. This works well for meetings I lead, but might not for everyone. Just remember that the point of brainstorming, as a means of getting information out, relies on a quick "brain-dump" style. In the early stages, don't get caught in detailed discussion of any of the points. Brainstorming is intended to identify potential ideas; analysis comes later.

Refer to Figures 1.10 and 1.11 in Chapter 1, which are sheets developed in upper-management interviews. These are the steps you should take:

1. Begin by inviting the technical staff to add bullets to both sheets.

2. After the application suggestions begin to slow, identify geographic locations of the hosts that run these applications. Ask your panel to describe the mission criticality of the application. Don't try to identify yet which users access which applications.

3. Return to the list of users and annotate them with the geographic location of the users. Use general terms, such as "branch office," and don't forget "telecommuters" or "mobile users." Get approximate counts of the user type with typical growth rates or counts, as shown in Table 3.1. From the perspective of justifying address space, you want to project growth after 6, 12, and 24 months.

TABLE 3.1. USERS AND EXPECTED GROWTH IN A REPRESENTATIVE COMMUNITY OF INTEREST—SALES.

Subapplication	Typical Locations	Users per Total Users (2 Years)	Typical Site (2 Years)	Sites (2 Years)
Inside Sales	Regional office			
Call center		200 (300)	50 (60)	4
Major account		10 (40)	2	5
Outside Sales	Mobile user	50 (150)	1	50 (150)*

Access via dial-in

On the first review of the list of users, some organizational structure might emerge. Sales, for example, is not monolithic. There are inside salespeople at fixed locations, divided into major account sales and call center sales. In addition, there are outside salespeople who are mobile.

As you begin to consider users, you are likely to run into something that electronic mail specialists call the *Santa Claus problem*. Electronic mail specialists refer to the Santa Claus problem in defining enterprise mail systems. During the Christmas season, children put letters into the postal mail addressed to Santa Claus at the North Pole. What is the postal service to do with them? Heartlessly return them, saying no such address? Simply throw them away? The actual practice is to send them to a group of volunteers to be answered.

The relevance of the Santa Claus problem is that it draws attention to the distinction between a functional name—Santa—and the personal name of the person who responds to queries. In networking practice, this is the difference between `hostmaster@company.com` and `jane_doe@company.com`. Jane is the current hostmaster, who replaced `richard_roe@company.com` and who is training `samuel_smith@company.com` as her replacement.

Users and Processes

You need to keep in mind the distinction between the person who works on a workstation and the workstation itself. A common convention, used with DNS names, is to identify users of that host by prefixing the host name with a user name, separated by the @ character:

```
socks@ovalofc.whitehouse.gov
```

A given person, and his characteristic workload, usually stays on one workstation. However, for any number of reasons, that user might move to another machine. The usual machine might be down. The user might be demonstrating something to another person and log in on the other user's machine. The user might be mobile.

Organizational changes also become involved; for example, the user might move to a different part of the organization and have new functions.

In organizations more traditional than Santa, the elves, and the reindeer, when email arrives addressed to `jsmith@company.com`, is it really intended for Jane Smith or the person who occupies Jane Smith's current job in marketing? What if Juan Gomez has replaced Jane in marketing because Jane was promoted to engineering manager?

One approach to dealing with the Santa Claus problem is to make a point of defining both personal and organizational user names. The latter is most useful for functions that receive lots of external email, such as `sales` or `help`.

DNS provides another aid for the problem of users moving among multiple machines. Detailed further in the section "DNS Architecture," DNS can provide mail exchanger information: one or more hosts in a named domain to which email can be sent, without knowledge of the specific host to which the user logs in. There still must be mechanisms for the internal user to log in to the mail host, validate his or her identity, and retrieve mail, but this is decoupled from the view of the outside world. The external world learns the mail gateway that serves the user workstation, rather than trying to send mail directly to the workstation.

The idea of separate views can go even further. In Chapter 7, "Addressing, Security, and Network Management," you will learn about the idea of *split DNS*, in which different name-to-address mappings are used inside and outside the enterprise.

Identifying Specific Servers

Table 3.2 shows the results of an initial inventory of the actual servers. Server names, as in this example, do not follow good naming practices if they are assigned casually.

"Flat" server names, such as `prod1`, are typical of an application environment where the names are first created for a small number of Windows hosts using NetBIOS. For the application topology to scale, the names need to evolve to follow a coherent hierarchical naming convention.

These names have many problems for use in a scalable application topology. Their problems include the flat structure that combines location and function.

TABLE 3.2. CURRENT SERVERS WITH NON-HIERARCHICAL NAMES.

General Function	Specific Server Function	Current Name
Email	Primary host: DC	`maildc`
	Dallas Regional	`maildfw`
	SF Regional	`mailsf`
	London Regional	`maillon`
	Bangkok Regional	`mailban`
	Sao Paulo Regional	`mailsp`
Production (includes manufacturing, order entry, and shipping	Primary host: Dallas-1	`prod1`
	Backup host: Dallas-2	`prod2`
	Standby-East: SF	`prod3`
	Standby-West: DC	`prod4`
	Manufacturing-Toronto	`mfg`

If obtaining the information can be done without slowing the process, note the protocol family (that is, IP, Novell IPX, AppleTalk, and Banyan) that the clients and servers use for connectivity. You will eventually want to know representative version numbers—version numbers are especially significant for Novell—and network interface card types, but this is at a level of detail that can unacceptably slow the brainstorming process. Details such as this can be filled in later.

Recognize, especially when dialup or Internet access is concerned, that you might not know what types of hardware and software the users have. Don't worry; the focus here is on applications. In Chapter 8, "The Existing IP and Non-IP Address Structure: Preparing for Remodeling," you will return to discussing the detailed inventory.

Services and Machines

Just as you began to impose some organization on the users, you are likely to discover that there is some structure among the applications. Accounts receivable and accounts payable are likely to be part of the same software package. There might be an integrated production system that deals with the entire cycle starting with order entry and ending with shipping.

In the first refinement of Table 3.2, establish DNS subdomains that identify the major sites and then use standard host names for the hosts at the site. An example of this is to standardize on `prod1` being a primary production host at any site and `prod2` being a standard name for a backup host. The next section, "Naming Machines," provides more general rules for host names. You'll see these refined names later in the chapter.

Naming Machines

You are now getting to the level of identifying the actual computers that run the services. Services and servers are different; services are software that runs on computers called servers.

Before actually assigning names to computers, it is worthwhile to read one of the classic real-world Internet documents, Don Libes's RFC 1178, "Choosing a Name for Your Computer." He identifies many operational problems that come from poorly chosen names. Some of his rules are dated, in that they were written at a time when timeshared servers were more common. A more current list of rules on what *not* to name computers includes:

- Don't overload other terms in common use. Naming a computer `host` or `computer` is incredibly confusing. This rule includes avoiding naming your computer after yourself, your children, your cats, and so on. A colleague told me of problems speaking of his "Sun" workstation rather than his "son."

- Don't use long names. Names longer than eight characters tend to be hard to remember, too long for fields in windows, and sometimes not supported in software. It's reasonable to have fields of hierarchical names be eight or so characters each.

- Avoid alternate spellings.

- Avoid trademarked names.

- Avoid names that duplicate names of domains.

- Avoid domain-like names.

- Don't use antagonistic or otherwise embarrassing names. Avoid acronyms that might translate into offensive phrases (for example, `foo`).

- Don't use digits at the beginning of a name.

- Don't use non-alphanumeric characters in a name. Underscores and slashes are special problems for DNS.

- Don't expect case to be preserved. Although UNIX systems are case sensitive, many other systems are not. My general practice is to use lowercase exclusively in creating names.

Libes also has some recommendations on things that are good to do in naming:

- Use words or names that are rarely used.

- Use theme names.

- Use real words.

- Always make room for an exception.

Making Names Hierarchical

In Table 3.2, you went from speaking generally of services to breaking out general services into specific applications functions, and eventually came up with a list of server names. These server names need to be made globally unique by adding DNS domain information to them, as shown in Table 3.3. The DNS convention in use establishes subdomains for each major site.

TABLE 3.3. CURRENT SERVERS WITH HIERARCHICAL NAMES.

General Function	Specific Server Function	Current Name	Hierarchical Name
Email	Primary Host: DC	maildc	mail.dc.company.com
	Dallas Regional	maildfw	mail.dfw.company.com
	SF Regional	mailsf	mail.sf.company.com
	London Regional	maillon	mail.lon.company.com
	Bangkok Regional	mailban	mail.ban.company.com
	Sao Paulo Regional	mailsp	mail.sp.company.com
Production	Primary Host: Dallas-1	prod1	prod1.dfw.company.com
(includes	Backup Host: Dallas-2	prod2	prod2.dfw.company.com
manufacturing,	Standby-West: SF	prod3	prod2.sf.company.com
order entry, and	Standby-East: DC	prod4	prod2.dc.company.com
shipping)	Manufacturing-Toronto	mfg	mfg.dc.company.com

One of the limitations of the original hosts.txt approach to name translation is that organizations independently created their own names, and these names could duplicate one another. Within the subdomains shown in Table 3.3, the regional site subdomains allow a machine to be unique within a subdomain.

Alternatives for Name Hierarchies

Geographic organization is not always the best way to delegate into subdomains. Table 3.3 shows a variant where the manufacturing and email groups are responsible for their own host naming. You might notice that the geographic names are not set up, in this example, as separate DNS levels.

Having functional group administration rather than administering at the geographic site level makes good sense for some organizations, because the functional groups are likely to know more about their data flow patterns and the name service infrastructure that best supports them. Functional groups are also more likely to match communities of interest.

In Table 3.4, the production administrator has introduced the convention that host names start with a location, such as dc, followed by a standard production host code. These host codes are:

- p1—The primary host running the integrated production system.

- p2—A backup host for the integrated production system. Backup hosts do not have the full capacity of a primary host and should be distinguished from p1 hosts.

- m1—A primary host for the manufacturing application only.

- m2—A backup host for the manufacturing application. No real instances of such backup hosts exist yet, but it is reasonable to reserve a name for them in the naming structure.

TABLE 3.4. CURRENT SERVERS WITH ALTERNATE HIERARCHICAL NAMES.

General Function	Specific Server Function	Current Name	Hierarchical Name
Email	Primary Host: DC	maildc	dc.mail.company.com
	Dallas Regional	maildfw	dfw.mail.company.com
	SF Regional	mailsf	sf.mail.company.com
	London Regional	maillon	lon.mail.company.com
	Bangkok Regional	mailban	ban.mail.company.com
	Sao Paulo Regional	mailsp	sp.mail.company.com
Production (includes manufacturing, order entry, and shipping)	Primary Host: Dallas-1	prod1	dfwp1.prod.company.com
	Backup Host: Dallas-2	prod2	dfwp2.prod.company.com
	Standby-West: SF	prod3	sfp2.prod.company.com
	Standby-East: DC	prod4	dcp2.prod.company.com
	Manufacturing-Toronto	mfg	torm1.prod.company.com

Naming When Organizations Merge

To see the flexibility of hierarchical DNS naming, assume that company.com has acquired another firm, firm.com. This new firm did not follow hierarchical naming conventions, and some of its server names duplicate existing company.com names.

Servers at firm.com, as shown in Table 3.5, have different functions than at company.com. The firm.com production servers run the applications to make widgets, where company.com manufactures blivits. All firm.com servers are capable of handling the full application load, so there is no reason to differentiate between primary and backup servers.

TABLE 3.5. *firm.com* SERVERS WITH NONHIERARCHICAL NAMES.

General Function	Specific Server Function	Current Name
Email	Primary Host: New York	mailnyc
	Dallas Regional	maildfw
	LA Regional	mailla
Production widget manufacturing	Primary Host: Chicago	prod1
	Backup Host: Dallas	prod2
	Standby-West: SF	prod3
Order Tracking	Primary Host: Chicago	ord1
	Standby-East: New York	ord2

Where company.com integrates manufacturing, order entry, and shipping, firm.com does not. The long-term direction of company.com is to develop an integrated server that will handle all these functions, and a naming convention should be established for this future application.

The production host naming convention needs to be extended:

- p1—The primary host running the integrated production system for blivits

- p2—A backup host for the integrated production system for blivits

- m1—A primary host for the blivit manufacturing application only

- m2—A backup host for the blivit manufacturing application

- w—A host for the widget manufacturing application

- s—A host for the firm.com order application

- int—A host for the future integrated application

Smaller changes are needed for the mail application, but they are needed. The mail administrator decides that mail servers from acquired companies will be suffixed with a code representing the acquired organization. Because company.com intends to integrate the mail systems, this works as an interim fix. Mail servers without a suffix are assumed to be part of the main mail system.

Even if you had retained the prod1, prod2, and so on convention, DNS could still allow some server names to be duplicated, as long as there were no duplicates in the same subdomain. A shortened example of handling duplicates is shown in Table 3.6.

TABLE 3.6. A MEANS OF HANDLING DUPLICATE FLAT SERVER NAMES.

General Function	Specific Server Function	Current Name	Hierarchical Name
Production (includes manufacturing, order entry, and shipping)	Primary Host: Dallas-1	prod1	prod1.prod.company.com
	Backup Host: Dallas-2	prod2	prod2.prod.company.com
	Standby-West: SF	prod3	prod3.prod.company.com
	Standby-East: DC	prod4	prod4.prod.company.com
	Manufacturing-Toronto	mfg	torm1.prod.company.com
firm.com	Primary Host: Chicago	prod1	prod1.firm.prod.company.com
widget manufacturing	Backup Host: Dallas	prod2	prod2.firm.company.com
	Standby-West: SF	prod3	prod3.firm.prod.company.com

The Integrated Naming Domain

Table 3.7 shows the integration of the two naming systems. There were duplicate names as long as the convention was flat, but changing naming conventions at the same time the firm.com names were integrated eliminated duplication. A simple way to accomplish this might have been to establish new subdomains for firm.com under company.com.

TABLE 3.7. INTEGRATION OF FIRM.COM INTO COMPANY.COM.

General Function	Specific Server Function	Current Name	Hierarchical Name
Email (general)	Primary Host: DC	maildc	dc.mail.company.com
	Dallas Regional	maildfw	dfw.mail.company.com
	SF Regional	mailsf	sf.mail.company.com
	London Regional	maillon	lon.mail.company.com
	Bangkok Regional	mailban	ban.mail.company.com
	Sao Paulo Regional	mailsp	sp.mail.company.com
firm.com mail	Primary Host: New York	mailnyc	firmnyc.company.com
	Dallas Regional	maildfw	firmdfw.company.com
	LA Regional	mailla	firmla.company.com
Production (includes manufacturing,	Primary Host: Dallas-1	prod1	dfwp1.prod.company.com
	Backup Host: Dallas-2	prod2	dfwp2.prod.company.com
	Standby-West: SF	prod3	sfp2.prod.company.com

continues

TABLE 3.7. CONTINUED

General Function	Specific Server Function	Current Name	Hierarchical Name
order entry, and shipping)	Standby-East: DC	prod4	dcp2.prod.company.com
	Manufacturing-Toronto	mfg	torm1.prod.company.com
firm.com widget manufacturing	Primary Host: Chicago	prod1	chiw.prod.company.com
	Backup Host: Dallas	prod2	dfww.prod.company.com
	Standby-West: SF	prod3	sfw.prod.company.com
firm.com orders	Primary Host : Chicago	ord1	chio.prod.company.com
	Standby-East: New York	ord2	nyco.prod.company.com

Traffic Considerations and Administration

Note the network administration function responsible for these users. The eventual DNS names will reflect delegation of network administration.

After endpoints are known, you must understand the traffic patterns among them, as well as user-perceived performance at the endpoints, before you can define the structure and addressing of the network that interconnects them.

As you discuss servers, annotate them with the criticality of the application and the protective measures used to ensure their availability. It might emerge that some high-availability services actually run on multiple, co-located mirrored servers. There might be cold or hot standby sites for the more critical functions. Server mirroring and standby facilities can require large amounts of bandwidth. When traffic analysis focuses on client to server flows, it is easy to miss potential large flows among servers.

Even applications of relatively low criticality still need file backup. Do the files get backed up to a specific backup server with removable media, or are the backup media created on the application servers? Backup traffic across LANs can be a major and often overlooked amount of network volume.

A first step to understanding traffic is to consider communities of interest and then analyze flow patterns within communities of interest. You can then unify the various communities of interest into a consistent application model.

Communities of Interest

Think of a *community of interest* as a set of users that uses a set of services and expects a certain level of service when using those services. The community of interest also imposes an identifiable workload on the network. One of the first goals of a network design is establishing requirements, and user expectations are among the most basic requirements.

Communities of interest usually have some relationship to the business organization. More traffic flows inside a community of interest than leaves it.

Begin by drawing blocks for the users and servers of which you aware. At first, you might want to draw arrows showing the flows among clients and servers. As your drawing evolves and includes all the communities of interest in the enterprise, drawing each flow will make the drawing hard to read. When your drawing is complete, you will just have blocks describing the client and server groups, as well as distribution and core functions. If you want to show flows on a complex block drawing, overlay these with transparencies over hard copy or a layered computer graphics tool.

In our first example, the Sales community of interest, shown in Figure 3.1, needs access to services including email, the catalog, and order entry. The arrows in the drawing show flows.

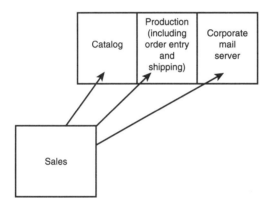

FIGURE 3.1. *A preliminary look at the Sales community of interest, showing flows. Begin the process by drawing individual user and server blocks. These will interconnect as the drawing evolves.*

It might or might not be appropriate to subdivide a community of interest into geographic parts. Geographic partitioning makes the most sense when there will be time zone variations in the traffic from different user groups. Again, do not confuse a community of interest with a network layout; a community of interest is generally location independent.

At the general design level shown in Figure 3.2, it is more useful to show user types that need different sorts of connectivity and draw in the distribution level blocks that provide this connectivity.

The core links regional servers and groups of users. There are arguments both for and against including central servers, such as mainframe databases, in the core part of the diagram. The argument for including central application servers in the core is that all other application information derives from them. The argument against placing these central servers in the core is that there might be information local to the central servers that should not leave their local environment, and putting them in a distribution block connected to the core allows you to specify filtering to keep that local information contained.

In Figure 3.2, I use my usual compromise. I place the directory service, which does name-to-address resolution, in the application core and put central servers at the distribution level.

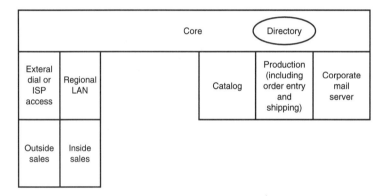

F IGURE 3.2. *Second refinement of the Sales community of interest, showing differentiat-ed user types with different distribution-level access requirements, the application core, and additional servers omitted in the first pass.*

After the basic community of interest is defined as a set of users and services, it is worthwhile to ask upper management if there are differences among the users. Should some users receive preferential system performance?

Depending on the organization's policies, it might be reasonable to split communities of interest into subcommunities that have different performance requirements. In our example, there are significant functional differences among Sales personnel in offices and in the field. Inside Sales personnel interact in real time with customers, so they need fast response. Outside Sales personnel tend not to retrieve information in the midst of a sales call, but use the network to place orders and receive updates for the large disks on their laptops.

Some special communities of interest might not be obvious, but must be considered. A good one is the disaster recovery service, in which the set of users stays the same, but the servers move to a "hot standby" system at a very different location.

You might observe that this is the same set of users and applications described for ordinary operation—why should it be a separate community of interest? The reason for separating this is the next stage of requirement analysis: describing end-to-end flows.

Flows and Traffic

Flows describe information relationships between sources and destinations. They join, or aggregate, into larger rivers of information.

Just as the water flow in a particular brook feeding a great river varies at times, specific source-to-destination flows might not actually be transferring data at a given moment. The existence of a flow does not mean that specific resources are dedicated to that specific association, merely that the information transfer system is aware of the requirement for carrying the flow.

Remember that a flow is one-directional, and an interactive session requires flows in each direction. Even batch-oriented, non-interactive flows for applications such as file transfer and mail do tend to be associated with a flow in the opposite direction. The reverse flow carries acknowledgment and possibly flow control information.

Our goal is to begin with understanding individual flows that are typical of the bulk of use and then aggregating these flows, or considering the set of flows among all similar users, as the basis of workload. Modern router operating systems include both explicit and implicit flow-based mechanisms, and it is easier to understand their details when flows are kept in mind.

A basic and useful characterization is to think of non-interactive and interactive flows. Non-interactive flows characteristically try to optimize communications for optimal use of bandwidth; they try to get all the bandwidth they can. Interactive flows, however, tend to want to optimize for minimal latency.

Your goal, in characterizing flows, is to be able to answer these questions:

- What is the burst bandwidth requirement? How about steady state bandwidth?

Bandwidth and minimum latency are related and inversely proportional. The minimum possible latency is the time it takes to transfer an application record at the bandwidth rate. This is theoretical and not achievable, because if nothing else, there will be speed-of-light propagation delays.

Other delays enter when considering loss and retransmission, time spent in flow control holds or waiting for acknowledgments, queuing for medium access, and so on.

- What sorts of topologies do the applications (or at least the endpoints) need?

- Is delay variability an issue? What error rate is tolerable?

Workload

It seems intuitive that networks cannot be designed rationally unless the workload they are expected to serve is known. It is also real-world experience that quantitative workload estimates are rather hard to find.

Although it is fashionable to look down at mainframes as inflexible monstrosities, they tend to have excellent software instrumentation. There is sometimes a cultural problem for network designers here. Often, the existing, hardware-oriented network operations staff is charged with upgrading to a general enterprise network. Operations staff do not always have ready access to capacity planning information kept by system software, such as SMF on IBM systems. Make sure the capacity planners and/or the NCP/VTAM system programmers participate in planning an IBM integration project.

Another source of workload information can be existing internetworking devices. Intelligent hubs can collect traffic on a per-port basis. Although they are substantially more expensive than pure passive hubs, these Layer 1 devices increasingly are comparable in price to Layer 2 workgroup switches. Workgroup switches have much more capability than intelligent hubs, but cost only slightly more.

In situations where workload has not been characterized, putting in intelligent hubs or switches as pure data collection devices can be extremely helpful. My general practice is to use workgroup switches rather than intelligent hubs. Remember that management stations are necessary to collect the information gathered by these devices.

Warning

In heavily loaded LANs with a small number of servers, insert switches with caution. Congestion on the shared medium might have been all that was protecting the servers from overload.

Whether you use switches or intelligent hubs, you want standard methods to collect data from them. This means that you query them with the Simple Network Management Protocol (SNMP), using SNMP to retrieve data from an appropriate Management Information Base (MIB).

Commercial monitoring tools are available that can passively plug in to a busy point on an existing network and analyze traffic. These can be expensive and require significant skill to use; analysis of their data is often part of a commercial network audit service.

Simply visiting a representative user and watching and timing what they do, with paper and a clock, can be quite informative. This is a worthwhile reality check regardless of what other traffic measurements are available.

When a significant part of the workload is general Web access, it can be hard to predict the traffic. Nevertheless, there are some practical ways to predict maximum load.

The cost of ISP connections is sufficiently high to be capped by budgetary factors. If, for a given site, all that can be afforded is a T1 line, that is the maximum speed at which any workstation can burst onto the Internet.

Tip

Although it can be reasonable and conservative to assume a user can burst up to the maximum WAN port speed, I confess to a prejudice that anyone with responsibilities for designing public Web pages should not get more than 14.4 KBps of bandwidth. To give Web designers huge bandwidth is, in my prejudiced opinion, a license for them to create Web pages that take forever to download at the speeds available to ordinary Internet mortals.

When the workload is transaction based, discuss the capacity of servers with the applications staff. Ignoring more precise queuing behavior, a first approximation of a single flow multiplies the transaction size, remembering input and output on a half-duplex LAN, by the expected number of transactions per second.

Break up the transactions into flows. If the medium is half duplex, client-to-server flows cannot overlap server-to-client flows.

Eventually, the addressing plan considers the number of servers that will coexist on a shared medium. Excessive bandwidth demands for the medium might suggest a switched, not a shared, medium. Switching, however, does not help if the aggregate transaction bandwidth exceeds the speed of the server's connection to the medium.

You just aggregated individual transaction flows. Before exploring the use of flow aggregation to characterize the overall workload, you need to consider whether your applications are such that a given user action will create multiple flows.

Flow and Packet Replication

When you analyze an order entry application, you might find the user typically enters 1800 bytes of order information and gets back 2000 bytes of response. This might suggest that the user action leads to two flows, one from client to server (C→S) of 1800 bytes and one from server to client (S→C) of 2000 bytes.

But what if this were a fault-tolerant application that kept mirrored databases on multiple servers? A user action, in this case, causes flows to replicate. If there were two servers, a primary and a backup, the flows would have to recognize these multiple destinations. They might do this in the following ways:

- The client is aware of the servers and, for a given user input, sends two flows: C→S1 and C→S2. Do note that each flow is constructed of multiple packets; the 1800 byte user input is too large for an Ethernet frame and a typical IP maximum packet size.

  Depending on the application design, there might be two full flows in response, with the client selecting the one to use. Alternatively, there might be S1→S2 and S2→S1 coordinating traffic, so only one server actually answers.

- The client is not aware of the multiple servers, and the server replicates the query and sends it to the backups.

- The client is aware of the servers, the network supports multicasting, and the client sends multicast packets that can be heard by all hosts. In this case, there is a single C→SG flow, where SG is the multicast group of servers.

  Even in this case, there are likely to be multiple response flows, possibly to keep the servers synchronized. Each server can respond independently to the query and let the client decide which response to use. The latter approach simplifies server coordination at the cost of increasing bandwidth.

Flow Aggregation

It is useful and meaningful to group individual flows into various aggregations. Globally, sets of flows can form a sensible application-oriented set of communities of interest. Communities of interest later will be used as the first method of sizing the parts of the hierarchy identified by address blocks, but you must keep in mind that these blocks can change.

Assume that certain flows are designated as high-priority interactive communications. If several individual user flows are treated this way, it lowers the workload in a router to treat those several flows as an aggregate when making flow-based forwarding decisions.

> ### Note
>
> *At an endpoint, there must be sufficient bandwidth, in each direction, to handle the aggregated flows expected between that endpoint and the rest of the network. You should be sure to consider both the average and peak aggregated flow volume.*
>
> *Peak traffic can be subtle to determine. From a pure application standpoint, it usually is reached an hour or so after a shift begins, as people get into their work rhythm. In a multiple time zone environment, however, several smaller peaks can coincide to make a large one.*
>
> *Knowing the aggregate of flows at a given point gives a check on the types of media that must handle those flows. The number of media needed, with parallel paths to achieve high bandwidth, has a direct effect on the amount of address space. Each path needs at least one prefix.*

System activities also can affect peak load. If backups are done across a network, they can produce huge bursts. Overhead from routing using older periodic update routing information exchange protocols, such as IP RIP and IGRP, can generate significant bursts, respectively, every 30 or 90 seconds. The service location mechanisms for workgroup protocols such as NetBIOS and Novell IPX produce significant overhead, which can be especially bad because it might be generated as broadcasts.

If there is a significant difference between peak and average aggregated flows, that might help in selecting the most appropriate transmission technology, especially in the WAN. Multiplexed services such as Frame Relay can have physical access lines sized to handle the peak, but subscribe to only enough capacity to handle the average load. Bandwidth-on-demand circuit-switched services also might be appropriate when peak and average differ significantly.

If peaks and averages are close together, dedicated circuit technologies might offer lower overhead than multiplexed services.

Realistic Bandwidth Requirements

Bandwidth requirements can be subtle. I dealt with some of these subtleties in a medical application that illustrates some common misconceptions about bandwidth.

A hospital wanted to move its radiologists to a building about one mile from the main hospital campus. An argument ensued about the amount of bandwidth that really was needed between the new offices and the campus.

At the heart of the argument were several assumptions:

- Radiologists are responsible for interpreting X-rays, CT and MRI scans, and so on.
- Digitized images from these procedures are large files.
- Because the files are large, radiologists need lots of bandwidth.

It was the third assumption that was flawed. Or at least it could be thought of as several related sub-assumptions.

Luckily in this case, I happen to be reasonably familiar with medical users and how they do their work. I played dumb and asked, "Tell me. We are obviously most concerned with emergencies. But let's say an unconscious crash victim arrives and needs an immediate head CT scan. It's 3 a.m. Does that scan get interpreted at the radiology office?"

"Of course not. We page the on-call radiologist in the hospital, who goes to the scanner room and gives a first impression while looking at the workstation screen."

"OK," I observed. So we definitely need a fast pipe between the scanner and the workstation in the on-call office. "But,

now let's consider someone with chronic low back pain, who comes in for a scheduled MRI. Does the on-call radiologist read that?"

"Of course not. That's handled routinely back at the office."

"And what's your turnaround time on those?"

"Oh, three to five working days."

"I see. Sounds like you really have three bandwidth requirements. There needs to be high bandwidth between the scanner and the local workstations. Radiologists who do the routine interpretations need high bandwidth between their workstations and wherever they get the image from…but they don't get it directly from the scanner. They get it from a disk farm in the radiology offices. The hospital does batch file transfers from the scanner's local disk to the disk farm."

At least a dedicated 10 MB pipe, and possibly 100 MB, would be needed between the workstations and their image sources so the radiologist could jump between images without delay—or even display motion. There are three to five working days, plus nights and weekends, available to transfer the image.

Let's assume the hospital queues up 100 images to be interpreted per day by each radiologist, and these images average a fairly generous 50 MB each. So, we have 5 GB, or roughly 40 GB, to transfer per radiologist over a three-day period. There are about 770,000 seconds in three days. To transfer those 40 GB, we need to average roughly 52 KBps per radiologist.

continues

continued

For 10 radiologists, a T1 (or less) is quite adequate between the two sites. People can perceive a minimum display of about 200 milliseconds. If the goal is to get the first image (for example, about 1 MB) to the screen of the workstation without noticeable delay, each workstation needs about 5 MBps of dedicated bandwidth to the server.

Switched Ethernet should be adequate. To be generous and allow for growth, as well as potential full-motion applications sensitive to latency, Fast Ethernet can be installed. There is little cost difference in new installations between interface costs for 10 and 100 MBps Ethernet. New wiring should conform to Category 5 specifications, which handles either 10 or 100 MBps.

We want to make sure the server has, to support 10 radiologists, a bandwidth adequate to serve 10*5 MBps, or at least 50 MBps. For the end users, the server port should run on Fast Ethernet on the end user station.

In addressing, the number of hosts per medium is a major driver of addressing design. When bandwidth, or other quality of service requirements, potentially limits the number of hosts per medium, this limitation needs to be known before detailed addressing design can occur.

Low-bandwidth users (see Table 3.8) can run interactive data and moderate multimedia applications on shared media in the 10 MB range.

As their bandwidth needs increase, their media need not change at first. Because a typical 10 to 100 user population on a shared Ethernet effectively has 50 to 100 KBps per user, using switches to give more bandwidth is a simple solution not requiring end system changes. The full effective bandwidth can be made available to individual users.

Increased speed, whether through dedicated switch ports on a 10 or 16 MBps medium, or through 100 MBps technologies, generally should be provided to servers before end users.

TABLE 3.8. REPRESENTATIVE BANDWIDTH BY INTERACTIVE APPLICATION.

Bandwidth	Application
64 KBps	Telephone quality audio in the public network. Compression can lower this.
100 KBps	Simple application sharing.
128 KBps to 1 MBps	Videoconferencing.
1.54 MBps	MPEG video.
8 MBps to 100 MBps	Imaging, broadcast quality video.
>100 MBps	Virtual reality.

An Application Model

You need to generalize the model you began by modeling the Sales COI to include the entire enterprise. To review, the levels of this model are:

- *Core*—Central servers and the functionality that leads to them and interconnects distribution servers. This is the *application* core and does not match the internetwork core that will be defined later.

- *Distribution*—Regionalized concentrating servers.

- *Access*—Functions that inherently need to be close to the end user.

An application-oriented model identifies the relationships among endpoints in a network. Either clients or servers can be at an endpoint. These clients and servers are joined by an application core. This core might be no more than the network infrastructure, but might also be an application-oriented hierarchy, such as a mail system.

The process of drawing the model has several steps. In Figure 3.2, you drew a community of interest as a client block and server blocks as a first approximation of the Sales community of interest. The first approximation has generic Sales users and two servers.

Discussing this first picture with the application staff should trigger more discussion and refinements shown in Figure 3.2.

Users live in the access tier. Looking at the requirements, there really are two kinds of Sales users: inside and outside. Figure 3.2 shows the refinement of the user type, as well as the core connectivity requirement, as a result of discussing the Figure 3.1 illustration with application experts. As such discussions are apt to do, this one reminds the staff that the production server, which tracks order entry, also needed to be added to the Sales COI.

There is need for a policy here that affects the bandwidth requirement. Should inside and outside salespeople get the same response time? Other policies are needed to define the access security policy for the different user groups.

There are functional differences in what the types of sales people do. Outside people have relatively low volume. Inside people have high volume and might need to be linked to the voice system.

Still at the application level, you can see that there are really two communities of interest within Sales: inside and outside. Inside salespeople are at regional centers and might need voice integration. Outside people need mobile access.

You still are not getting into specific network design, but you are getting more and more traffic patterns and requirements. Note that the external access service is a general, distribution-tier function, used by multiple communities of interest. It is worthwhile, in general, to distinguish between remote access by authorized users and general Internet access. The two functions generally should be quite separate, although new secure access techniques discussed in Chapter 7 make it more and more practical to allow access to internal resources through secure Internet connections.

Now, let us consider the additional requirements of Sales. Sales personnel need to access the catalog to describe the products they sell. They also need to access two parts of the production database, order entry and shipping, the latter to trace their orders.

Extending the Model Beyond Sales

Going beyond Sales, how do other organizational functions relate? The graphics staff actually builds the catalog, using input from engineering. Catalog databases, including company confidential information such as wholesale prices, are cached on internal servers. A subset of the catalog, which does not contain sensitive data, is on a public Web server protected by a firewall. Graphics prepares catalog entries based on information sent to Graphics by electronic mail from Engineering.

We live in a world of distributed computing. This leads to server-to-server communication as well as user-to-server communication. Server-to-server communication can be peer-to-peer or part of a hierarchy.

Traffic Among Servers

In estimating flow volumes, do not neglect server-to-server traffic. This traffic can be for database replication to caches, as the catalog here is copied to regions. It can be for pure backup. There can also be distributed computing. In this enterprise, some of the engineering computation runs from local processor to local processor in the engineering server farm. Other server-to-server communications shown in Figure 3.3 include backups, which are flows within the access level. Database updates from master servers to regional servers are flows that traverse the core.

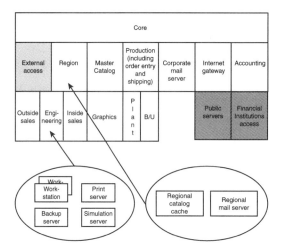

F IGURE 3.3.   *Server-to-server communications are part of the total workload and are easily missed!*

File backups in the production system are done to peer servers, while there is a master copy of the catalog in the graphics department. The "golden copy" of the catalog forms the highest level of a hierarchy, from which cached copies are replicated in the various regional offices and on the public catalog server. Depending on the requirements at each user site, the cached copies might be partial views of the master database.

External Connectivity

According to an old proverb, when the only tool you have is a hammer, every problem tends to look like a nail. Simplistic interpretation of hierarchy" often leads to awkward network design that tries to force everything into a singly routed tree. Don't try to solve every application topology with a single hierarchy. When you later learn about internetwork topology, again do not fall into the single hierarchy trap.

You want to maintain hierarchy in your *own* organization. There are several key reasons you might be tempted to break the hierarchical model:

- You have a heavy traffic requirement between two access-level servers.

- When you draw your enterprise using the core-distribution-access model, you find it awkward to split things into only three levels.

- You connect to business partners through private extranets or have Internet connectivity.

None of these reasons should cause you to break the model, only to interpret the model more generally. For the traffic management problem, remember that the application topology does not necessarily dictate the internetwork topology. Communications between points in the access layer should be drawn through the core, because the core is defined to be the mechanism of intersite communication. When you design the internetwork, you indeed might set up special paths for heavy flows, but detailed traffic management is not the focus of the application topology. The focus is on identifying flows among endpoints.

Next, the model is not meant to constrain. Just as the OSI model evolved to include sublayers for LAN architecture and a refined view of the network layer, it is perfectly reasonable to sublayer the application model. You might, for example, have workgroup-level servers such as printers and floor-level servers such as caches on the same building floor defined at the access tier.

External communications fits nicely into the model, if you accept the idea that each organization is structured as a tree; but the trees may overlap. Think of the external organization as an access-tier function. Your access to it might be controlled by your firewall, located at the distribution tier. Your various sites access the firewall through your application core.

The external organization's tree, as shown in Figure 3.4, is upside down with respect to yours. Your access tier overlaps their access tier. They control your access to their functions with their firewall.

Enterprise Core						
External access	Region	Catalog	Production (including order entry and shipping)	Corporate mail server	Internet gateway	Accounting
Outside sales	Engi-neering	Inside sales	Graphics	P l a n t		Public servers (ISP access)	Financial Institution access
						ISP distribution	Financial institution distribution
						Internet core	Financial institution core

FIGURE 3.4.   *External organizations, whether the Internet or private extranets, connect to your application hierarchy by overlapping at the access tier.*

For example, the accounting department communicates with a variety of external financial institutions—for electronic payments, payroll services, tax payments, funds transfer, and so on. Each of the external networks to which accounting connects might be a complex hierarchy of its own, but our enterprise is not concerned with the internal structure of those institutions' networks. The key is that each enterprise or ISP overlaps at the access tier.

Exchange of financial information often is a good application of an extranet, in which communications are secure and flow under bilateral or multilateral agreements. This contrasts with the public servers on the public side of the firewall, which are true general Internet applications, available to arbitrary use.

DNS: Mapping Between Internet Names and Logical Addresses

Actually sending packets, of course, requires that they contain a destination address. Because good application design requires that services be requested by name, not address, that name must be translated into an address before it can be used. The address corresponding to a name must be taken from an authoritative source of information.

In IP, names and addresses generally can be translated back and forth. There are basic cases in DNS where a name can map to multiple addresses, and there are advanced products that can do such tasks as dynamically change the address response to a name request.

The simplest name-to-address translation mechanisms are simple files containing a table of names with corresponding addresses. Cisco router configurations can contain IP host statements that have this effect. Common simple name-to-address translation files are /etc/hosts in UNIX and LMHOSTS in Windows.

Originally, name-to-address translation in UNIX systems was done through a simple file called hosts.txt. This was a simple list of host names and their addresses, but soon ran into scaling problems. In the original ARPAnet, the hosts.txt file was centrally controlled by the Network Information Center (NIC), and individual sites retrieved a new copy, typically at intervals of days. This was not sustainable as the ARPAnet grew.

In 1984, the DNS was defined. Early releases became stable, and a set of guiding documents was published. Over the years, public domain software for DNS evolved and improved. Numerous performance improvements entered both the software and the basic protocol.

In recent years, the DNS has had numerous enhancements proposed to deal with the much larger Internet. Enhancements are especially important in security.

There are technical enhancements of clear value. The value of some administrative changes, however, is more complex. The impact of these administrative changes greatly complicates the situation. There have been legitimate concerns about scaling of the top-level domain space and of the administration of top- and second-level domain space.

The DNS name problem is far more complex, from a business and legal standpoint, than address management, and this book can only skim the surface of the issues involved. The root, or the conceptual top of the DNS database tree, was under the control of the Internet Assigned Numbers Authority. Domain names and Internet addresses were administered by the NIC, under U.S. government subsidy.

As the Internet has become commercialized, the role of the U.S. government has been reduced. As budget cuts affect the U.S. government, it is eager to get out of the cost of supporting the Internet. Models to replace it, however, become complex, if for no other reason than the Internet is truly international, and a U.S.-guided solution is not appropriate as a long-term solution.

One model developed by the International Ad Hoc Committee (IAHC) establishes a structure for international registries, which actually record the allocations of domain names. At the time of this writing, in mid-1998, it is not a given that the IAHC proposal is the definitive solution. The situation remains complex politically and legally, in part due to many issues involving intellectual property rights to domain names. Participants in the IAHC plan have signed a Memorandum of Understanding for the generic top-level domains (gTLD-MoU) described below, and this agreement is kept by the International Telecommunications Union (ITU).

The gTLD-MoU organization, which freely describes gTLD-MoU as the Internet's worst acronym, establishes at the highest operational level a Council of Registrars (CORE), replacing the NIC as the top-level authority. CORE will guide multiple competing registries, of which one is a commercial spin-off of the existing NIC, operated by Network Solutions, Inc.

In the gTLD-MoU model, policy for the gTLD space will be initiated by a Policy Oversight Committee with members named by:

- IANA—Two appointments

- ISOC—Two appointments

- Internet Architecture Board (IAB)—Two appointments

- Council of Registrars (CORE)—Two appointments

- International Trademark Association (INTA)—One appointment

- World Intellectual Property Organization (WIPO)—One appointment

- International Telecommunication Union (ITU)—One appointment

- Representative of the Depository of the Memorandum of Understanding on the Generic Top Level Domain Name Space of the Internet Domain Name

- System (gTLD-MoU—the ITU)—One appointment

ISOC and IANA must ratify changes to policy, with review by a Policy Advisory Board (PAB) composed of the signatories of the gTLD-MoU. PAB members conceptually are a higher level than the POC.

You might think this is complex. It is. It is also controversial, and there has been an "AlterNIC" effort that competes with it, although with a very limited constituency. In 1997, an individual associated with the AlterNIC group publicized he had taken control of the DNS root as a protest. This individual has been arrested and criminal charges placed, with no resolution at the time of this writing.

The existing system for DNS has worked, but it must evolve. Readers are encouraged to monitor the constantly changing interests and policies involved. In contrast, IP address assignment has been relatively noncontroversial, although some issues have arisen and are discussed in Chapter 6, "Internet Failing: Details at 11."

A large part of the controversy involves resolution of conflicts between domain names and trademarks. It is unclear how this can be resolved legally and if current trademark law, national and international, is adequate for the process.

The Naming System as a Resource

From a technical standpoint, domain (that is, DNS) names are assigned from a high-level hierarchy. When assigned a domain, organizations assign subdomains within it.

Any registered domain name belongs to one of several *top-level domains* (TLDs). *Second-level domains* (SLDs) are allocated to individual organizations by the *registries* that actually administer the TLDs.

TLDs encompass several categories:

- "Generic." In practice, U.S. organizations have registered under one of the generic TLDs rather than the .us domain:

  .com for commercial enterprises

  .org for noncommercial organizations

  .edu for institutes of higher education

  .net for network service providers

- ISO 3166 country codes, such as .uk for Great Britain, .ru for Russia, and .de for Germany. The .us TLD is allocated to the United States, but has not been significantly used.

- .gov and .mil have been used by the U.S. government for civil and military organizations, respectively.

- .int for international organizations.

- A new group of TLDs defined under the gTLD-MoU effort:

  .firm for businesses or firms

  .shop for businesses offering goods to purchase

  .web for entities emphasizing activities related to the WWW

  .arts for entities emphasizing cultural and entertainment activities

  .rec for entities emphasizing recreation/entertainment

  .info for entities providing information services

  .nom activities for those wanting individual or personal nomenclature

The levels of the domain are written with the most significant on the right. Subdomains go to the left, separated by periods:

```
ovalofc.whitehouse.gov
```

DNS names map to the specific address of a host. Although DNS has capabilities to deal with the application level of routing email messages to specific users at a host, I'll defer that discussion until you understand the basic DNS architecture.

DNS Architecture

The database model used in DNS is modeled after the UNIX file system. The DNS model is intended to provide a consistent view of names, using names that are independent of the underlying network topology.

Performance is a significant concern in DNS design, especially given that the size and administrative nature of the application requires a distributed architecture. DNS was designed to be scalable over a wide range of platforms, although it might be reaching its limits in very large networks. One specific design goal was to allow the originator of naming data to balance the tradeoffs between accuracy and efficiency. These tradeoffs are realized in lifetimes applied to data, after which the receiver must get new copies.

Several architectural components make up DNS; they can be viewed in different ways:

- As *domain name space,* or the tree structure in which naming is defined.

- As *resource record*s attached to the naming tree, which contain information about the name. The set of information in all resource records in Internet-connected DNS servers defines the distributed DNS database. A specific DNS server contains its own domain's resource records and information learned from dynamic responses received from other domain servers.

- As *name servers* that provide information about all or part of the tree. In practice, the tree is distributed into a set of name servers, each having definitive knowledge about certain branches of the tree and additional knowledge on how to reach other definitive name servers. The definitive name server for a part of the tree is called the authority for that subset of the DNS name space.

- As client *resolvers* that retrieve information from name servers in response to requests from other programs. Resolvers appear as servers to applications, but act as clients of name servers.

It can be confusing, but DNS has both an *administrative model* and a *database model,* shown in Figure 3.5. The administrative model defines the abstraction of domain names from the root to the TLD, to SLDs issued to organizations, and to subdomains within those organizations. The database model deals with the storage of DNS information in files and servers.

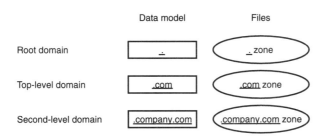

FIGURE 3.5. *Each level of domain is both an abstraction and a set of resource records in a particular zone file.*

The database model is the set of records that actually defines those domains as operational *zones*. Relationships among the major resource record types are shown in Figure 3.6. Domains are administrative; the databases that define their contents are in zone files. These databases are made of *resource records* (RRs), the contents of which are returned by queries in the DNS protocol.

Zone files begin with a Start of Authority (SOA) RR. Because DNS other than the root is a distributed hierarchical database, there must be one or more name server (NS) resource records that point to the next higher level of the hierarchy.

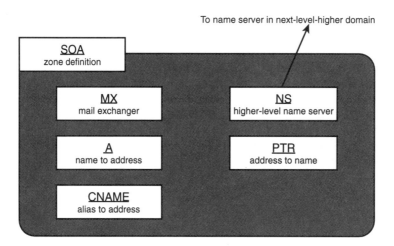

FIGURE 3.6. *Relationships among the primary DNS record types.*

Individual name-to-address mappings are described in A records. Aliases for addresses can also be established with CNAME records. Pointer RRs (PTRs) are used to enable translation of names to addresses. Queries can ask for information including the address associated with a name, or the name associated with a known address. The latter process is called *reverse mapping*.

Mail exchanger (MX) records define particular well-connected hosts to which mail can be sent from the outside, without knowing the specific host on which a user or process runs.

Primaries, Secondaries, and BIND

In the previous section, you learned that there is a distinction between the administrative and database models of DNS. The actual database definitions for a domain are kept in *zone files*.

For reliability and performance reasons, the DNS specifications define the idea of *primary masters* and *secondary masters* for zone files. Each domain has a single primary that is authoritative for that zone. Some number of secondaries periodically do *zone transfers*, updating their disk-based zone files to match the authoritative file. All administrative updates are done against the primary zone file. Both primary and secondary servers can answer DNS queries.

So far, I have focused on the server side of DNS. BIND also includes client software, called the *resolver*. Resolver, which is a general-purpose DNS client, sends DNS queries from general application clients and servers to the DNS servers.

BIND takes the primary and secondary model one step further, by adding caching-only servers. These have no disk-resident zone files, but after they have retrieved the results of a DNS query, they store it in main memory. Subsequent requests for the same information are answered from the memory-resident information, assuming it has not aged out.

Caching

Distributed applications in general, and name-to-address translation in particular, use caching to improve performance. The underlying idea is to answer queries as close to the source as possible.

When a client sends a request to a local server, if that server can answer the query, it goes no further. Otherwise, the local server refers the query to a higher-level server whose address it knows. At each higher level, the name server either answers the query or refers it upward in the hierarchy.

DNS makes a distinction between *iterative* and *recursive* searching in a hierarchy. The previously described behavior, where a server itself refers a query upward in the hierarchy and takes responsibility for getting the best possible answer, is recursive. The iterative model involves much less work for the server. In nonrecursive lookups, a server responds with the best answer it can give from its local files and cache, but does not query additional servers. It does, however, return to the client information on which servers might have more definitive information. The client then queries those servers and gets back the correct information or referrals to yet other servers. This is a perfectly reasonable approach for heavily loaded servers.

Whenever a server receives a positive response, it caches the response so it can answer subsequent requests without having to query higher-level servers. Entries in the cache eventually expire, according to the Time-To-Live (TTL) value in the received DNS response.

It is common practice to change TTLs to short values during a transition. Shortening TTLs for fault tolerance is a fairly complex issue, discussed later under "Round-Robin Load Sharing in DNS." A practical problem, however, is that most versions of BIND do not recognize TTLs less than 300 seconds.

Enhancements to Basic Name Translation

As both intranets and the Internet grow, network managers face scalability problems. There are issues of server performance, server availability, and congestion on paths to the servers. A natural approach to scaling is to have workload distributed among multiple servers.

Good application design should hide the details of multiple servers from the user. Various techniques have evolved to meet these needs, and many involve enhancements to the name-to-address translation mechanisms. Some are built in to application protocols themselves, such as FTP and HTTP. Others are optimized for high-performance transaction protocols running over UDP. Yet others are independent of the application protocol, but do assume that the application runs over TCP.

Several IP upper-layer protocols, including FTP, HTTP, and RPC, have redirection mechanisms. These techniques can make security filtering quite complex. Redirection also complicates understanding the workload as a set of flows, because what might appear to be a A→B request coupled with a B→A response can become A→B, B→C, and C→A responses, or even more complex situations.

Asymmetrical Routing: An Application Perspective

When an enterprise has multiple points of attachment to the Internet, it is almost impossible to avoid cases where the response from an outgoing query comes back at a different point from where the query left the enterprise. This does not mean anything is broken, but is a reflection of the reality of global Internet routing. The same sort of asymmetrical behavior can be caused by application-level redirection.

Most interenterprise routing follows a closest exit or hot potato model, as shown in Figure 3.7. When an ISP receives a packet to be forwarded to a given destination, it sends it out what it considers the best path to that destination. *Best*, in this case, depends on information available to the ISP, not what is truly the best end-to-end path based on complete information.

Your organization cannot significantly affect the routing policy of intermediate service providers with which you have no contractual relationship. This can be a very hard point to internalize if you are used to controlling all resources, as is typical inside an enterprise network.

From a traffic engineering standpoint, it cannot be assumed that a response flow will come back on the same line on which it left.

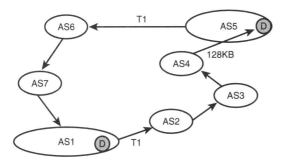

FIGURE 3.7. *Either application-level redirection or network-level routing can cause a response to come back on a different path than the request left.*

Round-Robin Load Sharing in DNS

A given name can have more than one address associated with it. Each address is in a separate type A resource record. In BIND version 4.9.3 and later, the server attempts to load balance among them by rotating the order of responses.

If there were three addresses for `a.company.com`—10.1.0.1, 10.2.0.1, and 10.3.0.1—the server would respond to three consecutive queries with the following sequences:

- `10.1.0.1, 10.2.0.1, 10.3.0.1`

- `10.2.0.1, 10.3.0.1, 10.1.0.1`

- `10.3.0.1, 10.1.0.1, 10.2.0.1`

This simply spreads the load over several servers. This process is unaware of the actual loading of the destinations, as opposed to methods such as DistributedDirector, described later in the chapter, and load-shared network address translation [RFC 2391], discussed in Chapter 6. Load sharing can add robustness, as long as the requesting client is reasonably intelligent. Assume that the client receives the second response in the preceding, and 10.2.0.1 happens to be down. An intelligent client would then try 10.3.0.1 and 10.1.0.1 before assuming that the destination is unreachable.

From the perspective of flows, DNS load sharing can result in flows being created to multiple destinations when a single one is expected. From the ingress perspective, these flows can be aggregated.

If there is more than one network path from the multiple DNS destinations back to the originator, the return flows might come in on different paths.

Say you have three mirrored servers for the xxx application at company.com. Round-robin DNS returns three addresses to the client. If the first server happens to be down, an intelligent client tries the third, and so forth. You also have an intelligent DNS management tool that detects hard failures of a given server and removes it from the active DNS.

If a local name server supporting the client had cached the name, the client might get the cached entry 1/2/3, and this and other clients would experience trying 1 and timing out. If the company.com name server put a short TTL on xxx.company.com, the cached entry would time out, the local name server would query again, and only the active server names would be returned.

HTTP Referral

On the Web, you commonly follow hypertext links. Clicking on one link does not ensure that the response will come from the Web server to which you're connected. If there are multiple Internet access points to your network, asymmetrical routing might take place.

In addition, the HTTP protocol includes several transaction redirection response codes in the 300 series, not all of which are supported by current software. Key among them are

301	Data requested by the URL have permanently moved. The response contains the new URL for the data.
302	Data requested were found by this server, but actually reside elsewhere. The response includes the URL where the data are located.

Remember to think of redirection as a possible source of additional flows. Redirection isn't necessarily bad. Your primary server might serve more as a directory and help pass more detailed requests to other servers you control. This can spread the workload over multiple machines.

Web Caching

Redirection is not the only way in which HTTP can have complex flow patterns. Web caching is increasingly common.

DNS round-robin process can create situations where more destinations than the expected one answer a query. Cache mechanisms, such as squid for WWW traffic, do the opposite: the cache selectively intercepts outgoing flows and responds to them far short of the original destination. The DNS round-robin process does have limitations, discussed in [ISC 1998].

Cache mechanisms can be part of firewalls, which are discussed in Chapter 7. The discussion here deals only with caches intended for performance improvement.

From an addressing standpoint, cache software such as squid sits between the end user and the destination, sometimes in the end user network but most commonly in an ISP. squid is a widely used freeware cache service [NLANR 1998]. The squid server intercepts requests for FTP, HTTP, gopher, SSL and WAIS services. It then logs in to the indicated server and makes the request on behalf of the original users, but keeps a copy of the server response. The next time an end user makes the same request, it is serviced from the closer squid cache server, not the more distant destination.

Web caching offers performance advantages and technical, business, and even legal challenges. The first question is how much it helps performance. Experience with squid suggests, as with so many things in information technology, that it helps with part but not all of the traffic. The user guide suggests that a relatively small disk cache, on the order of 2 GB, might help with 25% of general Internet Web destinations. Increasing the cache size does not give a proportional improvement, because the high-volume Web destinations fell into that initial 25%. Although a larger cache could hold more pages, those pages are less frequently used and are less likely to be retrieved from the cache before they become stale.

Not all queries are appropriate to cache. It makes little sense, for example, to cache the results of script execution on specific data, because these have one-time meaning. It makes little more sense to cache rapidly changing data such as stock quotations, at least in general caching systems that do not constantly invalidate old data. Sensitive information such as credit card authorizations should not be cached.

DistributedDirector

Yet another method that might return different destination addresses is Cisco's DistributedDirector product, which combines routing and utilization information with DNS. The IP address(es) returned by DistributedDirector to a DNS query are selected based on several metrics, including

- The exterior (BGP) metric

- The interior routing metric

- The random numbers-to-spread load

- Administrative preference

- Server availability

DistributedDirector makes sense when there are multiple servers that can carry out a user request. The difference between its approach and that of HTTP redirection is that DistributedDirector can redirect to alternate servers without a redirection function needing to be built into the application. This style of redirection is advantageous when there is no central navigation server, but when there are several identical servers.

FTP Redirection

HTTP can also result in other protocols, such as FTP, being invoked. FTP can do its own redirection. FTP separates its operations into control and file transfer. This is a very reasonable thing to separate, analogous to the separation of dialing and talking in telephony.

Control functions are directed to a well-known TCP port, number 21, at the desired server. After the server is contacted by the client, the server and client agree on a port and possibly new IP address to be used for the actual file transfer. By default, a FTP request involves creation of a single TCP data transfer connection to Port 20 of the server's address.

FTP servers in the real world, however, want multiple concurrent transfers. For this reason, FTP has the capability to override the default port and open data connections between arbitrary addresses and ports.

Earlier implementations had the client select a port to use on the server and send a PORT message to the server informing it of the port number to which the client would connect for the file transfer. This is not in keeping with reasonable security practices involving firewalls, because the selection of ports, in a secure environment, needs to be under the control of the server.

Alternatively, the client can send an FTP PASV command to the server, inviting the server to select a port, and possibly an address, to use for the transfer. The server informs the client of its selection. In either case, the problem from an addressing standpoint is that the client/server interaction can change the IP addresses expected by the original request [RFC 1579].

FTP has a complex setup process and runs over TCP. A connection-oriented transport mechanism such as TCP has higher overhead than UDP, and the RPC/PortMapper service is a lower-overhead alternative for well-defined, transaction-based applications.

Looking Ahead

In this chapter, you have looked at endpoints, and the traffic that must pass through them. The emphasis has been the applications in those computers at the edge of the network. By and large, the internals of the interconnecting network has been a magical cloud labeled "Here a miracle happens."

In Chapter 4, "Transmission System Identifiers and Logical Address Mapping: A View from the Bottom," you will drop down to a level that considers how those computers connect physically to the network, as well as the transmission system components of intermediate networking devices such as routers.

Chapter 5, "Classical IP Addressing: An Evolution," begins to explore the logical addressing structure that bonds together the application structure of this chapter with the transmission-oriented structure of Chapter 4.

PART II

Foundations of Network Addressing

Transmission System Identifiers and Logical Address Mapping: A View from the Bottom

Avian carriers can provide high delay, low throughput, and low altitude service. The connection topology is limited to a single point-to-point path for each carrier, used with standard carriers, but many carriers can be used without significant interference with each other, outside of early spring.

—D. Weitzmann

One policy, one system, and universal service.

—Theodore Vail

Well if I called the wrong number, why did you answer the phone?

—James Thurber

In designing internetworks, the usual emphasis is on logical addressing. But logical addresses are abstractions that travel over lower-level transmission systems, and these transmission systems often have their own systems of addressing. This chapter deals with those lower-level addresses and their relationships to logical addresses.

The bottom is always a fine place to start. Underlying this chapter is the little-known but useful architectural extension of the OSI Reference Model called the *Internal Organization of the Network Layer*, which provides a basis for systematic mapping between logical and transmission system addresses.

Standards Architectures and Protocol Development

Regardless of what one thinks of OSI as a solution, it does contain useful architectural methods. These methods did not freeze with the original OSI Reference Model.

Remember that OSI evolved in formal international standards bodies, whose roots were in telecommunications. These roots were largely in governmental national monopolies. Telecommunications providers classically interface to subscribers at the edge of the provider's "cloud," the details of which are hidden from the subscriber. Subscribers use signaling protocols to set up and receive connections from the cloud. Subscriber endpoints are identified by telephone numbers.

Do not become overly concerned because this information is hidden. Simply assume, for the initial analysis, that the provider network is magical and provides appropriate connectivity. The endpoint addresses in the wide area network (WAN) are the conventions by which user networks access it.

Also understand the underlying protocol model. In a local area network (LAN), the lower-layer protocols often are end-to-end, or at least map to real media. In a WAN, the lower-layer protocols are consciously not end-to-end, but intended to manage access between a provider and customer.

Taking a slightly tongue-in-cheek view of OSI development in the late 1970s, these organizations viewed all communications media as belonging to them, and they would tell subscribers how to connect to them. LAN development in the Institute for Electrical and Electronic Engineers (IEEE) was separate and largely did not affect the original OSI Reference Model published in 1984. Serious coordination between the two cultures was more of a mid-1980s matter. IEEE LAN standards work is IEEE Project 802.

A result of that coordination was the *Internal Organization of the Network Layer*, a document that relaxed the rigid boundaries between Layer 2 and Layer 3 of the OSI Reference Model and came up with a much more useful picture.

Ignoring the rather obscure OSI terminology for these new layers, the model, shown in Figure 4.1, is split into three parts:

- Logical addressing

- Medium or transmission system addressing

- Mapping between logical and transmission system addresses

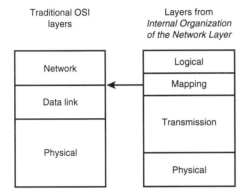

FIGURE 4.1. *Revised OSI model reflecting Internal Organization of the Network Layer extensions. The mapping function translates between medium-independent logical addresses and medium-dependent transmission system addresses.*

Logical addressing is what we usually think of as Layer 3: largely transmission system independent such as IP. The transmission medium address is the next level down.

As shown in Figure 4.2, IEEE further subdivided the transmission system for the LAN environment into *Media Access Control* (MAC) and *Logical Link Control* (LLC) at the data link layer. IEEE also divided the physical layer into *media-independent* (MDI) and *physical-media dependent* (PMD) sublayers. General physical layer and PMD functions tend to be implemented in different hardware chip sets.

WAN services, on the other hand, were usefully split into *persistent* and *transient* levels. Think of a five-button telephone to which is assigned a five-line hunt group, a group of five telephone lines with a single telephone number. The telephone number is the persistent identifier while the button that lights for a specific call is the transient identifier.

The distinction between LLC and MAC has allowed LLC to be a general buffer management mechanism that hides the timing-critical aspects of the MAC sublayer. LLC also provided a place for more general mechanisms such as upper layer protocol identification and optional retransmission.

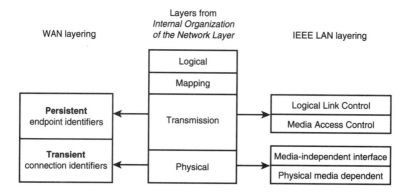

FIGURE 4.2. *WAN and LAN sublayering of basic OSI layers consistent with the Internal Organization and IEEE extensions to the OSI model.*

Transmission systems have their own addressing, distinct from the network layer. Their addressing models tend to fall into one of two categories, LAN or WAN. This categorization is not really based on the geographic scope of the transmission system, but on the underlying administrative model.

Figure 4.3 illustrates a typical WAN model, as might be seen with Frame Relay, X.25, or ATM. User organizations use access mechanisms to interact with a service provider cloud, the details of which are usually not visible to the calling or called user. Users have virtual circuits across the cloud.

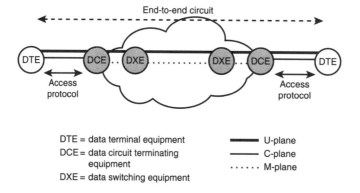

FIGURE 4.3. *Points of reference in WAN models. The DCE is the boundary between provider and customer responsibility.*

Even if the WAN service is of physical rather than virtual circuits, there still is a clear demarcation point between carrier/provider and user responsibility.

This demarcation point is logically inside the *data circuit terminating equipment (DCE)*. DCE is often assumed to stand for *data communications equipment*, but this is the formal standard meaning of the acronym. Special contractual arrangements are needed, in many cases, for the user organization to know the path taken through the provider network.

If, for reliability reasons, the user wants to have multiple circuits with no common point of failure, this takes specific engineering from the carrier, called *facility diversity*. This can be quite expensive. Some users have made the extremely dangerous assumption that leasing circuits from multiple providers inherently gives diversity. In practice, providers lease transmission facilities from each other and from "wholesale" providers. Diversity can be engineered when a specific organization is responsible for assuring it, but if the different carriers are not aware of each other, they may wind up leasing a common facility from a third party—a facility that can be affected by a single failure.

In contrast, all components of a LAN are operated by the same organization. Internetworking has its roots in the WAN culture, and it is worth reviewing the WAN concepts that shape communications.

The Influence of WAN History on Modern Networks

The engineering discipline of interconnecting communications systems began in telephony, with the nineteenth-century development of telephone switching. It evolved with the benevolent dictatorship of AT&T's Theodore Vail and his vision of universal telephone service, provided through a monopoly. Until the 1970s, data interconnection among computers was done over modems, using switched or dedicated telephone circuits.

Until the mid-1970s, much telephone service was provided by national monopolies or government organizations. These entities still had a deep commitment to technical standards, because their reality was that different countries, at the very least, would interconnect and would need a well-understood technical model for doing so.

The 1975 consent decree that split up AT&T in the United States accelerated the need for technical standards between telecommunications providers. The 1972 Carterfone Decision had struck a blow several years earlier, in a U.S. Supreme Court ruling that established the right of users to connect to telephone lines equipment that was not provided by the telephone company. In the 1990s, there is significant worldwide privatization of prior governmental monopolies and even more pressure for a common, well-defined architecture.

A drive toward common architecture, however, does not mean we have a single set of standards. Especially in the data area, there has been conflict between standards set by international telecommunications standards bodies, driven by telephony people, and the more informal but fast and effective process of the Internet Engineering Task Force (IETF), driven by data-network-oriented people. International telephony standards have been developed by the International Telecommunications Union-T (ITU-T), formerly the International Consultative Committee for Telegraphy and Telephony (CCITT).

Note

You might wonder why the abbreviation is CCITT, not ICCTT. This observation gives insight into the formal standards process. It was long a convention that standards bodies, whose official languages were English and French, spell out the names of the organizations in English, but use the abbreviation of the name in French. This cultural imperative for compromise, as opposed to the IETF's model of prototyping and rough consensus, slowed the international standards process. The OSI Reference Model and OSI protocols came out of these bodies, but the IETF Internet development process was faster and more responsive to real-world technical requirements.

Today, it seems that as many industry consortia develop telephony standards as does ITU-T. Important organizations doing this include the ATM and Frame Relay Forums. Nevertheless, the telephone model, evolved to include the Integrated Systems Digital Network (ISDN) architecture and protocols, is critical to modern networking.

Understanding the network model of the telephone system is a first step to understanding the current idea of the network layer. Consider a telephone number. Is there any change in the format of that number if it designates a single-line home telephone, a cellular car phone, or an externally visible line on a business PBX?

So it is with the network layer, which defines a set of logical addresses or locators. Connectivity can be defined among a set of network layer logical endpoints without immediately being concerned with the underlying physical nodes and their locations.

Network layer services interconnect both end systems containing the upper layers and the intermediate systems that make up the internal multiuser network. Logical addressing is one of the basic features of the network layer. Different network layer architectures and protocols tend to differ in several ways:

- The services provided by the network layer

- The types of entities addressed and the structure of their logical addresses

- Methods used to map logical addresses to and from physical addresses, and other infrastructure

End systems and routers have logical addresses that they use to transmit to one another. Before that actual transmission can happen, logical data units must be encapsulated in the format of the transmission system that connects the logical devices.

On the sending side, the lower-level transmitter must know

- The format of the lower-layer information unit

- The lower-layer transmission system address, or a procedure to obtain this

- Its own lower-layer transmission system address, if the transmission system requires that the transmitter put its own address into the source field of transmitted frames

- A convention to identify to the receiver what logical level protocol is in use

- Whether the path to the lower-level device is connection oriented, and, if so, know that the connection is up or know a procedure to open the connection

- Optional protocol-specific information

Internal Organization of the Network Layer

Originally, the OSI Reference Model described the data link and network layers as single blocks, without any internal sublayering. There also was an assumption that protocol functions would be easy to place either in the network layer or the data link layer. Relatively little known, early architectural experience showed a more flexible model was needed, and such a model was issued in a document called the *Internal Organization of the Network Layer*.

Stripped of the somewhat obscure OSI terminology, the revised model merges the upper part of the data link layer with the network layer, producing three layers:

- A medium-independent logical level

- A transmission level

- A "glue" level that maps between the two

Some of the OSI terminology is worth knowing, as it is used in various IP protocol specifications. The logical level address is the IP address in the Internet Protocol Suite and is called the *Network Service Access Point* (NSAP) address in OSI. Additional OSI terms refine the NSAP address concept, but are rarely encountered outside pure OSI networks.

A term that is seen fairly frequently is the Subnetwork Point of Attachment (SNPA) address, which is the transmission system address(es) associated with the logical address.

Logical addresses are assigned to router and end host interfaces. On end hosts, there is a supplementary transport identifier to identify one endpoint of the end-to-end path over which application data flows.

Addressing Assumptions

Separating the transmission subsystem's addressing from logical addressing extends beyond the simple physical endpoint identifier (for example, MAC addresses) into the useful distinction between persistent transmission endpoint identifiers (for example, X.121 address, E.164 ISDN, ATM Network Service Access Point [NSAP]) and connection identifiers (for example, X.25 logical channel number [LCN], ISDN terminal endpoint identifier [TEI], and ATM virtual path identifier/virtual circuit identifier [VPI/VCI]).

Dynamic mapping mechanisms here include the routine ARP, but also more subtle mechanisms such as LAN emulation and VLAN trunk identification.

Problems—or opportunities—created by new transmission technologies are discussed here. One such problem includes the local versus remote problem in partial mesh subnets. Another is the switch versus route decision with which *Next Hop Resolution Protocol (NHRP)* and other mechanisms attempt to cope. Yet other problems deal with transferring congestion notifications that are signaled on a WAN data link layer to end systems connected via a LAN.

The Local Versus Remote Decision

Traditional IP addressing has operated on a basic assumption called the *local versus remote* decision: If a given host shares a prefix with the source host, that destination should be reachable at Layer 2.

It then is necessary to perform *an address resolution* function (as shown in Figure 4.4) that maps the destination logical address to the transmission system address of the destination, before packets can be sent. Address resolution mechanisms discussed in this chapter deal with the problem of mapping the logical address of a device on the same transmission system to a transmission system address.

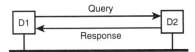

DL query contains DL's IP and MAC, DL's IP

DL response fills in DL's MAC address

FIGURE 4.4. *In basic address resolution, device D1 broadcasts a query intended for the device whose transmission system address it wants to know.*

In Chapter 5, "Classical IP Addressing: An Evolution," we will explore the problem of obtaining the logical address for one's own interface when the transmission system address is known.

If the prefixes—the part of the logical address used to make routing decisions—are different, the packet must be sent to a router to be forwarded. It is necessary to determine the logical address of the router and then perform an address resolution function that maps the *router* logical address to a reachable transmission system address. Address resolution mechanisms include those that find the router and also are involved in determining one's own logical address.

The basic assumption is true on point-to-point media and on multiaccess broadcast-capable media such as LANs. It is not true on on-demand media (for example, telephone lines) and on nonbroadcast multiaccess media such as Frame Relay.

To transmit at Layer 2, the Layer 2 address must be known. This is a trivial matter on point-to-point media and can be resolved with broadcasts on media that support broadcasting. Alternative techniques are needed to find the Layer 2 next hop address on nonbroadcast multiple access (NBMA) and demand media.

Figure 4.5 illustrates the basic local versus remote problem. In a traditional IP model, if R2 perceives itself to be in the same logical prefix as R3, it should be able to send directly to R3 using a Layer 2 mechanism. But the underlying transmission system is partial mesh, and there is no direct Layer 2 connectivity between R2 and R3.

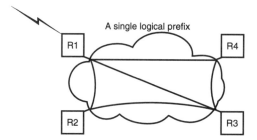

FIGURE 4.5. *A basic IP assumption, the local versus remote assumption, is not necessarily true on newer transmission systems such as Frame Relay or ATM.*

How does R2 learn it must communicate with R3 via R1? What are the performance implications for R1 if it needs to forward significant intra-subnet traffic? What happens if R1 fails?

An additional question, which most frequently arises on ATM media, is whether it is appropriate to route to the destination, possibly involving multiple hops, or to "cut through" a virtual circuit to the destination. Cut-through is not always a panacea, because although it might appear simpler and more efficient to cut through, there are resources and costs associated with setting up the virtual circuit. This introduces a need for the special address resolution function of the Next Hop Resolution Protocol for NBMA media. Before discussing NHRP, let us discuss the simpler case of address resolution over broadcast media.

Address Resolution

Let's deal with the general case of address resolution on broadcast media. There are four basic ways to learn the MAC address associated with a particular destination:

- Ask the device itself (that is, active query response)

- Look for preconfigured explicit information (that is, static mapping)

- Listen for periodic announcement of the device address

- Ask a well-known device such as a directory server

Different protocol families do this in different ways. IP, in general, relies on the Address Resolution Protocol (ARP) to ask the device itself. ARP does assume the underlying medium is broadcast capable, so this works only on LANs and on media where broadcasting is simulated.

Why, then, is address discovery an issue when stations know their network (that is, IP) address? The issue is performance. If two nodes are on the same LAN medium, they can exchange information directly only if they know each other's MAC-sublayer address. If MAC addresses are not known, the stations can communicate, but the benefits of the common medium are lost because the stations must use a router to communicate using Layer 3 addresses.

ARP assumes that the underlying physical network supports broadcasting. Such networks usually are LANs, but ARP can be used with other physical network technologies that allow multicasting. When a node wants to communicate with another node, and the transmitting node only knows the IP address of the desired destination, the transmitter builds an ARP request *protocol data unit* (PDU) and broadcasts it.

The ARP request, as shown in Figure 4.4, contains the sender's MAC and IP addresses, as well as the IP address of the desired definition. All listening nodes on the physical network compare the IP address in the ARP request with their own IP address.

A node recognizing its IP address then responds to the MAC address specified in the ARP request with a PDU containing both the responder's IP and hardware address.

After the originating node receives the ARP response, it stores the pair `<IP address, hardware address>` in an *ARP cache*. Subsequent messages sent from the sender to receiver use the hardware addresses stored in this cache. Entries in an ARP cache usually have a lifetime timer, and the host periodically flushes its ARP cache and sends a new ARP request to verify that the host is still present.

If no node responded to the ARP request, the sender can assume that the destination is not actually on the local medium. In principle, the sender then needs to find an appropriate IP relay to send IP datagrams to the ultimate destination. If the proxy ARP protocol is implemented by a router on the same medium and that router knows how to reach the desired destination, the destination will still be reachable.

ARP depends on MAC-level broadcasting to discover addresses. When a station wants to communicate with another station, it broadcasts the IP address of the destination and asks that it respond with its MAC address if it is on the same medium.

Routing protocols tend to understand point-to-point and broadcast media, but do not really understand NBMA. A common, but often expensive, workaround is *pseudobroadcasting*, in which a set of virtual circuits or other destination identifiers is manually configured. When a router sends a data unit with a broadcast destination address, the router copies it to the set of destination paths.

A single node broadcasting to all others is not uncommon in Frame Relay and X.25, but subjects the router to a significant processing load in copying the protocol data units. This copying overhead would be even more severe at ATM speeds. Some ATM switches support a point-to-multipoint organization where the switch does the packet replication at the cell level, in specialized hardware.

Some transmission systems, such as Frame Relay, have an out-of-band information channel that can be used to carry address management information. The Inverse ARP mechanism is an example of this.

ARP mechanisms, as well as more sophisticated mechanisms such as NHRP, are signaling interactions between end hosts and their local router or switch.

Configuration on NBMA Media

Because Frame Relay combines features of both the data link and network layers, its addressing structure does not immediately map into existing global addressing structure. In the IP, the Inverse ARP protocol [RFC 2390] was developed to help map between IP addresses and Frame Relay Data Link Connection Identifiers (DLCIs).

Inverse ARP assumes a DLCI is roughly equivalent to the LAN MAC addresses used in other ARP schemes. New DLCIs, and the corresponding virtual circuits, periodically activate in a Frame Relay system. The Frame Relay announcement of a new virtual circuit carries no information about the IP address of the other end.

The key difference between Inverse ARP and ARP is that Inverse ARP does not use a broadcast medium.

Signaling

If the underlying protocol is connection oriented, a connection has to be created before data can be transferred, much as you cannot have a useful telephone conversation without first picking up the phone, getting a dial tone, dialing, and having the called party pick up his telephone.

A rather useful product of ISDN and other telephony-oriented communications is an extended protocol reference model, which extends the two-dimensional OSI layered architectural model to three dimensions, shown in Figure 4.6. ISDN also has a functional model that shows protocol exchanges, shown in Figure 4.7. The OSI model was designed to describe user applications that begin at the top of Layer 7 and exit at the bottom of Layer 1. It really is application oriented and becomes awkward for describing the infrastructural protocols that operate only inside a layer, such as routing or call setup.

With the introduction of the Internal Organization and IEEE LAN models, as well as sublayering at layers above those of interest to us in this lower layer discussion, to say the OSI model truly has 7 layers is a bit superficial. When you think of these two- versus three-dimensional models, do not assume they have to apply to any specific number of layers. The ISDN and ATM reference models certainly are layered, but they do not have 7 layers.

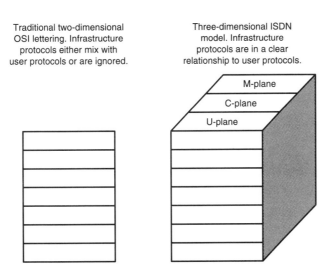

Traditional two-dimensional OSI lettering. Infrastructure protocols either mix with user protocols or are ignored.

Three-dimensional ISDN model. Infrastructure protocols are in a clear relationship to user protocols.

M-plane
C-plane
U-plane

FIGURE 4.6. *OSI versus ISDN model. Control and management functions are conceptually hidden behind user information.*

The three-dimensional model builds a cube from three protocol planes:

- *User-plane* (U-plane)—U-plane protocols carry user data from end to end. Most protocols shown in the OSI Reference Model belong to the U-plane. In the telephone analogy, it's the conversation between users.

- *Control-plane* (C-plane)—C-plane protocols interact between the end system and the ingress or egress device entering the transmission system. In the telephone analogy, it's obtaining dial tone, dialing, and ringing.

- *Management-plane* (M-plane)—M-plane communications are internal to the transmission system. In the telephone network, the analogy is setting up the end-to-end path through a sequence of telephone switches.

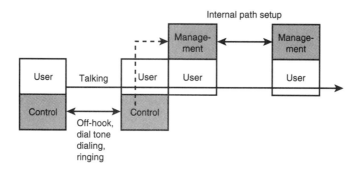

FIGURE 4.7. *ISDN functional model showing protocol exchanges among the planes at a given layer.*

Why a three-dimensional model? I find it helpful to conceptualize that I am looking at the model from the front. The U-plane is in front. I can describe user services with the understanding that the infrastructure protocols, at the C- and M-planes, are hidden underneath.

The idea of a C-plane protocol is very relevant to data as well as telephone networking. Even though the protocols involved might be connectionless, there are still needs for an end host to signal to other end hosts, or to ingress routers, before user data flow can begin. One C-plane mechanism is determining the transmission system address that should be used to forward to a given logical address. This is the process of address resolution, which works differently in detail on various types of transmission media.

One C-plane mechanism, for example, is NHRP. It is a mechanism for edge internetworking devices to determine whether they should route to a destination or open a cut-through path to it. Ingress routers query NHRP servers for the next hop transmission system address to reach a given destination. These servers have databases that identify the preferred method of reaching a destination, such as a direct virtual circuit at Layer 2 or the transmission system address of a next hop router (see Figure 4.8).

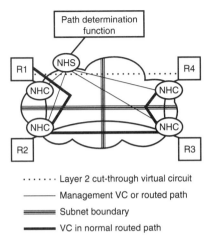

FIGURE 4.8. *NHRP makes database queries needed to make decisions on cut-through switching.*

Cut-Through Switching

When the underlying transmission system is connection oriented, the option might exist either to use conventional routing to reach the destination or to cut through a virtual circuit to the destination. A virtual circuit potentially offers better performance because it is an optimal Layer 2 path to the destination without potential Layer 3 overhead.

Unfortunately, the real situation is not that simple. Opening a virtual circuit takes time, adding to the latency before the first data unit can be sent. Monetary cost might be associated with additional connections.

Real-world equipment interfaces also have limits to the number of concurrent virtual circuits they can support.

What if a virtual circuit already exists to the destination? Should the sender multiplex communications onto that virtual circuit (VC) or open a new one? This depends on if the VC supports multiplexing from several data sources.

Standard cut-through techniques include Multiprotocol over ATM, discussed later in this chapter. Cabletron and other vendors have proprietary cut-through methods, such as Cabletron SecureFast.

Dial Servers

Servers to which users make PPP or SLIP connections often represent the set of point-to-point dial interfaces as hosts on a subnet. This subnet is contained within the terminal server.

Before address resolution can be conceptualized for a dialup server, it's necessary to understand the addressing model the server uses. There are two major models:

- Each connection to the server is a separate point-to-point logical network. The server acts as a router that forwards packets from each of these separate logical networks to an appropriate next hop network.

- The server represents a single multiaccess logical network. Individual dialups appear to be nodes on that single medium. The server bridges between dialups and routes to external destinations.

Upper-Layer Protocol Identification

Think of the tunneling mechanisms discussed in Chapter 2, "Principles Underlying Addressing," and generalize them beyond the transport layer. There are many cases where a lower-level protocol carries another, or where a protocol carries another one at the same layer. As an example of the latter, there are various schemes where a LAN bridged frame can be wrapped into a WAN protocol frame for transmission between LANs.

Whether a transmission system protocol is connectionless or connection oriented, the receiver needs to know what passenger protocol is carried by a received frame. This is often true in an apparently multiprotocol environment, as management and control protocols might need to be handled differently on receipt than protocols carrying user plane traffic.

In the common environment where more than one protocol family is present, the need to identify passenger protocols is even more necessary.

Connectionless protocols carry explicit protocol identifier fields. Connection-oriented protocols either might carry explicit identifiers or have a protocol identifier associated with the virtual circuit at setup time.

More Modern Mapping

Evolution of networking leads to several new ideas. The original concept of a logical address prefix mapping to a single medium fails to cover a wide range of practical applications. Consider the following combinations:

- Single medium, single prefix

- Single medium, multiple prefixes

- Multiple media, single prefix

- Multiple media, multiple prefixes

Figure 2.10 in Chapter 2 shows these graphically. The first remains most common. The second is also fairly common and is especially important when dealing with limitations in the logical addressing scheme.

In the latter of the multiple media cases, there is an additional requirement for address resolution. This requirement is internal to the system of linked virtual media and is invisible to the user. In this requirement, it is necessary to map end user MAC addresses to a trunk transmission system delivery mechanism identifier. In VLANs, this mapping is to a MAC address in the trunking system, while in ATM LAN Emulation, the mapping is to a virtual circuit.

Connectionless Services

In any connectionless communications system, the protocol data units must stand by themselves, carrying a full destination and a full source address. Connection-oriented communications, such as a telephone call, establish a context in which you can infer the sender of a message. In connectionless services like postal mail, you cannot tell who sent you mail unless there is a signature or return address.

LANs are the primary instances of connectionless transmission systems. It's informative to begin our fresh look at transmission-system-oriented addressing with LANs because they illustrate some key principles without undue complexity. LANs have at least two users and broadcast capability. This is a basic model assumed by routers; another basic model is point-to-point. See "Topology Terminology" in Chapter 2 for a discussion of these models. More complex LAN-like services include Switched Multimegabit Data Service (SMDS), ATM LAN Emulation (LANE), and virtual LANs. The first two of these services actually map a connectionless transmission model to an underlying connection-oriented transmission infrastructure. These complex services are discussed at the end of this chapter, after connection-oriented services have been presented.

All practical LANs today follow the IEEE 802 architecture. IEEE MAC protocols share a common endpoint identification scheme called the MAC address. They differ in their approaches to controlling access to the common medium and in the frame formats needed to support these approaches.

IEEE 802 MAC Addressing

The IEEE 802 project defines addressing at the MAC and LLC protocol levels. A 48-bit address format is used for all modern MAC protocols, although the bits of this address are transmitted differently by different MAC protocols.

MAC sublayer addressing uses a 48-bit address. The ordering of bits within frames varies with different MAC sublayer protocols such as 802.3 CSMA/CD, which is informally but not quite correctly called Ethernet, and 802.5 Token Ring.

The most significant bit called bit 1 has a common function in all MAC addresses. This bit is transmitted in different order in different MAC protocols. 802.3 and Ethernet transmit the least significant bit first, while 802.5 and FDDI transmit the most significant bit first.

Bit 1 of a MAC address is set to 1 if the address describes a multicast or broadcast group address and to 0 if the address is for a unicast individual address. Bit 2 is set to 1 if the address conforms to the global IEEE convention and to 0 if it is locally administered.

In the global addressing scheme, the first six hexadecimal digits of the address (that is, its first 24 bits, of which 22 are available as block identifiers) are assigned to specific vendors. These vendors, in turn, assign unique addresses to their products within the range of each block. The all-zero address is considered a null.

Globally administered addresses consist of a 24-bit part assigned to manufacturers and a 24-bit piece the vendor is responsible for keeping unique.

Given all the emphasis on universal addressing, why would we want to use local administration? There are two practical reasons, both of which might apply:

- System administration practices associate a certain MAC address with a specific user or location. In such cases, the addressing system would be useless if a MAC address changed whenever a board was changed for maintenance.

- Some network layer protocols, including those of DECnet, XNS, Novell, and Banyan, modify some or all MAC addresses to reflect Layer 3 information.

Locally administered MAC addresses can be set manually. In addition, there are several things that change a MAC address to which an interface responds from its globally administered one, which is "burned into" a read-only memory. Some interface types can have several active MAC addresses.

Redundancy schemes for protection against router failures tend to manipulate MAC addresses. As shown in the Cisco and Bay schemes discussed in Chapter

13, "Addressing in Routers," most such mechanisms define a virtual MAC address that can move among several routers. It is active only on the active router of a group of routers that back up one another.

Several non-IP protocols (DECnet, Novell IPX, XNS, and Banyan VINES) can manipulate the MAC addresses of router interfaces. They do so as part of strategies to allow routers to self-configure. These strategies can cause compatibility problems in multiprotocol environments, because, for example, DECnet's autoconfiguration might conflict with that of Novell. Details of these strategies are in Chapter 8, "The Existing IP and Non-IP Address Structure: Preparing for Remodeling."

IEEE 802.2 LLC

There are several variants of the IEEE 802.2 LLC protocol, but by far the most commonly used is LLC Class I. LLC Class II is used by some IBM and NetBIOS applications, usually on token ring networks. LLC Class III is a special-purpose variant intended for real-time process control in the Manufacturing Automation Protocol suite applications.

LLC Class I has fairly minimal functionality. Its major function is identifying the protocol carried in the data field of the LAN frame. The original LLC Class I protocol identification method was quite limited, but a useful extension was developed, so useful that the extension is also used for protocol identification with WAN data link protocols such as Frame Relay and ATM.

In the basic address specification, each frame contains two 8-bit fields: Source Service Access Point (SSAP) and Destination Service Access Point (DSAP). The first bit of these fields indicates whether the address is for a group (that is, broadcast or multicast) or for a specific protocol type. Only 7 bits, therefore, are available for specific protocol identification. There are far more than 127 protocols, so an extension mechanism was devised.

This method is called the *Subnetwork Access Protocol* (SNAP). A special value of the DSAP field, hexadecimal A0, indicates that a 5-byte SNAP field will follow the LLC header. The first 3 bytes of the SNAP field are an organizationally unique identifier (OUI) that identifies an organization registered with a standards body, and the last 2 bytes define a protocol specified by the organization corresponding to the OUI.

RFC 1490 describes the use of SNAP on Frame Relay, while RFC 2225 describes its use on ATM.

The Art of Services Formerly Known as WAN

Several of my close friends have a great interest in the period of American history between 1861 and 1865. Alert readers will notice that I describe that period exactly, but do not give it a name. From hard experience, I have found that safer with certain history buffs. Until I know the historian's background and beliefs, I don't know if it is most appropriate to refer to the Civil War, the Unpleasantness Between the States, or the War of Yankee Aggression.

And so it is with WAN services. It's safer and more accurate to refer to them not in terms of the wide or local area they cover, but in the relationships between endpoints and the transmission system. Traditional comments such as, "WANs are slow and LANs are fast," simply are not accurate when dealing with technologies such as ATM. Even speed-of-light propagation delay over longer distances does not clearly differentiate between WANs and LANs, because the per-bit propagation time on a short slow medium can be much longer than the speed-of-light delay on a long fast medium.

What remains accurate from the classic WAN model is the existence of a subscriber-to-provider relationship. In LAN models, a single network design includes all layers. In WAN models, the environment has at least three major subsystems:

- Calling user to provider

- Provider internal

- Provider to called user

WAN protocols have a scope that includes only their own subsystem. Access protocols deal with user-to-provider access, but the details of the caller-to-provider interaction are largely hidden from the provider-to-callee interaction.

Both called and calling users are aware of end-to-end, persistent identifiers. Additional transient connection identifiers are used in each of the two access domains; the transient identifier in the caller's access domain is independent of the transient identifier in the callee's office domain. We speak of the connection identifiers as having local significance and the endpoint identifiers as having global significance.

Local significance means the identifier is meaningful between a specific end system and the local access to the provider. Locally significant identifier 42 could appear at many access points without conflict. *Globally significant identifiers* are like telephone numbers, visible throughout the provider system and unique in that system.

Another characteristic of WAN services is that they are either *dedicated* or *switched*. Dedicated services are always available, while switched services, also a call establishment function, must be completed before switched services are available. Switched services are also called *demand services*.

Switched services can create connections using real media such as telephone circuits or can create them with virtual circuits at Layer 2. Virtual circuits that are intended for the use of individual sessions, and are connected and disconnected as needed, are called *switched virtual circuits* (SVCs). Virtual circuits that are explicitly configured and then are assumed to stay up indefinitely, like dedicated telephone lines, are called *permanent virtual circuits* (PVCs). The term *soft PVC* has come to describe virtual circuits that are kept up permanently after they are created, but use the same call setup procedure as SVCs.

Dedicated Lines and Protocol Identification

Addressing on dedicated lines between routers is simple, but not completely trivial. The various link layer protocols, PPP, HDLC, and LAP-B, do have address fields in the frame header. One end of the link is the Data Terminal Equipment (DTE) and the other is the data circuit terminating equipment (DCE). Dedicated lines supporting IBM protocols such as SDLC or BSC have much more complex identifiers.

In regular router-to-router communications, one issue is whether the data link protocol identifies the type of traffic in its data field. PPP and HDLC do have such fields. LAP-B does not, but the X.25 packet layer protocol can run above LAP-B and provide upper layer protocol identification.

Addressing Checklist for Dedicated Lines

☐ Data link protocol assigned

☐ Single or multiple protocol families per interface

☐ Keepalives required at Layer 2

☐ Special features needed: compression, encryption, and retransmission

☐ Address polling requirements

Circuit-Switched Transmission Systems

Circuit-switched transmission systems, such as the telephone network, dedicate bandwidth on real resources for the duration of the connection. Operating systems, especially of commercial routers, have mechanisms for creating on-demand connectivity over media such as ISDN and POTS. These mechanisms have two basic parts: the conditions that trigger the need for an on-demand connection and the actions by which the connection is made.

The most general way to look at transmission over demand media is that a demand medium is activated when some predefined event occurs. Classically, these triggering events are either:

- Arrival of designated frames containing packets with certain characteristics or frames eligible for bridging and meeting other characteristics. *Dial on demand* mechanisms are the usual way to realize a need for a medium to carry logical level information.

- Data link layer utilization. *Dial backup* and *bandwidth on demand* mechanisms bring up backup links to provide additional parallel bandwidth.

- Physical media status change. A backup interface initiates *dial backup* to create a backup connection. Physical level backup can be programmed on routers or done in external devices that connect between a router and the DCE.

The actions taken in response to these conditions are:

- *Dial backup,* realized as a change in electrical status on a designated interface that causes an external device to initiate telephone dialing or otherwise establish a connection.

- *Dial on demand routing (DDR),* in which a command string stored in the computer or router is sent to the external DCE. This might be a simple string or an interactive script composed of send and expected receive pairs.

A level of abstraction can be placed between the generic function of call initiation and the physical equipment involved. Cisco defined a generally useful abstraction of a *dialer profile* that links three elements:

- A *dialer interface* (a logical entity) configuration including one or more transmission system addresses each associated with a single logical destination.

- A *dialer map class* that defines all the characteristics for any call to the specified transmission system address (for example, telephone or ISDN number).

- An ordered *dialer pool* of physical interfaces to be used by the dialer interface. A given physical interface can belong to several dialer pools.

Dial Backup

Dial backup is triggered by physical or data link events. When the event occurs on a primary interface, the secondary interface is activated to help clear the event. When the event stops, the secondary interface can be deactivated.

Basic events that trigger dial backup are line failure and link utilization. Line failure is recognized as a loss of the carrier detect electrical signal, when one is present, or complete failure of the data link protocol. Link utilization events trigger when the percentage utilization of the link, measured at the data link layer, exceeds a configured threshold.

At the data link layer, a failure can be detected in several ways. On dedicated lines, most common is the absence of three consecutive data link keepalive messages. The Point-to-Point Protocol (PPP) monitors the ratio of frames received in error to total frames received and, if the ratio is above a programmed threshold, can disconnect the link.

Frame Relay local management interfaces should respond to `status_enquiry` messages with `status` messages that indicate a given PVC is down.

Some, but not all, LAN protocols give a specific indication of link failure. If an FDDI or token ring medium fails, such that a receiver does not receive a token within an expected time period, the receiver generates a `beacon` message.

Ethernet-family LANs do not have a Layer 2 keepalive. If you need to detect a failure on these LANs, the most common practice is to run a Layer 3 routing protocol on the Ethernet medium. If the routing protocol does not detect other routers it normally can hear, either by listening to periodic routing tables or *hello* subprotocols, it marks the link down. Hello protocols are low-overhead mechanisms in modern routing protocols, such as Open Shortest Path First (OSPF) and Enhanced Interior Gateway Routing Protocol (EIGRP). Think of a hello subprotocol as providing a Layer 3 keepalive function.

When any of these events take place, the data terminal ready signal is made TRUE on a configured backup interface. This is all the router does. The intelligence of the response depends on the intelligence of the DCE.

The basic assumption has been that the DCE is a modem or ISDN terminal adapter (TA) that places a call when DTR becomes true. In DDR, the phone number to be dialed resides in the router and is sent to the DCE via a C-plane mechanism. In dial backup, the extent of the C-plane protocol is a binary decision to bring up DTR.

Bandwidth-on-demand mechanisms open parallel calls to a destination, treating the multiple physical calls as one logical path. They are most often realized with multiple ISDN calls, so the term *dial backup* is not consistent because it is thought of in terms of pairs of interfaces. If the idea of dial backup is generalized to circuits rather than interface, its use on ISDN becomes consistent.

Dynamic Routing and Demand Media

Dial-on-demand routing (DDR) is triggered by the arrival of selected packets or frames at an outgoing interface. When the traffic arrives at that interface, the outgoing interface initiates C-plane signaling, sending the called phone number (stored in the router) to a DCE, initiating a Q.931 call request. A key difference between dial backup and DDR is that in DDR, full information on how to set up the circuit is stored in the router.

DDR connections usually drop when an inactivity timer expires. It sometimes can be difficult to get the interface to become inactive, unless care is taken to prevent routing updates or other network management overhead from keeping the interface busy even after there is no user traffic to send.

DDR is not intended for use with routing protocols that send periodic updates (for example, RIP or IGRP) or use an acknowledged hello protocol to verify connectivity (for example, OSPF, EIGRP, IS-IS). DDR works well with demand extensions to OSPF, which do not bring up the link unless it is specifically needed. DDR is most often used with static routing.

The problem with both periodic updates and hello subprotocols is that they defeat the fundamental purpose of DDR—reducing connection time charges to the times when there is something to say.

This is not to say that dynamic routing cannot run over demand media, but to do so requires a routing protocol designed for such operation. Recent versions of OSPF and RIP do contain extensions for demand media.

POTS

Dialup services, especially public Internet access providers, are undergoing explosive growth. This success represents a particular drain on the available address space, especially with a commonly used practice of assigning unique addresses to each customer.

Understanding data circuit setup over conventional analog dialups is a familiar starting point. There are two main means of triggering the call:

- *Dial backup*, in which pairs of physical devices are defined. When a triggering event takes place, the secondary interface of the pair raises an electrical signal, data terminal ready, to which an external DCE responds.

- *Dial on demand* using in-band call setup. In-band signaling methods include CCITT V.25 bis or *chat scripts* with Hayes-style command sets, coupled *with system scripts* for logging into the router.

Address Resolution in POTS

Dial links, both in POTS and ISDN, really involve two types of address resolution. The more important one is knowing what telephone number to call to reach a given destination address. This really needs to be static configuration information, because before the link is brought up, there is no connection over which signaling information can flow.

The second part of the problem deals with determining the caller's address after a connection is made. Local configuration information is really necessary for this and is in the form of a list of logical addresses and corresponding telephone numbers.

When you consider that a given host might call multiple hosts at various times, each of those hosts in their own address space, the complexity of the problem becomes obvious. It might be practical to have a fixed caller address for each called destination, but this practice is deprecated because it scales poorly for the Internet in general. Issues of determining the caller's address are detailed in Chapter 5.

Chat Scripts

With the advent of more complex modems, as with the Hayes command set, there were two stages of such interaction:

1. A *chat script* interacts between the calling system and its local modem.

2. Another script logs the caller in to the remote computer after a connection is established. This is sometimes called a *system script*. Chat scripts are made up of pairs of send and expect text strings.

Each pair can contain subexpect and subsend strings to handle exception conditions, where the expected response is not received.

Although a chat script tends to be required for modem dialing, system scripts are not as common, given the capability of the CHAP or PAP extensions to PPP. These can prompt dynamically for user IDs and passwords.

Addressing Checklist for POTS Dial Access

☐ Dialing mode selected

☐ Pool or single line

☐ Address mapping

☐ Line protocol selected

ISDN

Integrated Services Digital Network protocols are a set of mechanisms for obtaining 64 KB increments of bandwidth over a public telecommunications network. ISDN's architectural specifications include *functional groupings* and *reference points* that define the interconnection of functional groupings. The major functional groupings and reference points used in data networking are shown in Figure 4.9.

Remember that ISDN specifications are oriented to the telephone provider perspective, so both routers and end hosts are considered ISDN terminal equipment. *Terminal Equipment type 1* (TE1) speaks native ISDN protocols, while *Terminal Equipment type 2* (TE2) is a non-ISDN device that needs to go to a TA protocol converter. The R reference point actually is not defined by ISDN other than to say it is the native interface used by the non-ISDN device.

Native ISDN devices and TAs connect to the *Network Termination type 1* (NT1) at the S/T reference point. At the S/T reference point, you can define either point-to-point connectivity between the TE1/TA and the NT1, or you can have a "mini-LAN" that allows multiple TE1/TA devices to share the medium. TE1/TA devices on a shared S/T bus have individual subaddresses under the main ISDN transmission system address. These are roughly analogous to telephone extension numbers, except they can be called from the general ISDN network. Typical applications for subaddressing include using a single ISDN telephone number for a voice telephone, facsimile machine, and ISDN router.

The NT1 defines the demarcation point between customer and provider media. In the competitive telecommunications marketplace of North America, the customer can provide the NT1 device, so the U reference point defines the NT1's connection to the carrier end office. In regions where telecommunications is more regulated, the carrier provides the NT1, and the interface between the NT1 and the end office is chosen by the carrier.

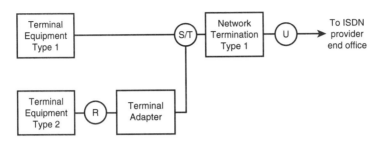

FIGURE 4.9. *Functional groupings such as NT1 and TE1 interconnect at reference points.*

64 KBps digital streams are the basic unit of digitized voice traffic, but can be used equally well for data. They can be aggregated into multilink channels of faster effective data rate. These 64 KBps streams are called Bearer (B) channels. Each B channel typically has an ISDN telephone number; sets of B channels can be treated as a hunt group.

ISDN interfaces multiplex B channels with various control paths called D channels used for signaling. (The *D* doesn't stand for anything.) Mixtures of B and D channels are realized in two broad physical interface types:

- *Basic rate interface (BRI)*—Two B channels and a 16KBps D channel

    BRI can appear at either of the following:

    S/T reference point realization, using a four-wire electrical interface on an RJ45 modular connector and including 48 KBps of overhead. S/T interfaces are point-to-multipoint and potentially involve subaddressing for the individual user devices on the shared bus.

    U reference point realization, using a two-wire electrical interface on an RJ11 modular connector and including 16 KBps of overhead.

- *Primary rate interface (PRI)*—Either 23 or 30 B channels plus a 64 KBps D channel

    23B+D—North American and Asia-Pacific usage provisioned over T1 facilities

    30B+D—European usage provisioned over 2.048 MBps E1 facilities

An ISDN TE implements U- and C-plane mechanisms. Before any user traffic flows, a control path must be established at Layer 2, using the Q.921/LAP-D protocol.

When an end host wants to make a connection request, this request is encoded into the Q.931 C-plane protocol, which is encapsulated into LAP-D (that is, Q.921) and sent to the local exchange.

Q.931 messages arriving at the local exchange, if valid, cause *Signaling System 7 (SS7)* M-plane messages to be sent by the telephone network to the exchange serving the remote user. SS7 is the principal M-plane protocol of public telephone networks, which, among many other functions, determines how a call is to be routed through the internal telephone network.

At the exchange switch, a Q.931 message is generated and sent to the called TE. Eventually, SS7 messages that indicate whether the call is answered return the caller's exchange and are translated into Q.931 messages to the end host.

LAP-D is a relatively complex Layer 2 protocol because it has several capabilities beyond simple call setup:

- Assigning transient identifiers to end equipment and creating a local addressing environment that supports subaddresses, comparable to telephone extensions. This environment allows several devices to share an S/T bus.

- Carrying low-speed X.25 packet data, interspersed with Q.931 control messages.

- Communicating with higher-level protocol translators and sending parameters to them.

Although ISDN's shared bus capability requires the D channel to establish addressing, collision avoidance is actually achieved through hardware-level B-channel conventions.

ISDN Endpoint Addressing

The ISDN network layer interface (used for call control) provided by the software conforms to the specifications for specific switch types defined by the ITU-T recommendation Q.931.

From a pure addressing standpoint, logical to transmission mapping on routers is done with static configuration statements. In practice, a number of supplemental parameters are needed in these statements.

Again, this is a standard protocol with persistent and nonpersistent identifiers. Persistent identifiers are defined by the E.164 specification. E.164 addresses are up to 15 digits long and begin with a country code.

The values of call setup parameters are dependent both on the carrier's switch type and the specific carrier implementation. The carrier defines them. Within most ISDN service providers, there is a person who not only knows the parameters in the form expected by the ISDN protocols, but the actual configuration statements needed on a particular router or host. Such people, however, can be hard to find.

> **Note**
>
> *Although the S / T interface (yes, I know I am being architecturally sloppy calling it that) needs four wires, it is on an eight-wire connector. The reason for the additional wires is for various options of electrically powering the NT and TE.*

Service protocol identifiers (SPIDs) might be required for communication through certain ISDN switch types. They identify the end equipment to the switch.

ISDN Addressing Checklist

☐ Circuit type required (BRI or PRI, reduced number of channels—for example, single B and D)

☐ Switch type

☐ SPID requirement

☐ Data link protocol for B channels

☐ When sending data over the D channel, X.121 address assigned

☐ X.25 packet layer parameters set, such as window size, packet length, and so on

LAP-D in Circuit and Packet Services

Most of the complexity of LAP-D comes from its role in managing multiple devices on a shared S/T bus. In other words, it is a multiplexing mechanism.

Think of the combined service access point identifier and transport endpoint identifier (SAPI/TEI) as a two-level hierarchy. SAPI effectively identifies the type of protocol or procedure that one of its subordinate TEIs speaks:

SAPI=0	Call control (that is, B channel setup)
SAPI=1	Q.931 user data packet mode over the D channel
SAPI=16	User data packets over D channel using X.25
SAPI=63	LAP-D protocol management

SAPI=0 has been the most important, both for data and voice applications. Subaddressed TEs all have SAPI=0. There has been a recent surge in SAPI=16 X.25 applications for low-volume dedicated accesses such as automatic teller machines and credit card authorization terminals.

TEIs identify terminal equipment. The ISDN specifications allow both fixed and dynamic specification of the TEI; dynamic assignment is generally more flexible.

Transient identifiers are 7-bit values called TEIs, which are fixed for certain devices, such as a telephone extension, or negotiated. TEI values are defined as

0–63	Manually configured; 0 reserved for point-to-point
64–126	Dynamically assigned via LAP-D negotiation
127	Broadcast

Additional provisioning questions arise for SAPI=1 X.25 data-over-D-channel applications. As noted in the ISDN addressing checklist, you need to set X.25 parameters including the X.121 transmission system address for X.25 networks.

Packet, Frame, and Cell Switched Transmission Systems

POTS is a circuit-switched technology with origins in the last century. ISDN is a 1980-vintage update of the same basic technology, with additional capabilities.

X.25 was introduced as a packet technology in the early 1970s. A class of *fast packet* services was introduced in the 1980s and 1990s and includes Frame Relay and Asynchronous Transfer Mode (ATM). Fast packet services are optimized for the newer digital and optical transmission systems with far better performance than X.25.

X.25 remains an excellent technology for running over poor-quality transmission systems, as might be found in rural areas or developing countries. It is also appropriate for long-delay satellite links.

X.25

Long established as a global WAN architecture, X.25 has both persistent endpoint identifiers and transient connection identifiers.

Persistent identifiers are defined by the X.121 specification. They are variable length numeric strings, written in decimal digits, and encoded as binary coded decimal (BCD). X.121 strings are up to 14 digits long. Public network identifiers always begin with a 4-digit data network identification code (DNIC). X.121 addresses must be configured on DTE interfaces.

Creating a call thus requires a connection to be made between pairs of X.121 addresses. These are spoken of as the *calling* and the *called* numbers (when spoken, the emphasis is on the second syllable of both calling and called).

An X.25 DCE can manipulate X.121 addresses presented to it, which is not uncommon for dial-in servers on public networks. The actual DTE's purported calling address can be replaced with an X.121 address associated with the terminal server. This prevents attacks based on forged X.121 addresses.

Subaddresses can be assigned to X.121 addresses, allowing an additional level of multiplexing. Most commonly, they are used to identify the specific dial-in asynchronous ports on an X.25 terminal server (that is, a packet assembler-disassembler [PAD]).

A specific connection is bound to local connection identifiers at each end. The calling DTE selects a potential connection identifier from a pool available to it, while the provider network selects a connection identifier at the far end, over which the incoming call request arrives.

Connection identifiers are locally significant 12-bit values, although using this many bits would be extremely rare. In practice, the 8-bit logical channel number field is quite adequate, although it can be extended by a 4-bit logical channel group number. The connection identifier is usually simply called the LCN.

X.25 has various rules for the permissible values of the LCN, which do affect configuration of the router. LCNs can be assigned to one of four functions:

- Permanent virtual circuits

- Incoming-only (can be initiated only by DCE)

- Two-way SVC

- Outgoing-only SVCs

If any PVCs are used, the lowest LCN value must start there. Only if there are no PVCs can the first incoming-only use LCN #1. In like manner, only if there are neither PVCs nor incoming-only SVCs can the two-way start with LCN #1.

Ranges set for LCN values can serve a tuning purpose. X.25 was developed for terminal-to-host timesharing, with end users entering characters at human typing speed. Given the natural pauses between user traffic, a significant amount of statistical multiplexing always was possible. Interleaving the bursts of traffic to and from various users often meant that the sum of user access speeds to the X.25-based terminal server (that is, the X.25 PAD) could exceed the speed of the link from the PAD to the X.25 ingress switch by a factor of 4 or more.

In computer-to-computer communications, there are no natural pauses caused by delays in typing. The sum of the throughputs of individual virtual circuits should equal, or only slightly exceed, the access link speed.

Throughput controls and class-of-service controlled access, although in the 1984 version of the X.25 standard, rarely are implemented. It is reasonably simple to limit the number of virtual circuits that can be created on the link. This can be done by limiting the virtual circuit ranges.

Assume you have two destinations that you commonly go to, and you expect the application to burst up to 32 KBps. Your access speed line is 64 KBps. If either end could randomly start the call, your channel number ranges could be set to:

- Permanent virtual circuits: 0 to 0

- Incoming-only: 0 to 0

- Two-way SVC: 1 to 2

- Outgoing-only SVCs: 0 to 0

Address Resolution in X.25

In most cases, manual configuration statements map the X.121 transmission system address to the logical address. There is no currently defined out-of-band mechanism over which address resolution queries could flow, nor is X.25 intrinsically broadcast capable.

U.S. military networks do have a convention for mapping between X.121 and IP addresses. This convention had specialized applications for IP over an underlying X.25 transmission system and never came into wide use.

Upper-Layer Protocol Identification on X.25

X.25 was developed long before today's multiprotocol environment. As such, it did not provide for carrying upper-layer protocols other than those of the X.25 protocol suite. As needs emerged to carry other upper-layer protocol traffic over X.25, proprietary and standard methods emerged to do this.

RFC 1356 prescribes a standard method for encapsulating upper-layer traffic over X.25. It provides the option for carrying either a single protocol type per virtual circuit or multiple protocols over a single virtual circuit. This choice continues in more modern protocols, such as *multiprotocol over ATM* (MPOA) [RFC 2225].

An apparently archaic feature of X.25—packet fragmentation—still has applicability in specific circuits. One of these is *packet fragmentation*, in which the X.25 MTU can be considerably smaller than the IP MTU. This is highly desirable on transmission media with a slow transmission speed or high error rate.

When PDUs of higher level packets, such as IP datagrams, are transmitted over X.25, they can be fragmented into sequences of multiple X.25 packets. This fragmentation does not interfere with protocol identification, because protocol identification is done at call setup time and is bound to the virtual circuit.

At call establishment time, the Call User Data field in the Call Request packet identifies the protocol. It contains, at a minimum, a one-octet Network Layer Protocol Identifier (NLPID). Values of special interest include:

- Hexadecimal CC, which indicates IP.

- Hexadecimal 81, which identifies the OSI CLNP.

- Hexadecimal 82, which identifies OSI ES-IS. The same virtual circuit can be used for CLNP and ES-IS.

- Hexadecimal 80, which indicates the IEEE Subnetwork Access Protocol (SNAP), as described in the LAN discussion earlier. Only a single protocol type should be supported over SNAP-identified links. In this mode, no protocol identification is carried in individual X.25 packets.

- Hexadecimal 00, which identifies a Null encapsulation used to multiplex more than one protocol over the X.25 virtual circuit.

In the mode specified by hexadecimal 80, no upper-layer protocol identification is carried in X.25 packets. When only a single protocol family is sent to a site, this clearly has better bandwidth utilization than the alternative multiplexed method. It allows per-protocol tuning and accounting.

Opening X.25 virtual circuits, however, has a performance impact on the encapsulating device. Most public data networks also charge for connection time, so a monetary cost results from opening multiple connections.

The multiplexed method, identified with a network-layer protocol identifier value of 00, must consume additional bandwidth on a single virtual circuit to identify different protocols. Each data unit of a protocol family is fragmented as necessary into an X.25 complete packet sequence. The first byte of this sequence contains a network-layer protocol identifier with the same values as specified earlier for the NLPID in the Call Request packet. If the value is hexadecimal 80, then the next five bytes contain SNAP information.

Addressing Checklist for X.25 Service

☐ X.121 addresses assigned to interfaces

☐ LCN ranges selected

☐ Single or multiple protocol per link

Frame Relay

Frame Relay is a widely used service. Although a switched Frame Relay service is being introduced, the great majority of Frame Relay implementations use a PVC model. Because there is no dynamic call setup, the distinction between persistent and transient identifier is less important than in other services.

As with ISDN, there are carrier-specific parameters, although they are less complex than with ISDN when using Frame Relay PVCs. Frame Relay SVCs, a new service, are considerably more complicated than PVCs. A key parameter, which can be set manually or automatically, is the management protocol used on each physical Frame Relay interface.

DLCIs

Frame Relay PVCs use locally significant DLCIs, represented as 10-bit fields. Illustrated in Figure 4.10, DLCIs identify local access to an end-to-end virtual circuit and quite commonly differ at both ends of the virtual circuit.

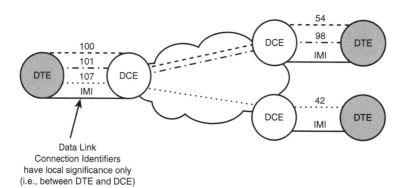

FIGURE 4.10. *Frame Relay end stations transmit to each other over end-to-end virtual circuits. Each station has a list of DLCI values that are associated with different endpoints.*

Frame Relay switches internal to the provider service have tables, shown in Figure 4.11, to map traffic arriving on one physical port, labeled with a DLCI local to that port, to an outgoing physical destination port and an associated local DLCI. Real-world Frame Relay services, of course, have more than one switch, but Frame Relay is not used to interconnect those switches. The specific technique used varies from provider to provider, but it is usually IP routing that encapsulates the Frame Relay frames or ATM virtual circuits.

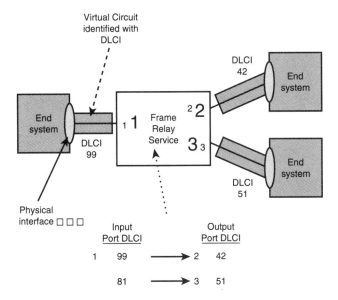

FIGURE 4.11. *The Frame Relay service is shown here symbolically as a single switch, although real networks have multiple physical switches. Tables map the DLCIs on incoming ports to what might be completely different DLCIs on outgoing ports.*

User-operated Frame Relay services can interconnect Frame Relay switches at Layer 2. If this is done, one interface in each connection is configured as a DTE and the other as a DCE.

In addition to DTE and DCE functions, Frame Relay specifies a *Network-to-Network Interface* (NNI). This is used to interconnect Frame Relay service providers. If the NNI is not implemented between providers—for example, if Frame Relay is simply tunneled through one provider using a dedicated line—management information might be lost and not delivered to local management interfaces.

Local Management Interface

The *Local Management Interface* (LMI) appears on a reserved DLCI. Three types are supported, and the Frame Relay service provider normally tells the customer which to use:

- Gang of 4, also called Frame Relay Forum LMI

- Annex A

- Annex D

Getting the LMI on the router to match the LMI on the provider's switch always has been a nuisance. In Cisco's IOS 11.2, the router can autosense the LMI the switch uses and autoconfigure the interface, subject to the following constraints:

- The router is powered up or the interface changes state to up.

- The line protocol is down but the line is up.

- The interface is a Frame Relay DTE.

- The LMI type is not explicitly configured.

Potentially, there can be 1024 values in a 10-bit field, so this is the absolute limitation on the often-asked question, "How many PVCs can I have per router interface?" This number is further reduced by reserved PVC values not available for general user PVCs, such as 0 for LMI, 1023 for Annex D management channels, and DLCIs 1-15 and 1008-1022 for other special functions.

This is still more PVCs than any plausible DTE can handle. Additional limitations come from performance and specific product design.

DLCI-to-Logical-Address Mapping

Static Frame Relay maps can become quite lengthy and difficult to maintain. Inverse ARP is now the default. The management interface of all Frame Relay indicates if a given PVC is available or down but does not contain information on the addresses reachable through that PVC. Inverse ARP extends the management interface to provide such information.

Ordinary ARP assumes that the underlying medium has a broadcast capability, which has to be simulated on Frame Relay with a heavy performance impact on the router. Inverse ARP does not impose this performance burden because it selectively sends information as a result of events on the management interface [RFC 2390]. This selective sending is directed to the known transmission system address of the destination.

On initialization, an interface on which Inverse ARP is supported should send an Inverse ARP request over every PVC on the interface. When the host learns that a new PVC has come up, the host should send an Inverse ARP request to the other end of the new PVC. These requests contain:

- The sender's transmission system address

- The sender's logical address

- The destination's transmission system address

- A zero-filled destination logical address field

Requests are then sent to the destination. On receipt, the destination handles this as it does a conventional ARP request, filling the destination logical address field and sending it to the sender. The Inverse ARP information is carried in the data field of the arriving frame, and the receiving station extracts the mapping information from it.

NBMA Issues for Frame Relay

Another important issue in Frame Relay and other NBMA transmission systems is the structure of the prefix to which the host addresses belong. The detailed structure of IP subnets is the subject of Chapter 5, but several points should be made here. Especially if an existing application runs on a LAN, there is a temptation to treat the entire Frame Relay system as a single NBMA subnet. Experience has shown this is generally a bad idea, certainly if dynamic routing updates run over the Frame Relay cloud. In most cases, each virtual circuit should be treated as a separate IP subnet. In some circumstances, it might be appropriate to group several VCs that have a single point in common as a point-to-multipoint subnet, but it is rarely, if ever, a good idea to deal with a partial mesh with no single hub point.

> **Note**
>
> Carriers should assign the DLCIs and tell customers about them. In the real world, this doesn't always work. Here's what sometimes happens:
>
> - The customer is told the correct DLCIs for each end, but they are reversed.
> - The wrong DLCIs are specified; there are active PVCs to the sites but on different PVCs.
> - The DLCIs have not been configured into the switch at one or both ends.

Upper-Layer Protocol Identification in Frame Relay

RFC 1490 prescribes a widely used convention for encapsulating arbitrary bridged or routed data in frames transmitted by Frame Relay services. It uses the SNAP field discussed earlier in LANs and X.25 applications, immediately following the Frame Relay header.

This method is especially popular in IBM applications, where a remote router encapsulates IBM protocol traffic and sends it via Frame Relay to a communications processor linked to a mainframe. If there are no other router applications at the mainframe site and the communications processor is sized to handle the Frame Relay traffic and is needed for other applications, this can save the cost of a router. IBM encapsulation is discussed further in Chapter 8.

Addressing Checklist for Frame Relay

☐ Management interface

☐ Number of DLCIs per access link. Relationships among access rate, CIR, and bursting understood

☐ DLCIs assigned

☐ Static or dynamic mapping

☐ Backup mechanisms

ATM

Many people think of ATM itself as more than it is: a mechanism for providing point-to-point and point-to-multipoint connections. It has endpoint and connection identifiers.

There are three potential formats for private ATM network endpoint identifiers, shown in Figure 4.12, and one for public network identifiers, shown in Figure 4.13:

- NSAP encoding of International Code Designator (ICD), a format that allows the registration of blocks for recognized international organizations

- NSAP encoding of E.164 public ISDN, which encodes the same E.164 phone numbers as the basic E.164 specification, but as 64 bits rather than 15 decimal digits

- OSI NSAP using ISO 3166 country codes, a format that allows the registration of national networks

- E.164 for public interconnection, using decimal encoding

A given ATM system can support the public E.164 format, all three of the NSAP encodings, or both.

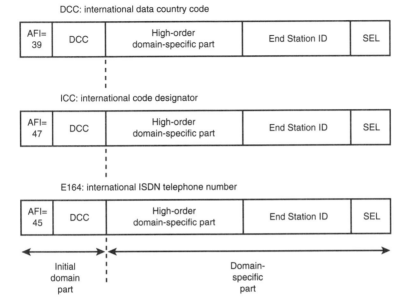

FIGURE 4.12. *NSAP formats for private ATM networks.*

Country code	E.164

FIGURE 4.13. *NSAP format for public ATM networks.*

ATM addressing format discussions speak in terms of the NSAP format. This can be confusing, because although the format of the OSI Network Service Access Point address is used, ATM does not use the OSI Network Service. The *encoding* of an NSAP address simply has proven convenient for identifying endpoints in a large network.

NSAP addresses for ATM applications are 20 bytes long. They are split into an initial domain part (IDP) and a domain-specific part (DSP).

In the IDP, the first byte, *the authority and format identifier (AFI)*, defines the layout and length of the rest of the address. DCC codes identify countries. ICD codes identify internationally recognized countries, although, somewhat confusingly, some governments have ICD values assigned to them. The U.S. government, for example, has 0004 for network research, 0005 for civilian agencies, and 0006 for military agencies. The E.164 15-digit format is defined for the largest network, the worldwide public telecommunications network.

The DSP includes fields relevant to routing the call inside the ATM service identified by the IDP. The *high-order domain specific part* gives information needed to reach a specific point with an end system identifier. The Selector (SEL) byte is not used by the ATM network, but can be used to send information meaningful to the end station.

Connection identifiers are significant on single hops between ATM devices. They are two part, composed of a VPI and a lower-order VCI. VPI/VCI combinations are remapped at each hop between ATM devices, as shown in Figure 4.14.

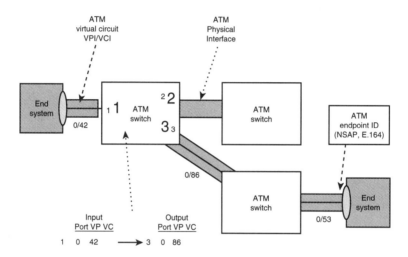

FIGURE 4.14. *ATM endpoint and connection identifiers.*

A LAN is connectionless, but ATM requires certain features to simulate a LAN environment for the users. One such feature is broadcast capability. Protocols wanting to broadcast packets to all stations in a subnet must be allowed to do so with a single call to Layer 2.

Several mechanisms exist for mapping end system addresses into an ATM transmission system. This mapping can be at the network or data link layer:

- Classical IP and ARP maps IP logical addresses to ATM transmission systems. The original specification in RFC 1577 has been superceded by RFC 2225, which consolidated RFC 1483 and RFC 1577.

- MPOA, which was originally specified in RFC 1483.

- ATMForum AF-LANE-0084-000, LAN Emulation.

ATM Adaptation

ATM adaptation layers (AALs) provide a structure for converting user information into ATM cells. AAL Types 1 and 2 are intended for user data streams with critical quality of service requirements, such as circuit emulation and compressed video.

In practice, AAL Types 3/4 and 5 map variable-length data link layer frames into fixed-length cells. AAL Type 3/4 allows the multiplexing of several stations on a single virtual circuit, at the cost of 4 bytes of overhead per 53-byte cell. This type must be used for SMDS.

AAL Type 5 is used for the majority of data applications. It has the constraint that only one source can send over the virtual circuit.

AALs can involve addressing; they certainly involve configuration to denote the identifier.

Addressing Checklist for ATM

☐ ATM address format chosen

☐ ATM addresses assigned to endpoint and switch ports

☐ Either PVCs setup or ATM dynamic setup supported

Emulated and Virtual LANs

Several transmission systems allow ATM-unaware devices to transmit over ATM transmission systems, either in a campus or long-haul environment. Other transmission systems, intended for building or campus awareness, allow classical LAN devices to communicate over high-speed trunking. Many implementations of VLANs, and above all their management systems, are vendor specific.

Assigning Devices to VLANs

Most commonly, a physical port on a VLAN-capable switch is manually configured to belong to a specific VLAN. Either the port can accept any MAC address from any device plugged into it or filters can be defined to accept or reject only specific MAC addresses.

Tables can also be configured with a list of MAC addresses and the VLAN to which they are to be assigned, regardless of the port to which they physically connect. Higher-layer protocol identifier values also can be used—for example, IP might go to one VLAN while AppleTalk would go to another.

In principle, even higher-level information, such as logical address, could be used for VLAN assignment. Functions such as this are not widely available and blur the already blurred boundary between switching and routing.

Trunking Technologies

Each of these systems is essentially an extended bridging technology, with a mapping of the edge system MAC address to an addressing construct in the trunk system. Addressing constructs can be MAC addresses or ATM virtual circuits. There are a number of vendor-specific variants, but common trunking technologies include

- *IEEE 802.10*—Inserts a VLAN identifier between the edge MAC and LLC headers for transmission over FDDI media. VLAN header information includes fields intended for encrypting the communications.

- *IEEE 802.1Q*—Inserts a VLAN identifier between the edge MAC and LLC headers for transmission over arbitrary media. Supports both VLAN tagging and frame priority tagging.

- *Cisco Inter-Switch Link (ISL)*—Prepends edge MAC frames with a VLAN identifier for transmission over Fast Ethernet or other media, as well as a MAC address for the transmission system.

- *Bay LattisNet*—An extension of the IEEE 802.1 spanning tree protocol, to include VLAN tagging.

- *SMDS*—Maps edge MAC addresses to ATM virtual circuits over AAL 3/4.

- *LAN Emulation*—Maps edge MAC addresses to ATM virtual circuits over AAL 5.

IEEE 802.10/802.1Q

Originally, the 802.10 protocol was developed strictly as a security standard for LANs. The tag field contained information that helped switches isolate the VLANs of different colors and pass cryptographic information. 802.10 assumed the trunk medium would be FDDI.

Cisco reused the 802.10 format for LANs without security, simply using the tag to keep track of isolated VLANs. This led to much controversy in the 802.10 committee, because 802.10 without encryption was felt by many to be a contradiction in terms.

Nevertheless, many felt that a standard VLAN method not requiring encryption did have a useful function. The 802.1Q committee was spawned from

802.10 work to work around the controversy. 802.1Q is essentially 802.10 without the encryption requirement. You cannot assume that an 802.10 implementation interoperates with an 802.1Q implementation.

802.1Q adds a *tag field* following the MAC header of a LAN frame, then recomputes the frame check sequence. The tag field contains a 12-bit VLAN identifier or a priority value.

Cisco ISL

ISL prepends a 26-byte proprietary header to the passenger frames and follows them with a 4-byte frame check sequence [Cisco 1996]. Passenger frames carry complete frames, complete with source and destination MAC addresses, which might be:

- Ethernet, Fast Ethernet, and Gigabit Ethernet

- Token ring

- ATM

- FDDI

ISL destination addresses are MAC addresses. The first 40 bits are in the form of a multicast address assigned to Cisco: 01-00-0c-00-00. The next 4 bits identify the passenger frame type, and the final 4 bits extend the frame type in a passenger-protocol-specific way.

The source address is the 802.3-format MAC address of the switch port from which the ISL frame originates.

SMDS

SMDS was introduced as an access mechanism to high-speed carrier facilities initially using DS-1 or DS-3 media, but in a manner upwardly compatible with ATM. It has its own layered architecture with addressing at two layers, one using E.164 addresses and the other using ATM VPI/VCI.

Although SMDS is not usually considered a VLAN technology, it really has the characteristics of one: a high-speed virtual trunking technology to which transmission system addresses are mapped. SMDS does seem to be losing ground in the marketplace, both to direct ATM services and to DS-3 access to Frame Relay.

Physical connectivity to SMDS services either goes from a router serial interface to an intelligent device called an SMDS data service unit or from a router ATM interface to an ATM switch.

SMDS supports both broadcast and unicast addressing. Its capability to handle multicasts and broadcasts makes LAN-like ARP practical as an address resolution mechanism.

If a protocol uses an ARP mechanism, it can dynamically discover SMDS addresses. Otherwise, it needs static mapping. After the topology is known, the medium appears to be full broadcast multiaccess and not subject to the NBMA issues seen in Frame Relay, ATM, and so on. The system may support true multicasting or the underlying router may replicate packets to simulate multicasting.

Multiple logical prefixes can be mapped onto the SMDS cloud. If so, it might be necessary to disable split horizon on router interfaces [RFC 1209].

LANE

ARP maps logical addresses onto MAC addresses. LANE uses a further level of indirection, in which it maps MAC addresses onto ATM virtual connections. This additional level of indirection is invisible to devices using MAC protocols, allowing the benefits of ATM to be used with existing LAN equipment.

LAN-based devices speak as they do today to routers and switches. Routers and switches implementing LANE, however, contain a function called the LAN Emulation client (LEC) that does the mapping of real MAC addresses into ATM addresses. Workstations and servers can also have LEC functionality, which gives them the impression of connecting to multiple LANs.

Most of the complexity of LAN emulation comes from how the LEC determines which LAN address to which a given destination address is mapped, and how the LEC forwards frames until the destination MAC address is resolved to a specific ATM address. Additional complexity comes from supporting multicast and broadcast MAC addressing.

LANE is a complex technology, and the discussion here does not attempt to get into the fine details of the internal protocols [ATMForum AF-LANE-0084-000].

Devices using MAC addresses do not see changes in the underlying ATM topology. From a system administration standpoint, the MAC-addressed devices can move from one emulated LAN (ELAN) to another, much as devices move from one physical segment to another. Functionally, ELANs and VLANs are the same thing; they are simply names developed by different standards groups. ELANs are VLANs that run over an ATM virtual circuit service.

Complementing LAN Emulation Clients, LANE has three server functions, which in basic LANE are single points of failure. The server functions are

- LAN Emulation Configuration Server (LECS)

- LAN Emulation Server (LES)

- Broadcast and Unknown Server (BUS)

In basic LANE, there is one LECS per system of ELANs and one LES and one BUS per ELAN. The IETF Server Cache Synchronization Protocol (SCSP) [RFC 2334], Cisco's Simple Server Redundancy Protocol, and the emerging Simple Cache allow multiple LECSs, BUSs, and LESs.

A LEC can belong to multiple ELANs. When a router does serve as a LEC for several ELANs, it can route packets between them.

LES and especially the BUS functions are CPU-intensive. In practice, the LES, BUS, and LECS run on the same box. For this reason, the usual practice is to put them on a separate processor with a fast CPU that does not provide direct user services. Depending on the vendor, this processor might be a workstation, a special-purpose processor inside an ATM switch chassis, or a "single-armed" router with a fast CPU and a single ATM interface.

Each emulated LAN corresponds to one bridged system. This might have one or more logical addresses mapped onto it by Layer 3 aware devices or might appear to be purely a MAC-address level bridging system. Basic LANE is not aware of Layer 3 addressing, although the MPOA extensions to it are.

Architecturally, the LECS can contain four kinds of entry in its database:

- Emulated LAN name–ATM address of LANE server pairs

- LANE client MAC address–emulated LAN name pairs

- LANE client ATM template–emulated LAN name pairs

- Default emulated LAN name

An LEC is the point at which conventional MAC-addressed devices interface to the LAN emulation system. On initialization, each LEC connects to an LECS and requests the ATM address of the LES that services the ELAN to which the LEC belongs. If the LEC belongs to more than one ELAN, it repeats the process for each.

LANE clients have several possible ways to find the LECS. The specific mode selected is a choice from the following list, which runs from most to least preferred:

- Locally configured ATM address

- Interim LMI

- Fixed address defined by the ATM Forum

- PVC 0/17 (that is, Virtual Path Identifier 0, Virtual Channel 17)

After the LEC contacts the LECS, the LECS returns the name and address of the LES that will service the LEC. A virtual circuit for carrying control information is set up between the LEC and its LES. The LES also adds the LEC to its point-to-multipoint virtual circuit to the set of its LECs.

In its tradition of confusing terminology, such as the LECS being different from more than one LEC, LANE has its own ARP mechanism. LE_ARP does *not* replace the ARP mechanism that binds a logical address to a transmission system address.

Remember that LANE appears as a bridging system to conventional MAC-addressed LAN devices on the LANs serviced by LECs. The LE_ARP is internal to the LANE environment and binds a MAC address at the LEC to an internal ATM address in the trunking system that provides the connectivity among components of the LANE environment.

Each LEC has a LANE ARP cache. This cache can be populated with manually configured static entries, with dynamic information learned from the LE_ARP mechanism, or both. When a LEC becomes active in a LANE system, it has no dynamically learned information. When no local information is available, the process to resolve the MAC address goes like this:

1. The LEC sends LE_ARP_Request to the LES for its emulated LAN, over the point-to-point control VC between EC and LES.

2. Assuming that the LES has no local cache information about the destination MAC address, the BUS forwards the request to all other LAN Emulation Clients in the ELAN, using the unidirectional point-to-multipoint VC from the LES to all of its clients.

3. Each LEC receives the request and checks its local tables to see if it connects the MAC address. If so, the LEC informs the LES of the ATM address that will reach the MAC address.

4. The LES caches the MAC-ATM correspondence and sends it back to the LEC that originated the LE_ARP.

5. The originating LEC now creates a bidirectional VC to the ATM address where the destination MAC address can be reached and starts passing the data to that LEC for delivery to the destination MAC address.

Although the LEC does not know the ATM address for the destination, it forwards the user data to the BUS, which floods the data to all other LECs. This is computationally intensive, and the BUS function usually is implemented on a processor separate from the main ATM switching fabric. The rationale for flooding information to potentially unknown, or even nonexistent, destinations, is that the LEC to which the destination will be connected has not had time to learn about a certain MAC address that will be reached through the LEC. Perhaps the MAC address is on the distant side of a conventional bridge from the LEC, or the LEC is simply in the process of updating tables when it receives the LE_ARP.

Of course, frames destined to multicast or broadcast MAC addresses should be flooded. The BUS does this flooding for such frames, using the same point-to-multipoint VCs it uses for unknown traffic.

MPOA

LANE is a pure Layer 2, bridged model, with all devices on an emulated LAN in the same Layer 3 prefix. LANE only can communicate among devices in the same Layer 3 prefix. MPOA extends the LANE model to support interprefix communication using high-performance direct ATM virtual circuits. Essentially, it is a hybrid of bridging and routing over an ATM transmission system or, in the preferred MPOA term, *virtual routing*. MPOA connects (routes between) ELANs.

If MPOA decides to cut through to the destination, it queries the Next Hop Resolution Server to get the ATM address for the destination of the virtual circuit it wants to create. MPOA has refinements that allow an existing virtual circuit to the destination to be multiplexed.

Looking Ahead

This chapter reviews addressing aspects associated with transmission systems, mapping transmission system identifiers to "black box" logical addresses. The next two chapters open the black boxes of IP addressing, beginning with classical methods and extending the discussion to new scalable techniques.

CHAPTER 5

Classical IP Addressing: An Evolution

Research is what you do when you don't know what you are doing, but you know that you don't know what you are doing.

—Wernher von Braun

Begin at the beginning, go to the end, and then stop.

—Lewis Carroll

History repeats itself; historians repeat each other.

—Philip Guedalla

Although the Queen of Wonderland could direct Alice to start at a clear beginning and go to a distinct end, logical addressing, as exemplified by the Internet Protocol (IP), is more of a journey than a destination. Internet newcomers often wonder what the brilliant designers of the original protocol had in mind and why the design has limitations when dealing with the size of the current Internet. Simply said, the current IP, version 4 (IPv4) evolved from 1970s-vintage protocols used in the original ARPAnet. The basis of the current version was defined in 1980, when personal computers and LANs were curiosities.

Even though IPv4 evolved in an Internet tiny by today's standards, at each stage of its evolution, there was a sufficient perceived need for backward compatibility that each early assumption of IP had to be preserved.

You probably have experience with IP addressing. If you are like most people in the industry, you did not learn IP addressing in a terribly coherent way. In this chapter, we concentrate on a model of IP addressing that describes what routers and end hosts really do, as opposed to focusing on confusing address notation and administrative mechanisms for assigning addresses. Classes, subnets, subnet masks, and dotted-decimal notation tend to confuse the basis of what really is an internally consistent process. The key to making IP addressing straightforward is always to think of the address as binary, not a set of decimal numbers.

Let's journey into the wonderland of IP addressing from the perspective of its most influential natives: routers. IP addresses have two functional purposes. The first and more obvious is logically identifying arbitrary points in a network. The second and subtle point is the role of the prefix part of the address: providing information to find the path to a specific point.

I have found it to be vastly informative, in understanding IP, not to concentrate on the artifacts and awkwardness of the evolved protocol, but to review the fundamentals of the original design. Key principles of that design still are valid.

How Did We Get Here?

Seen from the perspective of a router, IPv4 has changed little from its original design. Much of the complexity, as we will see, comes from administrative mechanisms used to assign address values.

Any IPv4 address is 32 bits long. Routers make decisions based on some number of contiguous bits of this address, starting with the most significant bit on the left. This part of the IP address is called the *prefix*.

In this book, when we look at an IP address in binary, the following convention is used for the meaning of bits:

- P—A prefix bit, which is considered in making routing decisions at the point in the topology we are examining. Realize that the same address will be evaluated with different prefix lengths at various points in the topology, just as a telephone number conceptually contains a country code, but that code is not considered inside that country.

- S—A subprefix bit that identifies a specific medium or group of media within a larger prefix. Think of area codes within the North American telephone hierarchy; they are a subdivision of the country code and in turn have subdivisions called exchange codes.

These bits can be *overloaded* in the sense that they simultaneously have more than one meaning. Bits can have both P and S meaning; the combination of the two locates a medium and host in the global Internet. The S bits alone, treating the P bits as a constant, can serve to locate a medium and host within an enterprise.

- x—A "don't care" bit from the perspective of routing at the point of topology we are examining.

- H—A host bit used to locate a specific host on a medium or to indicate the medium itself (rather than prefix for it) or the broadcast address for that medium.

Think of a postal address, which consists superficially of a street with a building number on the street. It is the job of routers to deliver packets to the final street, on which a destination host—the building— recognizes packets. Figure 5.1 shows an example to illustrate the process. Assume we route based on a single-bit prefix. The notation convention for this length is that it is a /1 prefix. This notation convention was introduced with the current practice for global Internet addressing, Classless Inter-Domain Routing (CIDR). You will see the motivations for CIDR in Chapter 6, "Internet Failing: Details at 11." At this point, we use the CIDR notation convention. You probably are familiar with an alternative convention, subnet masks. As this discussion progresses, you will see the relationship between subnet masks and CIDR notation. The CIDR notation, however, makes it much easier to see the underlying logic in IP addresses.

In a router, if the value of the prefix is 0, the packet leaves the router via interface 0. If the value of the prefix is 1, the packet leaves the router via interface 1. In other words, only the first bit of these IP addresses is considered in making routing decisions.

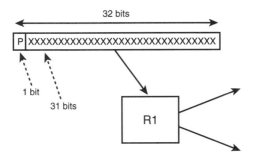

FIGURE 5.1. *Routing on a /1 prefix. The value of the P bit selects the output interface.*

A single-bit prefix gives us only one possible value. Staying with an essentially trivial example, assume that we have a 2-bit prefix and four possible destinations. Each of these destinations is identified by a value of the /2 prefix. These destinations could be reached with four interfaces on one router or with a tree of three routers.

Real-world IP addresses have at least 8 bits in their prefixes, and usually many more. Practical routers associate many prefixes with each outgoing interface. In Figure 5.2, the x in a prefix position represents a don't-care bit position in making forwarding decisions.

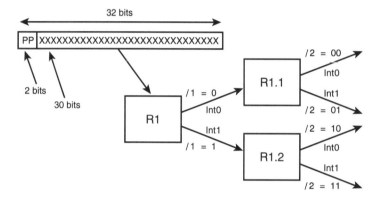

FIGURE 5.2. *Routing on a /2 prefix with a tree of routers.*

Another way to look at the don't-care mechanism is to remember that an IP address is always 32 bits long. If the prefix length (that is, /8) is subtracted from 32, the result is the number of don't-care bits for router decision making. In other words, decisions are made only on the prefix length number of bits.

The information shown in Figure 5.2 is stored internally in a router as a *routing table*, also called a *Forwarding Information Base* (FIB) or *Routing Information Base* (RIB). Table 5.1 shows a typical structure of this table for the router shown in Figure 5.2.

A minimal routing table contains a list of destinations and the output interface that should be used to reach them. In the sample routing table in Table 5.1, the Destination column contains the information needed to identify the destinations—prefix value and prefix length.

TABLE **5.1.** A ROUTING TABLE FOR **R1.**

Destination	Outgoing Interface
00 / 2	Int 0
01 / 2	Int 0
10 / 2	Int 1
11 / 2	Int 1

In these examples, the part of the IP address not included in the prefix bits used for decision making is composed of bits that identify the host on the destination medium or of bits that will be used for path determination hierarchically lower in the routing fabric.

IP Address Syntax and Semantics

In 29801, the original IPv4 specification was issued [RFC 760] with the intention of being compatible with existing ARPAnet addresses and providing growth for the future. *Growth*, in this context, meant the capability to interconnect over 200 networks.

This fixed prefix length meant that the remaining 24 bits could be used for host addresses. It was assumed that all host addresses in a given prefix were managed by a central computer such as a mainframe or were on the same LANs. In 1981, LANs were still primarily a research curiosity, as was the newly introduced personal computer.

Prefix, Prefix Length, and Host Fields

Meeting this interconnection requirement meant that a fixed 8-bit prefix field was quite adequate. The original 8-bit prefix structure is shown in Figure 5.3. Unfortunately, interconnection requirements grew quickly, and there were soon more than 200 networks. In 1981's RFC 791, a new convention was developed to have three standard prefix lengths of 8, 16, and 24 bits, shown in Figure 5.4.

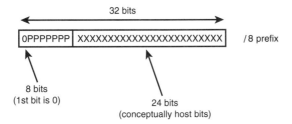

F I G U R E **5.3.** *RFC 760 fixed prefixes.*

> **Note**
>
> *Pay careful attention to this, because it will affect terminology later on: The original IP address prefix was fixed. With the introduction of different prefix lengths, it was no longer fixed, but variable. Variable length prefixes have been with us since the beginning of IP.*

RFC 791 controlled the values of the most significant bits (that is, leftmost) in the prefix to determine the prefix length. These bits were overloaded, in that they were part of the address, but also encoded how long the prefix was. The encodings are

- Addresses beginning with 0xxx are unicast with an 8-bit prefix. These were called Class A, although the idea of prefix classes is obsolete. Today, these are known as /8 prefixes.

- Addresses beginning with 10xx are unicast with a 16-bit prefix. These were called Class B and are now known as /16 prefixes.

- Addresses beginning with 110x are unicast with a 24-bit prefix. These were called Class C and now are called /24 prefixes.

- Addresses beginning with 1110 are multicast with a 28-bit prefix. These are called Class D.

- Addresses beginning with 1111 are reserved for experimental use and are called Class E.

IPv4 addresses were and are 32 bits long. The three standard unicast prefix lengths meant, respectively, there could be host fields 24, 16, and 8 bits long.

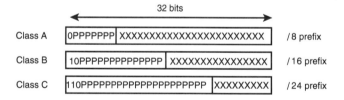

FIGURE 5.4. *RFC 791 variable prefixes.*

Features for Confusion: Dotted-Decimal Notation

Before discussing the structure of addresses, it is worthwhile to discuss the ways we talk about addresses. You, as a person, are unique. You, however, are addressed differently at different times by different people in a manner appropriate to the context. Someone might be addressed as "Mr. Smith," "Joe," or "Puppykins" in different addressing contexts.

In like manner, there are different ways to "say" the meaning of an address. The abstract semantics of an address deal with the meaning of *address* (for example, its membership in a specific hierarchy). *Abstract syntaxes* deal with human-readable notation for addresses. *Encodings* are machine-readable forms of the address used in protocol data units. Addressing authorities specify abstract semantics, protocols have specific encodings, whereas there needs to be a human-readable external abstract syntax for use by people.

Different architectures use these different ways according to their individual rules. All use some form of hierarchy to make addresses. Hierarchical organization might be intended simply to organize network administration or additionally to maintain worldwide address uniqueness.

IPv4 proper is encoded as a 32-bit binary string. Its abstract syntax, however, is called *dotted decimal*. Dotted decimal, unfortunately, is one of those things that seemed a good idea at the time, but definitely tends to confuse the situation. Its use is so widespread that it's impractical to phase it out directly. IP version 6 uses hexadecimal, a much more rational notation. Admittedly, dotted decimal is easier to remember than binary.

Basic Dotted Decimal

Even though the actual IP address is a 32-bit string, with prefix and host field sizes of arbitrary values, the dotted-decimal convention splits the address into four 8-bit octets such as `129.65.2.133`. These octets only have meaning in terms of human convenience and the administrative process of address assignment. The octets really are not seen by the routing process.

If we begin with the binary string

`10000001010000010000001010001111`

we can split it into four octets

`10000001 01000001 00000010 10001111`

Here is how it breaks down:

- Binary `10000001` has a decimal value of 129

- Binary `01000001` has a decimal value of 65

- Binary `00000010` has a decimal value of 2

- Binary `10001111` has a decimal value of 133

These four 8-bit values are written out as their decimal equivalents, separated by dots:

`129.65.2.133`

Historically, the class-based assignments of network numbers were done on an octet-aligned basis. This is obsolete. Most confusion about IP addressing comes from implying meaning to the octets.

Weighted Binary

There are some non-obvious conventions in converting between dotted decimal and binary. Look at the last octet in this example, 10001111, the decimal equivalent of which is 133. Let's assume that, for some reason, we need to split it into two 4-bit fields.

If you are a reasonably rational human being, proficient in binary and decimal arithmetic, you come to the apparently reasonable conclusions that the two fields would be 1000 and 1111, which, respectively, would have the decimal values 8 and 15.

This would be perfectly rational, and it also would be wrong for the first field. Dotted-decimal notation uses what is called the *weighted binary* convention. When a field is extracted from an octet, its bits must be evaluated in the same position, relative to the most significant bit on the left, in which the field started.

So in this case, the leftmost 4 bits must be evaluated as if they were

10000000

And the right 4-bit field must be evaluated as if it were

00001111

The proper value for these fields, if they were to be expressed as part of a dotted-decimal expression, would be, respectively, 128 and 15.

Subnetting and Subnet Masks

This limited range of three prefix lengths still proved inadequate, and *subnetting* was introduced as a means of providing more prefix lengths. At times, I look at traditional subnetting terminology as a means to full employment for consultants. At other times, I realize that it actually came from a sequence of just-in-time decisions on specific problems, not general solutions. In any case, the traditional subnetting terminology can be confusing.

Subnetting, when a large amount of confusing verbiage is stripped away, simply is a means of extending the prefix. This creates more prefix space. In practice, the original prefix is known at a high level of the hierarchy, and the extended prefixes are usually known only in the lower parts of the hierarchy.

Subnetting specifically moves the prefix rightward. It "borrows" bits from the host field and redefines their semantics to mean they are now part of the prefix.

"Traditional" subnetting (see Figure 5.5) introduced several terms that turned out to be rather complex. If one looks at the process introduced in RFC 950 not as a subdividing—subnetting—of existing networks, but more correctly as a general mechanism of prefix extension, the terminology becomes much simpler.

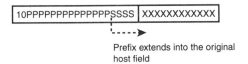

Prefix extends into the original
host field

FIGURE 5.5. *Traditional subnetting.*

The additional yet confusing terms are:

- Subnetting

- Bits of subnetting

- Subnet masks

In the classic RFC 950 method, *subnetting* is the process of further subdividing an assigned network number into a set of user "streets." It is a specific form of prefix addressing based on classful addressing, where addressing authorities assign network numbers to organizations, and the user organization extends the routing-relevant part by adding bits from the user field. In a classful system, this allocation is /8, /16, or /24.

The number of *bits of subnetting* m is the number of bits the prefix is extended by the network administrator, from the prefix assigned by higher authority. When *n* is the number of basic prefix bits, $m \leq (30 - n)$. The basic prefix is assigned by a higher-level administrative authority and given to a network administrator.

There are two ways to look at subnet masks:

- As a means of extracting the prefix from an arbitrary IP address, so the prefix can be used in routing decisions. In this case, the subnet mask should be considered a 32-bit string and a refinement to the *encoding* of IP addresses.

- As a convention for indicating the prefix length in the representation—the abstract syntax—of an IP address. In this usage, the subnet mask is a dotted-decimal expression of a 32-bit string. CIDR-style notation is far superior for this purpose. With CIDR, you can immediately see the hierarchical relationship between two prefixes, rather than needing to stop to decode a subnet mask.

Note

Confusingly, it is said that subnet masks are always associated with an IP address, even if the network associated with that address is not subnetted—that is, extended from a preassigned, hierarchically higher prefix. I prefer to use the term prefix length, because every IP address has a prefix length, whether subnetted or not.

Subnet masks should be viewed as one technique of prefix length notation. The slash or CIDR format, shown in Figure 5.6, is superior as a notation, but is not as widely deployed in software configuration tools.

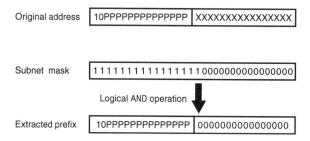

FIGURE 5.6. *Extracting a prefix with a subnet mask.*

The binary value of a subnet mask, as opposed to the use of subnet masks for a prefix length notation, is the basis of extracting prefixes from the destination address fields of packets to be forwarded.

You extract the prefix from an IP address by a bit-by-bit logical AND operation between the 32 bits of the IP address and the 32 bits of the subnet mask. Essentially, the subnet mask is a bit pattern that zeros out the host field of an IP address. The number of one bits in the mask is the length of the prefix.

One bits in the mask must be contiguous from the left. RFC 1812, the current "Requirements for IPv4 Routers" document, indicates that patterns such as `255.0.255.0` are now specifically illegal, although earlier specifications were vague on this point [RFC 1812].

Logically ANDing the two binary strings has the effect of zeroing out all bits in the host field of the address, producing the prefix. When a router looks at a specific host destination address in an incoming packet, it uses this logical operation to extract the prefix. The router finds destinations in the routing table not with specific host addresses, but with prefix values.

Using the prefix value rather than the specific host value is one of the fundamental strengths of routing. If specific host values were used, the router would have to track each address in the network. By using prefixes, the router only needs to track the much smaller number of prefixes, which are associated with destination media.

Note

The result of ANDing two bits together is 1 only if both bits are 1. All other combinations give a result of 0.

Relationships between subnet masks and prefix lengths are shown in Table 5.2, derived from RFC 1878.

The Original Administrative Model: Network and Subnet Numbers

In the original model for assigning IP addresses, the high-order part of the prefix—the /8, /16, or /24—was assigned by a single administrative body. This high-order part was called a *network number*.

Organizations assigned network numbers then would define subnets under them. When we speak of bits of subnetting, we mean the number of bits to the right that the prefix is extended.

The overall 32-bit address space is "owned" by an organization called the Internet Assigned Numbers Authority (IANA).

IANA, at first, delegated the detailed administration of the address space to the Network Information Center (NIC). Although the Internet received U.S. government funding, the NIC was a government-funded contractor, most recently Network Solutions of Herndon, Virginia. As the Internet grew, continental-level regional authorities replaced the original NIC. Regional registries are discussed in Chapter 6 and Chapter 9, "The Address Plan."

TABLE 5.2. A MASK AND PREFIX TABLE.

Expanded Mask Value	Prefix Length	Traditional Subnet Mask Length
10000000000000000000000000000000	/1	128.0.0.0
11000000000000000000000000000000	/2	192.0.0.0
11100000000000000000000000000000	/3	224.0.0.0
11110000000000000000000000000000	/4	240.0.0.0
11111000000000000000000000000000	/5	248.0.0.0
11111100000000000000000000000000	/6	252.0.0.0
11111110000000000000000000000000	/7	254.0.0.0
11111111000000000000000000000000	/8	255.0.0.0
11111111100000000000000000000000	/9	255.128.0.0
11111111110000000000000000000000	/10	255.192.0.0
11111111111000000000000000000000	/11	255.224.0.0
11111111111100000000000000000000	/12	255.240.0.0
11111111111110000000000000000000	/13	255.248.0.0
11111111111111000000000000000000	/14	255.252.0.0
11111111111111100000000000000000	/15	255.254.0.0
11111111111111110000000000000000	/16	255.255.0.0
11111111111111111000000000000000	/17	255.255.128.0
11111111111111111100000000000000	/18	255.255.192.0
11111111111111111110000000000000	/19	255.255.224.0
11111111111111111111000000000000	/20	255.255.240.0
11111111111111111111100000000000	/21	255.255.248.0
11111111111111111111110000000000	/22	255.255.252.0
11111111111111111111111000000000	/23	255.255.254.0
11111111111111111111111100000000	/24	255.255.255.0
11111111111111111111111110000000	/25	255.255.255.128
11111111111111111111111111000000	/26	255.255.255.192
11111111111111111111111111100000	/27	255.255.255.224
11111111111111111111111111110000	/28	255.255.255.240
11111111111111111111111111111000	/29	255.255.255.248
11111111111111111111111111111100	/30	255.255.255.252
11111111111111111111111111111110	/31	255.255.255.254
11111111111111111111111111111111	/32	255.255.255.255

Host or Don't Care	Hosts (-2 reserved)	Classful Equivalent
31	2048 MB	128A
30	1024 MB	64A
29	512 MB	32A
28	256 MB	16A
27	128 MB	8A
26	64 MB	4A
25	32 MB	2A
24	16 MB	1A
23	8 MB	128B
22	4 MB	64B
21	2 MB	32B
20	1024 KB	16B
19	512 KB	8B
18	256 KB	4B
17	128 KB	2B
16	64 KB	1B
15	32 KB	128C
14	16 KB	64C
13	8 KB	32C
12	4 KB	16C
11	2 KB	8C
10	1 KB	4C
9	512	2C
8	256	1C
7	128	1/2C
6	64	1/4C
5	32	1/8C
4	16	1/16C
3	8	1/32C
2	4	1/64C
1	2	1/128C
0	1	1/256C

The Evolution of IANA

At the time of this writing in September 1998, major restructuring of the IANA function is taking place, and the final form it will take has not been decided. The structure of *new IANA* (*nIANA*) will reflect the internationalization and commercialization of the Internet, as well as a new funding model for nIANA. See www.iana.org for the most current information on the evolution of IANA.

For many years, IANA was funded by the U.S. government as part of its networking research programs. IANA actually consisted of Jon Postel and a small staff at the University of Southern California. Because Postel is also the RFC Editor, IANA could be the central authority for avoiding conflicts among constants in protocols defined in standard RFCs. The Internet address space is one more set of numeric values that has to be allocated in a way that avoids technical conflicts. IANA, in my opinion and the opinion of most of the IETF, has done a superb job. Postel is widely respected in the Internet engineering community.

With the end of U.S. goveernment funding of IANA, a new model needs to emerge beyond those steps taken for interim funding. The U.S. government is helping this transition and working with many interests to form a consensus, driven by Ira Magaziner, a principal White House policy counselor. See the National Telecommunications and Information Administration's U.S. policy proposal, which can be found at www.ntia.doc.gov/ntiahome/domainname/6_5_98dns.htm.

New proposals focus on the control by *stakeholders*, or the various intermational government and commercial interests who are affected economically by the Internet. The evolving nIANA proposals seek to establish an international, not-for-profit organization that carries out the old IANA functions, but with guidance from a broader range of organizations than the funding agency of the U.S. government and the technical input of the IETF.

Host Field Conventions

When a host field of *m* bits is defined, 2^m-2 values are available for actual host addresses. In this context, a host can either be an ordinary end host or a router interface.

Two values are reserved and have special meaning. An all-zeroes value in the host field, sometimes called *this subnet*, effectively identifies the medium itself as opposed to any host on it.

It is the all-zeroes value—the "name of the wire"—that is stored in routing tables as the destination address. Routers forward packets to that medium to reach any host on it.

Packets sent to the all-ones host field address under a given prefix are broadcast onto the associated medium, assuming the medium is broadcast capable.

This value is called the *local broadcast* address of 32 one bits, usually written as the dotted-decimal value 255.255.255.255.

When a packet has the local broadcast address as its destination address, it is broadcast onto the medium on which it originates, but is not propagated to other media by routers. See Chapter 13, "Addressing in Routers," for techniques to convert a local broadcast to addresses that are propagated by routers. These techniques convert local broadcasts either to unicasts or directed broadcasts.

A broadcast sent to a specific prefix is called a *directed broadcast*. Directed, as opposed to local, broadcasts are routable. Packets with a directed broadcast address flow through the network based on their prefix, but are converted to a local broadcast when they reach the final destination medium.

Avoiding Directed Broadcasts

A trend to discourage use of the directed broadcast is developing. There is not a huge number of applications for it, and most of those, such as sending to mirrored replicated servers on a common medium, can be done with multicast addresses.

Directed broadcasts have been used as the basis of destructive hacking attacks on networks. If echo requests are sent to the broadcast address for a medium, the resulting broadcast is sent to all hosts and causes an operating system interrupt. Although an external communications link might not have the bandwidth to launch denial of service attacks on every host on a medium, only a single packet to the broadcast address can impact every host.

An Example

Three blocks of addresses are reserved for private use. *Private use* means that these addresses should never be seen on the public Internet [RFC 1918]. These blocks are normally described in dotted decimal:

- 10.0.0.0/8, the 8-bit block

- 172.16.0.0/12, the 12-bit block

- 192.168.0.0/16, the 16-bit block

In binary, we can expand the 8-bit block to

00001010 XXXXXXXX XXXXXXXX XXXXXXXX

Or the range of values

00001010.00000000.00000000.00000000

to

00001010.11111111.11111111.11111111

These binaries translate to the dotted-decimal range 10.0.0.0 through 10.255.255.255.

You are given an address, 10.169.100.20/13 in this block, and told it has a 13-bit prefix, which can also be expressed as 5 bits of subnetting. Expressed in dotted decimal, the subnet mask for a /13 prefix is 255.248.0.0. What is the prefix associated with this address?

To extract the prefix, write out the binary equivalent of 10.169.100.20 with the binary equivalent of the subnet mask immediately below it:

00001010.10101001.01100100.00010100
11111111.11111000.00000000.00000000

Applying a logical AND gives you

00001010. 10101001.00000000.00000000
     10.   169.   0.   0

Let's put the 10.169.0.0 prefix we have just extracted in context:

Prefix 10.169.0.0

Host value 0.0   Identifies the medium

Host values 0.1   Available for hosts through 255.254

Host value 255.255   Directed broadcast to this specific prefix

Basic Address Planning

In this section, we will begin by examining a single-site addressing system and then look at addressing for basic intersite connectivity. This simple example does not deal with methods for reducing routing table size, which are discussed in Chapter 6. Additional methods for optimizing the use of address space are discussed in Chapter 9.

Let's begin with the configuration shown in Figure 5.7, a single router that interconnects four LANs. This router might interconnect four floors or workgroups inside a single building. Assume that there are 40 user workstations and two print servers in each LAN. Workstations and servers are both hosts in IP terminology, so at least 42 host addresses are needed.

Total address space for LANs on router /24			
First /26 LAN Subnet	Second /26 LAN Subnet	Third /26 LAN Subnet	Fourth /26 LAN Subnet

FIGURE 5.7.   *Basic address planning for a single router.*

Remember that a router usually does not have a single network address of its own, but is treated as a collection of interfaces, one on each directly connected medium. This is true of IP, and most protocol families, with the exceptions of DECnet and Banyan VINES. In our IP case, there needs to be a router interface on each medium, bringing the total host requirement to 43.

Consider reasonable growth. If we assume 25% growth of user hosts, we would need space for an additional 10 hosts, for a total of 53.

Selecting the LAN Prefix Length

Look at Table 5.2 to find the number of host field bits that will contain this number of hosts. A 6-bit field suffices. You have justified a prefix length of /26 to locate this specific medium. In traditional subnet mask notation, this prefix length has a subnet mask of 255.255.255.192.

When using traditional classful addressing, which assigns addresses only on class A, B, or C boundaries, you have to round this up to a class C /24 block. In Chapter 6, you will learn the modern techniques of assigning addresses on arbitrary boundaries, not just the octet boundaries of classful addressing.

Address Requirements for a Single Router

You have four LANs connected to the router, so you need four media prefixes, each a /26. Table 5.2 shows that you need 2 bits to identify four prefixes. Together, the host field and the medium identification bits take up 8 bits. The 32-bit IP address, less these 8 bits, justifies a /24 prefix.

In traditional terms, this /24 is a class C block with 2 bits of subnetting. A better way to think of it, however, is that it is a /24 block containing four contiguous /26 blocks (that is, subnets). We can say these four subnets *summarize* into the /24.

For the prefix 192.168.1.0/24, address assignments are shown in Table 5.3.

TABLE 5.3. ADDRESS ASSIGNMENTS FOR /26 PREFIXES INSIDE A /24.

Binary Value of Last 8 Bits	Dotted-Decimal Address	Usage
00000000	192.168.1.0	Identifies the first subnet
00000001	192.168.1.1	First host on first subnet
	through	
00111110	192.168.1.62	Last host on first subnet
01111111	192.168.1.63	Broadcast for second subnet
01000000	192.168.1.64	Identifies second subnet
01000001	192.168.1.65	First host on second subnet
	through	
01111110	192.168.1.126	Last host on second subnet
01111111	192.168.1.127	Broadcast for second subnet
10000000	192.168.1.128	Identifies third subnet
10000001	192.168.1.129	First host on third subnet
	through	
10111110	192.168.1.190	Last host on third subnet
10111111	192.168.1.191	Broadcast for third subnet
11000000	192.168.1.192	Identifies fourth subnet
11000001	192.168.1.193	First host on fourth subnet
	through	
11111110	192.168.1.254	Last host on fourth subnet
11111111	192.168.1.255	Broadcast for fourth subnet

Contiguous Prefixes

It's worth reviewing the idea of contiguous prefixes. In Table 5.3, the three subnets are contiguous. Let's look at this more formally. Convert the two prefixes 192.168.0.0/26 and 192.168.0.64/26 to binary:

```
00001010.10101000.00000000.00000000
00001010.10101000.00000000.01000000
```

Observe that these differ only in the second bit of the last octet. Their first 25 bits are identical. Another way of saying this is that 192.168.0.0/26 and 192.168.0.64/26 are contiguous because they are inside the same binary block 192.168.0.0/25.

As long as the /26 prefixes are unique, they need not be contiguous for routing to work. The prefixes 10.11.0.0/26 and 171.16.0.128/26 would do nicely. Assigning a contiguous power-of-two block 192.168.0.0/25 for a site, however, is both easier to understand from the hierarchical addressing perspective and conveys other advantages (as we will see in Chapter 6). For this discussion, assume that multiple prefixes will be allocated in contiguous blocks.

Selecting the WAN Prefix Length

Let's make our little network more realistic by interconnecting the four sites with point-to-point lines, as shown in Figure 5.8. What is the host address space requirement for a point-to-point line?

Total classful address requirement: 5 x /24							
LAN address space on each router: /24 Total LAN space: 4 x /24 or one /22				Total address space for LANs on each router /28 needed – classful rounds up to /24			
Router 1	Router 2	Router 3	Router 4	First /30 WAN Subnet	Second /30 WAN Subnet	Third /30 WAN Subnet	Fourth /30 WAN Subnet
L L L A A A A N N N	L L L L A A A A N N N N	L L L L A A A A N N N N	L L L A A A A N N N				

FIGURE 5.8. *Basic address planning for four interconnected routers.*

Again, you need to define the host field size requirement. Two hosts plus the two reserved host values need a 2-bit host field:

PPPPPPPPPPPPPPPPPPPPPPPPPPPPPPHH

32 bits minus a 2-bit host field justifies a /30 prefix. Again referring to Table 5.2, the subnet mask for a /30 prefix is 255.255.255.252. We need four such interconnecting media, or the four /28 blocks are summarized:

PPPPPPPPPPPPPPPPPPPPPPPPPPPPPSSHH

In classful addressing, you cannot have more than one prefix length for a single network number. Because the LANs use a /26 prefix, you cannot use the same class C network number for the WANs. True, you have used up all the available address space in a class C with the LANs. But, under classless conventions, you would need to have an additional class C for the WAN links with /30 prefixes. You only need eight addresses, so you would waste 246 addresses in the second class C. This is unavoidable in classful addressing.

In practical enterprise networks, there are other requirements for blocks of address space, and preparing the overall plan is the thrust of Chapter 9.

Address Discovery

When I begin to learn a new networking architecture, I ask certain questions about addresses. Not all forms are present in all architectures. These questions are:

- What is my node's name? Its address, both Layer 2 and Layer 3?

- Given the name of an arbitrary node, how do I find the Layer 2 and Layer 3 addresses I should use to send to that destination?

- Are there any special conventions for locating and sending to routers and servers?

One's Own Host Address Configuration

A *host* is an unique locator in the Internet address space. *Host* does not imply a full application-through-physical layer stack. Physical computers often have more than one host address The exact mechanisms by which one's own host address is learned vary, depending on whether the information is

- Local to the host.

- In a server reachable with normal Layer 2 conventions. That is, the server is on a broadcast or point-to-point medium.

Static Configuration

In today's corporate world, mergers and acquisitions can have unexpected effects on networks. All too often, the building aspect is not even a remodeling, but a door abruptly cut between two rooms. In these days of corporate takeovers and splits, yet another problem is a wall suddenly erected inside an existing room. In this problem, a block of addresses had been assigned to one company, but the company splits. What addresses in the block should go to which new firm?

To participate in network layer activity, a network node needs to know its own network-layer address. It also needs to know the network address of others in the network and the physical-level addresses of other devices on the same medium. Each of these needs can be met by some type of address discovery mechanism. Address discovery mechanisms define the nodes of the network graph. Route discovery mechanisms, discussed in Chapter 6, define the paths between nodes. There are three basic approaches to address discovery, the first two of which are used in IP:

- Static or preconfigured, in which the address is known locally at initialization

- Active, in which the node requests its address from other nodes

- Passive or algorithmic, in which the entity does not initially know its address, but calculates it either from other locally available information and/or from information sent to it, unsolicited, by other entities

Hosts need additional information if they are to do effective work. Ideally, these include:

- One's own IP address

- Prefix length

- IP address of default gateway router

- IP address of DNS server

- DNS name of host

This information can be configured on a local disk, or part or all of it can come from servers. I strongly recommend the latter, as it is far easier, when changes need to be made—and they will—to make changes on one server than on 100 workstations. Server-based address management is discussed in Chapter 15, "Your Addressing Strategy: Integration for the Present and Planning for the Future."

Working with Classful Address Problems After a Corporate Merger

An enterprise with which I worked was formed from three merged companies. In each of the former companies, all aspects of network address assignment were done by a central group of experienced network engineers. These engineers assigned addresses to router interfaces, servers, and workstations. Because the first thing they did was test connectivity to the router, the router interface number was the first that was assigned.

Connectivity to servers was the next function tested. For a single-router medium, their convention was:

HOST ADDRESS(ES)	FUNCTION
1	Router interface
2 to (m+1)	m servers
(m+2) to (m+n+1)	n workstations

continues

continued

After the merger, the new central networking group was responsible for prefix assignment down to the subnet level, but not for host address assignment within prefixes. Individual LAN administrators were responsible for assigning the workstation and server host addresses from the prefixes sent to them by the networking group. Due to the haste of the reorganization, detailed addressing instructions were not sent to the LAN administrators.

A significant number of LAN administrators were selected after considering their technical backgrounds, and making decisions on such criteria as, "Your desk is closest to the router-thing. You are now the LAN administrator." Such backgrounds are not conducive to sophisticated address design.

Picture a novice LAN administrator sitting in front of a PC, following a checklist in a (fictional) book called *Really Basic Networking*: "Hmmmmm…it says enter the prefix…oh yes, that's on the piece of paper the network group gave me…*type type type*…OK…that's in. What's next?

"Enter the host number in the prefix. Host? Isn't that the person that greets you in a restaurant? OK. It's the number of the first computer in the network. Hmmmm…first computer…must be this PC; it's the first thing being connected."

Unfortunately, the novice LAN administrator didn't realize the router interface already had been assigned host number 1. The newly configured PC did indeed come up, but couldn't communicate with anything outside the local network because the PC's address duplicated the router's ID.

Some things in human nature can be circumvented by technical means, with varying levels of difficulty. The company with which I was working reduced a significant number of its problems by introducing a new numbering convention for router interfaces on a subnet with k host addresses:

HOST ADDRESS(ES)	FUNCTION
k (the last address of the subnet	Router interface
(k-1) to (k-m-1)	m servers
(k-m-1) to (k-m-n)	n workstations

Server-Based Configuration on Broadcast Media

To communicate effectively, an IP node must know its Layer 3 and Layer 2 addresses. If the node lives on a LAN, it presumably knows its hardware-defined MAC address, but may or may not know its IP address.

The way in which an IP node discovers its own network address, in practice, depends on its physical configuration. IP includes several address and path discovery mechanisms. Historically, the main address discovery protocols, which operate on a query/response model, are:

- *Reverse Address Resolution Protocol (RARP)*—Used to discover one's own IP address from an address server on the same medium, sending one's own MAC address in the request. RARP is discussed here for historical reasons; it has been superceded by the more versatile Bootstrap Protocol (BOOTP) and Dynamic Host Configuration Protocol (DHCP).

- *BOOTP*—Generalizes the idea of RARP to allow the address request to be routable to an address server on a different medium.

- *DHCP*—A superset of BOOTP that allows the address server to provide parameters beyond a simple address assignment.

Chapter 4, "Transmission System Identifiers and Logical Address Mapping: A View from the Bottom," discusses address resolution mechanisms needed to find the transmission system addresses required to send to other hosts' logical addresses.

Stateful Autoconfiguration: RARP, BOOTP, and DHCP

End systems without local configuration information need to obtain their network addresses using query/response methods. In practice, such diskless systems are only found on LANs, so the end systems know their MAC address. Diskless systems using Internet protocols use the Reverse Address Resolution Protocol (RARP) to learn their address.

As its name suggests, RARP is used when a station knows the MAC address, but not the network address, of another station. This is the case for diskless workstations, which have no local disk on which an administrator can preconfigure a network address.

RARP is thoroughly obsolete. It was replaced by BOOTP, which does not suffer from RARP's limitation of running directly over the data link layer. RARP information is not contained in an IP packet. It is a Layer 2 broadcast that contains Layer 3 information. Not being in a packet means RARP cannot pass through routers.

RARP servers must be on the same medium as their client, which can be a significant restriction. BOOTP and DHCP runs as a broadcast UDP packet and thus is routable. Figure 5.9 shows potential server locations.

BOOTP, in turn, has been replaced by DHCP. DHCP can return far more information than can BOOTP. DHCP servers, in general, are upwardly compatible from BOOTP. See the section "BOOTP/DHCP Relay Agent Operation" in Chapter 13 to learn how DHCP request broadcasts are routed to DHCP servers not on the local medium. Issues of using servers to manage address configuration are discussed in Chapter 15.

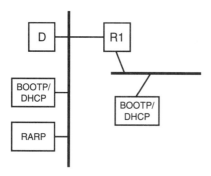

FIGURE 5.9.   *RARP, BOOTP, and DHCP all can provide addresses. RARP servers must be on the same medium as the client, while BOOTP and DHCP servers can be on the same or different one if connected by a router with a BOOTP/DHCP relay agent.*

RARP is sufficiently simple that it is worth looking at to understand how server-based address acquisition works. RARP is stateful, in the sense that the server remembers which addresses are assigned if a dynamic address pool is used. RARP, BOOTP, and DHCP all can return the same IP address each time, the lookup of the IP address being keyed to the requester's MAC address, or an IP address from a block of addresses. The actual method of selecting the address—from a pool or from a preconfigured table—depends on the capabilities of the server; the protocol itself does not limit this.

A node that wants to learn its IP address at startup time broadcasts an ARP request containing its hardware address. Structurally, the ARP request is a MAC-layer frame containing the requestor's MAC address in both source and destination fields, as well as a code identifying it as an RARP request and a field for an RARP server to fill in the network address. The RARP reply is very similar to the RARP request, except that the RARP server places its own hardware address in the source address field. There can be one or more RARP servers on a medium; the RARP requestor uses the first response received.

Configuration for Demand Media

Address resolution for dialup links normally involves binding an IP address to the connection, using the IP Control Protocol (IPCP) option of the Point-to-Point Protocol (PPP). The end station can propose an address for it to use, or it can ask to have one dynamically assigned.

In this practice, individual users announce their address to the access server using PPP's IP configuration option [RFC 1332]. The server can validate the proposed address against some user identifier or simply make the address active in a subnet to which the access server (or set of bridged access servers) belongs.

The preferred technique [RFC 2050] is to allocate dynamic addresses to the user from a pool of addresses available to the access server. Demand media are typified by dialup telephone or ISDN links. In Figure 5.10, D1 is an end user that connects to three different service providers' routers. When D1 is connected to R1, D1 wants to be inside the address space of the organization that operates R1, so other organizations know they need to go through R1 to reach D1. In like manner, if D1 wants to be reachable through R2's organization, or reach resources in that organization that are available only to addresses inside the R2 organization, R2 must be part of the R2 address space. The same situation exists with R3.

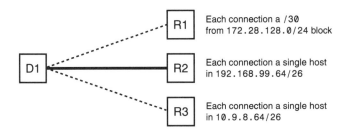

FIGURE 5.10. *IPCP demand configuration.*

The interface on D1 cannot have an address in a single prefix, but needs to be able to assume an address in the address space of the router to which it connects at a given time. This can be done through the dynamic address assignment mechanism IPCP.

Finding the Transmission System Address for Other Logically Addressed Hosts

After a station knows its own address, it will want to find other hosts. Protocols for doing this include:

- *Address Resolution Protocol (ARP)*—Used to discover the MAC layer address of a station on the same LAN for which the IP address is known. ARP assumes it is on a broadcast-capable medium.

- *Inverse Address Resolution Protocol*—Used to discover the transmission system address of another station on a nonbroadcast multiple access (NBMA) medium.

- *Proxy Address Resolution Protocol (Proxy ARP)*—Used to discover the MAC address of a station, on a different LAN, whose IP address is known. The remote LAN is assumed to be connected to the local one via a relay that responds to the MAC address of the remote station.

ARP proper, and its close relatives Proxy and Inverse ARP, are needed to find the address of arbitrary destination stations. Before a station can communicate with other stations, it must first know its own address. If it has its own disk files for configuration information, the station usually has a network address assigned statically by the local address administrator. If, however, it is diskless and must obtain its operating system executable image from another node, the network address is normally obtained as part of the operating system download.

Proxy ARP, shown in Figure 5.11, deals with the case where the destination station is not on the same broadcast medium, but the two media are interconnected by a router that participates in the ARP process. It is sometimes called the *ARP Hack* to show its ARP ancestry. It has two main purposes: providing more flexibility in address assignment and allowing for performance improvements by limiting the propagation of broadcasts. Proxy ARP is used in environments with multiple media that use ARP and are interconnected with a router. As with ARP, Proxy ARP is used when one node wants to send a MAC-sublayer message to another station Assume that there are two physical networks, A and B, interconnected with a router.

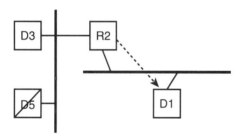

R2 will respond to D1 with R2's MAC address for ARPs
to queries for both
    D3
    D5 (which is actually down)
because R2 can reach the prefix common to D3 and D5

FIGURE 5.11.   *Proxy ARP responds to queries for hosts for which it knows how to reach their medium, whether the actual host is up or down.*

Both ARP and Proxy ARP are motivated by a desire for efficiency. If stations were unaware of each others' MAC addresses, they could still broadcast to devices and routers on the same medium. Broadcasts, however, place unnecessary processing loads on nodes to whom the broadcast is not directed. Even if the router was the only device to respond, there would still be two PDUs generated—one broadcast to the router and one sent by the router to the destination—for every information transfer.

Proxy ARP can create subtle problems. The router responds with its MAC address if it is aware of the prefix of the desired destination.

If that destination machine were physically connected to the local medium, but it was down for purposes of communications, the destination would not respond to the ARP query. The requesting host would realize that the destination was down after the response timed out and would act appropriately, either retransmitting the ARP query or deciding the destination was not reachable.

In the Proxy ARP model, however, the router responds to the ARP query if it knows how to reach the prefix on which the destination host should be located. This router takes no action to verify that the actual destination host is available. If the destination host were actually down, the requesting host would not know it. The requesting host would receive a normal ARP reply from the router and presumably would start sending to that destination. The router, in this condition, becomes a black hole for data to the destination. In most cases, the black hole does not persist because some higher-level protocol mechanism such as TCP times out, and the requesting host detects the failure through the TCP timeout mechanism.

Router Address Discovery

IP had long made the local versus remote assumption, as discussed in Chapter 4, that if a destination address were on a medium with a different prefix, traffic for that destination would be forwarded to a default gateway router. If the destination were on the same medium, then it was assumed the destination was reachable via Layer 2 mechanisms.

Which Default?

The terms *default gateway, default route,* and *default network* unfortunately mean different things.

The default router is a router on one's local medium to which traffic destined off the local medium is sent.

The *default route* is the routing table entry that matches all destinations, but is the least specific possible route and thus is the last considered. By convention, it is represented as the all-zeroes IP address, with a prefix length of zero, or `0.0.0.0/0`. This convention is respected in static routing and by the RIP, OSPF, and BGP dynamic routing exchange protocols.

Cisco's proprietary IGRP and EIGRP routing information exchange mechanisms

continues

continued

do not recognize the default route convention. Instead, they elect, or are configured with, one or more *default networks*.
These should be well-connected media
to which packets should be sent when
the next hop is not known. It is assumed
that a knowledgeable router is on that
medium. This default network mechanism is functionally similar to the default
route.

So an IP host must know how to reach a router on its local medium. The methods by which the host learns the address of the router vary considerably,
especially when more than one router might be present on the medium.

These methods, discussed below, include

- Static configuration of the default router address

- DHCP

- Internet Router Discovery Protocol (IRDP)

- Passive ARP

- Internet Control Message Protocol (ICMP) redirection

Most common is to have a statically configured router address. Some host
implementations allow multiple router addresses, but the general pattern is to
have a single default router address. DHCP can return a default router address
along with the host's assigned IP address.

When either static or dynamic configuration is used, if only a single router
address is known, the router becomes a single point of failure. Various vendors, such as Cisco and Bay, have proprietary techniques for defining a virtual
default router address that can move automatically from a failed router to
a backup router. These techniques are discussed in Chapter 13.

IRDP defines a pair of ICMP messages with which routers can announce themselves, and hosts can inquire about routers present on their medium rather
than waiting for a periodic router announcement. Although IRDP works, it has
not been widely deployed. Prior to the development of the IRDP standard,
Cisco implemented a proprietary Gateway Discovery Protocol (GDP). GDP is
completely obsolete and no longer supported.

A widely deployed method for finding the default router is to run the *Routing
Information Protocol (RIP)* on hosts. Such hosts run RIP in *passive mode*, where
end hosts listen to, but do not generate, routing information. The host assumes

that any host it hears, which does generate routing updates, must be a router. If that router advertises the default route, `0.0.0.0/0`, it can function as a default gateway.

Multiple routers can advertise the default gateway. Depending on the host implementation, if each router advertises the default route with the same metric, the host can either pick one as its default gateway or attempt to load-balance by sending packets to several routers, one after another in a round robin cycle.

Even though a given router might advertise the default, it might recognize situations when it should tell a host going to it to use a different, better router to reach a given destination. This is shown in Figure 5.12.

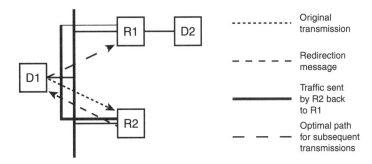

FIGURE 5.12. *An example of ICMP redirect.*

If host D1 wants to reach host D2, D1 begins with R2 as its default gateway and sends a packet destined to D2 to R2. Router R2 recognizes that it will forward the packet for the next hop to go towards D2 onto the same medium from which R2 received the packet from D1. R2 sends an ICMP Redirect back to D1, informing D1 that traffic to D2 should be sent directly to R1. D1 should cache this information and use it to send subsequent traffic to D2 via R1.

Classful Hacks and Pathologies

Remember that the original RFC 950 concept of subnets kept the subnet mask local to individual machines. The prefix length was not transmitted. There also was an assumption that only one subnet length would be used with any assigned network number.

Subnet Zero and the All-Ones Subnet

Look at these two apparently identical addresses:

```
10.0.0.0
10.0.0.0
```

Which is subnet zero of network `10.0.0.0`, and which is all of network `10.0.0.0`?

In a classful environment, when explicit prefix length information is not available, this is ambiguous. In contrast, is there any conflict in a classless environment, where we would say:

```
10.0.0.0/16
10.0.0.0/8
```

As long as the prefix length always is known, the zero and all-one subnets are perfectly legal [RFC 1812]. Their use is deprecated in some systems for the reasonable and conservative reasons that these subnets might inadvertently be redistributed into hosts or routers that remain classful and will not understand the subnets. Cisco, for example, internally has no problem with subnet zero, but requires that an explicit command, `ip subnet-zero`, be entered before the router accepts data entry of addresses that otherwise might go into subnet zero.

Some internetworking devices look at the "default mask" for classless addresses and really ignore specific mask information, falling back in preference onto traditional Class A, B, and C. This is a special problem because address allocation bodies assign pieces to different organizations of what was once a single network in the traditional Class A space [RFC 1878].

Secondary Addresses

Secondary addressing is defined as more than one logical prefix assigned to the same physical medium. Most of the reasons for doing this are limitations of a classful environment.

For example, the classful limitation of a single subnet within a major prefix (that is, a network number) can lead to having insufficient address space at key parts of the network. Consider a large campus network, on which most of the 8 workgroups have 10 or fewer nodes. Workgroups are joined by a backbone.

For the typical workgroup size, 4 host bits are needed. Assume that the site has been assigned a classical Class C block (that is, a /24 prefix). In classful terms, the site has a /24 with 4 bits of subnetting (that is, a /28 prefix in CIDR terms).

The customer service workgroup is significantly larger than the others, with 30 users. Following a strict model of 4-bit host fields with a maximum of 14 hosts each, three router ports, three separate media, and so on would be needed to support customer service. Performance considerations, however, indicate that the 30 users easily can share the same LAN.

Secondary addressing, shown in Figure 5.13, is one way to work around this problem. Without changing the fixed /28 prefix, three such prefixes can be assigned to the customer service LAN. The router interface needs an address in each prefix.

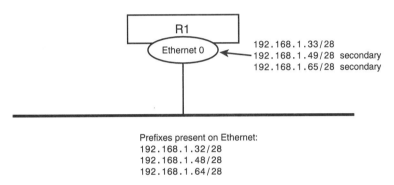

FIGURE 5.13. *Secondary addresses to provide more hosts on a single medium.*

By assigning three prefixes to the same physical medium, a total of 14×3, or 42, addresses become available in the customer service workgroup. Three of these are consumed by the router interface, but the 42 remaining addresses meet the requirement to have 30 local users.

Secondary addressing also can be used to heal discontiguous networks, a technique discussed next. See Chapter 13 for more applications of secondary addressing and details of its use.

Discontiguous Networks

In Figure 5.14, local configuration information on each router gives the prefix length. A dynamic routing protocol, the details of which are not relevant here, advertises all subnets.

Everything has worked well in this small enterprise network. Each router can build a routing table that tells it the next hop interface for each destination subnet. The routers are happy and content, cheerfully examining packets and forwarding them out the appropriate interface based on unambiguous information in their routing table. Each router advertised all its subnets to its peer. Subnet-level announcements were understood because each router had locally configured prefix length (that is, subnet mask) information. Let us assume that all these addresses were in the 10.0.0.0 prefix.

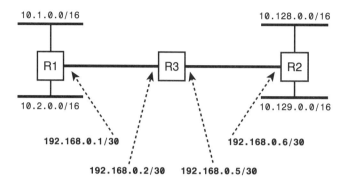

FIGURE 5.14. *An example of a discontiguous network.*

Confusion strikes the routing system when the enterprise merges with another and the new company becomes responsible for WAN connectivity. The new WAN organization uses its own network number for WAN links, 192.168.0.0/24.

Classful routing protocols do not make subnet-level announcements on interfaces with a different major network prefix. The underlying logic of this is that the distant peers would not have the subnet mask information to understand the subnet-level. Sending them detailed subnet information would simply waste bandwidth.

So, in Figure 5.15, neither R1 nor R2 make subnet-level announcements to their new peer, R3. Router R3 does know that elements of network 10.0.0.0/8 have been announced to interfaces S0 and S1 of R3. 10.0.0.0/8 is now a *discontiguous network*. 192.168.0.0/24 is the *partitioning prefix.*

One way to heal a discontiguous network is to assign a secondary address, in the discontiguous network, to every router interface along the paths between the discontiguous parts of the network.

As shown in Figure 5.15, when each router has local configuration information on the discontiguous prefix length, there is no longer a problem with discontiguous addressing. There is, of course, a vast amount of address space wasted in this example.

Secondary addressing can be a viable solution if there is a close organizational relationship between the discontiguous network router and the partitioning prefix router. If such a relationship exists, as might be found in merged companies, the administrators of the partitioning prefix will be willing to accept configuration changes to their routers. Changes such as adding the secondary addresses to heal the partition affect the R3 router's configuration in a way that does not directly help R3's operation, just the operation of the discontiguous network.

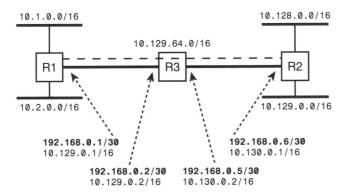

FIGURE 5.15. *Healing discontiguous networks with secondary addressing.*

Secondary addressing has limitations. With classful routing protocols such as RIP, it produces extra routing advertisements. Classless routing protocols such as OSPF and EIGRP, in existing versions, do not recognize routing relationships between secondary addresses.

Note

After one merger involving three companies, I saw up to seven secondary addresses assigned to core routers, in order to avoid discontiguous networks. It was inelegant, but it worked.

If the partitioning prefix belonged to a general network service provider, or an outsourced WAN provider, it would be far less likely that provider would allow its customer to change its router configurations. IP over IP tunneling, discussed in the next section, is a method transparent to the partitioning prefix routers and is useful in a number of situations when it is valuable to hide addressing information at the core of a network from its edges.

IP over IP Tunneling

A technique with a variety of applications, one of which is healing discontiguous subnets, is IP over IP tunneling. Various tunneling protocols have been implemented, including Cisco's Generic Route Encapsulation (GRE) [RFC 1701, RFC 1702]. The principle of tunneling also is used to carry non-IP protocols through an IP network, a use discussed in Chapter 8, "The Existing IP and Non-IP Address Structure: Preparing for Remodeling." Tunnels might also be used to provide cryptographic security, a topic in Chapter 7, "Addressing, Security, and Network Management."

In protocol tunneling, a *payload packet* is prefixed with a brief header for the tunneling overhead and then is wrapped in the *delivery protocol*. In IP over IP tunneling for the purpose of healing a discontiguous subnet, the passenger protocol is an IP packet originating and terminating on addresses inside the classful prefix that has been made discontiguous.

Obviously, tunneling increases the packet length and thus the overhead. When needed for connectivity, there might be no alternative to using it.

IP over IP tunneling's applications are not limited to healing discontiguous networks as illustrated in Figure 5.16. Perhaps the most common application of this technique is to carry private RFC 1918 addresses, or other addresses that are not allocated for global routing to the organization, over an ISP network.

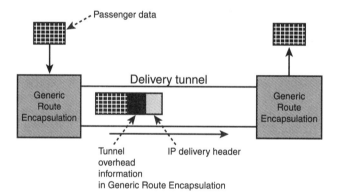

FIGURE 5.16. *IP over IP tunneling.*

The core routers see the packet as like any other with an address in the space used by the carrier protocol. The edge routers are in the address space used by the passenger protocol, with the exception of those edge routers that interface to the tunnels. Those tunneling routers need configuration information both from the carrier and passenger address spaces.

Tunneling can have a substantial CPU impact on the tunneling routers, although implementations exist that are quite fast enough to run at T1 speed or better. Because tunnels are most frequently used in the WAN, this speed suffices.

Some overhead bytes are added by the carrier headers, but it is a relatively modest number. A second 20-byte IP header is needed, and GRE has a fixed header length of 8 bytes and optional fields of up to 12 bytes more. So, GRE can add 28 to 40 bytes to each packet.

Another problem that can occur as a result of tunneling is that it can produce an increased number of fragmented packets. Assume that the *maximum transmission unit (MTU)* size on an interface is 1500 bytes. This defines the maximum length of the data field in an IP packet.

A payload packet arrives on an Ethernet interface and is of maximum length for that medium, 1500 data bytes. To tunnel it in IP, an additional 20 bytes of delivery protocol header and at least 4 bytes of GRE header are required. GRE headers are variable in length. Even at the minimum GRE length, the outgoing packet is 1524 bytes long and cannot be sent as one packet from the outgoing interface. It must be split into two packets, each with a delivery IP and GRE header. Ignoring the additional Layer 2 overhead to send two packets, the total overhead of GRE encapsulation is 48 bytes.

The fragmentation problem does not take place with all IP packets, but only those that are 1476 bytes or longer.

Points in a tunneled network are available for network management, but in a less than totally integrated way. `traceroute` from inside the passenger address space sees the entire tunnel as a single point-to-point medium. `traceroute` in the carrier address space does not see the passenger address space. A network management function in the carrier address space cannot `ping` passenger address points.

If there is an end-to-end security requirement, consider using a protocol such as IPsec that provides both address hiding and security. See Chapter 7 for a discussion of security tunneling.

These limitations still permit tighter network management than an older technique, IP unnumbered, which is discussed in the following section.

IP Unnumbered

There is little argument that assigning a point-to-point medium to a prefix large enough to accommodate a LAN wastes address space. Again, in the words of the old doctor, if raising your elbow over your head and slapping it hurts, don't raise your elbow over your head and slap it. If assigning a single, fixed-length prefix to point-to-point media is inefficient, use arbitrary-length prefixes to assign more appropriate lengths. More techniques for using arbitrary length prefixes are shown in Chapter 6.

IP over IP tunneling is a reasonably elegant solution. Another is IP unnumbered, shown in Figure 5.17. Notice that the serial interfaces in this figure have no addresses of their own.

IP unnumbered is a technique to "borrow" an address on a LAN to provide an identifier for an otherwise unnumbered WAN link. There are several ways to do this. On a Cisco router, a LAN interface is associated with the unnumbered serial link. See Chapter 13 for details. In Figure 5.17, each router associates its Ethernet address with the unnumbered serial link. As packets arrive on the serial link, they are routed to the appropriate interface or internal router process based on the destination address in the arriving packet. Through dynamic routing, each router learns of the address of the Ethernet on the other router and defines its own unnumbered serial interface as the outgoing interface to the destination Ethernet.

Other routers do not borrow an address from a real interface, but identify each end with a unique router ID, which is in the form of an IP address. This next hop is identified with a /32 route—a route to only one address.

Both routers configure their serial interfaces
as unnumbered paths to their Ethernets

FIGURE 5.17. *In unnumbered IP, both routers configure their serial interfaces as unnumbered paths to their Ethernets.*

Chapter 15 gives specific configuration examples. The underlying mechanism is essentially to create a virtual router with the unnumbered serial interfaces behaving as an internal bus.

The IP unnumbered technique has substantial operational limitations. It works between pairs of routers, rather than the arbitrary number of routers that IP over IP tunneling supports. The serial interfaces have no IP address that can be used as arguments of network management commands such as `ping` and `traceroute`. A busy LAN can have enough traffic to overwhelm a narrow WAN pipe between two routers.

Looking Ahead

As you have seen, the original classful style of addressing has many limitations. In Chapter 6, you will learn a variety of new *classless* methods. These add significantly more power, although some people find them much more complex than the classical approach.

If, whenever a classless technique seems complex, you remember to look at it in binary, almost all problems resolve quickly. The simplifying property of binary is why it has been so emphasized in this chapter.

There will be cases where it is impractical to convert from classful addressing. Network address translation is one of several techniques in the next chapter that can help cope with real-world deployment limitations.

CHAPTER **6**

Internet Failing: Details at 11

The machine gun is a much overrated weapon.

—General Sir Douglas Haig, 1914

Success is relative: It is what we can make of the mess we have made of things.

—T.S. Eliot

Pray that success will not come any faster than you are able to endure it.

—Elbert Hubbard

Look at your telephone. Has its number or area code changed recently? Have you had to learn new area codes to call? You have been experiencing the pains of telecommunications growth. Just as you have had to live with sometimes painful telephone renumbering in order to keep the telephone network operating, so does the success of the Internet mean that its users will occasionally be affected by measures needed to help it grow.

Originally, the Internet evolved from the ARPAnet, with the ambitious goal of interconnecting as many as 200 networks. Its continuing success, in many respects, has been its worst enemy. Its operational integrity has been jeopardized by what has seemed to be an avalanche of new routes entering the global Internet routing system. The operational means to manage uncontrolled growth, and avoid catastrophic failures of the global routing system, are based on addressing: the administrative issuance of addresses and the handling of routes to those addresses by service providers.

Both the general and trade press have sensationalized Internet problems and apparent limits to growth. There have been any number of breathless headlines on television news that the Internet is about to fail. "Details" on news shows, however, tend to present problems that can be circumvented, as long as the global routing architecture remains flexible. Such flexibility might require changes in addressing.

Chapter 5, "Classical IP Addressing: An Evolution," shows that the original classful assignment model simply was not necessary. Organizations should justify address space, at the very least, based on the number of hosts per medium and the number of media. In this chapter, we will continue to extend that model of defining the address structure, introducing *supernetting*—collapsing prefixes to the left—as well as *subnetting*—extending prefixes to the right.

I rather like the historical term *supernetting*, which was introduced in RFC 1338. In the global Internet, the term *classless inter-domain routing (CIDR)* has replaced supernetting as the name of the policy of *aggregation* of smaller address blocks into larger ones that are globally advertised [RFC 1519].

Complementing CIDR is another technique usually called *variable length subnet masking (VLSM)*. Whereas CIDR reduces the number of prefixes in the global routing system by collapsing small prefixes into large ones, VLSM tends to be used in enterprises that need more prefixes to describe their networks. You can think of VLSM as a method for subnetting a subnet into smaller, more numerous prefixes. It is especially useful when networks become more distributed and need many more prefixes to describe links to remote offices and small LANs at those offices.

Various refinements will follow in subsequent chapters until we write a detailed addressing plan in Chapter 9, "The Address Plan."

Current methods to scale the global Internet are, like democracy, messy but they work. RFC 2050, a guiding policy, speaks of addressing constraints as:

> largely the result of the interaction of existing router technology, address assignment, and architectural history. After extensive review and discussion, the authors of this document, the IETF working group that reviewed it, and the IESG have concluded that there are no other currently deployable technologies available to overcome these limitations. In the event that routing or router technology develops to the point that adequate routing aggregation can be achieved by other means or that routers can deal with larger routing and more dynamic tables, it may be appropriate to review these constraints [RFC 2050].

Applications of Arbitrary Prefix Lengths

Those of us who have worked in large organizations dread the practice of being micromanaged. Micromanagement consumes the resources of both the manager and the mismanaged and does not increase productivity. In like manner, the global Internet routing system works best when core routers know how to reach their peers, but do not concern themselves with the addresses that are subordinate to their peers. CIDR is an Internet address allocation policy intended to implement this policy of keeping the core routers from being overloaded with details.

VLSM, the other major application of arbitrary length prefixes, complements CIDR. VLSM is used by enterprise networks that need more prefixes to define large numbers of media with a small number of hosts, such as WAN links to remote sites and small LANs at those sites.

CIDR also includes a policy for allocating address space much more efficiently than did the classful addressing strategy described in Chapter 5. CIDR addresses are allocated on a basis of the amount of space needed, rather than the arbitrary administrative division into classes A, B, and C. See Table 5.2 for the sizes of CIDR block allocations.

Routers generally do not track the location of every host on their attached networks. To do so would be to lose the greater scalability routers offer over bridges.

The workload of a bridge that tracks all addresses in its scope is proportional to the number of devices, the number of MAC addresses. This is often written "on the order of," as in the following example:

```
O(#devices)
```

Because routers need only track prefixes, not devices, a router's workload drops to being proportional to the number of prefixes:

```
O(#prefixes)
```

Hierarchical organization drops the workload still further, at the cost of more administration of addresses to keep them hierarchical. If the addresses are split into areas, which are subsets of the address space, the work needed for area k is related to the number of internal and external prefixes visible to routers inside that area only:

```
O(#prefixes+#externals)
```

External routes are those not included in the area's range, but that need to be available in the area. A typical minimum external is the default route.

Creating More Prefixes Within Organizations

Many organizations received large allocations when there was no real constraint on acquiring address space and did not follow efficient address management practices. One enterprise has had the Class B, or /16 prefix, A.B.0.0, allocated to them for a number of years. After several corporate mergers and acquisitions, the enterprise is finding itself short on address space. Because the corporate architecture expects to use encrypted tunnels, the enterprise wants all its address space to be registered so the endpoints are compatible with IPsec. IPsec security tunnels are discussed in Chapter 7, "Addressing, Security, and Network Management."

The corporation also wants to use registered addresses because their business model now focuses on strategic partnerships rather than outright acquisitions of other firms. Because they will not take control of new business partners, they will be unable to renumber the address spaces of these partners. Assuming registered addresses prevents duplicate addresses in extranet and Internet communications.

Originally, the enterprise used a /24 prefix. A reasonably traditional yet hierarchical diagram of the enterprise's classful routing is shown in Figure 6.1. Figure 6.2 abstracts the drawing in Figure 6.1 into a block abstraction that makes it easier to see the addressing structure.

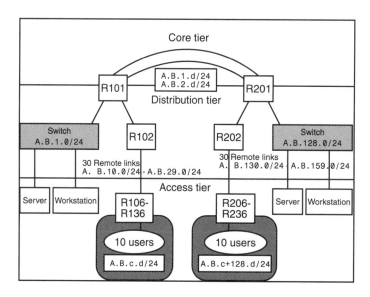

FIGURE 6.1. *Organization using a classful /24 prefix on a registered Class B address, A.B.0.0.*

The classful structure supports a prefix length that can accommodate large numbers of Ethernet or Token Ring users on headquarters LANs. There are two major campuses, each with two links to the other campus; the core links these two campuses. Each campus has a switch to support local workstations and servers, and a distribution tier router that provides access to remote sites. Each remote site has a small router servicing 10 users on a LAN. Version 1 RIP is used as the routing protocol, which does not support classless addressing and thus does not support subnet 0 (see Figure 6.2).

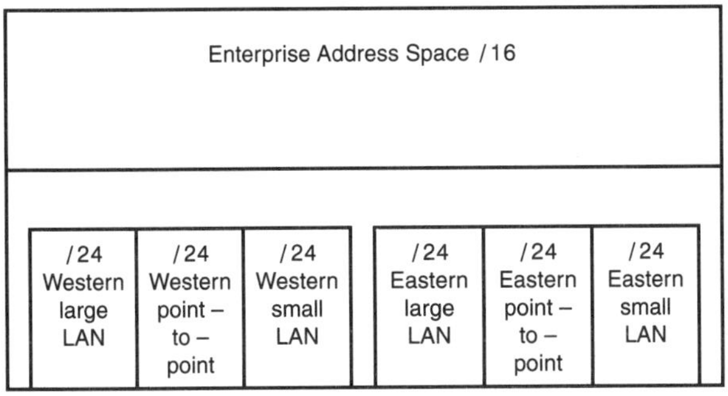

Enterprise Address Space / 16					
/24 Western large LAN	/24 Western point – to – point	/24 Western small LAN	/24 Eastern large LAN	/24 Eastern point – to – point	/24 Eastern small LAN

FIGURE 6.2. *A network topology drawing of an enterprise using a classful / 24 prefix on a registered Class B address,* `A.B.0.0`.

The classful subnet mask is `255.255.255.0`, which is used on large LANs, point-to-point links, and small office LANs. The network topology is hierarchical, splitting into a core, distribution, and access tier.

This organization expects significant growth not in large campus LANs, but in small offices. Each office needs a small LAN that supports 10 users, a router interface, and a Frame Relay virtual circuit that links it to one of the campus routers.

As a consequence of using a single subnet mask regardless of the host population on each, addressing is inefficient. The single subnet mask has been selected to be compatible with the LANs with the largest number of hosts. Figure 6.3 shows the number of host bits actually needed in various subnet assignments, even though 8 host bits are assigned to each prefix.

Customer addresses are in A.B.C.D/24

C (decimal value)
    D (binary contents)
0 - - - - - - - -

                        Not in use because current
                        classful routing does not support subnet 0

1 HHHHHHHH

                        Currently supports 200 hosts
                        and needs /24 prefix
2 000000HH

                        Currently supports 2 hosts
                        and needs /30 prefix

06fig03.eps
Bill K. 09/08/98 ISBN# 78700590

Figure 6.3. *Host field usage in current classful routing.*

Addressing requirements are simplified by the organization's policy about backup connectivity. The small sites do not have an alternate router connection, either dedicated or on demand. This reflects an operational philosophy that, because the small offices have no local technical support personnel, there is no one to diagnose whether there is a hub, router, or line failure. Each workstation has a modem and can dial a remote access server on one of the campuses.

The renumbering effort needs to use methods with minimal or no effect on the production network [RFC 2072]. The first step is to convert to a classless routing mechanism, which allows subnet 0 to be supported.

Because subnet A.B.2.0/24 is an internal link between two routers, with a redundant path to the other campus, it can be renumbered without affecting end users. Subnet A.B.0.0/24 is designated as the new home for point-to-point lines.

As Figure 6.4 shows, a point-to-point medium needs only two host bits. Subnet A.B.0.0/24 can, therefore, have its prefix extended 6 bits to the right, making 64 subnets available: A.B.0.0/30 through A.B.0.252. Each of these subnets has two host values available, one for each router interface. Taking a somewhat higher-level view than the details of the host fields in Figure 6.4, the pattern of prefixes that emerges is shown in Table 6.1.

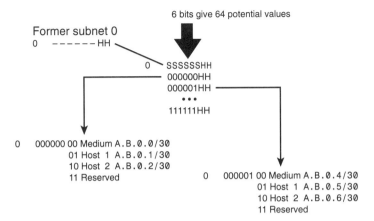

FIGURE 6.4. *Renumbering into the former, unused subnet 0 and given a /30 prefix, which is equivalent to the subnet mask 255.255.255.252.*

TABLE 6.1. PREFIX ADDRESS PATTERN IN /30 SUBNETS OF A.B.0.0.

Subnet Order	Binary	Dotted Decimal
1	00000000	A.B.0.0/30
2	00000100	A.B.0.4/30
3	00001000	A.B.0.8/3
4	00001100	A.B.0.12/30
...		
64	11111100	A.B.0.252/30

The router interfaces currently on the A.B.2.0/24 subnet renumber respectively as A.B.0.1/30 and A.B.0.2/30, and the interfaces are reactivated. The process is repeated for the other intercampus interface.

The prefix A.B.2.0/24 is made available when the point-to-point medium previously associated with it is assigned to the block of /30 prefixes under A.B.0.0/24. A.B.2.0 now can be made available for small LANs at remote sites, subdividing it into 16 /28 prefixes. After the point-to-point lines are renumbered into the former subnet 0, an existing /24 block is divided into /28 blocks for new small office LANs, as shown in Figure 6.5.

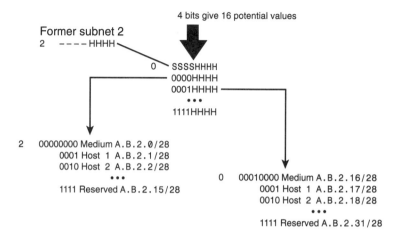

FIGURE 6.5. *Renumbering into the former subnet 2 and given a /28 prefix, which is equivalent to the subnet mask 255.255.255.248.*

In general, it is easiest to renumber starting with routers and new host installations. It is best to begin with point-to-point links, because these usually do not have end users on them.

Although it is possible to configure Frame Relay as a NBMA medium, routing usually works much better if you assign each PVC to a separate virtual subinterface, making each PVC its own /30 subnet—especially when the current frame environment is NBMA. Specific router issues in frame renumbering are discussed in Chapter 13, "Addressing in Routers."

Summarizing Inside Organizations

Summarization adds stability and improves router performance. Think back to the discussion of discontiguous networks in Chapter 5. Those situations happened largely because classful routing mechanisms automatically summarized at a classful network boundary.

In real-world practice, useful summarization is manually configured. Multiple levels of summarization easily can be involved. A group of small offices might have a single path each to a router at the edge of the dynamic routing system. In the example shown in Figure 6.6, the two campuses can serve as summarization points. The west campus can use the addresses A.B.0.0/18, and the east campus can use A.B.128.0/18.

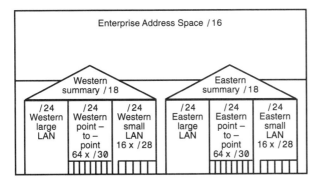

FIGURE 6.6. *Both the previously existing /24 blocks and the new /28 and /30 blocks summarize into /18 aggregate blocks.*

In turn, that router is part of a set of cooperating routers that share full information but only pass summarized information to higher levels of the hierarchy. Such a set is called an *area* in OSPF, and similar constructs can be defined in EIGRP and IS-IS.

Even if you haven't done formal addressing summarization, you've in all probability used very similar concepts. On the famous Washington Beltway near my home, there is an exit that says "95 North to New York." Does this exit take you to the state or the city of New York? At the level of detail seen in Virginia, it takes you to both. As you come closer to New York City, you start seeing more specific signs for destinations in the New York metropolitan area. But your basic decision to get on 95 North was based on the summary information that this is a path to all of New York state.

In like manner, a routing advertisement for an /18 block is a sign saying, "Take this exit to all destinations in the /18 range."

Area information aggregates into a backbone area, but summarization is not yet over. In a large organization, there easily can be a backbone of backbones. The organization, in turn, aggregates its routes before it advertises them to the general Internet.

An example of multilevel aggregation comes from the routing network being built for the U.S. Postal Service, which has approximately 38,000 routers. A post office serving a 5-digit ZIP code might have a /27 prefix. Groups of post offices in the same 3 digits of a ZIP code could aggregate into a /20. This /20 would include regional sorting centers. Larger groups of post offices, among which large shipments go by air, might in turn form the next level at a /14.

Eventually, the Class A block assigned to the Postal Service could be advertised at one or more Internet gateways as an /8.

Performance Problems Due to Using 10.0.0.0/8

One enterprise with which I worked had a single, very large campus with approximately 1000 subnets. They did not need registered addresses and thought they would simplify their lives by using private address space. Specifically, they chose 10.0.0.0/24.

Unfortunately, they did not consider that their routing protocol, RIP, summarizes automatically only on classful network boundaries. Within the scope of network 10.0.0.0, there was no summarization.

RIP does a dynamic update of its routing table every 30 seconds. These are in IP packets with a header length of 20 bytes, followed by an 8-byte UDP header. RIP proper has a header of 8 bytes, and each incremental route is 20 bytes long.

16×1000 is 16000 bytes of incremental routing information. Assuming an MTU of 1500 bytes—with 36 bytes of IP, UDP, and RIP—RIP only puts 50 routes into a packet. Using a back-of-the-envelope calculation that 50 routes fit into a packet, it will take 20 packets to send 1000 routes, or

approximately 21000 bytes. At 56 KBps, this takes about 3 seconds every 30 seconds, or 10% of the bandwidth. With interactive applications, anything expecting a response at about the routing update time would see an extra 3 seconds or more of delay, which is quite noticeable.

The situation was made even worse by the fact that there was a huge amount of Novell overhead at the one-minute mark. This came from both Novell routing and the Service Advertisement Protocol discussed in Chapter 8, "The Existing IP and Non-IP Address Structure: Preparing for Remodeling."

With appropriate summarization, only a small number of routes actually needed to be advertised. In fact, most remote offices only needed the default route to reach the main campus. RIP, which announces its full routing table at 30-second intervals, makes the problem much worse than a modern routing protocol such as OSPF or EIGRP, which only advertise changes to routing information.

Chapter 9 gives more examples of constructing summarization structures.

CIDR Aggregation in the Global Internet

CIDR, in its use in the public Internet, is both a means of managing routing overhead and of administratively assigning prefixes. Keys to understanding CIDR are the ideas of allocating blocks of addresses on non-octet boundary and provider-based allocation. Non-octet boundary allocation means that space is not wasted by giving Class B blocks to users that need less than 64 KB but more than 256 addresses. Provider-based allocation reduces the number of routes propagated in the global routing system, reducing the CPU and memory load on core routers.

CIDR is a policy for aggregating routes into major provider blocks. It is a forward-looking policy and recognizes that existing address space has not been allocated with CIDR in mind. Existing address allocations can be treated as exception cases for now, but the integrity of the global routing system requires that they be minimized.

As long as one major provider knows that a given host address is within the address space of another major provider, the first provider simply needs to know how to reach the second. The first sends to the second all those packets that have destination addresses in ranges associated with the second provider. To do this, the first provider does not know the internal routing of the second. The first provider reasonably trusts the second to know how to deliver packets to prefixes within its advertised address space.

There is a similar perspective for routers and hosts low in the hierarchy. As long as they know that the upper levels of their hierarchy will take them to other carriers, the low-level devices simply can default to the next higher level when they do not know how to reach a specific destination.

Insistence on keeping historically allocated space that is too small a piece for providers to desire to advertise has the potential of cutting off Internet connectivity for an organization. Organizations must realize that there is a cost associated with advertising routes.

Let's assume that the appropriate address authority decides to allocate a new address block, 221.255.0.0/16, and split it equally among four major carriers. To create more prefixes, you extend the prefix to the right. Moving it one bit to the right creates two parts and moving it two bits to the right creates four equal parts.

Note

Non-RFC 1918 addresses used in examples are not available for general use! They have been picked arbitrarily as examples only. There is a major difference between using an address in a book and potentially advertising it on the Internet when it has not been assigned to you!

As shown in Figure 6.7, Bits 17 and 18 of the prefix are overloaded in the sense that they serve multiple purposes. They identify an address as associated with the allocation of one of the four major carriers. This is highly desirable in reducing the number of routes the carriers need to advertise to one another. Figure 6.8 shows the reduced routes advertised among the carriers.

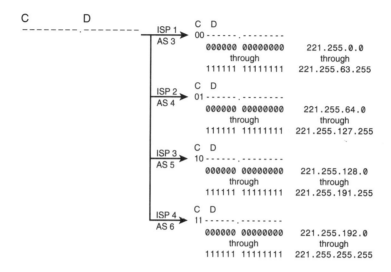

FIGURE 6.7. *A registry allocates parts of a block assigned to the registry to four major ISPs. The AS is an autonomous system number used by the Border Gateway Protocol (BGP), which is used to identify these ISPs in examples later in this chapter.*

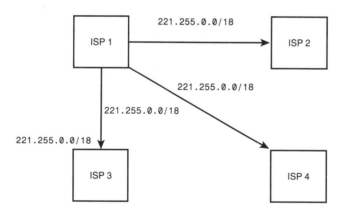

FIGURE 6.8. *Each ISP only needs to tell its peers about its entire block, not subassignments within it. For simplicity, only ISP 1's advertisement is shown.*

Assume that ISP 1 has 4 customers, each of which justifies 1000 hosts, and 16 customers each needing 50 hosts. In Figure 6.9, ISP 1 establishes prefixes to be assigned to its customers.

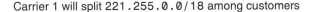

Carrier 1 will split 221.255.0.0/18 among customers

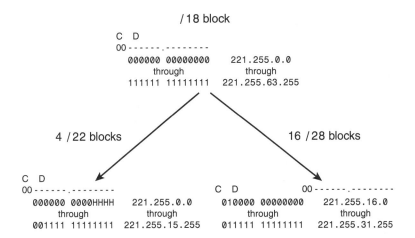

FIGURE 6.9. *After receiving an /18 allocation, the ISP assigns part of it as /22 prefixes and part as /28.*

Those customers can subnet as they please inside their assigned address blocks. ISP 1 knows how to get to the router that interconnects the ISP service to the customer, but ISP 1 itself usually does not know the details of the internal organization of its customers. Exceptions to this rule come when ISP 1 has contractual maintenance responsibility for the customer network or special load-sharing or path information is of concern.

Address Ownership

Address allocation has followed some of the principles of the American westward expansion. Until the Pacific Ocean was reached, there was always more land.

Early in the history of the Internet, there seemed always to be more address space. Until scalability limits of the Internet implementation were reached, there were always more address blocks that could be allocated permanently to organizations.

On a practical basis, *address ownership* had long been the model of Internet address assignment. In such a policy, enterprises request address assignments from a registry, receive a block assignment, and only relinquish this space if the enterprise decides the space is no longer useful to it. There also has been an underlying assumption that uniquely assigned addresses are *portable*—that they are globally routable and any ISP will accept them in any location.

Unfortunately, this policy, in an ever-growing Internet, does not reflect the reality of router implementations. Continued growth of the routing system, given the large installed base of working ISP routers, requires global address policies that minimize the (large) size of the routing table of routers that hold the full Internet routing table. Such routers are often called *default free*, and the set of such routers that exchange full information is called the *default free zone* (DFZ).

Life is not fair. To minimize the size of the DFZ router tables, each route must cover as many addresses as possible. The largest address blocks are allocated to major service providers because they service the largest number of addresses.

For technical reasons, some major carriers have limited the number of noncustomer routes they advertise to DFZ peers. These carriers also, for technical reasons, prefer not to advertise their own more specific customer routes. A route is more specific when it has a longer prefix length than another route. The detailed mechanisms by which BGP exterior routing selects routes is beyond the scope of this book. Refer to Table 5.2 when you need to know the sizes of various prefix blocks. The most specific route that generally is advertised is a /19, which can hold approximately 8,000 addresses. Although the /19 is the smallest unit of address space generally directly allocated, there is nothing magical about this length in terms of global routability. The address-allocating registries do not define what prefix length carriers will route. The carriers make that as a business and operational decision.

A distinction between the historical address ownership model and a more practical address lending policy, has evolved. Address registries *allocate* large blocks of address space to providers who have demonstrated the capability to utilize this address space. These providers *assign* portions of their allocations to their customers.

You might, for example, be a customer of ISP 1 that changes your Internet access to ISP 2. Prior to the change, you used a "borrowed" portion of ISP 1's address space. You need to renumber into ISP 2's address space. To assist in the transition, the ISP you are leaving usually gives you a 30- to 60-day grace period when they let you use some of their address space with the new carrier. You must coordinate with both ISP 1 and ISP 2 to be sure ISP 2 advertises this space and ISP 1 agrees to their advertisements.

In an address lending model, the assignee is required to return the address space when they change to a different service provider. In the classical ownership model, the address space was allocated directly to the customer and did not need to be returned.

Limitations of Address Ownership

The inherent problem of address ownership is that IP addressing and routing is a hierarchical system. The highest level of the hierarchy interconnects major providers, not individual customers. If the goal of the addressing is to provide information on how to reach a customer, the address must reflect the logical network topology. That topology is defined by interconnection, not organizational identity.

Owned addresses historically have been equated with portable addresses. In principle, having a portable address means an organization can change its upstream provider without having to renumber.

The underlying, and increasingly false, assumption here is that all upstream providers are willing to accept arbitrary customer-owned routes and advertise them to their peers. The more routes a provider has to track and advertise, the more work for their routers, and indeed their routers might be jeopardized by poorly administered customer route behavior.

Although various proposals keep surfacing for charging for route advertisements, the usual Internet practice is for major providers to discourage advertising their customers' routes. Instead, the major providers lend address space to customers and provide connectivity to their customers indirectly by advertising the customer address block as part of a larger provider block.

This practice does not really mean customers are locked in to a single provider. Although the address might not be portable, the customer's DNS domain and its names certainly are. Think of the relationship between portable domains and portable addresses as similar to everyday telephone practice. If I moved to California, I would still be Howard Berkowitz. My name would appear in the directories of the Californian telephone companies. I would not expect, however, to take my Virginia phone number to California.

Implementing Address Lending

In an address lending policy, portions of an allocated address space are lent, or assigned, from the allocations of large providers. The allocating provider provides connectivity to the assignee by advertising, to its DFZ peers, the address block in which the assigned customer addresses are contained.

The older address ownership policy exists in a reduced form. Providers can contract with their customers to advertise previously assigned customer address space.

In an address lending policy, if you—an assignee—change providers, you must return the address space and renumber into its new provider's address space. Most carriers provide a grace period for transition, typically a minimum of one month and a maximum of six months.

If your organization is a service provider, it could also sub-assign addresses. For example, a regional service provider could assign some of its address to local service providers. If the regional assigner changed its upstream provider, or grew to a point where it justified a direct allocation from a registry, the sub-assignees would have to renumber.

> **Note**
>
> *Renumbering is a fact of life. Network designs can and should be renumbering friendly. Renumbering can have fairly minimal impact when the infrastructure supports it, and it can be a huge problem when it is not planned for. Network address translation (NAT), discussed later in this chapter, can avoid renumbering in many cases, but is not a panacea.*

Renumbering is most likely to be of concern when the enterprise needs general Internet connectivity. Extranet and intranet situations are more likely to be able to operate with owned addresses, even though the capability to renumber still might become important.

A significant case is one in which an enterprise has Internet connectivity only through a firewall or other mediating gateway, which hides the internal address space from the general Internet. Later in this chapter, we will discuss the issues of private address space and network address translation. In Chapter 7, we will discuss more complex issues involving firewalls and secure tunnels. Suffice it to say, at this point, that private address space and address translation are very useful techniques, but do not solve all problems.

Global Internet Routing Issues

Without going too deeply into global Internet routing technology, we can state that the Internet is composed of *autonomous systems* (ASs). Although the definition of an AS has evolved, the current usage has the following characteristics [RFC 1930]:

- A set of routers and address ranges. These addresses are advertised as routes by BGP. Each AS selects the addresses it will advertise and accept on specific interfaces to other ASs.

- May be administered by one or more organizations, although only one organization sets the routing policy. Individual organizations manage their own address space, but must inform one another of their addresses.

- Presents a common routing policy to the global Internet. This policy is realized by the set of destination addresses to which the AS *advertises* it can route, and the set of destination addresses it will *accept* from other ASs.

If an AS adjacent to yours does not advertise a route containing your desired destination, you must not send packets meant for that destination to that AS. Even if the AS adjacent to you receives route advertisements from one of its neighbors, to which your AS is not connected, the adjacent AS is under no obligation to route your traffic to its neighbor.

Whether or not your neighbor accepts traffic for certain destinations depends on your neighbor's business, political, and other nontechnical factors, expressed through its routing policies.

Even more complex are the interactions of your traffic with AS on the path to your ultimate destination, but that are not even directly connected to your neighbor. If I am connected to AS1000, AS1000 is connected to AS2000, AS2000 is connected to AS3000, and my destination is AS4000 connected to AS3000, I have no general way to influence the routing policies of AS3000 and AS4000 unless I have a contractual relationship with them.

You might be used to enterprise networks, where your organization controls all resources, and there is a single person with overall authority. This is simply not the model of the global Internet or, indeed, many large companies. It is arguably the world's largest successful anarchy, and there is no single operational authority. It works because there is a set of collaborative relationships that enable it to work.

Distinguished Internet experts almost all have a story of explaining the workings of the global routing system to a corporate executive, who then smiles and says, "That's all very nice. And will you now put me in touch with the people that are in charge of the Internet?"

We emphasize these issues because addressing is intimately entwined in the means by which policies are enforced. Let's go through a relatively simple example to understand some sample relationships.

Autonomous Systems AS3 and AS4 are top-level providers in the default free zone of the Internet. Assume that this means they have effective connectivity with all Internet addresses. The address space shown in Figure 6.9 has been allocated to AS3: 221.255.0.0/18. A similar block, 221.255.64.0/18, has been allocated to AS4. AS3 assigns parts of its allocation to its customers, as either /22 or /28 blocks. The /22 blocks are:

```
221.255.0.0/22
221.255.4.0/22
221.255.8.0/22
221.255.12.0/22
```

Figure 6.10 shows how AS1 contracts with AS3 and AS4 for Internet connectivity. AS1 has a single physical link to each of its upstream providers, AS3 and AS4. AS3 is the primary external path, and AS4 is used only for backup.

> **Note**
>
> *Details of the BGP mechanisms that make AS4 the backup provider are beyond the scope of this book. For this example, assume that the more preferred path to AS1's address space is generally through AS3, even though AS4 advertises the more specific prefix of AS1.*

AS3 assigns—lends—the block 221.255.4.0/22 to AS1. To the rest of the Internet, AS3 does not advertise this prefix, but includes it in its 221.255.0.0/18 aggregate announcement.

AS1 also has a private peering relationship with AS2. This private link, in the view of AS1, is only intended for traffic between AS1 and AS2.

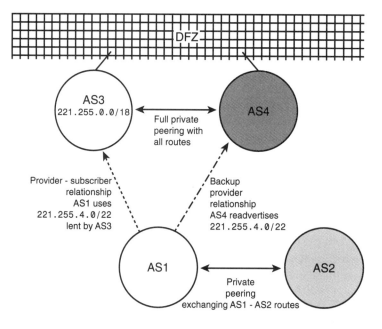

FIGURE 6.10. *AS1 is a direct customer of AS3 and uses provider assigned (PA) address space from AS3's allocation. AS1 also exchanges routes with AS2 under a policy that prefers the direct AS2 link, rather than the link to AS3, for traffic destined for AS2.*

In Figure 6.11, enterprise E100 does not have its own AS. The tag E100 is used simply to denote a subset of AS3's address space, because its only Internet connectivity is via AS3. It does, however, have redundant links to AS3. E100 appears to the Internet in general as part of AS3. AS3 is contractually responsible for assuring that at least one of the links to E100 always is available. E100 is simply an arbitrary label internal to AS3; it does not have meaning outside AS3. Remember the definition of an AS as a set of routers that presents a common routing policy to the Internet. AS3 makes all announcements of E100 addresses, so E100 has no policy independent of AS3.

AS3 assigned `221.255.8.0/22` to E100. Again, this is advertised by AS3 to the global Internet as part of AS3's aggregate, `221.255.0.0/18`.

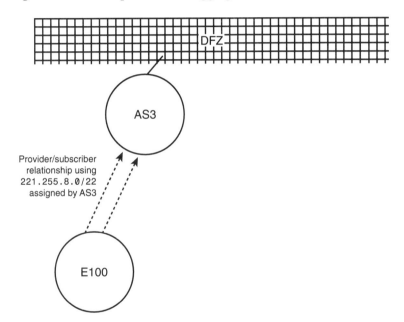

FIGURE 6.11. *Enterprise E100 does not need its own AS number, because all its Internet connectivity is via AS3.*

Figure 6.12 shows AS2's view of the world. This is, indeed, the connectivity. It might not work the way AS2 thinks it will.

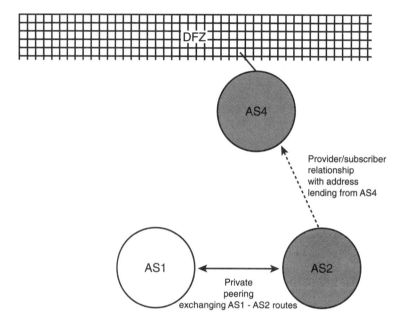

F IGURE 6.12. *AS2's Internet connectivity is via AS4. AS2 also has a private link to AS1, which is the preferred path for traffic destined for AS1.*

In Figure 6.13, AS1 and AS2 have a peer relationship with one another. This is intended to let AS1 and AS2 reach resources in each other. The network architect of AS1 understands this, but the AS2 staff thinks they can get backup from AS1 to reach AS3. AS1 does not advertise any of AS2's addresses to AS3, so AS3 doesn't know AS2 connects to AS1.

AS2 gets its Internet connectivity from AS4. The direct path to AS1 is preferred for all traffic to AS1 addresses.

AS2 only has a single link to AS4, so its connectivity is actually less robust than that of E100. E100 has dual paths.

Figure 6.13 unifies the various connectivity pictures. AS3 and AS4 are peers and freely exchange information. It is in their business interest that their customer bases be able to reach one another. This is called *full peering*.

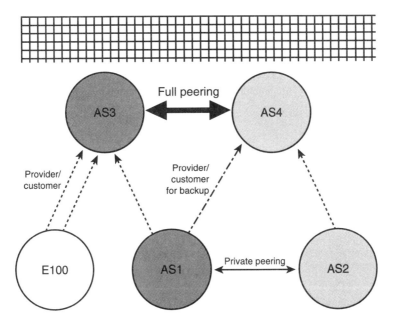

FIGURE 6.13. *All address allocations and assignments are shown in this figure. Because AS3's policies do not permit receiving AS4 addresses over the link to AS1, AS2's attempted transit through AS1 does not work, even if AS1 advertised them to AS3.*

The term *peering* unfortunately has become overloaded in Internet routing practice. One usage simply means two routers speak BGP to one another, but has no implication about the amount of routing they exchange. Alternatively, peering, in the sense of full peering, means two ASs exchange their full routing information without charging one another.

Full peering relationships are increasingly hard to find. Typically, they are found among service providers with a national or international presence. The more common relationship is a customer–provider one, in which the customer *buys transit* from one or more upstream providers. In general, this is charged at a flat rate based on the access line speed.

When a provider buys transit from another, the provider of transit service is considered upstream from the provider that resells the transit service. In general, if a provider is closer to the DMZ than you are, it is upstream of you.

Providers that make equal exchanges of routing information, without direct financial charges to one another, are considered transit peers.

Internet scalability is in many respects enforced by increasingly stringent policies and administration of the address space. Even if an enterprise network of today does not connect to the Internet, the addressing conventions of the general Internet increasingly are assumed in new products. In addition, organizations that do not have Internet connectivity today cannot predict changing business requirements that makes general, or specific, Internet connectivity appropriate.

Resource Scarcity

Several factors have threatened the Internet, but it always seems to have survived. Huitema [Huitema 1995] uses the lovely term *just in time* to describe the culture of solution in the Internet. The first factor that threatened the Internet is that there was a shortage of Class B network numbers. Class C is too small for a network of any appreciable size, but Class B is too large for the average enterprise.

From a performance, rather than an administrative, perspective, the limiting factor has been the capability of core Internet routers to handle a full, default free, Internet routing table. Historically, as Internet growth took off, the capability of routers to handle additional growth doubled roughly every 18 to 24 months, but the number of routes doubled every 5 to 9 months.

At first, this capability limitation was simply one of memory. The obsolete but well-proven Cisco AGS, for example, had a maximum RAM size of 16 MB.

Note

This example is not meant to criticize Cisco. People, and overly eager sales representatives, often focus unreasonably on the performance of a manufacturer's highest-performance router. The majority of the market does not need this capability and would pay dearly for it. Cisco, for example, recently shipped its millionth 2500 series router, a small, inexpensive router much more characteristic of the marketplace. In the same period, it started shipping the 12000 series router, intended for the very high end. These are different requirements; don't judge a router company's suitability for your specific need based on products at the opposite end of the performance envelope.

As the global routing table grew in size, the computational load grew and CPU power became more of an issue. Although the Cisco 7000 could hold 64 MB of RAM, its 68040 processor was limited. The next generation of Cisco routers could hold 128 MB of memory and used 100 to 200 MHz RISC processors both in the main processor and interface processors. Bay has had a different architecture in which the concept of a main processor is deemphasized. Both approaches work.

In the following generation of high-end routers, such as the Cisco 12000 or Ascend GRF, route computation engines have been separated from packet forwarding engines inside high-end routers. Current routers intended for large carriers are able to keep up with a current routing table of approximately 50,000 entries. For major ISPs, the limitation is now the forwarding performance of the routers, or the recomputation of the routing table when routes rapidly change states.

Still, router technology cannot keep pace with uncontrolled growth of routes. This has been controlled by the CIDR process of allocating address space not on a traditional class boundary, and by the process of provider-based aggregation. CIDR was introduced in 1992, and gained momentum among major network operators [RFC 1517, RFC 1518, RFC 1519, RFC 1520].

As an example of CIDR savings, in October 1995, AlterNet advertised 3194 routes. After CIDR aggregation, AlterNet advertised 799 routes, a saving of approximately 75% [Partan 1995].

Local Address Space: Private and Bogus

RFC 1918 defines a block of *private* prefixes that should never be routed on the global Internet. Providers should, but do not always, filter them out when received from customers. The private prefixes are:

- `10.0.0.0/8`, equivalent to an old-style Class A block

- `171.16.0.0/12`, equivalent to 16 contiguous Class B blocks

- `192.168.0.0/16`, equivalent to 256 contiguous Class C blocks

Private address space is not a panacea. Potential problems arise when connecting to other organizations that have used private address space. What if your organization used `10.0.0.0/8`, but now wants to connect to a business partner who also used `10.0.0.0/8`? Double network address translation, discussed later in this chapter, is one workaround, but this situation needs careful analysis.

One of the fundamental assumptions of IP is that addresses are globally meaningful: the end-to-end assumption. In a pure private network, use of the RFC 1918 address space still meets the end-to-end assumption, assuming the network has no view of the outside world, and the network administrator assures that addresses inside the network are assigned uniquely.

Private address space refers to a specific set of addresses intended never to be on the Internet. This set has been explicitly allocated for that purpose by the Internet Assigned Numbers Authority.

Some users arbitrarily picked address ranges for use in their internal networks. They assumed they would never connect to the Internet, so it made little difference what they picked. Address space that is used, but has not been allocated to an organization, is called *bogus.*

IPsec, discussed in Chapter 7, assumes that the endpoint IP addresses are unique. This approach is counter to that of network address translators and firewalls that deliberately break the association between inside and outside space.

Bogus Address Space

Another problem is bogus address space. In this case, organizations might have picked prefixes at random to use inside what is assumed to be an isolated network. The prefixes they picked variously have not been assigned at all or have actually been assigned to other organizations. Of course, this works technically when an organization is isolated, but is incompatible with any external connectivity.

Note

Although some organizations have been able to advertise addresses that do not belong to them, especially unassigned space, there is ongoing work in the Intercontinental Engineering Planning Group (IEPG) and other operational groups to work with address authorities to establish cryptographic authentication for address ownership.

After authentication is in place, routers can reject address space advertised by other than the organization authorized to do so.

Other use of bogus address space is more malicious. Senders of unsolicited commercial email—spammers—can use it to hide their theft of mail relaying services, or simply to avoid complaints. Hostile crackers can launch denial of service attacks from seemingly untraceable bogus addresses.

Operational Oddities Produced by Private Address Space

Operational oddities can be seen when service providers use private address space internally. This is a more marginal violation of the assumption of end-to-end significance. It works, but it can make troubleshooting more difficult.

As shown in Figure 6.14, Providers A and B use registered addresses on all of their public interfaces, but use private address space in their own backbones. A traceroute from User 1 to User 2, however, shows the sequence:

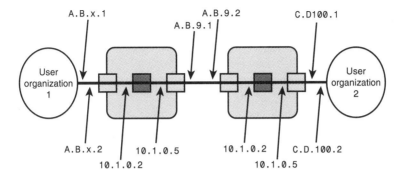

FIGURE 6.14. *Although customers and providers use registered address space (light and dark gray) on their external interfaces, both providers use private address space (white) inside their routing networks.*

Address	Function
A.B.x.1	User 1 border router
A.B.x.2	Carrier A edge to backbone
10.1.0.2	Carrier A internal hop
10.1.0.5	Carrier A internal hop 2
A.B.9.1	Carrier A edge to carrier 2
10.1.0.2	Carrier B internal hop 1
10.1.0.5	Carrier B internal hop 2
C.D.100.1	Carrier B edge to user
C.D.100.2	User 2 border router

Normally, if you see the same address more than once in a `traceroute`, you are seeing a routing loop. In this case, there is no loop, because carriers A and B have both used space from `10.0.0.0/8` internally. The complexity added to troubleshooting is a good argument for ISPs using registered addresses on all their router interfaces.

> **Tip**
>
> *Please don't use the nonprivate addresses used in classes and textbooks in your networks. Use RFC 1918 values. Several generations of Cisco courses used networks including* 131.108.0.0/16 *and* 202.222.5.0/24. *These are really not available for general use!*
>
> *These addresses were released by Cisco, but have been reassigned to other organizations that use them in production. Such organizations do not appreciate what they consider hijacking of their address space.*

Network Address Translation: Opportunities and Limitations

Network address translation is an evolving technique that provides a practical means of dealing with certain addressing problems. It also violates a basic principle of the Internet: the end-to-end model, in which IP host addresses have global significance. This definitely has negative affects on security mechanisms and introduces operational problems that complicate troubleshooting and may still not be fully understood.

Address leasing, in a CIDR context, is the main alternative to address ownership and the potential of global routing collapse. Address leasing, however, often involves the negative operational impact of renumbering. The original NAT paper [RFC 1631] introduced an *address reuse* alternative:

> Place network address translators (NATs) at the borders of stub domains. Each NAT box has a table consisting of pairs of local IP addresses and globally unique addresses. The IP addresses inside the stub domain are not globally unique. They are reused in other domains, thus solving the address depletion problem.

Experience has shown that there are even more powerful ways to use NAT, but there are even more complexities in its use. In addition to being a means of avoiding renumbering, variants can conserve registered address space and provide means of load sharing. NAT is widely used as part of firewalls. At the very least, however, its violation of the end-to-end model conflicts seriously with newer end-to-end security mechanisms discussed in Chapter 7.

Network Address Translation is sometimes described as a simple swapping of internal to external IP addresses, but it must do more than that if it is to work. Figure 6.15 shows fields at OSI Layers 3, 4, and 7 that can be affected by NAT. Layer 7 fields are not translated by pure NAT, but can be affected by changes at Layer 3 or 4.

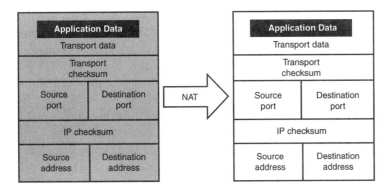

FIGURE 6.15. *Various types of NAT can affect protocols at multiple OSI layers.*

At the most trivial level, NAT cannot just replace source and destination addresses. It must compute a new IP header checksum reflecting the new addresses.

Remember that TCP and UDP also have checksums. These checksums cover the data part, but also include the IP source and destination addresses in their checksum calculation. A NAT, therefore, has to recognize IP packets that contain TCP or UDP packets and change the TCP or UDP checksums to reflect the changed IP packets.

At the application layer, there are issues where application protocols carry IP addresses in data fields. NAT alone does not understand application protocols and does not deal with such things as FTP redirection with the PORT command, as discussed in Chapter 3, "Application Topology: Naming Endpoints." Other applications carry IP addresses in data, including multiplayer games, SNMP, database protocols such as SQL*Net, DNS, and so on.

To understand the function of NAT, however, assume that it is transparent to all protocol mechanisms and examine some scenarios for its use. You will find that the simple model of inside-address-mapping-to-outside-address-mapping is insufficient for using NAT effectively in real network design. Figure 6.16 shows the basic structure of a NAT. In the basic types of NAT, translation is specified independently in each direction of flow. Some load-sharing NAT technologies might have linkage between the directions of flow.

The usual practice is to think of NAT as having an *inside* and an *outside*. If private address space is being used, it usually is considered to be on the inside. In Figure 6.16, it is assumed that there is a one-to-one mapping between inside and outside addresses, and port numbers do not change.

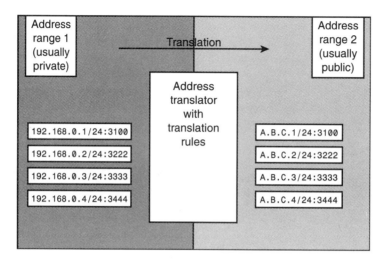

FIGURE 6.16. *A basic NAT system has inside and outside address ranges, with mappings explicitly configured for each direction of flow.*

If the clients are on the inside and the desired servers are on the outside, the problem you are trying to solve with NAT is to work around the inside addresses not being compatible with external space. The external space might be the general Internet, but a not-uncommon case comes up when two organizations use RFC 1918 private address space, but need bilateral (that is, not through the general Internet) communications.

In this scenario, you also might be trying to find a way to minimize your requirements for registered Internet addresses.

Static Basic NAT

Static NAT has manually configured mappings between inside and outside address spaces. The inside is called a *stub domain*. Basic NAT restricts a network topology so that the stub domain is accessed either through a single border (that is, NAT) router or a set of border routers whose address translation tables are synchronized. Figure 6.17 shows the address mapping in basic NAT. The addresses change but the ports remain constant. Both network and transport layer checksums need to be recomputed in the NAT process.

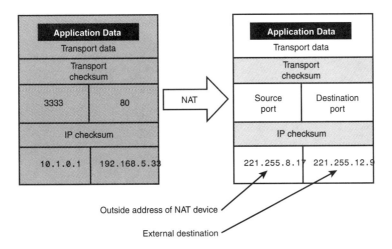

FIGURE 6.17. *Both addresses and checksums need to change in basic NAT.*

Inside Clients, Outside Servers

There is a fairly trivial case here: You have received an adequate allocation of public space, but it's operationally inconvenient to renumber individual hosts. Do not confuse this case with one in which you are trying to enforce a security policy. NAT alone provides no particular security.

Assume, in this case, that your routing policy causes the NAT to advertise the default route inside. Traffic to all unknown destinations thus flows to the NAT device.

Figure 6.18 shows this case. When a packet from the inside reaches the NAT, the NAT substitutes a registered address on the outside of the address for the source address. It then forwards the packet into the general Internet.

The NAT has a static table that maps external addresses into internal addresses. When a packet is received by the outside, the NAT substitutes the internal address for the destination address and forwards it to the inside.

Bilateral Communications with Double NAT

A slightly more complex case, shown in Figure 6.18, can be useful in bilateral communications. This involves two NAT devices and an agreement on a shared address space. This shared address space, as shown, can also be part of the private address space.

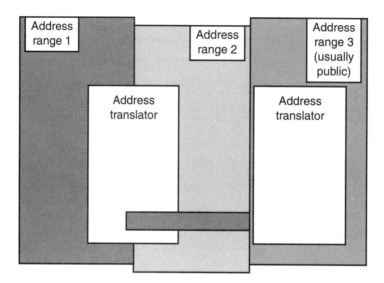

FIGURE 6.18. *Three sets of addresses are involved in double address translation. Mappings from each private address space to the white interconnection address space need to be coordinated, but not all the details of addressing in each private space.*

Double, in this context, means there is a first translation from the inside space of one organization to the agreed shared space, and a second translation from the shared address space to the inside space of the second organization. The two address translators can use basic NAT or any of the more advanced NAT techniques described in this chapter.

Basic NAT

Basic NAT does avoid renumbering, but it does not necessarily save registered address space if there is a one-to-one mapping between stub and registered addresses.

Tip

One-to-one fixed mapping can be useful during the consolidation of merged enterprise networks, or possibly during renumbering into a new ISP. It is of less general utility for connecting to the general Internet.

Basic NAT and Backbone Partitioned Stubs

Remember the idea of discontiguous subnets presented in Chapter 5? A similar problem can arise with NAT, where there is not one neat stub domain, but there are geographically dispersed campuses, each using the same unregistered address space. Although each of the campuses could independently use NAT to translate to registered addresses, this is often undesirable because each campus would need its own NAT device.

An alternative, shown in Figure 6.19, is to treat the set of stub campuses as a *backbone-partitioned stub* and treat them as a single address domain, interconnected by IP over IP tunnels.

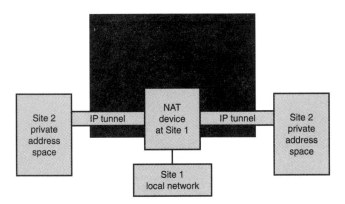

FIGURE 6.19. *The tunnels are known to the private side. The public side only sees the registered addresses of the tunnel endpoints.*

Three sites share a common private address space. Packets arriving at the NAT device at Site 1 can be sent out a local interface to Site 1 destinations or sent over an IP over IP tunnel to either other site.

The external interfaces of IP tunnel leaving a stub domain needs a registered address. This sort of tunneling adds another level of addressing. Packets routed across the public backbone contain the source and destination addresses of the outside tunnel interfaces. When packets are delivered to the destination NAT, the tunnel IP header is stripped away, and the destination address from the encapsulated packet is used to reach the final destination.

Network Address and Port Translation

To conserve addresses, there needs to be a many-to-few mapping, not a one-to-one mapping as shown in Figure 6.20. If not all internal addresses need external connectivity at the same time, it is reasonable to have fewer registered than unregistered addresses and create temporary mappings between the two. To maintain the uniqueness of sessions that were previously defined between unique source address-destination address pairs, we now need to map between source address/port and destination address/port pairs. The outside destination sees a unique source address/port pair that is associated with an outside address on the NAT device.

Because port as well as network address translation is involved, the term NAT is no longer adequate. RFC 2391 calls the process *network address and port translation (NAPT)*. Cisco calls it *port address translation (PAT)*.

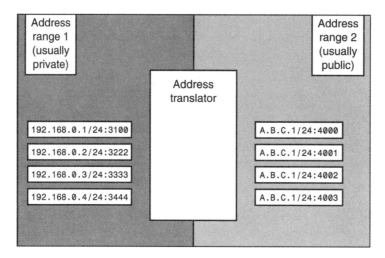

FIGURE 6.20. *There are usually far more addresses on the private side than the public side. Each side, however, has the same number of endpoints, defined as an address/port pair.*

Figure 6.21 shows representative packet flow in NAPT.

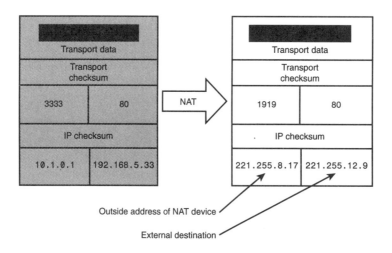

FIGURE 6.21. *Both ports and addresses change. Transport and network checksums, of course, also need to be recomputed.*

General Session-Level Issues in NAPT

NAT documents distinguish between *session flow* and *packet flow*. These usages have different intent than the flows discussed as a means of characterizing traffic in Chapter 3.

> **Note**
>
> *Session-level NAT might seem similar to proxies seen on firewalls. The two are different, because a proxy terminates a session from an inside host, creating and managing a separate session to an outside host. NAPT, on the other hand, is conceptually transparent to the end-to-end session, although it substitutes addresses in packets belonging to the session. Proxies are discussed further in Chapter 7.*

Session flows conceptually are connection oriented, and the flow direction defines the direction in which a session connection was established, with respect to a specific interface. Session flows usually are established from a client to a server.

TCP-based session flows have a distinct session establishment and teardown phase, but UDP flows do not. A sufficiently intelligent translating router can impose state on a set of UDP flows and create a pseudo-connection. Packet flows are unidirectional. They really are very similar to the unidirectional traffic flows discussed in Chapter 3. A typical client/server session involves at least two packet flows, one from client to server and the other from server to client. In the context of NAT discussion, packet flows do not necessarily have known Quality of Service (QoS) or traffic characteristics.

Using NAT on the elements of a session involves both inbound and outbound packet flows within that session. Packets associated with a specific session are identified by:

- Source IP address.

- Packet protocol type. Defines whether the packet carries TCP, UDP, ICMP, and so on.

- Source port.

- Destination IP address.

- Destination port.

> **Note**
>
> These five components might look familiar. They should, because they are the basic identifiers of the flows described in Chapter 3. NATs that involve ports effectively operate on flows. Just as NAT breaks the end-to-end significance of IP addresses, it breaks the end-to-end characteristics of flows. This is not necessarily a problem, but it needs to be considered when you are trying to do end-to-end capacity planning.

TCP Session Handling

A NAT, router, bastion host, or other device can recognize the start of a TCP session when it sees a packet with SYN but not ACK bits set to one. It is at session (that is, connection) establishment type that the stub address (and port, where appropriate) is bound to a registered address and port. The translator retains the state of the actual stub address and the registered address it sends to the outside to identify packets from the internal host. In like manner, the translator remembers the address the internal host used to reach it and the external address to which this internal destination address needs to be mapped.

The type of translation can be one-to-one or many-to-few on an address basis, or many-to-few with port translation. Other than the first, statically mapped case, there needs to be binding and unbinding at the start and end of each session. Safeguards also are needed to protect resources against sessions that fail and do not properly release the session.

After state is established, translation tables exist for each direction of flow. Packets traversing the NAT go through associated header processing, such as checksum changing.

Ordinary TCP sessions terminate when either end sets the RST bit, or both sides acknowledge a packet containing a FIN bit. Adding an age timer to the NAT, however, is prudent. If a given TCP session does not terminate gracefully, an aging mechanism eventually releases the port number used for the session.

UDP Session Handling

Without additional higher-level protocol information, there is no way the NAT can recognize the start and end of a non-TCP session. Application proxies, discussed in Chapter 7, do have the additional information to do so, but application proxies do not run on NAT routers.

Session lifetime is useless in a dynamic NAT environment, where outside addresses have been bound dynamically to inside addresses. The best that can be done is to release bindings that have not been used in some configurable period of time (for example, 1 minute) or have a rule that releases bindings starting with the least recently used.

Load Sharing and NAT

In Chapter 3, you saw that DNS can be used for load sharing across several servers. Basic DNS, and especially BIND, might not offer sufficiently short TTLs to accomplish this. DistributedDirector was one proprietary approach that removes some of the DNS-based issues, which often assume that all servers have the same capacity; DistributedDirector has an administrative weight mechanism, which allows the system administrator to set preferences as to which server is used first.

You can load share with DNS-based or NAT-based techniques, or use both. They can be complementary.

Before discussing the specific mechanisms that pass load to servers, which can operate on addresses or ports, it is worthwhile to examine some of the mechanisms that select the server onto which work is to be distributed.

There are a great many potential algorithms for load sharing. To understand the principles involved, think first of algorithms where the network cost of reaching a server is not significant, and server workload becomes the only factor considered. These are the *local* family of algorithms. Next, consider more complex topologies where the cost of reaching a server is significant. Algorithms that consider network cost are *distributed*.

These algorithms break into two further categories: the *non-intrusive*, where the intelligence to select servers is completely in the load-sharing device, and *intrusive* algorithms, where the servers explicitly send selection information to the load-sharing device.

Load-sharing algorithms need to know whether real hosts are in fact available. Assigning sessions to hosts that are actually down is possible in simple algorithms. An algorithm that weights hosts by output traffic can lead to the extremely silly, but logical, conclusion that a dead host that emitted no traffic was the least loaded and thus best for new sessions.

Load-sharing implementations need to test periodically that servers are still alive. Although `ping` has serious limitations for estimating quantitative performance, it is generally adequate for qualitatively checking if a host is up. Of course, if there is an intrusive mechanism between NAT and server for monitoring performance, timeouts in such mechanisms would also detect black-hole servers.

Local Load-Sharing Algorithms

Local load-sharing algorithms apply when the network cost of reaching a server in the pool is negligible, as would be the case when the server pool is on a local LAN or switched subnet. Local load-sharing algorithms include the following [RFC 2391]:

- *Round-robin algorithm*—This simplest algorithm distributes sessions to servers in a wrap-around sequence. This might be adequate when all hosts are of equal power and all requests are of equal intensity.

- *Least load first algorithm*—In this approach, the LSNAT tracks how many sessions have been assigned to each server and assigns each new session to the server that currently has the least number of sessions. The advantage of this method over round-robin is that it does not have to wait for the full round-robin cycle; if a session on a given server terminates, that server becomes immediately available to accept a new session. Like round-robin, least load first assumes all servers are equally capable and all sessions consume equal resources.

- *Least traffic first algorithm*—If the volume of traffic directed at a given server is a reasonable representation of actual server load, this algorithm is an improvement over the least load first method.

- *Least weighted load first algorithm*—This approach combines the round-robin and least load first methods. Cisco's LocalDirector product uses a variant of this. Least weighted load considers the load on each server, based on a loading factor assigned to the type of traffic. It also considers a configured capacity value for each server.

  The algorithm then calculates a utilization value for each server. It multiplies each current server by the weighting factor for the type of session, for each of the sessions on that machine. It then adds together the weighted session load for each server and divides this by the capacity of that server. This results in a weighted load figure for each server. The algorithm picks, for the next session, the server with the lowest weighted load.

- *Heuristics using intrusive probes*—The previous approaches use various heuristics to guess the load on servers. Heuristics cannot substitute for actual measurement. A simplistic approach is to ping the servers and use the one with fastest response.

  ICMP-based pings, however, are quite limited in their accuracy of predicting load. Routers often treat ICMP at their lowest priority, which does help protect against ICMP flooding attacks by hackers.

A much more accurate method involves application-level monitoring of the servers by the load-sharing NATs. The load-sharing NATs might send a predefined application transaction and measure its response time, or could use an application-specific measurement protocol. SNMP is another possible method for the load-sharing-aware device to inquire about host loads. It periodically polls the hosts, with the added advantage of dead host detection.

Distributed Load-Sharing Algorithms

Load sharing still can work when the server pool is geographically distributed, as long as the load-sharing mechanism can also consider the network cost of reaching a given server. Again, the servers are expected to be in a single stub domain, although that could be a backbone-partitioned stub domain. Some representative ways to consider network cost are:

- *Weighted least load first algorithm*—Multiply the cost of network access to the server by the number of sessions assigned to the server. The server with the lowest product would be preferred for the next session assignment. If a server fails or is not accessible through the network, an infinite cost to reach it is assumed.

- *Weighted least traffic first algorithm*—Because sessions include different amounts of workload, a simple session count is not as accurate as one that considers traffic. A relatively simple improvement to the previous algorithm, easy to implement on routers, is to estimate network load by the number of bytes or packets sent to the server. In this algorithm, network access cost is multiplied by traffic volume to produce a cost to use each server. The server with lowest cost is selected for the new session.

These distributed methods can be generalized to include the non-intrusive or intrusive local load-sharing algorithms, which take more application factors into consideration. The preceding two distributed methods are there primarily to illustrate how network cost can be considered.

Application-aware proxies, discussed in Chapter 7, can have even more knowledge of application load.

Load Sharing with Outside Client Address Passthrough

A variant of NAT, called *load shared NAT* (LSNAT), offers a load-sharing mechanism at the transport/network level rather than the DNS level. The term *LSNAT* is misleading because it implies there is no port translation. Whether or not ports are translated is irrelevant to its key mechanism, which is passing through the address of the real client to the real server; translating the virtual server address to and from the real server address on the inside of the LSNAT function, on the other hand, is relevant. Nevertheless, I will use LSNAT because it is the term the RFC uses.

When considering LSNAT-style load sharing, remember that it emphasizes providing a pool of servers capable of servicing requests. In its local form, it does not easily provide mechanisms for increasing reliability by mapping the user request to geographically distributed servers. More advanced variants can combine with DNS- and routing-aware mechanisms to increase reliability as well as performance.

As shown in Figure 6.22, the LSNAT function is visible globally as a server address. It is actually a virtual server. When a client request arrives at the LSNAT device, LSNAT translates the destination address, transparently to the client, and passes it to a server in the LSNAT device's server pool.

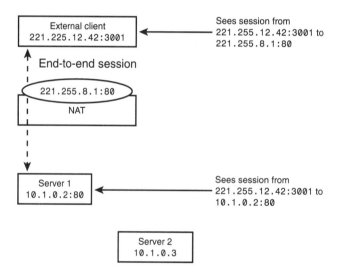

FIGURE 6.22.   *A load-sharing network address and port translator.*

LSNAT devices, in their basic form, do have topological restriction. It has been suggested that all request/response traffic in a single session must go from the real client to one specific LSNAT to the server. It is conceivable that multiple routers could be used, but they would need to be tightly synchronized.

LSNAT builds on NAPT, but adds intelligence to the port mapping function. Also, general NAPT is oriented toward outgoing requests from the stub domain to the outside, whereas LSNAT emphasizes incoming requests to a virtual server address.

As currently conceived, LSNATs operate at the session level, so they cannot easily change server hosts during a session. There are potential workarounds to this, including using a multicast address as the server pool destination, with coordination between the servers as to which actually answers the request. For highly fault-tolerant applications, more than one server conceivably could answer the NAT request, and the LSNAT device could decide which to pass to the client. Typically, if servers are identical, it would be the first response received by the server pool side of the LSNAT.

This general topology restriction suggests that LSNAT functionality belongs on a single NAT-capable border router, with the server pool inside the stub domain. LSNAT violates the Internet end-to-end model in the same way that basic NAT does. There is no requirement that the addressing in the stub domain be private, only that all access to the servers go through the NAT.

In basic LSNAT, an arbitrary external client attempts to establish a session with what it believes to be a server. In reality, it is attempting to establish a session with the virtual server address of the outside interface of the LSNAT.

The LSNAT device, based on internal criteria, redirects the external request to a specific internal server in a server pool. Unique connections are established from the LSNAT device to the pool server for each request, translating addresses and ports as needed.

Load Sharing with Virtual Server Address Passthrough

Adding the complexity of port as well as address translation gives additional flexibility. In particular, adding port translation removes many topological limitations between the real servers and the NAT.

LSNAT devices translate inbound addresses from `<real client address & port, virtual server address & port>` to `<real client address & port, real inside server address & port>`. You might notice that the server needs to respond to the real client address in a LSNAT system. Assuming the servers do not participate in routing, the only realistic way for the servers to send to an external address is to use a default route.

In load-shared NAPT (LSNAPT), as shown in Figure 6.23, you define a virtual server address as that of an external interface of an LSNAPT router. Incoming sessions translate from `<real client address & port, virtual server address & port>` to `<virtual server address & port, real inside server address & port>`.

The LSNAPT device is aware of session relationships. When it receives a packet from the outside client, it passes this to the inside server as if it came from the virtual server. LSNAPT can change the inside server address at any time with UDP-based protocols and with TCP-based protocols if a suitable connection exists.

When the inside server sends a packet back to the LSNAPT function, the LSNAPT device can translate the port number that the inside server thinks is the destination port on the outside virtual server address to the actual destination port to which the real outside client is sending.

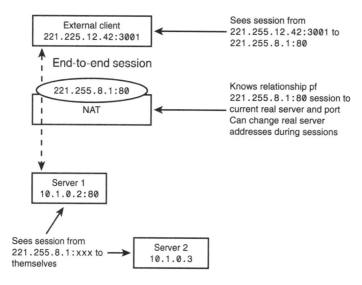

FIGURE 6.23. *LSNAPT.*

By replacing the real client address with the address of the virtual server as the address source seen by the inside, the real server can use multiple paths to return responses. Quite complex routing can provide multiple paths to the LSNAPT router.

There remains the basic topological constraint that there is only one LSNAPT router, but there can more easily be multiple internal paths to it. A LSNAPT router can direct traffic to an internal server inside the private address space of a stub domain, or direct the traffic to a third-party server using registered addresses and WAN connectivity.

The additional complexity of LSNAPT allows greater scalability because new links can be dropped into the routing system without a problem. As long as new client links can get to the virtual server address, the addition of these links is transparent to both servers and clients.

An architectural limit on LSNAPT comes from the number of available client TU ports on the virtual server address. TCP and UDP have a 16-bit port field, of which ports 0–1023 are reserved for well-known services, and 1024–2047 prudently should be reserved for vendor-specific services. That limits a virtual server address to supporting approximately 62 KB addresses, which should not be a practical limitation.

Even if the 62 KB port limit does become a restriction, LSNAPT could combine with DNS-based load sharing of *virtual* addresses and allow the load to be shared over multiple virtual server addresses with a common DNS name.

Protocol Mechanism Incompatibilities with NAT

Many of the complexities of NAT come not from the IP translation proper, but from the effects of address translation, and the more general idea of multiple address space, on the passenger information carried by IP packets in their data fields.

For example, the checksums of TCP and UDP are calculated to include a *pseudo header* that contains the IP source and destination address. The original NAT RFC presents some clever, low-overhead ways to fix the checksums in both IP and the transport layer protocol, the details of which are beyond our present scope. Simply remember that there is more than a simple address swap involved in even basic NAT processing.

A simple address swap would fail because literally swapping the address only would not recompute the IP header checksum. The next receiving IP interface would discard the packet because it had a checksum that did not match the header, computed, as it was, on the old IP addresses.

So NAT functions have the minimal additional requirement of IP header checksum recomputation. In practice, they must pay attention to other factors. TCP and UDP, for example, both have checksums. These checksums are based on the end-to-end segment before IP fragmentation, if any. The checksum includes the original source and destination fields of the original IP packet, not just the TCP or UDP part.

If the IP addresses change without changing the TCP or UDP checksums, the TCP or UDP PDUs are delivered with correct IP checksums, but are discarded because the higher-level checksums fail.

Higher-level protocols that embed IP addresses in application layer protocols fail when going through classical NAT. You have seen examples of such application mechanisms—such as FTP and HTTP redirection—in Chapter 3. Quite a number of multiplayer interactive games embed IP addresses as part of an integrated multicasting function. The failure of games to work can be a shock to consumer-oriented ISPs that install NAT.

Remember the discussion of FTP redirection in Chapter 3. The address to which FTP redirects traffic is not in the IP header of the FTP packets, but is an ASCII-encoded string inside the data field of the TCP PDU. A pure NAT does not understand application layer protocols, so it cannot look inside this data field to translate the redirected IP addresses.

FTP redirection, and similar protocol mechanisms where IP addresses are carried in the application layer data field, fail when going through a pure NAT. True, embedding lower-layer information in upper-layer fields is a technical violation of layering principles, but that rarely constrains protocol designers. For application protocols with embedded IP addresses to work properly, it is necessary to have a translator more powerful than NAT. Application proxies have this capability, because they understand the application protocol. Such proxies are discussed in the "Bastion Hosts and Stateful Screening" section of Chapter 7.

Layer 2 Versus Layer 3 in Providing Internet Services

Especially inside large provider networks, the traditional IP destination-only model of packet forwarding might not be adequate for scaling. Most large providers, in practice, have mixtures of Layer 2 and Layer 3 forwarding [O'Dell 1996]. For example, there is a practical need to have large amounts of bandwidth between exchange points or internal ISP superhubs. Peers at exchange points advertise and accept large numbers of routes, which do not always aggregate.

Intracarrier Paths

From the perspective of a customer to a provider, it is highly desirable to aggregate addresses as one moves higher in the routing hierarchy. It is perfectly reasonable for the provider to aggregate irreversibly, because the provider simply knows it needs to route everything with a specific prefix to the customer.

This isn't necessarily true inside the provider network, or even in large enterprises, when trying to route traffic based on flow characteristics. There seem to be fashions in networking, much as the fashion gurus dictate whether hem lines will be up or down. The earliest internetworking, in the telephone system, was at the physical or data link layer. Bridging, the next major evolution for data networks, operates at Layer 2. Routing, at Layer 3, replaced bridging in the WAN. Yet newer initiatives, sometimes overly zealous ones, pushed Layer 2 switches in flattened networks.

Current thinking uses complementary Layer 2 and Layer 3 technologies. In enterprises, workgroups are linked by routing, often inter-VLAN routing, but use Layer 2 connectivity inside the workgroup. Inside the workgroup, Layer 2 switching offers a "turbocharge" to obtain high bandwidth at low cost.

Large ISPs also turbocharge their Layer 3 networks with selected Layer 2 technology, but ISPs emphasize Layer 2 technology in their cores. There is also a tendency in ISPs to have a limited number of path determination servers that pass routing information to large numbers of forwarding devices. The latter tendency has long been the case in the telephone network, where most switches do not know how to forward paths until they obtain routing information from an SS7 server. Current IETF work on *multiprotocol label switching (MPLS)* provides a framework for communication between path determination and forwarding engines.

Large ISP networks tend to differ in their external and internal routing infrastructures. This is one of the arguments for what is variously called IP switching, tag switching, or, in the IETF, MPLS. By whatever name, this function creates a short, fixed field that can represent the next hop for a multiplicity of Layer 3 and higher information, yet be processed completely by fast Layer 2 forwarding mechanisms.

MPLS has some similarities to MPOA, as discussed in Chapter 4, "Transmission System Identifiers and Logical Address Mapping: A View from the Bottom," but has a different emphasis. MPLS mechanisms have some type of label distribution protocol (LDP) that identifies a soft state that aggregates certain flows or routes, assigns a label to it, and sends this label to the Layer 2 forwarding engines.

The general pattern is that the large ISPs begin with a Layer 3 network and then use Layer 2 technology to interconnect their major internal interconnection points. If they offer Layer 2 services such as Frame Relay, the Layer 2 network to provide may be combined with the network that interconnects their superhub interconnection points.

Layer 2 and Layer 3 technologies mix in exchange points, discussed next. Understanding the role of exchange points in external routing is important from an addressing standpoint. In IPv6 addressing proposals discussed in Chapter 15, "Your Addressing Strategy: Integration for the Present and Planning for the Future," metropolitan exchanges form a distinct level in hierarchical addressing for the global IPv6 Internet.

Exchange Points

ISPs interconnect with private interconnects, or at *exchange points* variously called *metropolitan area exchanges*, *network access points*, or simply *exchanges*. As shown in Figure 6.24, exchanges are hybrids of Layer 2 and Layer 3 technologies.

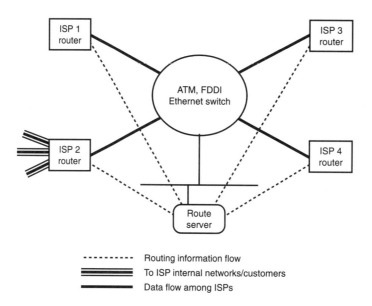

FIGURE 6.24. *Basic parts of an exchange are feeder routers, a Layer 2 switching fabric, and a route server.*

By whatever name, they have several common components:

- Participating ISPs that provide routers to connect to the switching fabric

- A switching fabric, which is most often a high-performance local switch, but also might be a geographically distributed ATM cloud

- A route server that exchanges routing information with the ISP routers, but does not forward packets

The significance of this structure is the clear separation of routing and forwarding. ISP routers exchange routing information with the route server, rather than directly exchanging routes with one another. The route server can help enforce routing policies.

The main data transfer, however, goes between pairs of router interfaces connected to the switching fabric. These transfers might go as MAC-layer unicasts, or over ATM PVCs.

Multicast-friendly exchange points are being explored, where the switching fabric is optimized for multicast. These are apt to be co-located with existing unicast exchanges and have interdomain multicast traffic routed through them.

Depending on the rules of the specific exchange, there might be direct physical connections among various provider routers. Such private peering arrangements do not go through the switch fabric.

In general, exchange participants have been ISPs only, not end customers. This might be changing, as it makes sense to have large server farms or Web caches at major traffic sites. Such servers can be operated by providers rather than an end user organization. The Digital exchange in Palo Alto, California (PAIX) is one exchange that has successfully offered co-located server space.

Looking Ahead

This chapter begins with a discussion of what are not CIDR/VLSM extensions to IP addressing, but are a way of generalizing the original design. You might now realize even better why the presentation of IP addressing in Chapter 5 emphasizes the binary nature of IP addresses rather than the more traditional presentation using dotted decimal.

A large part of this chapter deals with NAT, its variations, and its applications. NAT is a more profound change to the traditions of IP than is CIDR/VLSM, because NAT breaks the end-to-end significance assumption long implicit in IP design.

In Chapter 7, you will see how different security mechanisms take quite different views of end-to-end significance. Firewalls with address-translating bastion hosts violate this in the same manner as NAT, but they also contain application proxies that can work around some of NAT's protocol incompatibilities. The IPsec cryptographic tunneling mechanism requires end-to-end significance. Layer 2 tunneling rather sidesteps the entire issue.

CHAPTER 7

Addressing, Security, and Network Management

There is no technical solution to a management problem.

—*Gary A. Desler*

I wouldn't belong to any club that would have me as a member.

—*Groucho Marx*

The Internet was designed to trust the kindness of strangers. If it is to be considered a mission-critical system for which compromise is a serious problem, it must evolve and will necessarily become more secure...train tracks, especially unprotected tracks in rural countryside, are easy to sabotage, and with grimmer results than network failure, but such incidents are rare.

—*Martin Libicki*

From a network operations perspective, your users are rather uncaring. If they cannot get their work done, they really don't care if the network doesn't work because an evil hacker broke in and destroyed the software, or if a backbone transmission facility is so congested it cannot pass user data. Your users don't care why; they simply want to have services available when they need them.

Your users, therefore, don't care whether you use security techniques or network management techniques to ensure that they get the services they need. You should budget for both areas of service, under the broad category of ensuring service.

Although the goal of user service is common between security and network management, there are differences in the techniques they use to provide user service.

> **Note**
>
> *Above all else, security is a management problem. Top management must support security and network management efforts.*
>
> *All security mechanisms are based on accountability and audit. In a secured system, someone must always be responsible for any action, and there must be a way of validating who did what to whom.*
>
> *Security never stops. New threats always emerge; it is the classical military or sports problem that the defense must react to the offense. Audit mechanisms and procedures are your friends; they tell you how effective your security and network management has been.*

A detailed discussion of security, of course, is far beyond the scope of this book. The focus here is how addresses are used by security mechanisms, and how security mechanisms affect addressing. Security policy, however, is so important that it deserves a bit of attention. Think back to the executive expectations you researched in Chapter 1, "What Is the Problem You Are Trying to Solve?" and be sure you understand the policy implications of those expectations.

Security Policies

A security policy states the assumptions of top management about who is authorized to access which organizational information resources. It might have additional language that explicitly identifies unauthorized activities, such as launching denial of service (DOS) attacks.

In the broadest policy terms, a secure environment is one in which a set of services (or information) is provided to authorized users and not provided to unauthorized users.

The sort of network failures that network management deals with result in denial of service. Conventional network management tools help prevent or repair denial of service problems caused by accident. So, the set of objectives that drives the security policy and budget also drives the network management policy and budget.

Addresses in Security and Network Management

Perhaps the most fundamental requirements for a security system to work are to be able to identify users and track their behavior. In many environments, the process of user identification is closely associated with assigning addresses to them, especially in dialup access.

After the address is assigned, it is often used as a primary identifier for the user. This works in environments where there is no security threat, but IPv4 packets have no built-in method to authenticate the validity of addresses. The IPsec security mechanisms, which were developed as part of IPv6 work and retrofitted to IPv4, do provide address authentication.

Link-level encryption effectively authenticates addresses, if it can be assumed that the sender on the link has a valid encryption key.

There are many circumstances in which it is dangerous to trust an address. Yet many mechanisms, such as SNMPv1 network management, often rely only on addresses as identifiers. Without stronger identification, these mechanisms cannot be fully trusted. New versions of SNMP contain their own cryptographic authentication mechanisms.

Another issue where security and addressing can conflict is that IP addresses are assumed to have end-to-end significance. If these addresses are changed by network address translation devices or firewalls, which are invisible to upper-layer protocols, upper-layer mechanisms that depend on IP addresses can break.

Firewalls themselves might assume that the source address of any IP packets arriving at the firewall is the true source address. This assumption does not work with various tunneling mechanisms, both for security and those that carry IP traffic with hidden addresses.

Secure Communications and Threats

Security tools help prevent deliberate denial-of-service attacks, but also prevent additional problems such as:

- Disclosure of information

- Theft of information

- Alteration/replay/duplication of information

Some definitions are needed:

- *Threat*—An adverse event

- *Risk*—The likelihood of a threat's occurrence

- *Incident cost*—The cost associated with the occurrence of a threat event

- *Exposure*—The real cost estimate, or the incident cost weighted by risk

Especially as internetworking clients connect to the public Internet, but also as they interconnect to business partners and even among business units of the same enterprise, security becomes more and more of a concern. Before you can design security solutions, you must first understand what security means.

Many people focus on security as a means of preventing the disclosure of information. They picture the wily hacker as a person out to read confidential files. In actuality, security threats are much broader than information disclosure. The denial-of-service or theft-of-service attack is more common from the outside; information disclosure and alteration is more commonly an inside problem with disgruntled employees.

Before Internet connectivity was widespread, the most critical threats to enterprise networks were internal. Security consultants constantly warned about disgruntled employees.

I have observed that the best way to keep employees from becoming disgruntled is to practice a reasonable management style. With tongue in cheek, I often ask executives, "What are you doing to keep your staff gruntled?" When this phrasing triggers a double-take, I point out that the only real way to have security inside an organization is to obtain the willing cooperation of the staff. Keep staff aware of security issues and sensitive to outside threats.

So what are the characteristics of successful secure communications? I remember them with the 5-S mnemonic coined by Dennis Branstad, then at the National Institute for Standards and Technology:

- *Sealed* to protect against unauthorized modification. *Unitary integrity* mechanisms seal messages.

- *Sequenced* to protect against unauthorized loss or modification. *Sequential integrity* mechanisms ensure that the sequencing of records is not altered.

- *Secret* so it cannot be disclosed without authorization. *Confidentiality* mechanisms protect the information from unauthorized eyes.

- *Signed* to ensure the correct identity of its sender. *Authentication* and *digital signature* mechanisms verify the sender is who she claims to be and that the sender attests to the authenticity of the information.

- *Stamped* to protect against delivery to an incorrect recipient. *Receiver authentication* mechanisms verify the receiver, and *non-repudiation* mechanisms certify receipt.

The Weighted Risk Model

A rational security budget comes from identifying potential threats and weighting them by the probability of their occurrence. Such tradeoffs are shown in Figure 7.1. An airline reservations system, for example, might cost its organization $5,000 of revenue per minute of downtime. If a particular threat that could cause networkwide failure has a one percent chance of occurrence, a solution that costs less than $50 per minute is cost effective.

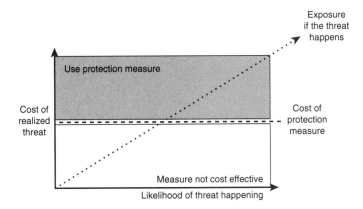

FIGURE 7.1. *Weighted risk: Consider the cost of protection versus your exposure for each risk.*

Different protection measures protect against different threats. The better protection measures protect against multiple threats, ideally both deliberate and accidental. If your goal is to ensure your service continues to operate under all threats, you certainly could surround your data center with antiaircraft guns and missiles to deal with the threat that a deranged pilot will crash a 747 into the building. Be sure to place these defenses far enough away so that the plane, when shot down, doesn't crash into your data center. The land for such defenses might be a bit expensive if your data center were in downtown San Francisco.

Alternatively, you could protect against a single attacking 747 and earthquakes by establishing a backup data center in New York City.

Never forget that denial of service can result from deliberate attacks or random failures. If the goal is to ensure that users can reliably use resources, security and network management both contribute to reliable usage. Security measures protect against the deliberate, whereas network management techniques protect against the accidental. But if your network never works, you really don't need to worry about security.

After the threat and budget are defined, then and only then should tools be selected. You might, for example, decide you need three alternate paths between two endpoints to reach the desired level of reliability.

> **Note**
>
> It is a good idea to use redundant facilities, but when you select them, be sure they are truly redundant. Dual router power supplies connected to the same circuit breaker are no more reliable than the common power circuit. Multiple data lines that leave your building through the same telephone company cable are all vulnerable to being dug up by a backhoe.

Internet Security Considerations

Martin Libicki of the National Defense University has written extensively on "information warfare." He tries to put this threat in perspective, observing that both railroad sabotage and devastating Internet attacks have happened. Nevertheless, he says, "by creating a dense aura of magic around hacking, it raises the status of professional paranoids" [Libicki, 1995].

The Internet was developed as a research environment where trust among its users could be assumed. Paradoxically, it was also developed to test a model of connectivity that could be robust under nuclear attack. Discovering that your network nodes are, in a short period of time, becoming mushroom clouds is to discover the ultimate denial-of-service attack.

In today's Internet, the threat of denial of service is much more from the users than physical catastrophes. The original Internet protocols, however, did not presume a major hacking threat, and safeguards were not present, were trivial, or were afterthoughts. Newer Internet protocols contain much more security.

Security Mechanisms

Security mechanisms are, in their simplest form, things that decide whether information meets the criteria to flow through a given interface or process. Information flow restrictions are supplemented by things such as auditing or logging systems and methods for identifying users. Cryptography is an enabling technique for a wide range of flow and identification methods.

Cryptography: A Brief Review

An encryption algorithm takes understandable *plaintext*, manipulates it based on the value of a key, and produces unintelligible *ciphertext*. Decryption reverses the process by applying a key to ciphertext and producing plaintext.

The combination of an algorithm, the platform it runs on, and the keys form a *cryptosystem*. Administrative procedures, especially involved in key distribution, are an enormously complex issue in security systems.

Keys are used in two major ways. When the same key is used for encryption and decryption, the cryptosystem is called *symmetrical*. The key forms a *shared secret* between sender and receiver.

Note

Shared secret mechanisms are the usual mechanism for authenticating dialup user identities prior to address assignment. See the discussion in the section "Secure Address Assignment" later in this chapter.

Asymmetrical cryptosystems use different keys for encrypting and decrypting. Asymmetrical systems can be (but are not required to be) public key systems. In a public key system, either the encrypting or the decrypting key is made widely available, depending on the application of cryptography.

Confidentiality

James Bond and other spy thriller movies often show parties communicating using codebooks taken from a safe or a typewriter-like cipher machine into which a secret key was set. This is the classic model of shared secret cryptography.

Shared secret mechanisms can provide both confidentiality—prevention of disclosure of message contents—and authentication. Authentication is implicit in the assumption that only authorized parties possess the keys. For shared secret to be useful in communications, the parties need to be known to one another so they can agree on a key to use. Shared secret has the administrative complexity that the keys must be distributed before they can be used.

When public key encryption is being used to provide confidentiality, the sender uses a public key to encrypt information that needs to be protected. In other words, the plaintext is secret, as is the decrypting key. There is a mathematical relationship between the encrypting key and the decrypting key that allows only the authorized receiver to decrypt the ciphertext.

Authentication

In digital signature applications, where the concern is that the sender's identity is verified, the sender encrypts public information, such as his name, with a secret encrypting key. The decrypting key is public. If a receiver can retrieve the public information using the decrypting key, the sender's identity is validated.

> **Note**
>
> *An increasing number of digital signature applications can be expected to be seen within the global Internet addressing and routing structure. To cope with the problem of organizations advertising address-es not assigned to them, there is active research on how address assignment authorities can sign alloca-tions, and the organizations that actually advertise these can sign the signature as well. Secure DNS uses digital signatures.*
>
> *When DNS information can be authenticated, it can be useful for basic checks on the source of an address. Double DNS lookup is a method that has long been used to validate the source of requests, a method that becomes much stronger when digital signatures prevent tampering with DNS databases.*
>
> *In double DNS lookup, an application server extracts the source address from a request packet and does a reverse lookup of that address, obtaining a domain name. This domain name is then looked up, and the resulting address range should include the received source address. If the reverse lookup does not work, or the addresses from forward and reverse lookup do not match, the packet is suspect.*

Firewalls

Perhaps the most popular buzzword in security technology is *firewall*. Properly, a firewall is a set of security components that sits between the protected inside network and outside users. These users can access the network through dialup links, the Internet, and so on.

Routers are an important component of firewall solutions, but are not the only mechanism in a comprehensive firewall. In selected environments, simple router-based filtering can provide appropriate security, but limitations must be understood.

Cheswick and Bellovin describe the firewall as "a hard crunchy shell around a soft chewy center" [Cheswick 1994]. The soft chewy center is the set of resources the firewall protects. This analogy deals with a simple black-and-white view of the world; things are either trusted and inside the firewall or untrusted and outside it.

I find a more complex, if somewhat mixed, metaphor to be useful in dealing with more complex firewalling. At the first level of metaphor enhancement, think of a hard crunchy shell surrounding an onion, with each level of the onion being a different level of sensitivity. Some services in a company are intended to be available to the public, but in a controlled way. Other services are never to be available to the outside world.

Sometimes, when cutting into a real onion, the chef finds that it is not a single symmetrical set of layers surrounding a core, but made up of two or more cloves, each with its set of layers. In many network environments, access to certain selected resources must be restricted inside the organization. By only slightly strained analogy, both the moderately and highly sensitive resources are protected by the outer skin of the onion, but the different communities are separated inside. This separation is invisible from the outside.

Major firewall components include:

- Screening routers that use filtering logic to permit or deny network layer packets to flow through the firewall.

  Routers typically are the fastest devices in a firewall system. They do not maintain information on user connections to applications, which is more the job of the slower bastion host.

- Authentication challenge servers, such as RADIUS or TACACS+.

- Personal identification devices used as authenticators. These include one-time password generators, such as products from Security Dynamics and Enigma Logic, biometric devices that check fingerprints or other personal characteristics, and individually generated paper lists of one-time passwords.

- Accounting and audit trail mechanisms, which can be trusted disks or even printers.

- Bastion hosts, such as the public domain `ftwk` or commercial-grade Gauntlet from Trusted Information Systems, Firewall/1 from Checkpoint, and so on.

Routers with access control features are sometimes called firewalls, but that is a simplification. On a boat, safety features include fire extinguishers and life jackets. Although both are appropriate for their intended tasks, it would be unfortunate if one depended on a fire extinguisher for flotation, or used a plastic life jacket to snuff a gasoline fire. In like manner, different security features complement one another in networks. These various features often operate at different OSI layers. Routers provide security at the network layer. Bastion hosts are application routers that provide security at the network layer. Encryption devices can operate at the data link or network layers.

Figure 7.2 shows an idealized architecture in which routers screen the bastion host, an internal screening router between the dual-homed bastion host and public networks, and an external screening router between the bastion host and the protected inside network. The external screening router has a physical connection to the outside, to the bastion host, and to the demilitarized zone (DMZ) network. A secure perimeter network connects the bastion host with the internal screening router.

Note

In traditional firewall systems, the public hosts (for example, WWW, FTP) are on a LAN between the external router and the bastion host. This is called the demilitarized zone (DMZ).

Bastion hosts can be dual homed, separating the DMZ and perimeter networks, or a single-homed "traffic cop" on the DMZ. Single homing, also called screened host, *is less secure than the dual-homed* screened subnet *method [Chapman, 1996]. Newer bastion hosts can have more than two interfaces and put public hosts on a LAN interface that is reachable only through the bastion, allowing much greater control over access to public hosts.*

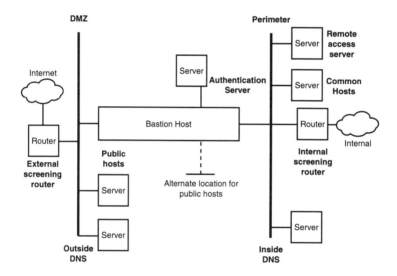

FIGURE 7.2.   *Not all components here need to be in separate boxes; this is an idealized architectural view of a full-featured, screened-subnet, dual-homed firewall.*

Note

Although it is most common to see public hosts, such as Web servers, on the DMZ, an increasing number of bastion hosts support three or more interfaces. In such configurations, public hosts are on their own medium. The traditional DMZ, between the external screening router and the bastion host, might contain a DNS or no servers at all.

It can be a reasonable economy, when the risks are understood, to use a single router (with enough interfaces) as the interior and exterior screening router functions; the bastion host is still desirable in this scenario. Alternatively, there can be additional screening routers inside the protected network to give extra protection to specific projects or organizations.

Screening routers are sensitive parts of the firewall. Many organizations disable the virtual terminal login into such routers and use secure modems on the auxiliary console port if remote access is needed. Screening routers complement bastion hosts, protecting them from attacks including denial-of-service attempts based on flooding the network layer. They can also help in protecting against TCP sequence prediction attacks that "hijack" existing connections. There are many other protocol threats they can help protect against, such as smurf attacks, which flood a target subnet with ICMP requests directed to the subnet-specific directed broadcast address, causing a huge number of responses.

New threats constantly emerge, and it is impossible to detail or anticipate all of them here. An authoritative source of information on threats is the CERT Coordination Center at www.cert.org. Obviously, if the router vendor doesn't support a protection measure, you can't use it. Keep track of your vendor's security announcements. Major router vendors usually are highly responsive to identified threats.

Overloading the Poor IP Address

IP addresses are intended to be identifiers to manage packet forwarding at the network layer. Unfortunately, they are so ubiquitous in networking that they have been *overloaded*, or used for multiple purposes. Some of the additional semantics that have been loaded onto the poor IP address include identifying the source of data and identifying managed objects for network management.

Unfortunately, IP addresses easily can be forged, either at the origin or at intermediate points. Realistically, if there are no additional means to validate an IP address received through the public Internet, you cannot assume it comes from the claimed server.

Most means of validating Internet addresses are cryptographic, as discussed later in this chapter. If a purported user account is associated with the address, that can be used to provide some authentication.

You can give more trust to addresses generated on machines your organization physically controls and whose traffic has reached you either over media you physically control or through cryptographic communications under your control.

Many corporations, especially multinational ones, like to have a corporate classful network number. They assign an almost trademark-like significance to an arbitrary number, even if the address block is used principally inside the enterprise network and is generally not visible on the public Internet. Such usage is especially common with the early participants in the global Internet, who received Class A allocations at the beginning. It is a practice that adds no significant protection and wastes globally routable space.

Several IP hacking attacks involve the attacker masquerading, or spoofing, the address of an internal host that has some level of trust. A fairly simple counter-measure is to assign addresses such that an internal network address *never* is allowed in from the Internet, unless Internet connectivity is cryptographically protected.

If you use classful addressing, do not assign addresses in your assigned net-works to traveling users. If absolutely necessary, use filtering to deny the sub-nets assigned to Internet users from coming directly into your network, or give no special privileges to machines with such addresses.

Tighter security can be applied to users that dial in to a remote access server you control, because you can force authentication and you control the IP address that is assigned. Layer 2 tunneling, discussed later in this chapter, can extend your dialup security to remote points.

Stateless Screening

The idea of *state* is a common one in computer science. A function that main-tains state establishes an initial condition and then remembers changes to it. A TCP connection, for example, is *stateful* in that it has basic states of disconnect-ed and connected.

A *stateless* function is one that makes a new decision, with no consideration of prior history, on each new piece of information. IP routing is stateless in that a new decision is made on how to forward each packet.

Connection-oriented communications are stateful whereas connectionless com-munications are stateless. Connection terminology has a meaning beyond knowing or not knowing prior history. A connection also implies a commit-ment of resources.

Stateless screening involves applying pattern-matching criteria against a unit of information, such as a frame or a packet, and making a decision on how to handle that unit without any other contextual information. Such screening can be extremely fast, and hardware can be optimized to do it.

As illustrated in Figure 7.3, the components of a filtering system include the rules, the pattern-matching and selective forwarding mechanism, and optional logging.

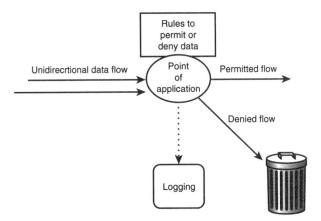

FIGURE 7.3. *The basic components of stateless filtering are applicable to Layer 2 and Layer 3 filtering mechanisms.*

Bay Networks has a reasonably clear terminology for this function. The part of a configuration file that defines the matching rules is a *template*. The part of a configuration file that enables the processes of matching and actions taken upon matching is the *filter*. Cisco is less consistent on its terminology, but the term *access list* is most often used for the pattern match rules; on the other hand, a wide range of commands, most commonly *access group* but including a confusing range of others, invoke filtering in a specific place. See Chapter 14, "Selective Forwarding Inside Routers," for more detail on filtering.

Data Link Layer Packet Filtering

You will find actual configuration guidance in Chapter 12, "Addressing in Hubs and Switches." This section gives the principles that underlie the vendor-specific mechanisms.

Depending on the router architecture, you might be able to apply data link filters, then packet filters, on the same data. Bay explicitly allows this as the path goes first to Layer 2 processing and then to Layer 3. On a Cisco interface, as soon as the protocol of a received packet is known, it is sent either to a Layer 2 or a Layer 3 process and only then are filters applied.

An alternative strategy, applicable to many vendors, is to apply data link filtering on a switch and packet filtering on a router.

Router Packet Filtering

The major router-based security function is stateless packet filtering, which permits or denies data flow based on addresses and other criteria. Most commercial routers have a wide range of such filtering mechanisms, for both IP and non-IP protocols. You will find actual configuration guidance in Chapter 14.

In general, each protocol family has one set of capabilities that applies to unicast traffic with specific destinations and other sets of capabilities that apply to broadcasts and other management functions such as routing updates.

The general approach to filtering is to define global rules with pattern matching statements and activate them on interfaces with appropriate enabling statements. Specialized filtering can also be activated under routing processes, console lines, and other functions.

The Internet Protocol Security Option

Several features, originally intended for military use but applicable in appropriate commercial environments, make security decisions during routing. The *Internet Protocol Security Option* (IPSO) prevents IP datagrams of high sensitivity from being forwarded to untrusted subnets, regardless of other routing criteria [RFC 1108].

There can be useful nonmilitary applications for IPSO. In general, it is inferior to cryptographic methods, but it is one more of those tools that can be exactly what you need for a special circumstance.

In Figure 7.4, top secret (TS) hosts can send TS traffic only to hosts on TS subnets. On TS net 1, the TS host also is trusted to generate secret, confidential, and unclassified traffic. This host can send S, C, and U traffic to the S net or U traffic to the U net. The router rejects attempts to send TS traffic to a net with a lower maximum classification.

The S host can send S traffic to either TS network. The U host can send U traffic to TS1 or S, but not TS2.

TS2 operates in the *system high* mode, in which all traffic is assumed to be of maximum sensitivity. As a result, both the minimum and maximum sensitivity levels on TS2 are TS. Packets of lower sensitivity levels are assumed to come from a host that is not cleared for TS and are not permitted.

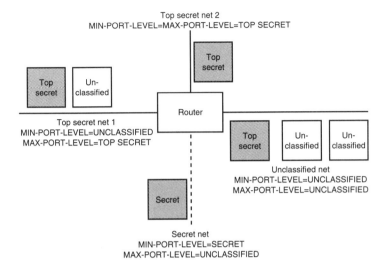

FIGURE 7.4. *An Internet Protocol security option configuration for a hospital.*

IP Security Options

As shown in Figure 7.4, a hospital wants to control access to material of different sensitivities. It is not practical to install cryptographic protection on the individual workstations or terminals.

Prescriptions can be created only on patient wards and physician offices. LANs on each floor are treated as top secret by their router. Workstations on these LANs are not IPSO-aware, but the router on their LAN marks them top secret before passing them to other subnets. In addition, some floors have dumb terminals. Terminal servers for these terminals have their LAN side connected to the TS LANs.

The clinical laboratories can create reports and send them to clinical units, such as patient wards and the pharmacy. Laboratory LANs are treated as secret. Again, the hosts on these LANs do not directly support IPSO; the routers enforce IPSO and label laboratory-generated

packets secret. Secret packets are permitted onto S and TS subnets.

The business office cannot see clinical information, but does have the right to see patient billing information that needs to be kept off the public LANs. Router interfaces serving the business office are treated as confidential.

Only one host type needs to be IPSO aware: a server that generates billing information and the patient directory. It is on a top secret interface, but the router interface trusts IPSO fields set by the host. The interface allows top secret through unclassified traffic to flow from the host onto other networks.

The hospital has various public access workstations that give access to the patient directory and to educational materials on an unclassified server.

Bastion Hosts and Stateful Screening

You can think of a bastion host as an extension of a network address translator, typically operating at the port translation level. Although a NAT device is essentially a permissive device that translates everything it can, a bastion host is restrictive. It examines traffic between the inside and outside and passes only that traffic that meets security criteria.

This is a functional similarity that might not be exact. But both NAT and bastion host devices can be considered specialized routers. A bastion host might not do address translation, but it does forward based on more specific criteria than a routing table.

As part of a firewall system, bastion hosts complement screening routers by providing a framework for user-level authentication, by protecting the inside network from flooding, and by a variety of other mechanisms. These hosts work closely with user authentication devices. They might use stateless screening or a variety of proxy methods. Proxies are stateful.

Typically, a bastion host is implemented on one or more stripped-down UNIX servers, which only run the bastion software and minimal system software. Some products run on dedicated boxes using a special-purpose operating system.

Proxies normally are incompatible with end-to-end encryption. If your security policy permits, it is possible for the proxy to decrypt traffic, apply criteria, and then re-encrypt traffic intended to be forwarded.

Although it might be a temptation to put World Wide Web and similar servers on the bastion host, this is not good practice. If a Web server is hacked—and this can and does happen—the bastion is now vulnerable. Public servers belong on the DMZ network between the external screening router and the bastion host, or possibly on a third or fourth interface of the bastion host.

Circuit Proxies

Circuit proxies are very similar to the NAPT function discussed in Chapter 6, "Internet Failing: Details at 11." They operate on TCP sessions; the circuit that is referred to is the TCP virtual circuit. Circuit proxies differ from NATP in that they terminate the TCP sessions at each side.

Contrast Figure 7.5 with Figure 6.20 from Chapter 6. You will find them to be quite similar. The mapping table in the NAT is roughly equivalent to the rules implementing security policy in the bastion host.

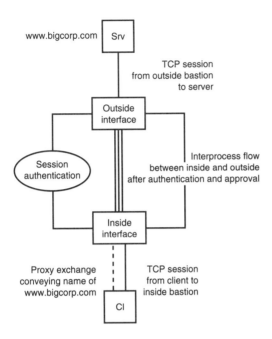

FIGURE 7.5. *Circuit proxies have inside and outside TCP processes joined by validation mechanisms inside the bastion host.*

A classical circuit proxy terminates a TCP session on the inside and uses interprocess communications within the bastion host to link it to another TCP session on the outside. The client needs to pass the true destination address to the proxy server, using manual login to the proxy server or proxy-aware client software.

The Cisco PIX advertises that it is not a true circuit proxy, but rather a stateful packet screen aware of TCP and able to substitute the appropriate TCP header checksum.

The advantage of a circuit proxy is that it works for any TCP-based application and is relatively low in overhead. It is limited in its capability to enforce application-related policies and to cope with application protocol problems due to address translation.

In general, an inside client establishes a TCP connection to one side of the proxy, and the proxy then applies tests to see if the flow should be permitted. This can include a password or other challenge to the user, authenticating the client identity and granting access if an authenticated identifier comes from a known user.

After access is granted, the proxy sets up an internal flow to the other side of the bastion host and creates a TCP session to the destination. This is done with port mapping as in NAPT.

A challenge of implementing the proxy is how it knows the ultimate destination of the TCP session. The inside user is connecting to the proxy server, so it needs to send packets to the destination address of the bastion host interface, not the ultimate destination.

There are several ways the proxy could know where to go:

- The bastion host could act as a router advertising the default route. In this case, clients put the real destination address in their packets.

- The user could explicitly log in to the bastion and issue commands to log in to the destination.

- Client software could be aware of the proxy's existence and negotiate with the proxy to give ultimate connection information, invisibly to the user.

The problem is more complex when coming inbound from an untrusted network, such as the Internet. Cryptographic protections, at the very least on session authentication and preferably at the packet authentication level, should be used.

Stateful Packet Screening

Stateful packet screening might appear to be connectionless NATs, but in actuality they impose and use a pseudo-connectionless structure on traffic.

There are various implementations, each having different knowledge they impose to create structure. A trivial example is that for every packet sent from source 1 to destination 2, a packet, or a sequence of packets, is expected in response. The responses have source address 2 and destination 1.

A stateful packet screen, for this case, notes the outgoing packet and creates an inbound access list for the expected response, a list that permits the response to enter. This inbound access list has an associated lifetime, so if there is no response in a reasonable period of time, the list is canceled so that unexpected traffic cannot pass through it.

If real-world protocols were sufficiently simple that a query packet only had a single response packet, stateful packet screening would be simple and powerful. Unfortunately, the real world is not that simple.

Without substantial knowledge of application layer protocols, it is difficult to predict the number of packets that will be returned in a response. Protocol redirection mechanisms can also make it hard to predict the source port number or source address of response packets.

Several commercial products do, in fact, have stateful packet screens that are aware of application layer protocols and use this awareness to produce suitable response filters. There is a difference between a stateful packet screen that uses application awareness to create filters and a true application proxy as described in the next section. An application proxy interacts with the application protocol, potentially blocking certain application operations or manipulating the application protocol fields. Application-aware stateful packet filters and application proxies both are useful techniques. The former might be faster, but the latter has more intelligence and can deal with such situations as the interaction of NAT with application protocols that embed IP addresses in application data.

Application Proxies

Application proxies, as illustrated in Figure 7.6, go well beyond NATP in that they understand the actual application protocols such as FTP or HTTP and do not simply infer things about sessions through the characteristics of transport protocols such as TCP and UDP.

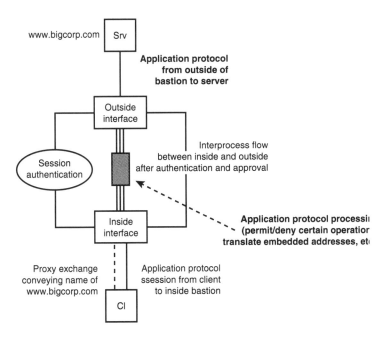

FIGURE 7.6. *Application proxies have a topology similar to that of a circuit proxy, but also do application layer processing.*

Many of the DNS extensions discussed in Chapter 3, "Application Topology: Naming Endpoints," and the NAT protocol incompatibilities mentioned in Chapter 6 can be solved with application proxies. The downside of application proxies includes:

- A specific proxy must be written for each application type.

- The bastion host needs more complex processing power to handle the application protocols. Whereas NAT devices add delay in microseconds, much as does a router, complex proxies might add milliseconds of per-packet delay and have a longer connection establishment time.

Traffic-Aware Proxies

Without trying to go into all the characteristics of a traffic-aware application proxy, you will want to note its characteristics in terms of the application requirements you developed in Chapter 3 (see Figure 7.7).

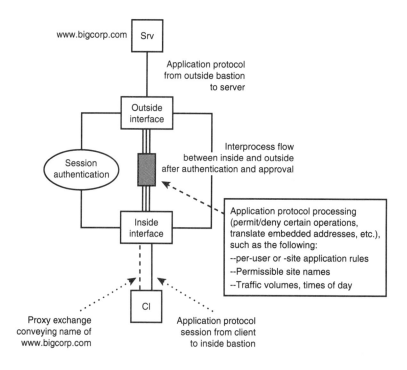

FIGURE 7.7. *Traffic-aware proxies have a topology similar to an application proxy. They need additional configuration to set traffic policies.*

Proxies of this sort may be aware of:

- Server name and/or address, and if these names are permitted or denied for a specific client

- Volume of data to be transferred

- Type of data transfer (read, write, and so on)

- Time of day of transfer

A traffic-aware proxy has all the capabilities of an application proxy. Its additional capabilities include restricting the sites to which a user can connect and placing basic controls on the data transfer. It does not attempt to check what is in the data.

From the addressing and naming standpoint, there might be significant administration involved in keeping the permit/deny tables of the traffic-aware proxy current.

Content-Aware Proxies

Content-aware proxies understand the application protocol, but also look inside application data fields for selected keywords that match rules to permit or deny application-level forwarding.

Although the usual perception of a content-aware proxy is something that scans text for "bad words," such as sexually oriented terms that should not be seen by children, appropriate content filters can scan for IP addresses or DNS names. Specialized content-aware proxies could scan binaries to search for viruses or disallow binary transmission.

Access Control Mechanisms Involved with Addressing

It is a reality in most existing networks that IP addresses will be used as unique identifiers and trusted to identify objects. Although more sophisticated attacks can spoof IP addresses of established sessions, the most vulnerable situation is at initial address assignment time.

When a host asks to be assigned an address or claims it has an address in your address space, you can trust that host to varying extents. LAN-connected hosts inside your buildings generally are the most trusted. Hosts dialing into modem or ISDN server pools are less trusted, but usually can be trusted more than machines coming to you from the general Internet.

Basic dynamic address assignment is done with DHCP on LANs and with the IPCP subprotocol of PPP on-demand WANs. DHCP has no standard security features used to validate the request. PPP has PAP and CHAP available for security, but these are not required when IPCP is used, and CHAP and PAP are not fine-grained security measures.

If intruders were to gain access to your network, either because your dialup access was not secure or the intruder defeated the access authentication process, they could acquire a valid address from DHCP. With a valid address, address-based filtering does not restrict illegal access. It might be reasonable, if you have good authentication methods, to consider this an unlikely event. If it is a matter of concern, this is one more example of why no one security component can be a total solution. Keeping such intruders from penetrating application hosts relies on host-based, not network-based, security measures.

More complex authentication mechanisms such as TACACS, TACACS+, and RADIUS can be used to secure the process of dynamic IP address assignment. Again, these emphasize dialup access. Extensions to DHCP do include the idea of a digital signature to validate the user.

Note

Dynamic IP address assignment can be coupled with dynamic DNS update. Neither the base DHCP nor dynamic DNS update contain cryptographic authentication. You need to do a risk assessment to see whether you can reasonably run without authentication. If you need authentication, it must be explicitly available in the products you use.

Some vendors have worked around the DHCP-DNS security problem by requiring that both DHCP and DNS servers run on the same physical machine. All DHCP-DNS interaction is done by interprocess communication inside the machine. Although this restricts configuration flexibility, it does shield the DHCP-DNS interaction from potential attackers on the network.

Another, longer-term approach is to use digital signatures to authenticate the DHCP client request as well as the messages between the DHCP and DNS servers.

Secure Address Assignment

TACACS was introduced somewhat informally and documented and deployed by Cisco. RADIUS is newer and in the IETF Standards Track. TACACS+ is a set of proprietary extensions to TACACS, by which Cisco apparently tries to keep a qualitative edge over RADIUS. TACACS+ is a different protocol from TACACS. Each has advantages and disadvantages. TACACS+ may be more common in enterprises, whereas RADIUS is more common in ISPs.

In practice, RADIUS and TACACS define both the protocol used between access servers and RADIUS/TACACS authentication servers, and characteristics of the databases in the authentication servers.

Both TACACS and RADIUS servers can invoke other servers in satisfying a login request. A very common service type is one that validates a one-time user password (for example, S/Key) or encrypted user password (for example, Security Dynamics' ACE server for SecurID). TACACS and RADIUS also can act as a proxy DHCP client to obtain addresses for WAN-attached clients.

PPP, IPCP, CHAP, and PAP

PAP and CHAP are two authentication protocols used during the initialization of IP over PPP. PAP relies on a shared secret between the client and the network access server (NAS). In PAP authentication, this is sent in cleartext rather than ciphertext. CHAP is significantly more secure because the actual secret is never sent across the wire. The CHAP server, which might or might not be the RADIUS or TACACS server, sends a random challenge string to the remote client. The client encrypts the string and sends it, along with a CHAP ID and user name, back to the server. If the string is correctly decrypted using the expected key, the user is validated.

After the user is validated, either an address can be allocated with IPCP or the process can go to a second stage of more precise validation with RADIUS or DHCP. IPCP packets have a client address field into which the client either places an address it wants to use or the value `0.0.0.0` to indicate that it wants the dialup server to assign an address for this particular connection. Figure 7.8 shows this address acquisition.

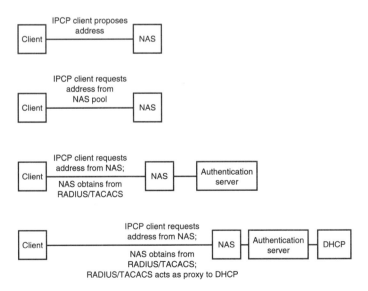

FIGURE 7.8. *IPCP address sources: Alternatives in obtaining an address for a PPP client.*

The server responds with a confirmation and either a dynamically assigned address or an acceptance of the proposed address. If the proposed address is not acceptable, the RAS (Remote Access Service) clears the connection attempt.

When second-stage authentication is done with RADIUS or TACACS, a validated username and password obtained from IPCP are passed to the authentication service. The authentication server can go through additional validation, using an encrypted or one-time password challenge and response.

RADIUS

Remote Authentication Dial In User Service (RADIUS) is "a protocol for carrying authentication, authorization, and configuration information between a Network Access Server which desires to authenticate its links and a shared Authentication Server" [RFC 2138]. Like DHCP, RADIUS is a client/server mechanism that can return configuration information to the user.

For our discussion, it is of particular importance that the configuration information returned can include an IP address to assign to the client. The RADIUS server can assign addresses from a pool of addresses it manages, or it can act as a proxy to a DHCP server.

RADIUS can send SLIP or PPP users such parameters as IP address, subnet mask, MTU, desired compression, and desired packet filter identifiers.

DHCP can send a wide range of options back to the address-requesting client. These options are somewhat LAN oriented.

PPP can set an address, but is limited in the number of additional options it can send back. RADIUS and similar mechanisms are able to provide a large number of more dial-oriented parameters.

TACACS and TACACS+

TACACS is an alternative authentication and credential service. Although not a formal Internet standard, it was widely available. Originally, it was developed by the U.S. Defense Department, but was only informally documented. Cisco deployed TACACS in its products and documented it on an informational basis in RFC 1492 by Cisco.

Cisco put significant extensions into the protocol and servers for TACACS and called this TACACS+. TACACS+ is integrated into Cisco network management products, although there are third-party servers for it as well.

Nevertheless, the IETF has chosen RADIUS as the standard terminal access control mechanism, and it is reasonable to assume the industry will focus on RADIUS for enhancements. Given Cisco's market position, TACACS+ is apt to remain strongly supported. Many network access servers support both RADIUS and TACACS+, and possibly other authentication protocols such as TACACS and Kerberos.

Controlling Access to Network Infrastructure

It's worth noting that the source IP address of management packets ranging from Telnet to SNMP to TFTP is often used as a means of validating access to network infrastructure. You should be aware that IP address validation only protects against rather casual attackers. The only serious protection involves cryptographic authentication with IPsec or link layer encryption, or the use of the new SNMPv3 protocol with its own authentication mechanism.

Split DNS

Some organizations provide added security with a split DNS, with a public DNS server in the DMZ containing only public server information, which is synchronized with a full DNS server inside the protected area and accessed through the bastion host and internal screening router (see Figure 7.9).

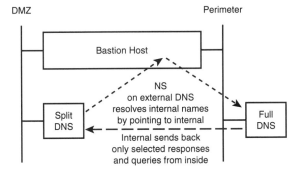

F IGURE 7.9. *Split DNS for an environment with private and public address space.*

The inside DNS responds to internal client queries with the actual address of the desired host if the host is internal, or with the address of the inside interface of the bastion host if the destination is external.

A mirror image takes place at the outside DNS, which returns the actual address of hosts on the DMZ or the outside bastion host address for all other machines [Cheswick 1994]. In practice, the outside DNS is usually manually configured, because it has a small number of definitions. Individual installations have written scripts to coordinate entries in the inside and outside DNS.

Secure Tunnels and Addressing

As you can see in Figure 7.10, there are multiple ways to establish tunnels. Layer 3 address translation, as part of a firewall, is generally incompatible with secure tunneling methods. You might determine that they are run through adequately protected facilities such that you trust them, or they might use bulk encryption at the data link layer. Layer 2 tunneling, at the cost of additional overhead, can be compatible with bastion hosts.

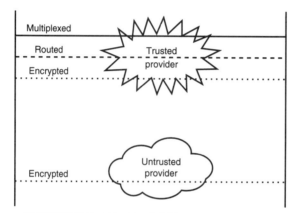

Multiplexed

Routed

Encrypted   Trusted provider

Encrypted   Untrusted provider

Mechanisms for carrying encrypted data
Layer 3.5/4: IPsec
Encapsulated Layer 2: L2TP
Layer 2: Method-specific

FIGURE 7.10. *Multiplexed tunnels run at the physical or data link layer. Routed tunnels are likely to need encryption using higher layer mechanisms such as IPsec.*

Bulk data link encryption, using a variety of methods, can run only on a single WAN link. It is simple to configure but fairly inflexible.

IPsec

An assortment of end-to-end security mechanisms has been developed under the general term *IPsec*. RFC 1825 describes these mechanisms in a general security architecture for IP. IPsec security mechanisms, originally developed for IPv6, have been adapted to be usable both with IPv6 and IPv4. These mechanisms run at Layer 3.5 in that they are connectionless and passed as option fields in IP packets, but are originated and primarily evaluated at endpoints.

Most cryptographic systems to date have aimed at producing confidentiality and, by extension, authentication. Some systems specifically are intended for authentication only. IPsec's designers consciously separated the authentication and confidentiality capabilities to help the techniques be available on a worldwide basis.

For a variety of reasons beyond the scope of this text, governments tend to be uncomfortable with cryptography in general. When pressed, they tend to accept the need for authentication.

IPsec is a set of protocols that sets up one-way *security associations* between trusted endpoints. Shown graphically in Figure 7.11, endpoint relationships can be:

- Host to host

- Host to security gateway

- Security gateway to security gateway

As shown in Figure 7.11, administration of key information is simplest when cryptographic information needs to be distributed to the least number of computers. This is the case when only the gateways contain keying information. If the gateways are not trusted by end users, cryptographic information needs to be distributed to the end hosts.

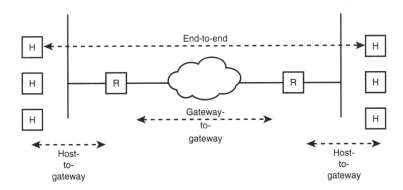

FIGURE 7.11. *The scope of trust in IPsec can be between end processes in hosts, between hosts, or between trusted gateways.*

IPsec assumes end-to-end significance of IP addresses. A real-world alternative might be using IPsec to implement trusted Virtual Private Networks (VPNs) between firewalls. In such a model, there is no longer true host-to-host trust. There is trust from host to security gateway, from security gateway to security gateway, and from security gateway to destination host.

If an organization truly wants to use only host-to-host trust, it cannot use private address space for its secure hosts [RFC 1825].

> **Note**
>
> Widespread use of host-to-host IPsec has enormous implications for the global address space. Host-to-host IPsec modes that do not trust an intermediate gateway/firewall cannot use private addresses that are then translated, on a many-to-one basis, between private and public addresses.
>
> This potential address demand might be alleviated in multi-organizational private networks that obtain registered address space that explicitly is not globally routable.

Security Associations in IPsec

Architecturally, IPsec works through one-way *security associations*, shown in Figure 7.12. Just as an interactive session needs at least two flows, one in each direction, to be described in the flow-oriented terms of Chapter 3, bidirectional security sessions need two security associations. Within the context of this book, security associations can be considered addressing constructs in the same way that flows are addressing constructs. Both flows and security associations define relationships among sets of entities with addresses. Both add information to a simple list of addresses, the order of the addresses in both cases, traffic and quality of service in flow specifications, and security rules in security associations.

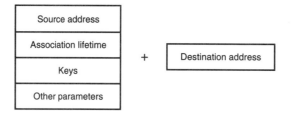

FIGURE 7.12. *Security associations are based on addresses, but they also add semantics to the simple endpoint address.*

Security associations are based on addresses, but add semantics to the simple endpoint address. Depending on the flow application, there might or might not be a visible flow identifier. IPsec security associations are explicitly identified with the combination of a destination address and a Security Parameter Index (SPI). Destination addresses can be unicast or multicast IP addresses.

Security associations, in a very broad interpretation, are address-like constructs. More specifically, they identify endpoints of associations. Security associations are defined with reference to specific receivers. Logically, this means a single unicast receiver normally selects the SPI value. SPI selection becomes somewhat more complex when dealing with multicast groups. Although there is a single multicast group address, some real system has to select the SPI and share the SPI value with other members of the same multicast group.

A SPI has certain required or recommended parameters in all cases. It always must contain certain parameters for authentication header (AH) and Encapsulating Security Payload (ESP) implementations. It can contain other parameters meaningful between the implementations. No matter whether AH, ESP, or both are in use, parameters always contained in the SPI include:

- Source address(es) of the security association. This could be a unicast address or a wildcard if more than one sender can use the same security association with the destination. Again, remember that the destination address can be a multicast or unicast address.

- Lifetime of the security association and of the key or the time at which a key change should take place.

- Sensitivity level (for example, secret or unclassified) of the protected data.

Additional parameters are specific to AH or ESP use. These include identification of the authentication or encryption algorithms in use, the key to be used, and information on cryptographic initialization conventions. They do not include additional addressing information.

If multiple senders send to multiple members of a multicast group, there is no authentication of the sender unless the senders use unique SPIs for each sender. Some applications require data origin authentication, whereas others do not. If data origin authentication is needed, unique SPIs must be set.

Authentication depends on the contents of the IPsec AH. The AH can appear in one of several ways:

- A header of an unencrypted IPv6 packet

- A header following an IP header

- Before the ESP header in a transport-mode ESP packet

- As a header inside the encrypted part of a tunnel-mode ESP packet

Confidentiality services require ESP, which contains a cleartext header that tells how to decrypt the encrypted body part of the ESP. If IPsec is operating in tunnel mode, the encrypted part contains addresses of the encapsulated packet. Tunnel mode is especially useful between security gateways, where a single tunnel can carry the traffic among multiple hosts. Tunnels can traverse the untrusted Internet—it is presumably trusted firewalls that create problems for tunnels, or vice versa. They can be used to create virtual private networks across the Internet.

Addressing Aspects of Tunnel Versus Transport Mode ESP

From the addressing aspect, there are two IPsec modes, shown in Figure 7.13. Tunnel mode creates an encrypted tunnel between two hosts. These hosts can be end hosts or security gateways. When the tunnel is between two gateways, it provides a proxy service for hosts in the trusted domain.

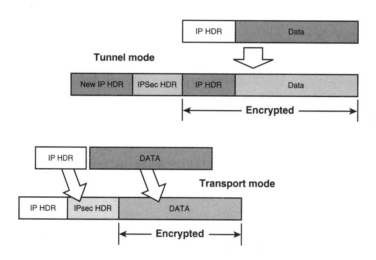

FIGURE 7.13. *Tunnel mode increases the size of each packet, but allows more flexible addressing than transport mode.*

Note

When tunnel mode is used between security gateways, it can conserve addresses if those security gateways also have a NAT function. Transport mode needs registered addresses to function across the Internet. Although transport mode does not conserve addresses, its advocates prefer the trust model that puts the sensitive parts of cryptography onto end hosts, rather than trusting gateways.

Cryptography is CPU intensive. The burden for a single host's traffic might not be great, but when a router needs to do the cryptographic processing for many hosts, that can impact router performance. Host-resident cryptographic processing reduces load on the router.

Widespread use of transport mode could very well reduce the trend of lessened registered address requirements for enterprise networks. This trend has arisen with widespread address translation on firewalls with NAT functionality. If the firewalls no longer can translate, the address space requirement jumps.

Growth in requirements for unique end host identifiers is likely to accelerate demand for IP version 6. As you will learn in Chapter 15, "Your Addressing Strategy: Integration for the Present and Planning for the Future," although IP version 6 addressing strategies have not yet been standardized beyond the basic 128-bit address size, it is likely that addresses will be dynamically assigned and will have a part that uniquely identifies the end host and a part that gives global information on how to route to that end host. It is the latter part that goes into global routing tables, so that using the larger IP version 6 address does not necessarily impose a significant load on global routing resources.

Tunnel mode ESP preserves the IP address of the originating host, as the source address in a packet that is completely enclosed in the encrypted field of an ESP data unit. The ESP is placed in another packet with its own IP header, and this header and its addresses are actually used to route the information end to end. No relationship needs to exist between the unencrypted carrier packet addresses and the addresses in the encapsulated packet inside the encrypted ESP.

There are applications in which it is desirable to conceal not only what is being said, but who is saying it. The technique of obtaining information from knowledge of traffic patterns is called *traffic analysis*. Military organizations tend to be quite concerned with traffic analysis, as it can be almost as important to know that the aircraft carrier *USS Nimitz* is transmitting from a location near you as it is to know the contents of its messages. Concern with traffic analysis is not limited to the military. Consider the value of knowing there is a sudden burst of traffic from an oil prospector to a home office, which might mean oil has been found—and perhaps an eavesdropper can file a claim before the prospector can do so. Sudden surges in financial information among banks or stock exchanges might be useful in predicting market trends.

Transport mode does not preserve the original host header. Instead, it inserts the ESP into the IP packet just before the IP data field. Appropriate headers are re-created at the receiver.

Layer 2 Tunneling

Simply because a user can access general Internet applications does not necessarily mean the user is generally present, from a routing standpoint, on the Internet [RFC 1775].

Other user access is opposite to this: enterprises can use the widespread ISP infrastructure to allow their users access to internal corporate resources, without making them generally available. Some of these resources can use AppleTalk, IPX, or other non-IP protocols. Enterprise resources can internally use non-registered private address space.

A standard Layer 2 secure tunneling protocol, L2TP, is being developed by the IETF, based on the earlier separate L2F proposal from Cisco and the PPTP proposal from Microsoft. Its model provides for access via an ISP, but the actual addresses at the endpoints of the tunnel are assigned dynamically from the home system's address space.

The protocol runs PPP over an IP access, so any upper-layer protocol that can run over PPP can run over L2TP. The intention is to make the PPP tunnel appear to the home site as would a direct dialup connection. User authentication is independent of the ISP, although authentication might be needed to create the initial dialup connection to the ISP.

An L2TP remote user connects to a network access server (NAS) at an ISP. The ISP can authenticate the remote user simply to find whether virtual dialup is needed. If L2TP is used, the user name indicated in CHAP or PAP is mapped to the home gateway distant endpoint. Using L2TP does not mean the POP cannot accept non-L2TP dialins. The login is passed either to L2TP or other access mechanisms depending on the user ID entered.

After the ISP POP identifies the traffic as L2TP to a given home gateway, an L2TP gateway to that home gateway is needed. Such a tunnel is created for the first user session. After a tunnel exists between the ISP and the home gateway, additional user connections can be multiplexed onto it. Each user is allocated an addressing construct called a multiplex ID (MID).

A user connection request is passed, identified by the MID, to the home gateway. The home gateway can either accept or reject the new session. The session request can contain CHAP or PAP information that lets the home gateway authenticate the access request. This request can also contain PPP LCP negotiation information.

If the connection is accepted, a mechanism now exists where arbitrary frames can be received at the ISP POP, stripped of any data link information needed to carry information from the remote user to the POP, encapsulated into the L2F protocol, and forwarded over the carrier mechanism to the home gateway. On receipt, the Home Gateway strips the L2F information and passes the de-encapsulated information to the appropriate protocol handler that normally would accept dialed calls.

Conventional PPP dialups allocate an IP address to the user from a pool in the ISP's address space. These addresses might not be compatible with the home enterprise's address space, either because they might be private IP addresses or non-IP addresses. Because L2TP gives the impression of a data link service, the home system remains unaware of ISP addressing. The client is assigned an IP address that belongs to the address space of the home gateway, not the ISP.

SNMP Network Management

SNMP version 1 architecture was fully standardized in 1990 [RFC 1157]. Version 2 was not widely deployed. Both were perceived to have serious limitations in security, especially in their incapability to provide cryptographic authentication for commands that change the state of the managed objects. Version 3, which was issued as an IETF Proposed Standard in 1998, corrects these deficiencies but is a new specification [RFC 2271]. This discussion focuses on the widely deployed Version 1.

SNMP finds things using IP addresses. Network management applications often map IP addresses to DNS names in their long term databases and reports, so a name associated with more than one IP address, at different times, creates problems. Associating a name with multiple addresses, however, is exactly what happens with DHCP dynamic addressing with lease times for the addresses. Even when addresses are assigned statically, SNMP databases can become inconsistent after static addresses are renumbered.

Network address translation can pose another problem for SNMP, because SNMP packets embed IP addresses in the data field. If the database consistently uses the inside IP address as the SNMP identifier, and the inside address remains stable, this might work. A special concern is that some network management software generates its license key based on an IP address on the management station. If no packets match the range of addresses associated with the management station, the software can refuse to run.

Some vendors, such as Bay, base their box management on SNMP. Others, like Cisco, have SNMP as an adjunct to their command language.

It's essential to understand the addressing relationships among the various SNMP components:

- Managers

  GET/SET clients

  TRAP servers

- Agents

  GET/SET servers

  TRAP clients

  Proxy agents

SNMP Managers

In SNMP version 1, there are two manager functions: the GET/SET client that sends GET/SET commands to managed objects, and the TRAP server that receives asynchronous TRAP messages from managed objects. The manager sends the GET/SET messages to port 161 on the managed object. The manager listens for TRAP messages on manager port 162.

Although the administrative model of SNMP version 1 contains only one manager entity, there is no specific requirement that the two functions be on the same IP address. More complex models exist in SNMP version 2 and version 3 (see Figure 7.14). Managed objects are explicitly configured with the address of a UDP 162 trap server.

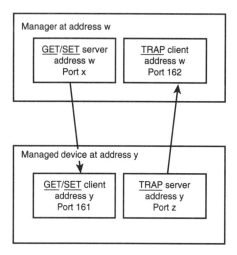

FIGURE 7.14. *Addressing relationships among managed devices and managers.*

In the SNMP version 1 protocol, the managed objects really don't care about the source address in GET/SET packets, as long as the SNMP password is correct. You can supplement this security with packet filters that check for valid source addresses. Packet filters, of course, do not cryptographically validate the source address.

Addressing Constructs in the MIB

There very well might be additional addressing-like constructs in the device identified by an IP address. Assume that the managed device is a router. From the pure architectural perspective described in RFC 1812, a router has no unique address of its own; it is only a collection of interfaces. Management commands should be able to be sent to any interface.

But in reality, at any moment, one or more real interfaces of the router might be down. A common practice is to define an internal address as the address of the "box" itself, rather than any of its operational interfaces. Such an interface is called a *loopback address* by Cisco or *a circuitless interface* by Bay. This address is reachable by any of the real interfaces of the router, as long as that internal address is advertised into the routing system.

Basic Interface Relationships

A given device has one or more interfaces. The MIB for an object contains the Interfaces Group. Key elements of this group are:

- ifNumber is the number of interfaces present on this host, regardless of their up/down state. There are ifNumber entries in the interfaces table of the system. This number can increase if, for example, additional interface boards are plugged into a router.

  The interfaces table contains more detailed information on each interface. Formally, it is a SEQUENCE of the IfEntry object type. An individual entry is addressed within the device MIB as IfEntry, indexed by some value ifIndex that is less than or equal to ifNumber.

- ifIndex is a unique value for each interface, in the range between 1 and IfNumber (see Figure 7.15). These values must remain stable after each initialization of the network management system. You might see the numbers increase, however, after reconfiguration operations such as inserting or removing interface cards.

- Another interface entry is ifPhysAddress, the transmission system address for the interface. Examples of such addresses include MAC addresses, Frame Relay DLCIs, and so on.

- ifSpecific references medium-specific additional MIB information, which might contain supplementary addressing.

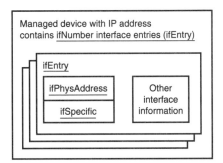

FIGURE 7.15. *A given monitored host has one or more interfaces.*

Evolution in MIB Interface Concepts

The original MIB has proved limited in the types of interfaces and interface relationships it can describe. Originally, there was assumed to be a one-to-one correspondence between physical interfaces and logical addresses.

But what if the physical interface is a single interface, over which ATM or Frame Relay runs, with each virtual circuit defined as a separate prefix? What if an IP address maps to a multilink PPP interface, with multiple physical interfaces assembled into a single data stream?

The most recent evolution of the Interfaces Group is in RFC 2233 and provides mechanisms to cope with other than one-to-one relationships between physical interfaces and logical addresses. The Interface Group is extended to deal with other problems that result from newer technologies, such as counters that overrun quickly on very high-speed media.

SNMP Agents: Regular and Proxy

Agent functions   are in the devices being managed by SNMP. The agent translates the abstraction of a MIB reference in the SNMP packet to the real equivalent software, hardware, or alternate reality in the managed device. Agents reply to manager commands and queries.

Most commonly, this is a function in the managed box, where MIB variables are mapped to local data structures. It is possible, however, to have the SNMP function in one device and the actual managed resource in another device linked by some local form of communications. An example of this sort of thing might be a rack mount of modems, where SNMP functions are in a common control card and the actual modem management commands flow over a bus.

In such a case, the control function is considered a *proxy agent*, and there is a mapping between MIB variables identified by IP addresses and the addresses of managed devices. The proxy may very well control non-local managed devices through proxy-specific communications channels, such as analog dialup and tone signaling.

To map SNMP to local functions, you need to be sure managed devices are configured properly with the information they need.

Remote Monitoring

Remote monitoring (RMON) operates at a lower level than SNMP and indeed is controlled by SNMP [RFC 1271]. Whereas prior SNMP MIB information tends to require a good deal of protocol knowledge by the agent, RMON is closer to traditional standards protocol analyzers such as the Network General (now Network Associates) Sniffer.

RMON Version 1

The original RMON specification defines nine groups of variables that can be monitored by RMON, and Figure 7.16 shows how some groups can be viewed as subgroups of others. Not all groups contain explicit MAC address information.

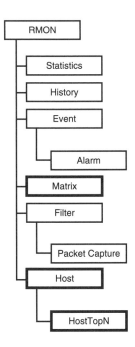

FIGURE 7.16. *The unshaded RMON groups contain MAC address information, either specific host addresses or source/destination pairs.*

RMON's groups are:

- The Statistics group contains statistics measured by the probe for each monitored interface on this device.

- The History group records periodic statistical samples from a network and stores them for later retrieval.

- The Event group controls the generation and notification of events from this device.

- The Alarm group periodically takes statistical samples from variables in the probe and compares them to previously configured thresholds. If the monitored variable crosses a threshold, an event is generated. A hysteresis mechanism is implemented to limit the generation of alarms, by setting a threshold trigger point. The alarm is generated by a value exceeding this point. Subsequent events above that level, as long as there are no intervening drops below it, do not generate additional alarms.

  This group consists of the `alarmTable` and depends on the Event group.

- The Host group contains statistics associated with each host discovered on the network. This group discovers hosts on the network by keeping a list of source and destination MAC addresses seen in good packets promiscuously received from the network.

  The hostTopN group, which depends on the Host group, is used to prepare reports that describe the hosts that top a list ordered by one of the statistics. The available statistics are samples of one of the base statistics over an interval specified by the management station. Thus, these statistics are rate based. The management station also selects how many such hosts are reported.

- The Matrix group stores statistics for conversations between pairs of MAC addresses. As the device detects a new conversation, it creates a new entry in its tables.

- The Filter group allows packets to be matched by a filter equation. These matched packets form a data stream that can be captured or can generate events.

  Requiring the Filter group, the packet capture group allows packets to be captured after they flow through a channel. This group requires the implementation of the Filter group.

RMON Version 2

The original RMON was much like early protocol analyzers. It monitored traffic based on MAC address, but did not know about higher layer entities. Certainly, routing-level diagnosis needs to track network layer entities. Performance monitoring and troubleshooting for the application level is also highly desirable, and there are far too many vendor-specific application protocols to rely on the IETF to produce MIBs for them.

RMONv1 emphasized Layer 2 addressing in recognizing and organizing the data it captured. It was not a general Layer 2 tool, however, in that it defined endpoints in terms of MAC addresses. RMONv2 extended its Layer 2 model to include WAN and generic Layer 2 protocol support.

RMONv2 extended the basic Layer 2 matrices to track information by Layer 3 address. It captures the same sort of information it does at Layer 2, such as packet error counts.

It also adds the capability to define application monitoring, which really means layers above the network layer. From the addressing standpoint, this offers the capability to monitor on transport port numbers or actual application layer fields.

All these extended recognition capabilities are done by extending the definition of filters in RMON. Filters essentially are recognition rules for fields and their values. RMONv2 allows these rules to be defined in terms of an offset from the start of a protocol header, with provisions for dealing with variable length headers.

Looking Ahead

There is a close association between security and network management. Each can impose requirements on network addressing. Although this is a book on addressing, please remember that IP addresses are, at best, extremely weak identifiers for the purpose of authentication. They can only be trusted thoroughly after cryptographic authentication.

PART III

Drawing the Addressing Architecture

CHAPTER 8

The Existing IP and Non-IP Address Structure: Preparing for Remodeling

Idealism is fine, but as it approaches reality the cost becomes prohibitive.

—William F. Buckley, Jr.

The metaphor of the melting pot is unfortunate and misleading.
A more accurate analogy would be the salad bowl, for, though the salad
is an entity, the lettuce can still be distinguished
from the chicory; the tomatoes from the cabbage.

—*Carl M. Degler*, Out of Our Past:
The Forces That Shaped Modern America

Stand ye in the ways, and see and ask for the old paths,
where is the good way, and walk therein.

—Jeremiah 6:16

Before the backbone can be designed, you need to know what is at the edges. You then need to consider how you will carry non-IP protocols, or poorly numbered IP traffic, across the backbone.

You might have an existing backbone, or perhaps you are first building one to link growing edge sites. Possibly, you might have multiple backbones for different protocol families, especially if you run IBM networking as well as IP.

Our emphasis in this chapter is on the legacy physical networks, as well as the current IP addressing structure.

Support costs are a major part of overall network cost, and legacy mechanisms tend to be among the most expensive to support. Principal among these support costs is that of network design and configuration control. Chapter 6, "Internet Failing: Details at 11," introduces the need for conscious addressing design and management, which will be detailed further in chapters on network management and configuration control.

Your Multiprotocol Environment

A basic assumption in this book is that backbones principally use IP routing, possibly supplemented with some direct Layer 2 connectivity with Frame Relay or ATM. Nevertheless, there are perfectly valid reasons to have other routed protocols in an enterprise backbone.

Most of the sections of this chapter provide guidance on addressing considerations in different protocol families. They will prepare you to take an inventory of your present environment. You'll find worksheets for that inventory at the end of the chapter. Some protocol families, such as AppleTalk, DEC's Local Area Transport (LAT), default NetBIOS networking on Microsoft systems, and older Novell systems, simply do not scale well to the wide area. IBM networking expects to control its own network resources, but it can be far more economical to have only one set of network resources over which all protocols run. These can be made to work on an IP backbone with various forms of tunneling. Application gateways might be a better choice.

When part of an enterprise network, the key problem in NetBIOS, Novell Internetwork Packet Exchange (IPX), and AppleTalk networking is to make sure that endpoints can find one another. In these protocol families, hosts and clients search for one another by name. The result of this search is an address. In most cases, these are not IP addresses, so you need to ensure that you implement ways to map these addresses to IP addresses and provide mechanisms for the non-IP protocols to reach the IP tunneling or other mechanism.

You need to decide whether you will use *ships in the night* (SIN) routing for your non-IP protocols or tunnel these in IP and rely on IP routing for path determination. In SIN routing, more than one protocol family's native routing protocols coexist in the same network, but do not interact with one another.

Good examples of pure routing protocols that might run separately are the protocols for IP and for DECnet Phase IV. There also are integrated routing protocols, such as IS-IS that handles IP, OSI, and DECnet Phase V. Cisco's EIGRP handles IP, AppleTalk, and Novell.

Another range of alternatives is to use Layer 2 connectivity for non-IP protocols, such as Frame Relay with RFC 1490 encapsulation or ATM with MPOA encapsulation, discussed in Chapter 4, "Transmission System Identifiers and Logical Address Mapping: A View from the Bottom."

LAN Protocol Multicast Resource Discovery

The major protocol families, called desktop, workgroup, or LAN protocols, historically have had much less of an idea of specialized name resolution services, such as DNS, than the IP protocol family. Their basic mechanisms have involved some type of broadcast or multicast among client and server endpoints. In some cases, routers are involved in this process of name resolution, but they mimic endpoints when doing so.

As the workgroups grow, and, more importantly, interconnect to other workgroups in a large enterprise, there have been distinct trends to add directory services to the protocol families. Directory functions can be either in native directory services or in migrating application protocols to an IP world where they can use DNS.

Static and Proxy Resource Location Services

Native, broadcast-based resource discovery protocols assume that the client and server interact directly. Routers can pass along information, but they are viewed more as passive conduits.

> **Note**
>
> In routing, a black hole is a destination that appears in routing tables, but, when traffic is sent to that destination, the traffic is discarded. Black holes can be configured deliberately. Although a detailed discussion of the use of black holes in routing is beyond the scope of this book, intelligent use of them can increase network stability.
>
> The principle here is that certain packets cannot be delivered and sending them causes a destination unreachable message to be generated for every one of these packets. Given that this message is generated by some router—a distant one if routing information about unreachability is not propagated and a local router if such information is propagated—there is a design tradeoff between the overhead of tracking detailed reachability information and the overhead of passing some traffic that could be discarded earlier if some unreachability information were known.
>
> In large networks, it is usually better to avoid the detailed tracking overhead, which avoids the need for constant recomputation of routing tables.

Because the broadcast-based mechanisms tend to produce a lot of overhead, various strategies for reducing overhead have been developed. These tend to be alternatives to lower-overhead directory services, but have the advantage that they can be implemented in routers without disturbing a large number of hosts. The following are some of these strategies:

- Filtering, to prevent queries or announcements from going where there will be no response or other interest.

- Static definition, where a local router has a fixed definition of the location of the endpoint and will respond as if it were the endpoint. The router does not know if the endpoint is actually reachable and becomes a black hole if the endpoint is not reachable. Such definition can require significant configuration setup and maintenance.

- Proxy resource resolution, where the router pays attention to the content of broadcast or multicast requests and saves the response. When subsequent queries are made, the proxy server answers them from a local cache. Again, the proxy might not have the most recent information, so black holing is a possibility. A compromise is to put a lifetime on each cache entry and periodically resolve the cached resource entry when this timer expires.

How helpful filtering can be to you depends on the structure of your communities of interest. If there are many communities of interest, and services that are only used within the community, filtering can be extremely helpful. If you have large numbers of servers that need to be seen everywhere, you cannot filter out their existence. In such cases, you want to look at more efficient resource location protocols or static/proxy mechanisms.

Black hole behavior by static or proxy responders might not be as important an operational problem as it first seems. Think about the operational realities. If a user cannot reach a resource, he calls the help desk to complain. The user behaves in the same way if the resource is actually down, if the service mechanism is pointing at it incorrectly (for example, it has moved and static definitions have not been updated), or if a proxy points at a correct location but connectivity to that location has been lost.

To diagnose a user report of this sort, the normal procedure is to test connectivity to the user. If the user is unreachable, then there is a network problem that needs to be fixed. If the server is unreachable, again there is a network problem. If the server is reachable but the service is down, a host problem needs to be solved. Independent network management tools might already have been monitoring the server, and the help desk might already know about the problem.

So, if a proxy or static definition causes user traffic to be black holed rather than getting an immediate unreachable message on the workstation, does that really slow the process of troubleshooting? If it does not, then proxy or static definition are valuable operational tools.

Legacy IP

Your existing address space, shown schematically in Figure 8.1, consists of:

- Registered address space

- Private address space

- Possibly bogus address space not assigned to you

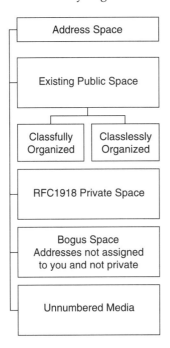

FIGURE 8.1.   *Using this structure, you can get a high-level view of your existing addresses.*

Figure 8.1 illustrates the address space present in your existing environment, focusing on media rather than individual hosts. You use this structure to present the results of your inventory of existing resources.

The inventory might be manual, using procedures and worksheets in the "Taking Inventory of Your Environment" section of this chapter. If you have network management software, it might have an autodiscovery mode in which it detects and records the active addresses in your network.

> **Note**
>
> Be careful in using autodiscovery. It's best not to leave it on, but to turn it on for specific inventory projects. Autodiscovery can generate a substantial amount of traffic.
>
> Autodiscovery can have especially nasty consequences when your network includes autodialed links. I had a client who installed autodiscovery in their network, and didn't check carefully that it only ran on dedicated media. The client configured the autodiscovery program to run every five minutes, just before a long weekend.
>
> When the operations staff came back after the holiday, they discovered the autodiscovery program had placed a call from the U.S. to Japan, every five minutes. These calls simply confirmed the other end could answer its phone. The resulting telephone bill was impressive.

You will want to look for potential problem areas. These include:

- Use of bogus addresses (that is, things outside the private address space that have not been allocated to your organization)

- Private address space that might need external visibility

- Classful address usage that can cause discontiguous networks

- Classful address space that wastes significant address space

- Unnumbered interfaces that might be hard to manage

- Duplicate addresses

In Chapter 9, "The Address Plan," you will come up with a plan to minimize the effect of these problem areas, generally through renumbering.

Microsoft Networking

Newer Microsoft systems default to IP—rather than less scalable alternatives—as their networking protocol. The characteristics of NetBIOS upper layer protocols, however, permeate Microsoft networking, even as there is movement to IP- and DNS-based architecture.

> **Note**
>
> Fully scalable Microsoft networks use IP as their network protocol. The challenge in implementing IP-based solutions is not to lose the NetBIOS resource location methods critical to most applications written for Windows, and at the same time to gain the use of scalable, IP-oriented applications.
>
> Older Microsoft networks have NetBIOS name services that run directly over the data link layer, or over Novell IPX. If the backbone is IP, you need to think through how to handle these with tunneling. Yet another alternative is to minimize carrying the NetBIOS overhead through the backbone, using local definition and proxies instead. The latter alternative is labor intensive unless considerable effort is spent on developing installation-specific scripting. This effort probably would be better expended on IP migration.

At the OSI application layer, Microsoft's major protocol is *Server Message Block* (SMB). SMB, in turn, uses the NetBIOS programming interface, which essentially provides an OSI session layer service. NetBIOS runs over a variety of lower layer stacks, a nonroutable one called NetBIOS Frame Format or NetBEUI, Novell IPX, or TCP/IP. Many Windows applications, however, do not go through SMB, but directly use NetBIOS.

> **Note**
>
> *NetBIOS was designed in 1984 and was intended for small LANs of perhaps as many as 250 hosts and as few as 30. Unfortunately, many PC-based applications have grown in popularity, but their networking support has not grown apace.*

NetBIOS is relatively independent of the underlying stack, although it is broadcast intensive and tends to have major scaling problems. Given the model of a single broadcast domain, it isn't terribly meaningful to have identifiers for specific media. There is no equivalent to the IP convention of representing the medium itself with a prefix with a zero host field.

As shown in Figure 8.2, NetBIOS can be mapped to a variety of networking protocols. The default, non-routable stack has been NetBIOS Frame Format (NBF). It's common industry practice to call NBF NetBIOS and to treat NetBIOS communications as non-routable. The stack of NetBIOS over NBF is termed NetBEUI, but this term is used far less than NetBIOS.

Both Microsoft and Novell support NetBIOS over the Novell IPX network layer protocol. The Novell aspects will be discussed in their own section, later in this chapter. Microsoft's protocol stack for running NetBIOS over IPX is called NWLink. The dotted line in Figure 8.2, inside the NetBIOS block, indicates both Novell and Microsoft support NetBIOS over IPX. NWLink still floods broadcasts as does NBF. It encapsulates these broadcasts in IPX Type 20 packets.

Figure 8.2 shows the overlapping protocol environments of Microsoft and Novell operating systems. The lowest level is the hardware driver: Open Datalink Interface (ODI) for Novell and Network Device Interface Specification (NDIS) for Microsoft. Microsoft-supported protocols are drawn above NDIS.

The NBF format in the stack is not routable, but needs to be bridged. The asterisk on NBF reminds us that a nonroutable protocol still can be carried through tunnels in an IP network.

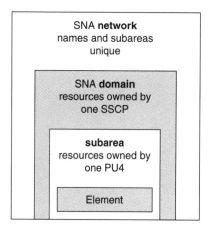

FIGURE 8.2. *Microsoft and Novell proprietary stacks are converging. Both protocol families are moving to native IP as their network layer protocol, but non-IP protocols will be around for years.*

Note

The broadcast model is intuitive and simple to set up, but simply doesn't scale well from a performance standpoint; and it often presents security concerns in an enterprise network. The key to getting NetBIOS under control is to impose an application hierarchy. Think about which hosts actually need to see which servers.

There are a great many bridged NetBIOS systems in operation. NetBIOS bridged frames can be carried in IP-based virtual bridging systems, or using data link switching. Bridged systems are broadcast intensive, although router operating systems can reduce this load with various filtering and proxy mechanisms. Migrating the NetBIOS upper layer to an IP stack doesn't just improve the connectivity, but also adds functions for reducing broadcasts.

Using RFC 1001/RFC 1002 procedures, NetBIOS can be encapsulated over TCP/IP. Microsoft calls this *NetBIOS over TCP* (NBT). Such encapsulation is not ideal from a performance standpoint compared with native TCP/IP stacks, but has significant compatibility advantages for NetBIOS applications not written for the TCP interface. *Winsock* is a native Microsoft interface to TCP. Microsoft and Novell are evolving to systems that use native IP as the network layer.

Resource Location

NetBIOS names are unstructured strings up to 16 characters long, although Microsoft's implementation limits them to 15. They can map to an individual (that is, unicast) or group address. In the original NetBIOS implementation, broadcasts resolved these names to MAC addresses. The newer methods resolve them to IPX or IP addresses.

Microsoft's restriction on name length is due to use of the last byte as a resource identifier. This is much like a port number for TCP or UDP.

It might be a good idea to introduce hierarchical naming conventions, but this is not implicit in the protocol specification. Figure 8.3 shows an example of NetBIOS name filtering with filters to control the propagation of broadcasts. Such filters would be implemented on routers and would prevent requests from propagating into areas where it is known they never would be responded to.

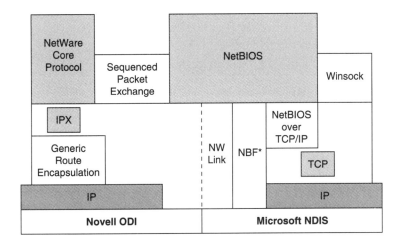

FIGURE 8.3. *Hierarchical NetBIOS naming and filtering.*

Microsoft has a wide range of capabilities for mapping NetBIOS names to either MAC or IP addresses. The first implementations used either preconfigured static definitions or broadcast to find the destination or, as a slight improvement, a main browser.

The original NetBIOS service location method, beyond pure any-to-any broadcasting, is the *LAN services browser*. A broadcast-based method, this method elects one machine in a broadcast domain to maintain a list of all services available in that broadcast domain. It offers the advantage of not requiring explicit host address tables to be managed.

The next method is LMHOSTS name resolution. LMHOSTS is a flat file associating NetBIOS names with IP addresses. It is available on non-NT systems. In its most basic form, each host has a full file of IP addresses of other hosts it needs to reach. It has the advantage of not being broadcast based, but requires substantial manual management whenever a host address changes.

Windows Internet Name Server (WINS) was added in Windows 3.5. This permits a NetBIOS name to be resolved to an IP address, by appending a DNS domain name to a NetBIOS name and resolving the resulting fully qualified domain name (FQDN) through DNS. WINS acts as a DNS client.

To understand which of the many methods a given Windows machine uses for name resolution, you need to know its node type:

- *H-node* is the default for most modern software. It looks for a NetBIOS name server and goes into P-node if it finds one. If it cannot find one, it uses B-node. It continues to poll for a nameserver and switches back to P-node when one becomes available.

- *B-nodes* use broadcasts for name registration and resolution.

- *P-nodes* use a NetBIOS name server for name registration and resolution.

- *M-nodes* use broadcasts for name registration; they try to resolve names first with broadcasts and only try the name server if there is no response. If there are no broadcast responses, the node switches to P-node status.

- *Microsoft-enhanced nodes* use Local `LMHOSTS` file or WINS proxies plus Windows Sockets `gethostbyname()` calls. `gethostbyname()` tries local `hosts` files and UDP/IP name requests, in addition to the usual NetBIOS types of name resolution.

Microsoft has been evolving its networking support to be IP-, and thus DNS-, based.

For WINS to work, the NetBIOS name and the host part of the DNS name are the same. DNS then can map names to addresses. Microsoft supports this with the Enable Windows for DNS Name Resolution option in NBT configuration.

One reason to use WINS rather than DNS name resolution is that WINS is dynamically linked to DHCP. We will discuss the ramifications of the decision to use WINS in Chapters 10, "Addressing and Name Services," 11, "Addressing in End Hosts," and 15, "Your Addressing Strategy: Integration for the Present and Planning for the Future."

Windows NT 4.0 extended name resolution to full DNS support. NetBIOS resources can be accessed by an IP address or a DNS name that contains the NetBIOS shared resource name.

Management and Name Resolution

In a Microsoft environment, each host can be part of a *Windows workgroup*, which is a not terribly scalable arbitrary collection of hosts. With workgroup support alone, you are generally limited to broadcasts for name resolution.

Windows domains establish servers that can do name resolution and, to a certain extent, impose hierarchy on Windows naming. A domain is a defined set of NT servers, of which one or more machines are domain controllers.

Trust relationships exist among Windows domains. In a small network, this can be reduced to the simplicity of having only one domain. A somewhat more complex trust relationship is to have a global domain, in which each domain trusts every other domain. A configuration error in one domain can affect other domains in a global environment.

More controllable, but more maintenance-intensive, structures include a master domain, which is trusted by subordinate domains but does not trust any subordinates. This can be extended to a multiple master domain structure in which the master domains trust one another and the subordinates of each master trust it.

A more scalable approach uses the Windows domain structure. Each client in a broadcast domain has a pointer to the primary domain controller (PDC). The PDC, in turn, has the master host table of all hosts in its domain and also the PDC IP addresses for all other domains. Clients know the PDC address either from locally configured information in LMHOSTS or from a DHCP response that includes a WINS address.

Remote Access

The Windows *Remote Access Server* (RAS) provides PPP and PPTP access to Microsoft environments for both servers and clients. Although it supports clients connected by SLIP, Microsoft does not recommend using SLIP because SLIP lacks security features.

RAS acts as a NetBIOS gateway and can provide remote access to NetBIOS resources accessed using NetBEUI/NBF, IP, or IPX. Essentially, it is a special-purpose router. RAS servers receive ARP requests from serially connected clients, establish host routes (that is, /32 prefixes) to them, and act as ARP proxies. They also can act as DHCP proxies, accessing a LAN-attached DHCP server, then setting client parameters using IPCP.

When clients connect to the RAS, the IP route tables in the clients are modified to prefer the PPP server over an existing default gateway on a LAN. In other words, local routes are made less preferable than remote ones, unless there are explicitly defined static routes to local resources.

IBM Networking

In this section, we'll consider the following IBM protocols:

- IBM protocols that preceded Systems Network Architecture (SNA) protocols, primarily binary synchronous communications (BSC) but possibly including special-purpose applications such as travel agent/airline reservations

- SNA

- NetBIOS (see also the discussion in the "Microsoft Networking" section)

- Data link switching:

  Legacy (DLSw) [RFC 1434]

  Data link switching (DLSw+) [RFC 2114, RFC 1795]

- Advanced Peer-to-Peer Networking (APPN), the IBM next generation after SNA

Historically, IBM protocols have not been generally routable by non-IBM devices. SNA does have hierarchical network layer addresses that could be routed, but BSC has no concept of a logical address. In practice, BSC and much SNA needs to be tunneled. APPN does include IP-like routing.

Note

Classical IBM networking assumes dedicated transmission media, or controlled dialup. It definitely does not have the concept of adaptive, network-centric routing. Your challenge is to provide a backbone over which IBM edge protocols are carried transparently. You can minimize some of the overhead with static or proxy definition of resources and by locally terminating the IBM data link acknowledgments and relying on TCP for retransmission.

IBM addressing is significant to capture in that the devices you use at the edges must be aware of host naming and addressing.

Binary Synchronous Communications

BSC is an old protocol family, but is still found in certain niche applications. These applications generally have followed the First Law of Plumbing: "If it doesn't leak, don't fix it." One of the most common of such niches is automatic teller machines (ATM, but not the high-speed sort) in North America. BSC also appears on old remote batch equipment. Both X.25 and BSC are used with point-of-sale devices such as credit authorization terminals and intelligent cash registers.

By the time such machines became common in Europe, IBM's SDLC protocol, part of SNA, was available. IBM's Synchronous Data Link Control (SDLC) Layer 2 protocol was introduced in 1974. European banking networks were implemented with SDLC, but there was no pressure to convert operational North American networks to SDLC. In fact, there is and was a distinct lack of desire to change mission-critical banking networks that worked adequately for their purpose. Widespread use of BSC in banking networks drove internetworking vendors to continue to add BSC support to new products. North American teller machines commonly shared a relatively low-speed, multidrop analog line over which the BSC protocol ran. There has been a recent trend to replace such low-speed functions with X.25 packets sent over ISDN Basic Rate Interfaces that only implement the D-channel. 0B+D channels are less expensive than the usual 2B+D that provides two 64 KBps channels.

Systems Network Architecture

SNA has logical addresses, but until fairly recently, the practice in carrying them through a backbone involved tunneling their Layer 2 addresses. Synchronous Data Link Control (SDLC) addresses are 1 byte long, and Logical Link Control, Type 2 (LLC2) on Token Ring uses standard 48-bit MAC addresses.

SNA, obviously, is well established in large enterprise networks. It is a strongly hierarchical architecture, with major components shown in Figure 8.4.

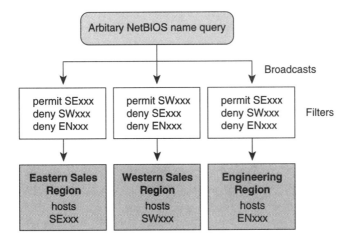

FIGURE 8.4.   *IBM scopes of control and address components.*

At the highest level is the *SNA network*. In most architectures, network refers to a destination to which you can route. In SNA, this term means something totally different: an administrative scope in which names and addresses must be unique. An SNA feature called *SNA Network Interconnection (SNI)* links separately administered SNA networks; it is a combination of NAT and name translator.

Below the level of the SNA network is the SNA domain. In SNA, a domain is the set of resources owned by a System Services Control Point (SSCP). An SSCP is an architectural concept, implemented in software as the Virtual Telecommunications Access Method (VTAM) that runs on mainframes. SSCP functionality is built in to the IBM AS/400 operating system.

At the next hierarchical level below the SSCP are SNA *subareas*. What happened to the area? No one knows. SNA doesn't define them. Subareas are the basic elements of SNA routing, very roughly equivalent to destination prefixes. In software, they are the set of communications resources under the direct control of a 37x5 series processor running the Network Control Program, or the local communications resources controlled by a mainframe or an AS/400.

SNA logical addresses are two-part addresses split between subarea and element numbers [Ranade, 1995]. A subarea can be considered the set of resources under the control of one instance of the NCP running in a 37x5 communications controller. There are three formats of the element address, which is subordinate to a subarea:

- *16-bit network addressing*. The number of bits assigned to subarea and element is specific to an SNA network, but is configured for that network. System programmers can configure more areas containing lesser number of elements, or fewer areas with more elements.

- *23-bit extended network addressing*. This had a constant 7-bit subarea field and 15-bit element field.

- *31-bit extended network addressing*, requiring Virtual Telecommunications Access Method (VTAM) 3.2 on the host and NCP 4.3.1/5.2.1 on communications processors. This has a fixed 16-bit subarea field and 15-bit element field.

Data link switching (DLSw) and Advanced Peer-to-Peer Networking (APPN) actually work with the SNA addresses. DLSw assumes it will run over a routed IP network, whereas APPN has its own native routing.

A variant of tunneling is *protocol translation*. As Cisco uses the term, there is a frame-level interface at both ends of the tunnel, but the content of the frame is delivered in a data link protocol different from the one in which it originated. This is particularly common when carrying IBM protocols over an IP carrier system. The most common such conversion is between SDLC used on WAN media and LLC2 on LAN media. LLC2 is most often found on Token Ring LANs, but can appear on any medium type.

Strategies for Handling SNA

In working with IBM SNA networks, the most important thing to realize is that these networks do certain things very well, if not necessarily in the least expensive way. Like any internetwork, the IBM environment needs to meet the expectations of its users.

Expectations tend to be quite formalized in the mainframe culture and usually are in a written service level agreement (SLA). SLAs include requirements for interactive application response time, overall availability, and so on.

IBM system software is heavily instrumented to be able to monitor compliance with SLAs. It also gives excellent workload data and allows planning staff to predict, well in advance, when they will need new resources to continue meeting the SLA. It would be very nice if we had such hard information in the IP world!

Unfortunately, the nature of the IP world is such that SLAs are much more difficult. SNA networks typically are optimized for a limited set of well-defined strategic business applications. They can make the best environment for a well-understood application. Internet systems, however, tend to emphasize flexibility over pure performance. Their underlying flexibility might help the availability of SNA services implemented over router-based IP networks.

Native IBM SNA has a short timeout, after which SNA sessions fail. This is actually reasonable given the original SNA design, in which all routes are established by the mainframe at session connection time. Even if alternate paths exist, the session must fail and a new end-to-end route must be established for the alternate paths to be used.

In the real world, tradeoffs need to be made between user-perceived availability and cost of fault tolerance. Router-based networks can have higher availability than traditional SNA networks, because they can reroute around failed paths without losing the SNA session. Traditional SNA networks, as opposed to APPN networks, cannot do this.

Hosts connected over a router-based internetwork, however, drop sessions if the routing convergence time is longer than the SNA session timeout value, unless special measures are taken to spoof timeouts. Session failure means the users have to log in again and will lose data of the transaction in progress. The impact of such losses has to be weighed against the cost of preventing them.

Before we discuss the internals of the network for carrying SNA traffic, you need to understand the alternatives in preparing SNA upper layer traffic for carriage over the underlying router network. Only after this is done does it make sense to talk about the characteristics of routing networks for carrying IBM traffic, possibly along with traffic of other protocol families. Always remember these two key functions: preparation for carrying traffic and the actual carriage of traffic over the general-purpose router internetwork.

Preparing for Transit

Assuming a centralized mainframe environment, the best way to think about preparing for transit is as the nature of the IBM device interface at the remote and central site ends. The most common IBM interfaces are SDLC and Token Ring.

IBM networking began with serial line connectivity; Token Ring came later. IP router-based means of carrying SNA over a routed network generally look like these media to IBM hosts.

When you use routers to carry IBM traffic over an IP-based network, the problem you are trying to solve is to carry the end-to-end SNA units. The first architectural choice is whether or not you will preserve the frames on an end-to-end basis. DLSw does not preserve frames, but preserves end-to-end data units. Serial Line Tunneling (STUN) and Remote Source Route Bridging (RSRB) do preserve frames.

There are three main ways you can handle SNA traffic:

- Set up connectivity for Layer 2 information, which uses the same physical interface type at both ends.

- Use SDLC at one end and Token Ring at the other. Cisco calls Layer 2 connectivity that uses the same interface type *protocol tunneling*, but calls connectivity with different Layer 2 types *protocol translation*. Don't confuse IBM-oriented protocol translation with the Cisco Protocol Translator software product, which translates among application-level terminal protocols.

- Use DLSw. Originally, DLSw was a proprietary IBM mechanism documented in RFC 1434. In its current multivendor form, defined in RFC 1795, DLSw+ carries end-to-end SNA information, but does not preserve Layer 2 information. DLSw+ cooperates with the end data link mechanisms, but terminates the Layer 2 protocol, extracting higher-level protocol information and encapsulating it in TCP/IP for transmission. At the distant end, the SNA information is extracted from TCP and inserted into the appropriate data link protocol. IBM software at both ends is unaware of DLSw+. Bay and IBM implemented both basic DLSw [RFC 1434] and DLSw version 2 [RFC 1795].

Traditional SNA/SDLC

Respecting the oldest form of SNA networking, let's return to the pure SDLC case. When SDLC devices are at both ends, the appropriate Cisco feature to interconnect them is Serial Tunneling (STUN). Bay emphasizes DLSw and APPN for carrying SDLC traffic.

If the front-end processor (FEP) interfaces are owned rather than leased, SDLC interfacing can be a cost-effective method. The key decisions to make in managing SDLC deal with handling acknowledgments and polls. In general, local acknowledgment is most beneficial with relatively slow lines—64 KB and less.

A special case of STUN deals with connectivity between NCPs: multilink transmission groups. Although Format Identifier 4 (FID4) transmission groups use SDLC, they are tuned differently than Format Identifier 2 (FID2) SDLC links serving end devices. FID4 has an adaptive windowing protocol that tunes itself quite nicely without assistance from local acknowledgment. Multilink SDLC transmission groups should be avoided unless they are the only way to get adequate bandwidth or a means of fault tolerance.

Token Ring

IBM 37x5 front-end processors and associated software historically have been priced by their interface count. The more interfaces, the more expensive the FEP is in operational cost.

Because Token Ring interfaces are faster than SDLC interfaces, more devices can connect through a Token Ring interface. In general, replacing SDLC with Token Ring interfaces reduces the cost of operation. This might change with IBM pricing policies.

Now, let's consider Token Ring devices using the LLC2 data link protocol. Things stay relatively simple if both the central and remote ends are native Token Ring devices. You would configure RSRB at both ends. RSRB itself, however, is less scalable but upwardly compatible with DLSw+.

The Cisco IOS feature that lets remote SDLC devices connect to Token Ring ports on an FEP is SDLLC. SDLLC is not itself an abbreviation, but a name produced by overlaying the abbreviation SDLC over the abbreviation LLC. The chief reason to use it is that you can minimize the number of physical interfaces on an FEP by using Token Ring, and IBM software and hardware costs depend on the number of physical interfaces. Token Ring interfaces are the fastest on a 3745. Although much faster than SDLC links, they still can be a bottleneck because their 16 MBps rate is much less than the rate of the IBM channel.

Reverse SDLLC preserves the investment in owned SDLC ports on FEPs when the newer remote devices use LLC2.

Just as SDLC devices are concerned with timeouts and delay, so are LLC2 devices. Do not assume that SDLC and LLC2 local acknowledgment timer values are identical. LLC2 assumes that it is running over a LAN and can constrain the timer ranges more tightly. It is not implausible that the default timers for end-to-end acknowledgment could cause timeouts for LLC2 but not SDLC. With IBM default values, LLC2 times out after 14 seconds.

The original IBM LLC2 devices were PCs. Token Ring LANs were introduced not for mainframe use, but for IBM PC connectivity. In the IBM PC LAN system, connectivity between clients and servers did not involve a mainframe. IBM's model for extending Token Ring over wide area networks is based on bridging. In the classical IBM model of bridging over WAN media, half bridges are linked by a SDLC connection.

Token Ring support was added to mainframe systems in a manner that required the least change to VTAM and NCP. Specifically, stations on LANs were modeled as stations on dialup links (that is, VTAM switched major nodes). This is the history behind seemingly bizarre IBM configuration parameters that describe dialing to LANs. You can't use the hexadecimal digits A–F in traditional IBM MAC addresses, because these digits are not valid in telephone numbers!

PC Connectivity

If the network grows, remote devices remain true PCs, and there might be scaling difficulties. Many of these stem from the original Token Ring support on mainframes, which views PCs as SNA physical units. There is a basic 256 physical unit limit on the IBM channel to which FEPs attach.

Several methods exist for reducing the number of IBM device addresses seen by the mainframe. In general, they map the PCs as logical units onto a physical unit that is seen by the mainframe, avoiding the physical unit count limit. Care needs to be taken with preserving manageability of the PCs, because traditional IBM network management applications such as NetView track physical units, not logical units. In most gateway products, the logical unit mapping/ concentration function appears as a MIB, and the PCs are visible to SNMP-based managers.

Token Ring devices have MAC addresses, which typically are locally administered rather than burned in. Addressing conventions that indicate a given MAC address is locally administered are in the "IEEE 802 MAC Addressing" section of Chapter 4. These MAC addresses are identified as dial numbers in IBM software definitions, because the software reuses dialup code to deal with LAN stations. Some IBM fault-tolerance schemes deliberately use duplicate MAC addresses, only one of which is active at a time. Although this can be a valid approach, it might be incompatible with router-based MAC address caching schemes and Token Ring LAN switches.

Frame Relay to the Mainframe

Yet another way to connect to the mainframe is to use Frame Relay directly into a FEP. In other words, with this technique, there are routers at the remote sites but not at the data center. This is called RFC 1490 encapsulation, although there are IBM extensions to that RFC. Again, it is an appropriate technology for certain niches. Multiple router vendors support it. The ideal situation for using 1490-style encapsulation is replacement of an existing IBM private line network connecting a data center that has no non-IBM protocol applications. At this data center, there would already be a high-performance FEP running NCP 7.1 or later or other reasons why such a FEP is justified.

If there isn't good reason to upgrade the FEP, it might be more cost-effective to use Frame Relay as the means of connectivity between a data center router and remote site routers and then connect the router to the mainframe using Token Ring on a 37x5 or a direct channel interface. Token ring attachment is available from most router vendors.

Novell IPX Networking

Novell IPX is a connectionless network protocol used in Novell NetWare environments. It is a derivative of the generally obsolete Xerox Network Services protocol family and is optimized for workgroups. Novell is migrating its higher-level protocols to run natively over IP. NetWare 5.0 will be native IP, as opposed to the current NetWare IP that encapsulates IPX packets in IP. The latter encapsulation, illustrated in Figure 8.2 with the overlap of IPX over IP, is distinct from general tunneling mechanisms such as GRE.

At present, Novell offers an IP stack for its upper layer protocols. This stack encapsulates IPX within IP packets.

> **Note**
>
> *Like Microsoft networking, the challenge in working with Novell networking is managing the overhead of resource locations optimized for broadcast LANs. Novell is migrating away from the IPX environment; NetWare 5 is natively based on IP.*

Layer 2 Addressing Issues in Novell Networks

A LAN complexity seen in the real world involves various versions and configurations of Novell NetWare. This protocol suite can use four different types of framing on Ethernet-style LANs. The different frame types were the defaults defined for products developed for different versions of NetWare:

- Ethernet Phase II

- 802.3 MAC frame with no LLC ("raw" 802.3)

- 802.3/802.2 LLC-1 with SNAP Ethernet compatibility, preserving the Ethernet type codes in the SNAP field

- 802.3/802.2 with standard LLC use

Although native Novell relay servers support these different types, the different types might confuse other products.

On FDDI and Token Ring LANs, there are fewer choices, but a choice still needs to be made between basic LLC and SNAP encapsulation. The different encapsulations potentially can coexist on a common physical medium. It is assumed that an individual Novell server will not have more than one physical interface on the same LAN. Routers, in this context, are a special case of server. The same MAC address is copied to all interfaces of the server, and the network address is generated by prefixing a network number to the software-defined MAC address.

> **Note**
>
> *Split horizon is a technique used with some older routing protocols. It is a means of loop prevention and essentially is a rule that says, "If you first learn about a destination from information received on one interface, never send information about the destination out the interface on which you first learned about it." This creates a problem with NBMA networks, such as Frame Relay with two virtual circuits defined on the same physical router interface.*
>
> *Assume a core router with virtual circuit 1 goes to destination A and virtual circuit 2 goes to destination B. There is no direct connection between destinations A and B. To get from A to B, traffic must be relayed through the router. There are routers at sites A and B, which rely on the core router to tell them about other reachable destinations.*
>
> *Assume the router learns about destination A on virtual circuit 1. By the split horizon rule, you would not send a routing announcement out the same interface, so you would be prevented from announcing destination A to the router at site B and, vice versa, for destination B being announced to site A.*

> *With older IP protocols such as RIP and IGRP, one solution is to disable split horizon on the physical inter-face. Native Novell and Apple routing do not know how to disable split horizon.*
>
> *As a consequence, neither Novell nor Apple work properly with NBMA networks. The usual solution, dis-cussed in Chapter 13, "Addressing in Routers," is to define routing in terms of virtual rather than physical interfaces. Each virtual circuit is assigned to a separate subinterface.*

On dial or dedicated point-to-point media, it is most appropriate to run IPX over PPP. This requires a unique host name at each end, from which addresses are negotiated.

IPX/Novell Network Addressing

IPX addresses have two basic parts: a 32-bit network number and a 48-bit node number. The network number is the prefix used by routing [Chappell 1993]. In recent Novell software that uses later releases of the Novell Link State Protocol (NLSP), network numbers can be aggregated. Address aggregation is a funda-mental technique for scaling IP networks, as discussed in Chapter 6.

In Novell networks, you see some network numbers that appear on no physical interface. This is quite normal. In Figure 8.5, network numbers 1 and 2 are called *external network numbers*, which actually appear on interfaces.

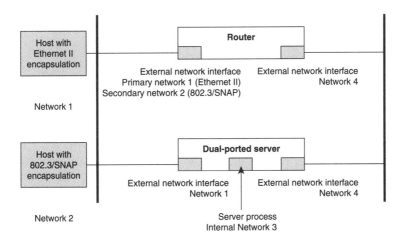

FIGURE 8.5. *Novell environments have both internal and external network numbers. Multiple network numbers can appear on the same medium when different frame types are in use.*

Note

Novell network numbers are customarily in hexadecimal. Although Cisco's configuration language nor-mally follows the convention that any numeric value not preceded with 0x is decimal, the ipx network *statement's argument is assumed to be hexadecimal.*

On workstation clients, the hardware MAC address usually is overridden by a locally administered MAC address. This is entered into a driver configuration file, such as NET.CFG or NETx.COM in Novell.

Naming in Novell Networks

To understand the role of naming in the Novell context, you must understand that there are multiple Novell stacks. The purest Novell names are involved when Network Core Protocol is the basic application stack.

RFC 1234 prescribes a method for encapsulating IPX packets so they can traverse IP-based internetworks, intermixed with true Internet traffic. To IPX, the Internet is a lower layer environment similar to a LAN. Where IPX packets are wrapped inside LLC and MAC frames for the LAN, they are wrapped in IP datagrams for the wide area, as shown in Figure 8.6. These IP datagrams are then wrapped into whatever frames are needed in the internetwork.

IP header	UDP header	IPX header	IPX data

FIGURE 8.6. *Current NetWare IP support for IPX encapsulates NetWare upper layer information in IP/UDP.*

Network Core Protocol Names and Their Resolutions

Network Core Protocol names are up to 48 characters long and have no inherent hierarchy. Up to NetWare 4.x, the Novell name distribution model had significant scaling problems. Certain of these problems can be alleviated with router software features. As the system designer, you need to make a tradeoff between controlling Service Advertisement Protocol (SAP) announcements on routers and upgrading to host software that generates only incremental SAP updates rather than the huge table every 60 seconds.

In IPX, nodes broadcast queries asking for a device of a given type. Assuming that an appropriate server on their own medium hears them, or a router on their segment hears the request and forwards it to a server, the server returns the logical address of the desired device. Novell logical addresses contain the medium address of the desired device. If the network number of the desired device is the same as that of the requesting device, Layer 2 reachability is assumed, and the MAC address of the destination is extracted from the logical address.

When a NetWare client requests a service, it broadcasts a *Get Nearest Server* request that is answered by the server or a router acting as a server. The response is to the topologically closest server.

In large networks, SAP traffic can become huge. One hundred servers, not a large number when each printer is a server, can saturate a 64 KBps line with SAP broadcasts for approximately 10 seconds per minute.

After the client attempts to access the server, establishing initial communications with it, the server can redirect the client to another instance of the same server type.

Emulated NetBIOS Names

In addition to the Network Core Protocol stack, Novell has a stack that supports applications that use the NetBIOS programming interface. NetBIOS messages are encapsulated in IPX packets, which are routable over any network that routes IPX. Accepting the additional overhead of IPX encapsulation in IP, it is possible to run Novell NetBIOS over an IP backbone without changing application stacks.

There is one caveat to NetBIOS over IPX: Unless static or proxy mechanisms are used, you have to allow IPX Type 20 packets to flood. If you do not filter these broadcasts, you have introduced the overhead of a bridged broadcast domain to a routed one.

AppleTalk Networking

AppleTalk is the proprietary networking architecture defined by Apple Computer Corporation. Although the term *AppleTalk* is often used to describe Apple networking using the twisted pair interface supplied on Macintosh computers, that interface is properly called *LocalTalk*. 802.3 connectivity is called *EtherTalk*, and 802.5 is called *TokenTalk*.

AppleTalk properly refers to protocols at the network layer and above. AppleTalk has had two major versions, Phase 1 and Phase 2. This discussion assumes Phase 2; Phase 1 has long been obsolete. Phase 2 was introduced with the Mac Plus. It is an interesting contrast to IP and OSI, because it is built to comply with a very different set of goals. The most important goal in AppleTalk is that the network structure should be invisible to the end user. AppleTalk equipment, especially individual user workstations, is as self-configuring as possible.

Conscious design decisions were made to emphasize self-configuration over performance. Other design decisions assumed that workstations primarily would communicate within a single organization; unique global addressability of AppleTalk devices was not a goal.

AppleTalk assumes a LAN environment with relatively small numbers of devices on each LAN. Each medium has its own network number; more than one network number can be assigned to a single medium. Zones aggregate network numbers (for example, a zone might comprise all the LAN cables, each with their own numbers, in a large building).

AppleTalk Addressing

In AppleTalk, addresses are assigned dynamically, and users have no fixed address. To varying extents, this notion of dynamic address assignment is characteristic of workgroup protocols. In the sections that follow, the addressing constructs for AppleTalk are discussed at the medium and host levels, and then we look at AppleTalk's unique concept of zones.

Device and Medium Addresses

AppleTalk addresses are hierarchical and contain a 16-bit network number and an 8-bit node ID. As shown in Figure 8.7, one or more network numbers are assigned to each medium in a contiguous sequence, called a *network number range* in the AppleTalk architectural specification and a *cable range* in most router documentation. Cable ranges are equivalent to IP subnets in that they are the identifiers for media.

End Station and Router Interface Addresses

AppleTalk network addresses are combined with socket addresses to define the actual destinations for packets. These values are dynamically assigned and map to network visible entity names.

End station addresses, and most router interface addresses, are assigned dynamically through an address discovery process. AppleTalk uses a zero value to show that a network or node number has not yet been assigned, resulting in the following examples of AppleTalk addresses:

- `0.0`—No network or node address assigned.

- `0.1`—Node assigned but no network.

- `1.0`—Network assigned but node assignment not yet done. Also refers to all routers on a medium.

- `1.1`—Network and node numbers assigned.

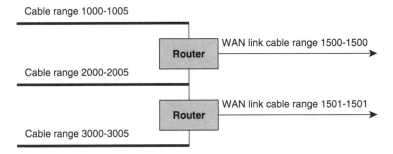

FIGURE 8.7. *Cable ranges are roughly similar to the "this subnet," or prefix with a zero host field, in IP. Most interface addresses are dynamically assigned.*

At least one router in each system must have its addresses manually assigned; this *seed router* can become the direct or indirect source of addresses for all other devices (see Figure 8.8). Both the dynamic assignment and mapping between transmission system and logical address are done by the AppleTalk Address Resolution Protocol (AARP). Be aware that if the seed router becomes isolated from part of the network, the part that cannot reach it cannot assign addresses.

Zones and Network Visible Entities

Network addresses and cable ranges are hidden from end users. The only addressing constructs visible to AppleTalk users are *zones* and *network visible entities* (NVEs).

Formally, a *zone* is an arbitrary set of network numbers; a node can belong to more than one zone. Figure 8.9 gives an example of zone usage. In Figure 8.9, a building is shared by engineering and accounting groups, with engineering on the second and third floors and sales on the first floor. Each floor has a shared printer, so two "floor" zones are established. An engineering database is shared between the engineering groups on both floors, so all engineering workstations have access to it but accounting nodes do not. WAN links are in a separate zone.

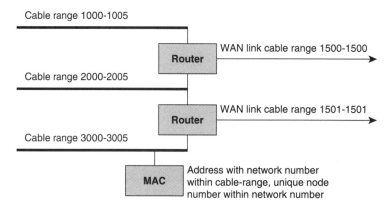

FIGURE 8.8. *As long as a seed router is defined, all other addresses are generated without manual configuration.*

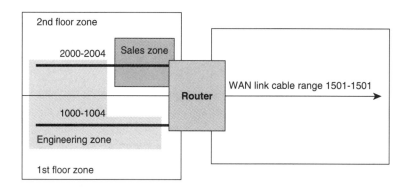

FIGURE 8.9. *Three zones—sales, engineering, and second floor—are present on the second floor cable and two zones—engineering and first floor—are present on the first floor cable. Engineering overlaps both cables.*

Be aware that there is no strict hierarchical relationship among zones, networks, and media: A medium can have multiple network numbers belonging to the same or different zones. There are a few constraints:

- Network numbers in a cable range must be contiguous.

- Both a cable range and a zone must be defined before anything can be routed to a given medium.

Individual Appletalk devices are assigned object names, either by default or by explicit configuration. NVEs are structured triplets composed of the names of an AppleTalk object, device type, and zone name. They are character strings up to 32 characters long, with the format

`objectName:typeName@zoneName`

NVEs are mapped dynamically to endpoint identifiers. They need not be strict unicast identifiers, because NVEs can contain wildcards. `=:typeName@*`, for example, refers to all instances of `typeName` in the requester's zone. These wildcard conventions can become quite complex, because AppleTalk is intended to be able to follow name matching rules appropriate to languages with different alphabets and local collating conventions.

AppleTalk in Backbones

AppleTalk generally does not scale well as a backbone routing protocol. There are several ways to make it run in the wide area.

Apple's solution is to use the Apple update-based routing protocol (AURP), which tunnels AppleTalk routing information through an arbitrary IP network. Only changes to the topology are sent, which removes the major scaling barrier of native RTMP routing.

A Cisco-specific alternative is to use Enhanced IGRP (EIGRP) for AppleTalk, which also can carry Apple routing information. The advantage of EIGRP over AURP is in having a single routing mechanism to configure. You do need to enable AppleTalk on each interface where you want EIGRP for AppleTalk routing.

A third alternative is to tunnel RTMP and ZIP, but filter them extensively at the edge of the backbone. An alternative to IP tunneling is to use Frame Relay PVCs to carry well-filtered AppleTalk over a Layer 2 network.

> **Note**
>
> Like IPX routing, AppleTalk routing does not know how to disable split horizon. As a consequence, it does not work properly with NBMA networks. You should assign only two hosts to Apple network numbers implemented over Frame Relay. You'll probably want to use unary cable ranges, such as 1500-1500.

Digital Equipment Corporation Protocols for Networking

Digital Equipment Corporation, or its successors in Compaq and Cabletron, defined a networking architecture called Digital Network Architecture (DNA). DNA specifications have been issued in Roman-numbered phases, the most common of which is Phase IV. Phase V DECnet uses a significant number of OSI rather than proprietary protocols.

DECnet is the software that implements DNA on DEC computers. It has version numbers written in decimal. For some reason beyond the understanding of ordinary mortals, DNA phase numbers and DECnet version numbers are out of synchronization. DECnet version 5 implements DNA Phase IV, and DECnet version 6 implements DNA Phase V.

Note

In industry practice, people refer to DECnet Phase IV, which is really DECnet Version 5, as an implementation of DNA Phase IV. In this text, I call the entire protocol family DECnet.

DECnet is a general-purpose network architecture, oriented toward interconnecting timesharing hosts, that is well proven in networks with tens of thousands of hosts and hundreds of thousands of end users. DECnet is designed to work well over arbitrary media, both WAN and LAN.

Local Area Transport (LAT) is a specialized protocol developed by Digital Equipment Corporation to complement general-purpose DECnet. LAT is not part of DECnet.

Note

DECnet is quite scalable as a WAN protocol. It's often reasonable to let it coexist with IP.

LAT, on the other hand, really should not run outside a local environment. Designed to operate on a single Ethernet between a terminal server and a VAX, it has extremely short timeouts.

DECnet Network Addressing

DECnet is fully routable. It uses hierarchical routing. Addresses are 16 bits long, split into a 6-bit area number and a 10-bit node number.

DECnet's addressing is different from that of most other protocol families, other than Banyan and OSI. It does not include a concept of a medium address such as an IP prefix. Rather, the area number identifies a set of hosts; routers are a subset of these hosts. Hierarchy is introduced with the ideas of Level 1 and Level 2 routers. Level 1 routers only know about addresses inside their own area, whereas Level 2 routers know about other areas.

DECnet Phase V replaced the proprietary DECnet protocols, at OSI Layer 3, with OSI protocols. Its basic network layer protocol is the OSI Connectionless Network Layer Protocol (CLNP). Its routing protocol is the OSI Intermediate System–to–Intermediate System (IS-IS) protocol. DECnet Phase V continues to use DEC-defined protocols above the network layer.

An extended version of IS-IS, called dual or integrated IS-IS, handles both IP and CLNP. Several major Internet service providers use IS-IS as their main IP routing protocol, so IS-IS is widely supported. Enterprises that now run DECnet Phase IV have, as one migration strategy to an all-IP network, the option of upgrading to DECnet Phase V and running integrated IS-IS.

LAT and MOP

LAT is a specialized protocol family meant to complement DECnet. LAT is optimized for interconnecting asynchronous device servers, to which terminals and printers are connected, to a DEC computer across a single Ethernet cable. LAT and the associated Maintenance & Operations Protocol (MOP) are deliberately not routable and are not intended for use over a WAN, or indeed over LANs interconnected by routers.

Note

Do not confuse Cisco's uppercase Protocol Translator software with what Cisco calls the process of protocol translation. The Protocol Translator feature can be used to create tunnels for unusual protocols, both symmetric and asymmetric.

DEC's LAT protocol, for example, is extremely timing sensitive. As mentioned previously, its sensitivity was a reasonable design choice because it was intended for a very narrow niche. In the real world, organizations try to use any given protocol for things for which the protocol was not intended, and LAT is no exception.

DEC Protocols in Backbones

DECnet can be carried in IP encapsulation, or run as a ships in the night (SIN) protocol coexisting with IP. As discussed in the sidebar "Strange Interactions of Multiple Protocols," very strange things have been known to happen to routers when DECnet runs in certain router configurations that have the properties:

- There are no LAN interfaces on the router.

- DECnet coexists with other protocol families that assume they will derive addresses from MAC addresses. Novell IPX is the most common here, but issues also may emerge with XNS or VINES.

An unusual thing about DECnet is that it modifies all MAC addresses on the router to reflect the DECnet logical address. The algorithm for this, to put it mildly, is arcane.

Assume you are trying to determine the MAC address to be generated for DECnet node 257 in area 15. Convert the decimal area number to a 6-bit binary value:

001111

and convert the node number to a 10-bit binary:

0100000001

Now, concatenate the two strings, the area bits in the most significant position, to form a 16-bit binary string. Convert this string into hexadecimal digits:

0011110100000001

3 D 0 1

You now have two byte values in hexadecimal, 3D-01. Swap the positions of these two bytes to give 01-3D.

These swapped two bytes form the low-order bytes of a MAC address, with the high-order part being a standard DEC prefix:

AA-00-04-00-01-3D

A DECnet host goes through this process whether or not it has physical LAN interfaces.

Strange Interactions of Multiple Protocols

This DECnet convention can lead to odd problems, stemming from the reality that, although router vendors work hard at building multiprotocol routers, the individual protocol families do not assume that they will coexist with other protocols.

Assume that you have a Cisco router with serial interfaces only, and you need to route DECnet and IPX on it. DECnet creates a MAC address in the manner just described, whether or not there are interfaces that have burned-in MAC addresses.

If the router has no interfaces that have native MAC addresses, IPX routing needs a manually defined MAC address lookalike so that it can create the node number part of IPX addresses. If the same router is running DECnet, the MAC address in the ipx routing statement *must* match the MAC address computed by DECnet.

Problems are most apt to occur when DECnet is started after IPX is running. The two protocols can work together; it is just a matter of being sure some finely detailed parameters do not conflict with one another.

DEC was one of the strongest advocates of OSI and indeed is today a leader in IPv6.

DECnet Phase V

Whereas DECnet Phase IV uses proprietary network layer protocols, Phase V uses the OSI Connectionless Network Protocol as its network layer, along with OSI routing.

OSI and ATM Network Addressing

OSI network addressing is intended to deal with much larger address spaces than IP version 4. As a network layer protocol, it is not widely used in the marketplace, other than in some specialized niches such as SONET management.

It is worth understanding the detailed structure of OSI addressing, because the *format* of the OSI NSAP address is extensively used in ATM networking. See the "ATM" section of Chapter 4. In addition, autoconfiguration mechanisms introduced in OSI are seen in other protocol families such as DECnet, VINES, and IPv6.

OSI's network layer protocols include the *end system hello* and *intermediate system hello* messages. End system hello packets announce the existence of hosts, primarily for network management. Intermediate system hello packets provide the keepalive function for monitoring routers, but also are the basis of autoconfiguration for end hosts.

Router hellos also are important in DECnet, not for end system autoconfiguration but for router discovery. Hosts must be configured with a logical address. Sending nodes learn the address of a router on their segment by listening to periodic hellos from routers. After a router address is known, the end station sends a unicast to the designated router, but continues to listen to the medium. If the router redirects the unicast to another router that provides a better path than the designated router, the host hears that packet and learns the other router is a better way to reach the destination. The host uses that other router for subsequent transmissions to the destination.

VINES and CLNP are similar in that devices learn about other devices by listening to hellos. They differ in that most OSI end systems autoconfigure. In OSI CLNP, no destinations are reachable until an intermediate system hello is heard. If an end system hello from the destination is heard, that ESH contains the MAC address of the destination node, which is cached. Otherwise, the end station sends to a router, after it learns the router address by hearing the router announce itself in an intermediate system hello.

A VINES station learns which devices are present on its own medium by listening for periodic end system hellos and intermediate system hellos. It gets its actual address, however, through an interaction with a VINES server or a router acting as a proxy for the server.

Semantically, Network Protocol address information has two main components: the initial domain part (IDP) and the domain-specific part (DSP). Figure 8.10 graphically depicts how the IDP defines the DSP. The IDP is further divided into an authority and format identifier (AFI) and an initial domain identifier (IDI). As specified in Table 8.1, the AFI gives the format of the rest of the address.

TABLE 8.1. AUTHORITY AND FORMAT INDICATOR VALUES.

AFI Value for Decimal Encoded DSP	Binary Encoded DSP	DSP Address Type
36	37	X.121 (X.25 family, including X.25, X.21, and X.75)
38	39	ISO DCC country code
40	41	F.69 Telex address
42	43	E.163 analog telephone number
44	45	E.164 ISDN telephone number
46	47	ISO 6523 ICD organization code
48	49	Local network defined
50	51	Local network defined

In networks using IS-IS, AFI Type 47 is seen most often. Types 39, 45, and 47 are used in ATM networks.

When written for human reading, AFIs have two decimal digits. They are variously allocated by ISO, CCITT, or both in joint agreement; reserved and not to be used; and reserved for a family of addressing conventions already in use.

Addressing authorities identified by the AFI prescribe the syntax of the DSP and administer the assignment of semantics. Binary octets, decimal digits, character, and national character syntaxes can be used. IDIs abstractly have a variable number of decimal digits. Encoding, or syntax, might be significantly different in the manner a user or administrator externally specifies it, and the way it is encoded into packets.

Numerous ways exist to encode NSAPs. One popular method, for which a U.S. government example is shown in the following section, allows self-configuration of devices on a LAN. This is also used as an ATM endpoint identifier in private ATM networks.

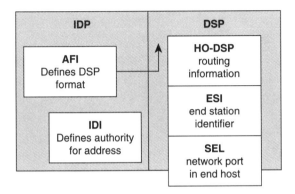

FIGURE 8.10. *Relationships among fields in an NSAP header.*

A General NSAP Example for CLNP

Understanding the exact procedure of self-configuration requires knowledge of routing protocols, which is beyond the scope of this book. Simply assume that the MAC sublayer address of a device can be prefixed with information on how to find this address in the overall address space. The basic idea is that end hosts can listen for announcements from routers, which contain an (IDP) and a high-order domain-specific part (HO-DSP). The end host knows its own MAC address and prefixes this with the IDP and HO-DSP. A 1-byte selector field is appended.

These examples show NSAP usage in CLNP networks. Figures 4.12 and 4.13 in Chapter 4 show examples from ATM networks.

International Code Designator Format

Figure 8.11 shows an example of the International Code Designator (ICD) format for NSAPs, as administered for the U.S. government. This reflects extensive experiments with OSI in the U.S. governments, using the specifications of the Government OSI Profile (GOSIP). In general, there are only niche applications of OSI in government networks today.

Figure 8.12 reviews the steps in determining an actual address. In the ICD space, which begins with the AFI value 0x47, ISO delegated IDI codes 0x0005 and 0x0006 to the U.S. government (as NIST), which, in turn, delegated civil agency code 0x0005 administration to the General Services Administration and military code 0x0006 to the Defense Information Systems Agency (DISA). Code 0x0004 is delegated to the OSINET interoperability research network.

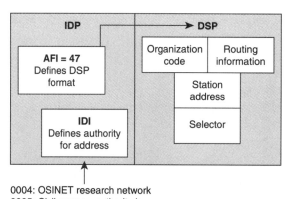

0004: OSINET research network
0005: Civil agency, authority is
        General Services Administration
0006: Military agency, authority is
        Defense Information Systems Agency

FIGURE 8.11. *An example of an NSAP address with U.S. GOSIP field values.*

Following the IDP, the DSP begins with a 1-byte domain-specific identifier. A
3-byte administrative authority (AA) field follows; the value of this field is controlled by the organization with the ISO-assigned IDI. In this example, GSA
assigns AA values in the ICD 0x05 space, whereas DISA administers AA values
in the ICD 0x06 space. Another way to say this is that any public NSAP that
begins 0x470005 is a U.S. government address administered by GSA.

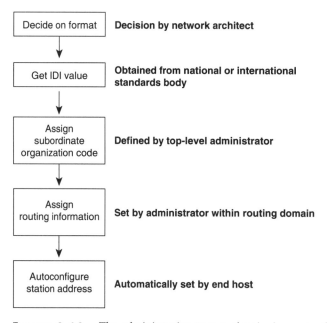

FIGURE 8.12. *The administrative process of assigning parts of an NSAP address.*

A representative administration might be the Internal Revenue Service, which then administers the rest of the address. The next 2 bytes are reserved, followed by a 2-byte routing domain identifier, and a 2-byte area identifier. In the Internal Revenue Service OSI network, there are 10 tax regions, a headquarters region, and a network test laboratory. Each is a separately administered routing domain. The area identifier identifies an actual group of routers and addresses.

This string of bytes, from the AFI to the area identifier, forms the HO-DSP.

The next six bytes are the end system identifier, and the last byte is the selector field. The selector field is significant only at end hosts and is similar to a TCP port number with the caveat that it only identifies a network layer process in the end host. There is a separate port number associated with OSI transport protocols.

ATM Use of NSAP

ATM endpoint addressing uses four variants of the NSAP address:

- ISO Data Country Code

- ISO International Code Designator

- ITU-T (former CCITT) E.164 private

- ITU-T E.164 public format

Figure 4.12 shows the choices for private networks; the discussion that follows gives more details on field usage within those alternatives. Figure 4.13 shows the public network format. Private networks are required to support the first three types, whereas public networks either must support the fourth or the first three types. The first three are data oriented in that they contain a 6-byte end station identifier that often, in practice, is a MAC address. The ICD format was described earlier in this chapter.

Data Country Codes

Data country codes (DCCs) are associated with national addressing authorities. The IDP has an AFI that is 0x39 and a 2-byte IDI with a value from the ISO 3166 country code space. The DSP is identical to that used with the ICD format.

E.164 Private

The full NSAP version of this format begins with an AFI of 0x45, and the IDI is an 8-byte, binary-encoded field. It is followed by a DSP composed of an RD and AREA field, followed in turn by the 6-byte end system ID and a selector field.

E.164 Public

As shown in Figure 8.13, there is no AFI field; the address begins with a 4-byte country code administered by the International Telecommunications Union. A variable-length binary-encoded-decimal DSP follows, which can be up to 15 decimal digits long. The DSP is a national number, much like an X.121 address or E.163 telephone number, whose format is specified by the national authority.

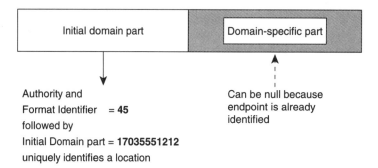

FIGURE 8.13.   *An E.164 format example, using hypothetical address values.*

X.25 Networking

X.25 is an old network layer protocol family that still has important niche applications, aside from its use by existing applications. It was designed for terminal-to-host applications and still can be quite efficient in that role. The X.25 Fast Select facility is widely used for transaction processing, such as credit card authorization. It is optimized for operations over media with combinations of low bandwidth, high error rates, and long delays.

There might be a resurgence of X.25 usage as X.25 data transmission over ISDN D channels replaces the existing analog connectivity of automatic teller machines and point-of-sale terminals.

You might want to distinguish between X.25 used as a transmission subsystem to deal with poor media and when the application expects X.25 functionality in its applications. Applications that use X.25 might need awareness of X.25 addressing. If X.25 underlies IP, the X.25 addressing should be transparent to applications.

When X.25 addressing is a consideration, it might be necessary to translate X.25 addresses to reflect changes in the underlying service.

An example of this involves translating local to public X.25 addresses [Berkowitz 1988] in a user organization that established a convention that a zero in the Data Network Identification Code (DNIC) part of an X.121 address meant that the address was part of a local address space. This is illustrated in Figure 8.14. The DNIC identifies an internationally unique code for an X.25 service provider. In this address space, the first three digits of the X.121 address identified an X.25 switch, and the last four digits identified a port on that switch.

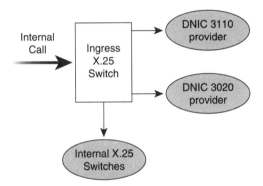

FIGURE 8.14. *You can select X.25 carriers based on the DNIC.*

If the DNIC part of an address is nonzero, switches are programmed to route that call to a gateway serving to the external network identified by that DNIC. Address translation software would translate external references (for example, 3020–888–0001) to internal references (for example, Port 9999 on Switch 999). Although an internal network user at 997–0002 would see a direct circuit to 3020–888–0001, that virtual circuit was actually composed of circuits between the user and the ingress switch, and a switch port that looks like a DTE to the carrier.

General-purpose intercomputer networks using proprietary protocols still exist in many enterprises. These networks are not built to the most current standards but are real resources on which organizational operations depend. They cannot be replaced without careful thought. Although there are a great number of technologies used, some of the major ones in use are:

- X.25 subnetworks

- Proprietary subnetworks

In the past, before use of IP was widespread in enterprise networks, one strategy for migrating from proprietary to standard protocols was to convert the proprietary protocol to run over X.25. This still might be viable for old applications with proprietary protocols in that there might be a way to convert the protocol to X.25 but not to IP. X.25, of course, can be tunneled over IP as a second step that allows you to run the old protocol in your IP backbone.

X.25 preceded the introduction of IP and most workgroup protocols, and X.25 networks have been operational for many years. For this reason, most vendors have interfaced their proprietary network architectures with X.25.

In many vendors' product lines, you will find two types of X.25 interface: one which runs the vendor's proprietary upper layer protocols over X.25 and another which provides an X.25 interface to proprietary lower layers. Proprietary protocols, Internet protocols, and X.25 PAD protocols all flow over X.25 DTE interfaces to the network, however that network actually is implemented.

The X.25-over-proprietary configuration lends itself to transition schemes where X.25 is used as the subnetwork underlying more modern protocols, and the proprietary protocol, in turn, is a subnetwork underlying X.25. This is not necessarily an efficient way of doing things, but it can be a way to do things at all.

The proprietary-over-X.25 configuration can be treated as a way of tunneling proprietary protocols through an open network. In mixed proprietary/X.25 environments, the conversion function can be considered part of the X.25-based service or part of the proprietary service; it can be transparent to one of these services.

Remember that existing X.25 networks might provide services without exact functional equivalents in modern protocols. Some of these features include asynchronous terminal support and the Fast Select facility.

For example, dumb terminals might represent a significant investment in a real environment and be well served with X.25 PAD devices. New networks can preserve the investment in these terminals by providing protocol encapsulation for packet assembler-disassembler (PAD) traffic, rather than forcing the terminals to become intelligent devices that directly support TCP/IP. The X.25 PAD protocol converts character-oriented traffic to packets, much as the `telnet` protocol for IP does. The PAD protocol can be more efficient than `telnet` in some low-speed applications.

An X.25 optional capability called Fast Select is an acknowledged datagram protocol often used for simple query/response applications such as credit card authorization. Whereas low-volume credit authorization terminals are apt to use dialup facilities, moderate- to high-volume terminals have long been connected to X.25 networks using dedicated lines up to 9600 KBps.

ISDN specifications have always provided for low-speed packet data sharing the D channel with signaling information, but this was rarely used. The facility was not used primarily for administrative reasons; carriers could not price it competitively to dialup service.

Recently, there has been a surge of interest in using X.25 over the D channel to carry transactions using Fast Select. The major area of application seems to be replacement of multidrop analog lines with automatic teller machines.

Taking Inventory of Your Environment

To understand your existing environment, it is often best to begin by taking a physical inventory. The current technology review should consider:

- Building wiring

- Typical and extreme numbers of hosts per LAN

- Wide area network service agreements in place

- Existing routers

- Other existing internetworking technology, including bridging, X.25 packet switching, repeaters, and so on

- Host-based routing

Figures 8.15 through 8.19 show worksheets that are a basic guide for collecting information on the existing physical network. More detailed worksheets, later in the chapter, deal with the transport of specific protocol families over this network and the transport requirements in the evolved network.

An Inventory ID field appears in all the worksheets shown in Figures 8.15 through 8.19. It is a unique identifier for the row in the worksheet.

You might choose to use a commercial network management database product. If so, it will have its own conventions for inventory identification, which you should follow.

There is no standard convention for inventory ID. It might be no more than a sequence number drawn from a list. When allocated, it should not be reused for a long time, if ever.

One relatively simple way to allocate the inventory IDs is to put a number on each new worksheet and increment it by a line number. A "status" column can indicate if the ID is in a planning stage, is operational, or has been retired.

Although it's not unreasonable to include the identifier of a network management function or center in the inventory ID, do not become tempted to make any user location information part of the inventory ID.

It might be useful to put the inventory ID in the form of a DNS name. Such a name doesn't need to be easily human readable, but simply a machine key. For example, let's say the domain `example.com` has three management centers: M1, M2, and M3. Each management center maintains databases, one for each of the four worksheet types in Figures 8.15 through 8.19. Lines in the worksheets could be named `linenumber.managementcenter-worksheettype.example.com`.

Figure 8.15 is a guide for collecting information on your existing dedicated lines. It assumes that lines are point-to-point. If they are not point-to-point, indicate that they are multidrop in the Medium Type column and put a reference to a list of drops in the Location 2 column. Alternatively, you can modify the form to have a column for each drop, although this can become unwieldy with many drops.

It might appear that a great deal of information is requested about the DCE devices. If you interpret addressing broadly, however, this will make sense from a management standpoint. The industry trend is to have devices manageable by SNMP, and devices often have proprietary MIB extensions. Knowing the device type tells you how to access these extensions, which are keyed from the device's IP address used by management.

Figure 8.16 is a worksheet for recording information on your local area networks. The topological assumption here is that each LAN will appear in a primary wire closet and also serve an area of a building.

This worksheet is intended to gather information on physical LANs. Virtual LANs can spread across multiple physical media. A column of the worksheet lets you record which VLANs can appear on which physical media.

Inventory ID	Status	Location 1				Location 2				Medium Type	Circuit ID	Endpoint ID	IP Addressing				Novell/IPX Addressing			AppleTalk Addressing			Other Protocols Present				
		Site	DCE Name	DCE Management ID	DCE Type	Site	DCE Name	DCE Management ID	DCE Type				Authority	Prefix	Length	Hosts Now Used	Aggregate Network Number	Network Number	Encapsulation	Aggregate Cable range	Cable range	Zones present	IBM SDLC	DEC LAT	VINES	CLNP	NetBIOS

FIGURE 8.15. *A dedicated line worksheet.*

Inventory ID	Status	Wire Closet ID	Area Served	VLANs Present on Medium	Edge LAN, VLAN trunk, or mixed	Medium Type	IP Addressing				Novell/IPX Addressing			AppleTalk Addressing			NetBIOS			Source Route Bridging	Other Protocols Present
							Authority	Prefix	Length	Host Count	Aggregate	Network Number	Encapsulation	Aggregate cable range	Cable range	Zones present	Name Prefix	Name Resolution Method	Name Resolution on Server	MAC Address Prefix	IBM SNA / DEC LAT / DLC / VINES / NetBEUI / Other Bridged Protocols / XNS

FIGURE 8.16. *A LAN worksheet.*

Inventory ID	Status	Location 1				Location 2 to m (separate lines)				Medium Type	Circuit ID	Endpoint ID	IP Addressing				Novell/IPX Addressing			AppleTalk Addressing			Other Protocols Present							
		Site	DCE Name	DCE Management ID	DCE Type	Site	DCE Name	DCE Management ID	DCE Type				Authority	Prefix	Length	Hosts Now Used	Aggregate Network Number	Network Number	Encapsulation	Aggregate Cable range	Cable range	Zones present	IBM BSC	IBM SDLC	DECnet	LAT	VINES	CLNP	NetBIOS	XNS

FIGURE 8.17. *An NBMA media worksheet.*

Figure 8.18. *A demand media worksheet.*

NBMA PVC networks, as in Frame Relay and ATM, are similar to dedicated lines, but with a point-to-multipoint topology. The worksheet in Figure 8.17 is intended to help you capture information on these media. It also can be used to capture information on analog multidrop lines.

Demand media include analog dialups, ISDN dialups, and switched virtual circuits. Your dialup analog and ISDN lines, as well as switched virtual circuits created in ATM, X.25, or Frame Relay, should be inventoried using the Figure 8.18 worksheet. It assumes that these media are tracked by the transmission system's endpoint address, such as telephone numbers, ATM NSAP addresses, and so on.

Inventory ID	Location	Device Name	SNMP IP Address	Interface ID	IP Addressing		Novell/IPX Addressing		AppleTalk Addressing		NetBIOS	Source Route Bridging
					Prefix	Length	Network Number	Encapsu-lation	Cable range	Zones present	Name Prefix	MAC Address Prefix

FIGURE 8.19. *An internetworking devices worksheet.*

Figure 8.14 is a means of tracking the relays that interconnect media described in the other worksheets. Relays include routers, bridges, and switches. You might want to customize this worksheet to reflect your physical internetworking devices. Worksheets for each standard configuration, with blanks for each interface, are quite useful.

In filling these worksheets, your first goal is to gather the physical information.

After you know your physical topology, the next step is to understand your existing physical environment. There is an assumption here that every medium, bridge, and router has IP capability, even if IP is not the routed/bridged user protocol stack present. Virtually all industry network management tools assume IP addresses are present.

Some information requested by the worksheets is not strictly relevant to addressing. This information, however, is highly relevant to network design and operations, and it seems silly not to collect it when going through the pain and suffering of a detailed inventory.

If you develop your own software to manage this information, remember a basic rule: never rekey the same information (unless it is a retrieval key).

Expect the Unlikely When Taking Inventory

Taking inventory goes beyond counting the devices on your LANs. It's an excellent idea to go through telephone bills and call each number you are billed for. If a computer answers, try to log in to it. You might find modem lines in individual offices, which could represent significant security vulnerabilities.

You also might find lines that ring but do not answer. Other lines might not be in use at all, but your organization is still being billed for them. At the very least, this can indicate a bad modem or computer port. Stranger things happen.

I happened to conduct one telephone line inventory while in the network control center. Not only did some lines ring without answering my test line, but I heard some muted ringing. It seemed louder in some parts of the control center than in others. Eventually, even though my colleagues began to conclude I was acting more strangely than normal, I brought in a stethoscope and started listening to the walls. The ringing definitely was coming from behind one of the walls. Lifting a tile in the raised floor, I found that one of our building contractors had misread the blueprints and put up some drywall in front of one of our less frequently used modem racks.

Looking Ahead

Networks interconnect things. To come up with reasonable designs, the designer must first know approximately what functions and/or components must be interconnected.

Real networks have to be built for the real world, where Murphy's law applies. Experience is an important teacher here and teaches that reliability and flexibility are best designed into networks, not added on as an afterthought.

The information you have collected in this chapter is the starting point for Chapter 9.

CHAPTER 9

The Address Plan

Ah, Love! Could thou and I with Fate conspire/To grasp this sorry Scheme of Things entire,/Would not we shatter it to bits— and then Re-mould it nearer to the Heart's Desire

—Omar Khayyam

Peace is present when man can see the face that is composed of things that have meaning and are in their place. Peace is present when things form part of a whole greater than their sum, as the diverse minerals in the ground collect to become the tree.

—Antoine Saint-Exupery

Realists do not fear the results of their study.

—Fyodor Dostoevsky

There are several goals in developing an address plan, regardless of whether public or private address space is used. Above all, the address plan should be maintainable because, after WAN costs, people costs are the largest part of a network's life cycle cost. The address plan should intelligently balance stability, optimality of routes, and performance.

You need to decide what your policy is regarding the Internet visibility of your addresses. Starting from the IP address space shown in Figure 8.1 (in Chapter 8, "The Existing IP and Non-IP Address Structure: Preparing for Remodeling"), what exactly is the problem you are trying to solve?

What Is the Problem You Are Trying to Solve?

At this point, it's very useful to have a drawing of the network architecture you want. Obviously, for a complex network, this won't fit on one page.

Documenting the Architecture of the Goal

You will want a very high level of network structure. See Chapter 3, "Application Topology: Naming Endpoints," for a basis for this. You need to evolve the application hierarchy into a networking hierarchy, as shown in Figure 9.1.

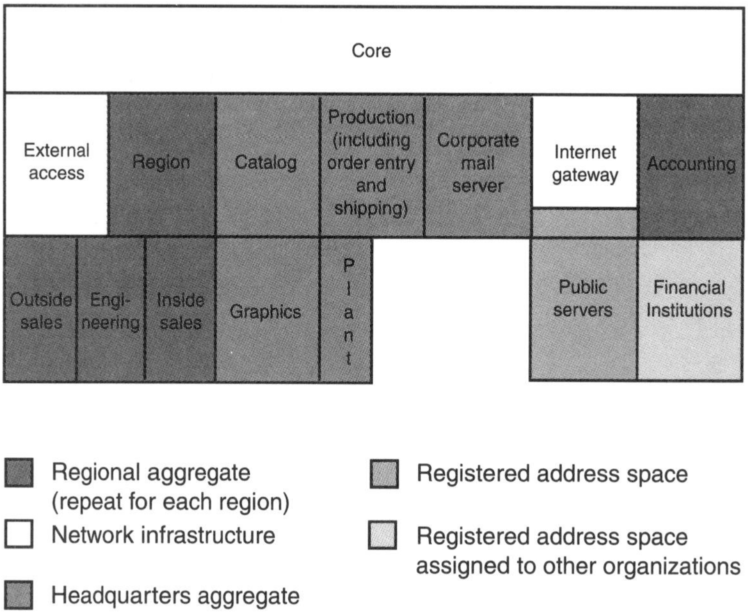

FIGURE 9.1.   *The application hierarchy is now a networking-oriented one.*

Later, when the addressing plan calls for narrative descriptions, you can say "core" or "region 2 distribution." Within each of the blocks of the diagrams you create, you can identify network topology. Ideally, you could color code or otherwise visually designate which media need registered addresses and which will use private addresses.

Simply because a host needs Internet or other outside access does not necessarily mean it needs a registered address of its own. It could communicate through some type of network address translation or proxy function, sharing outside addresses of the translator (see the upcoming section "Traffic Considerations").

If you have a security policy that requires end-to-end authentication, each of your hosts with external connectivity will need a unique registered address.

Documenting the Architecture of the Present

If you have existing address space, you will want a present-network drawing that shows address space to be renumbered.

Figure 9.2 builds from Figure 8.1. You will need to think about which of your addresses have the following characteristics:

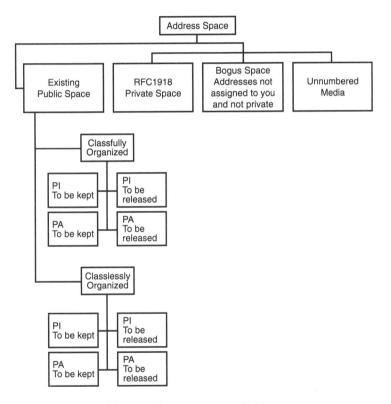

FIGURE 9.2. *Address requirements, new and old.*

- Are visible *only* inside your enterprise
- Should be hidden inside your enterprise (this is *not* the same as the previous point!)
- Need to be visible to the general Internet
- Need to be visible to specific external users

- Need to access arbitrary destinations on the general Internet

- Need to access destinations in specific external sites

Reviewing the Inventory

Begin with the list of media in Figures 8.15 through 8.19 and round the number of hosts per medium up to the smallest value 2^n-2 that is large enough to contain the number of hosts. In other words, if you have 1 to 6 hosts, you round up to 2^3-2. If you have 7 to 14 hosts, you round up to 2^4-2. Record these adjusted media requirements in Figure 9.3. This table is the basis for your current address space description in your request for address space.

Supernet					Number of Hosts							
Top level	Midlevel	Prefix	Location	Length	Current		Time 1		Time 2		Time 3	
					Count	Utili-zation ratio	Count	Utili-zation ratio	Count	Utili-zation ratio	Count	Utili-zation ratio

Legend for Status Codes				
CR = current registered	CP = current private	CX = current registered to be released	FR = future registered being requested	FP = future private

FIGURE 9.3.   *This worksheet extracts the IP part of the inventory sheets you did in Chapter 8 and forms the basis for the current usage part of new address requests.*

Sort the adjusted media by numbers of hosts per medium. You have just established a list of potentially needed prefix lengths. Modify the table to include additional columns if you have more than two levels of summarization, which is perfectly reasonable in large networks.

Repeat the process of deciding how much host space you need on each medium, considering planned growth, both in media and hosts per medium.

Most organizations find they have the following three or four commonly used prefix lengths:

- A big LAN for switched or bridged environments, typically 126 or more hosts (that is, a /25 or shorter prefix). Be aware that some host software might not understand prefixes shorter than /24 in the classical Class C space, 192.0.0.0 through 223.255.255.255.

- A WAN /30 prefix for point-to-point links.

- A SOHO prefix, usually /29 or /28, for small and home offices. Note that individual dialup users tend to be represented as a single host that is not explicitly considered by routing; instead, the dialup server treats all hosts as a pool.

- Possibly a medium LAN seen at medium-sized offices.

Try to reduce the number of prefix lengths to three or four. You might find you need a larger number of levels of aggregation, but these tend to be less confusing because they do not touch individual hosts.

If, for example, you had a mixture of /29 and /28 prefixes for SOHO applications, it is probably best to standardize on /28 in all but the largest networks.

Cleaning Up Problem Areas

When you think about your present address design, you should definitely consider problems that might be present and how they can be fixed. Typical problems include the following:

- Bogus address space

- Registered address space that is now visible on the general Internet and should be completely hidden from all external eyes

- Registered address space that is now visible on the general Internet and should be visible only to specific business partners

- Unnumbered interfaces, which can be hard to manage

- Current private addresses, the management of which you want to outsource

Potentially Overloaded Prefixes

In reducing the number of prefix lengths, one of the first places to look is at the shortest prefixes (that is, those with the largest number of hosts). It is entirely possible that some prefixes are too long for ideal performance, or might have potential limits to growth. Table 9.1 is a table where you can establish some of these limits.

TABLE 9.1. LIMITING FACTORS FOR SUBNET SIZE.

Prefix Length	Usable Host Addresses	Limiting Size Factors
/30	2	Optimal size for point-to-point
/29	6	
/28	14	12 hosts is an upper limit on 200 MHz PCs on a shared 10 MBPS Ethernet
/27	30	20 hosts is a comfortable upper limit for ISA bus, 66 MHz PCs on a shared 10 MBPS Ethernet
/26	62	
/25	126	Beginning of broadcast radiation concern given heavy broadcast/multicast
/24	254	Limit of classful awareness if address in Class C range
		Probable upper limit from broadcasts (<200 preferred) if Apple, NetBIOS devices, or many NetWare servers issuing SAPs, are present
		Default limit of bridge entry count in IOS bridging
/23	510	Usual limit for IP devices
/22	1022	Recommended upper limit for IP
		VLAN port size on Bay 28xxx switches*
/21	2046	IETF estimate of upper size of multiserver NHRP system
/20	4094	
/19	8190	Typical minimum globally routable prefix
/18	16382	Pushing extreme range of bridge size
/16		Catalyst 5000 boxwide table size

Traffic Considerations

Some tradeoffs might need to be made for media with heavy traffic. Analysis might show that if the permissible number of hosts on a medium are all active, the underlying medium might not have the bandwidth to handle the traffic.

To maintain the prefix structure, it might be necessary either to decrease the number of hosts per medium (and thus lengthen the prefix) or to increase the capacity of the medium. Capacity increase can involve LAN switching on 10 or 16 MBps facilities, or movement to 100 MBps or faster facilities. Traffic factors certainly can affect a switch. You need to consider both fabric speed and server port speed.

Let's say you have a switch with a 1 GB fabric and 100 ports. If the switch is a full nonblocking crossbar, this will work if all ports are 10 MBps. Assuming a half-duplex environment, there are 50 flows through the switch, and each path can run at $1^9/50$ or 20 MB each. This still works with full-duplex at 10 MB each.

Be sure your addressing is consistent with the traffic that can move over real media. If a user application needs 500 Kbps of bandwidth averaged over time, and you have a single server connected via 10 MBps Ethernet, that server can only support 20 users. 20 users, one server, and one router interface justify a /27 address prefix, which can hold up to 26 hosts.

How Many Addresses Can Your Bandwidth Support?

If you connected the server to a 100 MBps switch port and connected the hosts to 10 MBps switch ports, the theoretical maximum number of users in the subnet represented by that medium would be 200, which would justify a /24.

If you could load share among four identical servers, each connected through the same switch at 100 MBps, you would have the potential of justifying a /22 to support 800 potential users.

If you asked for a /22 with a single server, you could not justify the address space given the capabilities of your hosts.

Both DNS and Load Sharing with Network Address and Port Translation (LS-NAPT) methods may apply, singly or in combination. LS-NAPT, discussed in Chapter 6, "Internet Failing: Details at 11," can reduce requirements for registered space. If LS-NAPT servers are at different sites, there presumably is a need for registered space to interconnect them, if virtual private networks are used.

Variable Length Subnet Masking (VLSM) and Classless Inter-Domain Routing (CIDR) are the accepted Internet conventions for dealing efficiently with different prefix lengths. In limited cases, it might be useful to use several classful prefixes to deal with legacy equipment, each prefix of a different length. Such strategies easily introduce pathologies such as discontiguous networks.

Note

Remember that VLSM lets you use the all-zeros and all-ones subnets. Not being able to support all zero and all one subnets can be construed by registries as inefficient address space use.

If a single prefix length is used throughout the organization, some LANs will not have enough host space and others will waste it. This is especially true in the large subnets created with microsegmenting switches, which connect each host directly to a switch port and thus provide large amounts of bandwidth, allowing many devices to connect. In a non-VLSM environment, the best simple approach often is to have a mask that fits the small-to-average LAN and handle the large LANs by assigning multiple subnets to each large LAN.

If a single prefix length were used throughout an enterprise, and this length were adequate for the most common number of hosts per medium, a great deal of space would be wasted on media with low host counts (for example, point-to-point lines). Other large media, or simulated media such as a Layer 2 switching system, could very well not have enough host space.

Before VLSM, one way to approach this was to use a prefix length that fit the most common host count requirement. This became the basic quantum of internal address space allocation. When there was a particularly large requirement for hosts on a medium, additional prefixes were assigned to the medium as secondary addresses. The technique frequently works, but may have both performance and host interoperability problems.

Point-to-point lines were often handled as special cases not requiring any prefix, using the ip unnumbered option. Again, this works, but can be difficult to troubleshoot.

Submitting the Justification

When registered addresses are used, the address plan must follow the principles of RFC 2050:

- *Conservation*—Routable prefixes are a limited resource. They need to be allocated in a manner that gives a perception of fairness, while recognizing operational realities and historical practices. Although historical assignments might have been wasteful, the current goals are to be frugal in assigning space and to avoid hoarding address space.

- *Routability*—There is no value to Internet addresses if the global routing system fails. With present deployable technology, the only way for that system to have a good chance of working is to use hierarchical allocation, primarily provider based. Address allocation policy is limited to establishing an environment that has the potential of global routability. Whether a given address prefix is or is not globally routable will still be governed by the operational policies of the organizations providing routing service.

* *Traceability*—Registration addresses advertised on the global Internet must be traceable back to a registered assignment, if global troubleshooting is to have any real chance of success. Registration also prevents duplicate address assignments.

There is no simple formula for creating your addressing plan. RFC 2050 recognizes that conservation and routability are often conflicting goals. Service providers and end users can also have conflicting goals. Registries, and registry policy, need to balance the needs of the different consumers of address as well as those of the global system. In the real world, registry staff needs to have increasingly large amounts of engineering and business information to make reasonable decisions. Increasingly, network managers need to be able to collect and present this information.

The overall Internet space is under the control of a governing function called the Internet Assigned Numbers Authority (IANA). Only the largest address requests are dealt with by IANA; most assignments are done in large blocks by the following three regional registries:

* *Americas*—American Registry for Internet Numbers (ARIN; www.arin.net)

* *Europe*—Reseau IP Europeens (RIPE; http://www.ripe.net)

* *Pacific Rim*—Asia-Pacific Network Information Center (APNIC; www.apnic.net)

ARIN is a not-for-profit spin-off of the former Network Information Center (NIC), which was operated under contract by Network Solutions. The old NIC is being replaced by separate DNS and address registries. Some DNS registries are for-profit, and there is potential competition among them.

Address registries are seen as a service that does not lend itself to competition and needs the tight control of a technical monopoly. Regional address registries might suballocate address space to national registries, service providers, and local registries. The different regional registries have different systems of delegation.

In the Americas, there are at present two national registries, in Brazil and Mexico. In Europe, however, RIPE delegates registry functions to organizations at the level of Internet service providers (ISPs). European countries often contain multiple registries.

> **Note**
>
> *Just as tax auditors become suspicious when they see all deductions as an even number with lots of zeros, registries are suspicious when all requests are at the /8, /16, or /24 levels. They are suspicious that the address requirement was justified for administrative convenience rather than effective address space usage. Most often, you will see address wastage when addresses are allocated on the traditional classful boundaries. In this previous example, however, there is a dangerous address shortage.*

The current addressing policy defined by RFC 2050 distinguishes between the allocation of address space and its assignment. *Allocations* are made by registries to ISPs, which further *assign* them to end users. There might be special cases where registries both allocate and assign to end users, but these should not be common. Criteria for direct allocation by a registry to a user organization include the following:

- The organization does not plan to connect to the Internet, but its requirements would not be met by RFC 1918 private address space. One example of this is a business consortium linking independent partners over a private network.

- The enterprise homes to multiple address spaces, with no favored connection. For example, a university might connect to several research consortia autonomous systems (ASs), as well as to multiple service providers.

> **Warning**
>
> *All registries warn that allocations made directly by registries are not guaranteed to be globally routable. The highest probability of routability is associated with provider assigned space.*

- Actual requirements for IP address space are very large, typically /18 or longer.

RFC 2050 establishes general guidelines for the information registries required to evaluate requests for address space. Regional registries implement specific templates for use in submitting requests to them.

High-Level Information

For the registry to process the request, it must identify the requesting organization and the technical contact for the request. The contact for the request might not be the same as the actual user of the address space. For example, a local ISP registry might submit the request on behalf of a customer. Because address requests can be evaluated among all divisions of an enterprise, this high-level description should identify the ownership of the requesting organization.

Current Usage

You need to satisfy the registry that you are using currently assigned space in an efficient manner. Registry policies vary, but typically 80% of the assigned space should be in use before registries will do a supplemental allocation. Figures 8.15 through 8.19 should have captured most material you need to document this.

Tip

Registries ask for information on current and previous. You specify this part at an aggregate level—totals of address space you used. In this section, you also identify any address blocks you have returned, in the interest of global address conservation.

This is expected to be in tabular form, following the Current Address Space Usage Template, and include growth projections for additional hosts on the currently allocated subnets. APNIC makes a useful distinction between address space allocated to customers and to your internal infrastructure.

Both APNIC and RIPE ask specific questions about whether you have used efficient practices in your address management. Such practices include use of RFC 1918 private space, use of the all-ones and all-zeros subnets, CIDR-style supernetting, and so on.

Regardless of the registry, it's a good idea to point out that you have used your allocated space wisely. You might want to point out any address-conserving dynamic allocation schemes.

Write a general description of the network topology and then discuss the routing plan used with it. Your routing plan should identify the dynamic routing protocol(s) used and any special considerations such as hosts or routers that only handle a subset of a protocol. The practical question here is not the specific routing mechanisms used, but ensuring that classless routing is used and identifying and justifying exceptions to a classless environment.

Note

When a registry allocates a block of space, not only does it have a starting address and prefix length, such as 192.168.0.0/10, but it also has a network name. Network names are used in various global Internet tables and databases.

The network name is specified by the requesting organization in its allocation request. For ARIN, network names are up to 12 alphanumeric characters in length and can contain a dash (-). APNIC allows names to be up to 25 characters long, but it might be prudent to restrict them to 12 in the event software that refers to network names is restricted to the ARIN length.

Registries recommend that subsequent name requests should clearly be continuations of the first, such as internet-block-1, internet-block-2, and so on.

Network name blocks have no relationship to DNS domains and must not end in a top-level domain identifier such as .com.

Another aspect of the routing plan description is identifying the prefixes to be externally advertised and the places these are to be advertised. Such places are upstream ISPs, exchange points, and bilateral and multilateral peers.

Registries also want to ensure that the number of hosts and media used to justify the address space request reflect reality. The old days in which you could justify a Class B address to have two network octets, one subnet octet, and one host octet to "make things easy to write" are long gone. Even static addressing for dialup hosts is considered a matter of administrative convenience and will not be accepted as a justification for space.

ISPs might ask their users to provide addressing plans. If the ISP's users have inefficient address plans, registries can deny additional allocations to the ISP.

Proposed Usage

Registries expect deployment plans before granting additional space. These certainly reflect the top management guidance we talked about in Chapter 1, "What Is the Problem You Are Trying to Solve?" but also consider detailed deployment, renumbering, and so on. The following are key elements of the proposal:

- A description of the topology, routing, and how new addresses will be introduced into it.

- Total number of addresses requested, identifying the count and utilization ratio at initial allocation, and the numbers and ratios that will be used in 12 and 24 months. Some registries will want shorter-term projections as in three or six months.

- Criteria for assigning address space. For example, the requester might identify some number of "large site switched LANs," which will have a minimum immediate population of 100 hosts, 200 in 12 months, and 400 in 24 months. Your plan should include masks and number of hosts per medium. You have the information in Worksheets 8-1 through 8-3 to create this, when coupled with management guidance about growth you obtained with the Chapter 1.

- A list of all subnets on the network with subnet masks or prefix lengths, numbers of hosts at each time period, and a description of the subnet's function such as POP 3 access server or customer 1 server farm. Again, the worksheets serve as a basis for structuring this information.

Although RFC 2050 suggests if subnetting is not used, "an explanation why it cannot be implemented is required," it is difficult to imagine why a registry would accept a nonsubnetted design. Remember that the smallest unit of address space generally allocated by a registry is a /19, which needs 4,094 current hosts. The performance and reliability of a 4,000+ host, "flattened" network would be questionable, so it is hard to imagine a nonsubnetted request of that size. If a network is sufficiently small that it can be handled completely at Layer 2, it is probably too small to justify other than provider-based address space or private address space. Exceptions might be considered if the network is based on advanced switching technology such as ATM or flow/tag switching.

Although /19 is the most common direct registry allocation, there are cases when smaller CIDR blocks might be allocated. APNIC, for example, usually assigns /22 blocks to new ISPs.

Modifiers to the Address Plan

You get your address space assignments from private address space, from an ISP, or directly from an address registry. Large organizations might have an internal group that simulates an ISP; you negotiate with this organization just as if it were a true external ISP.

Address space from a registry is justified from the bottom up, basing the justification on the numbers of present and planned hosts on media. The justification is refined with requirements for aggregation, alternate connectivity, and so on. Even if you are obtaining space from an ISP rather than directly from a registry, it's a good idea to prepare a justification. If your upstream service provider itself needs more space, your justifications will help with its request. If you change providers, the justification will help get new space delegated to you.

Note

Registries usually allocate under a slow start rule, giving out the minimum address space that is justified by information in the request. Their preference is to allocate minimum address space at first and then make additional allocations based on demonstrated usage. ARIN and RIPE generally require justification for a /19, basing their estimates on 12- and 24-month utilization. APNIC wants six- and 12-month utilization projections, but usually grants a /22. ARIN has an experimental procedure for ISPs that makes it easier to make the initial CIDR block globally routable. Don't plan on requesting a large initial allocation simply for reasons of global routability; this is not adequate justification.

continues

Future allocations will not necessarily be in the same CIDR block, so it is a good idea to have a renumbering-friendly environment in place from the beginning.

After you have gotten an initial allocation, registries check that you have used most of it before allocating new space. Their primary check is the RHWHOIS or SWIP databases in which you record, in a public structure, the allocations of your space.

As you assign blocks to your customers, be sure you keep the associated RHWHOIS or SWIP entries current. Don't wait until you need more address space.

Public Versus Private Address Space

Even when you use private IP addresses, the justification process is a worth-while exercise. It reflects best current practices in administration and design.

In addition, your business requirements might change such that some of your private address space needs to become externally visible. If this happens, your address usage should be something you can justify.

Note

In my experience, too many people fall into a trap of saying, "Let's not worry about all the detail of address justification. Let's just put everything into network 10.0.0.0 and translate on the firewall."

It seems so easy to do. There's no need to do fancy subnetting when address space is effectively unlimited, as it is with a /8 block, or a traditional Class A. But an increasing number of business and technical issues might come back to haunt you.

There are several things wrong with this approach. First, fine-tuning an address plan includes the route aggregation and summarization that are important to overall network stability. There are good technical reasons not to fall into the trap of putting all address boundaries on a dotted-decimal octet boundary. If you find that all your prefixes are /8, /16, or /24, there is a strong chance you haven't thought through your design.

Second, there is an increasing number of cases where private address space and network address translation might not be an appropriate solution. These include end-to-end cryptography, outsourced network management, and some virtual private network designs. Even if you never need to connect to the general Internet, what if you need to interconnect with a new business partner that also numbered into the 10.0.0.0/8?

Forcing a network design into /16 and /24 subnets of a private network is rather like insisting on feeding baby foods to adults. Some adults need baby food due to digestive problems. I confess to a certain fondness for strained plums as a dessert and have been known to use baby foods as convenient purees while doing complex cooking. But to insist that baby food is appropriate for all adults is analogous to insisting that all adults should eat nothing but baby food.

Dynamic Assignment

RFC 2050 specifies that reserving specific IP addresses for individual dialup users does not constitute a justification for address space. There is a guiding principle that addresses will be assigned dynamically for the duration of a connection and then returned to the pool.

In practice, this means that address blocks are assigned to dial access servers. Depending on the particular server implementation, an address might be associated with each dial-in port of the server, a single pool might be established inside the server, or the pool and address assignments might come from an access control server such as RADIUS. RADIUS address assignment is discussed in Chapter 7, "Addressing, Security, and Network Management."

Emerging IP mobility methods might create a tunnel from the access server to an IP address on a home LAN. In that case, there is no IP address assignment from the server to the user.

The engineering plan of your address request should specifically state that you are using dynamic address assignment for individual dialup users. This is yet another way to show you are using space efficiently and increases the probability that your request will be accepted.

Static address assignments are more acceptable for routers that make periodic or on-demand connections to an upstream service provider. Assigning static addresses to router WAN ports amortizes the static address over multiple LAN addresses that gain access through the router.

Dynamic assignment of only the addresses that are actually needed is not limited to dialup users. Remember that registries are concerned with conserving globally routable address space. If you use NAPT to reduce the number of addresses needed for external connectivity, make sure to mention this in the justification.

Multihomed Routing

Multihoming means many things, but a significant meaning in address allocation is providing multiple Internet access paths for an enterprise or nontransit ISP [Berkowitz 1998a]. As shown in Figure 9.4, a multihomed organization of this sort connects to at least two upstream service providers. All the upstream providers advertise the organization's address space to their upstream and peer providers.

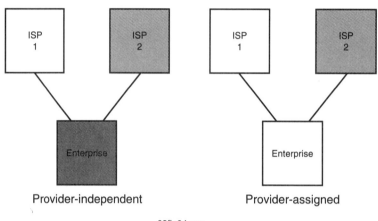

09fig04.eps
Bill K. 09/14/98 ISBN# 78700590

FIGURE 9.4.   *Multihomed address space.*

Conceptually, it makes no difference whether the enterprise's address space is an assignment from one of the providers—that is, a *provider assigned* (PA) space—or is directly assigned to the enterprise as *provider independent* (PI). In the real world, this is much more complex.

PI space is much more flexible from a business standpoint because the organization does not have to renumber if it changes providers. The chief problem with PI space, however, is that a PI block assigned to an organization newly connected to the Internet tends to be small. It might be only the set of addresses on the organization's firewall DMZ and be only a /24, /25, or longer prefix.

Some major ISPs filter out route advertisements longer than /19, unless they are generated by a directly connected customer. This means that the specific organization addresses do not propagate through such major carriers, unless they are /19 or shorter (that is, with more hosts) prefixes.

There is no general solution to this problem. Although a /19 today is assumed to be the longest prefix generally routable in the Internet, there are no guarantees that in the future, the magic length might not become /18. Registry policy does not guarantee routability.

In the interest of overall routability, it might actually turn out that PA space is more useful because the PA space is part of a larger block to which prefix length restrictions do not apply. If you plan to make it easy to renumber in your network, appropriately using dynamic address assignment, linked DNS/DHCP, and so on, changing to a different PA block might be less of an obstacle than it seems.

Realistically, if you have a multihoming requirement of this sort, get advice from a service provider or consultant experienced with multihoming address practices. When you submit the address request, indicate that you intend to multihome and identify the providers that will advertise your address block.

Examples

Several examples will illustrate how you collect the information to construct an address request. The discussions in this section focus on enterprises because special considerations exist for ISPs. ISP examples are presented later in this chapter.

A Small Firm

To understand the justification process, begin with a simple case. Imagine that yours is a small firm that has a single location with 20 workstations that want occasional Internet access. These workstations connect to three local servers. You intend to establish a public Web presence. Figure 9.5 shows this simple case. The small firm is a flat network that has no plausible subnets at this point, although the servers might move onto a subnet if there is significant growth.

It's a good idea to keep this simple. The number of workstations and servers required is reasonable to connect to a switch. Twenty clients and three local servers might be a bit high in traffic for a single 10 MB shared Ethernet, so use a shared 100 MB hub or simply bring the devices into a switch, putting at least the servers on 100 MBps ports.

You could simplify things enormously by outsourcing your Web server and Internet connectivity to a local ISP. Depending on availability requirements, the service provider would place one or more routers, with one or more lines, on your site. Your responsibility would end at the LAN interface to the router(s).

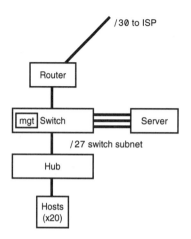

FIGURE 9.5.   *A small firm using PA space with a single user subnet.*

In practice, the addressing requirement is not large enough for you to request an independent address allocation from a registry. You would have address space assigned from your upstream provider's allocation. Before delving into the actual address requirement, consider how the addresses will be used and managed.

All your workstations, and preferably your servers, should get their specific address assignments from a Dynamic Host Configuration Protocol (DHCP) server. It's preferable that this server should be on your LAN, but if you are looking for the simplest possible operation, the DHCP server could be at the ISP, and the router could be configured to forward DHCP client broadcasts to the DHCP server.

Warning

Remember to include router interfaces and management interfaces of switches in the total number of hosts.

If the switch is managed, either from one of your client workstations or from the ISP, it needs an IP address for its own management function. This IP address is assigned to a management interface that either can be configured as part of your main subnet (that is, in-band management) or on a separate subnet (that is, out-of-band management).

There also needs to be an IP address assigned for the router port on the LAN. The router port address is on a different subnet, presumably a /30.

This network is sufficiently small that in-band versus out-of-band management makes little difference from a performance standpoint—although you will see in the example "Architecting an Enterprise" that out-of-band makes sense for large networks.

In this case, the ISP does management, and there is only one local subnet for the ISP to reach, so in-band probably is reasonable. Another reason to use in-band management is because adding a second subnet would require a routing function to send management packets to one interface and user traffic to the other.

You have one broadcast domain—one subnet—in your actual enterprise. The router needs one interface in the LAN and one on the WAN link back to the provider. For the WAN link, you need a single /30 prefix for a point-to-point link implemented as a dedicated circuit, ISDN line, or Frame Relay PVC. If the ISP is responsible for the router, it normally manages the addressing on the WAN side.

It is your responsibility to determine the addressing requirement on the LAN. An inventory of the current usage shows the following breakdowns and counts of hosts:

Clients	20
Servers	3
Switch management port	1
Router port	1
Total	25

This doesn't allow for any growth, but to keep the example simple, that is a problem for another day. Refer to Table 5.2, where the smallest prefix size that can contain 25 hosts is a /27, which has 30 usable host addresses. The traditional subnet mask associated with a /27 is 255.255.255.240.

In this simple example, the utilization ratio between hosts used and available space is 25/30, or 0.83. This would be considered quite good utilization, still allowing for 20% growth.

With this small address requirement, you could not justify a direct allocation from a registry, so there is no need to prepare detailed justifications. Still, this is good practice for the justification process. Some ISPs might ask their subscribers to provide some level of justification, because registries consider the efficiency of use of subscriber space when the ISPs ask for more address space to be allocated to them.

> **Note**
>
> *This discussion does not consider whether to use public or private address space. When doing your address planning, please don't fall into the trap of assuming you will always use private space with address translation. Network address translation is not compatible with all applications. It works in many situations, but avoid the temptation that it can always be used to avoid complex addressing.*
>
> *Registries do not look kindly on address justifications that are administratively convenient to set up as a numbering plan, but not efficient in address usage. Remember, you can always define an efficient address plan and use private address space, and go through rather simple renumbering if you need to convert to public space. If you did not use efficient addressing, renumbering is much more painful.*

A More Complex Justification

The organization illustrated in Figure 9.6 has a corporate site with 1,000 users and a server farm with 20 machines. It now has 20 remote sites with an average of six remote users at each site.

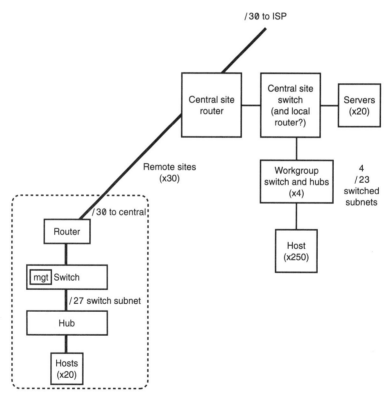

FIGURE 9.6. *A more complex organization, using PA space with subnetting.*

There is good business justification that the number of sites will grow 50% in the next year, and each remote site will double its number of users. The central site will increase its user count by 25%, but will double the number of servers.

Remote Site Requirements

Giving a /28 to each remote site allows an additional five users to be added, with no additional servers or network infrastructure. Fifty percent growth would only require three more addresses, for a total of 12 hosts.

This is really on the edge. The utilization ratio, which is the number of hosts used divided by the number of hosts possible in the prefix, is 0.86 with a /28, but 0.40 with a /27. A typical goal is a 0.50 ratio. If you reasonably feel that there might be more servers or managed devices at remote sites, or that some of the sites might have more users, the /27 is probably reasonable to request.

WAN and Central Site Requirements

Remember that the number of sites will grow as well. There needs to be a LAN at each site and a WAN link from the central site to each remote site.

Assuming Frame Relay PVCs or dedicated lines, you need 30 /30 WAN prefixes to connect to your 30 remote sites, each remote LAN with a /27.

At the central site, there are 1,000 users and 20 servers. Let's look first at issues in addressing for the user workstations.

User Addressing

Two hundred fifty users per subnet is extremely close to the 254 hosts available in a /24. That number of users leaves no growth for workstations, nor does it allow for placing servers on user subnets.

Although a /23 would give more flexibility, it might conflict with some assumptions in your host software. If your addresses were in the traditional

Class C space (that is, 192.x.x.x through 223.x.x.x), and your hosts did not understand CIDR, they could only directly address half the hosts on the medium. They would need to go through the router to reach the other half, increasing the workload on the router and doubling the number of packets appearing on the LAN.

If your hosts had this limitation, and it was not practical to upgrade their software for CIDR awareness, a better approach might be to renumber them into 12 /25 subnets. These 12 blocks could be aggregated with another /25 for the server farm, a management subnet, one subnet further divided into /30 subnets for remote access, and one spare. Such aggregation would call for a /21 for the central site and lines leading to it. The server and management subnets are lightly utilized in this example, but the 12 user blocks would force you to the next power of 2 to get a CIDR block that contains all the address space for your headquarters.

Server Addressing

What about the server addressing? There are two basic approaches to addressing servers at a single campus. The first, traditional approach is routing between user and server subnets. An alternative approach is installing VLAN-aware NICs in the servers, so that each server—or the appropriate subset of servers—appears on each user VLAN.

There is no question that routing works. Without VLANs, there needs to be an interface on the router for each of the user subnets, one for the server farm and one for a management subnet if one is used. These interfaces are in addition to those needed for WAN connectivity to the remote sites.

VLAN-aware NICs would flatten the network, yet still provide broadcast isolation for workstations on the VLANs. The servers, of course, would see all broadcasts on all VLANs. In this context, VLAN awareness includes both connectionless VLANs such as ISL and ATM LAN Emulation (LANE).

Traffic must be considered before leaping to use VLAN-aware NICs. VLAN-aware NICs have physical 100 MBps or possibly 155 MBps interfaces. If the aggregate of workstation-to-server traffic on all VLANs is greater than the bandwidth of the physical NIC, you have to provide additional NICs, if the software supports multiple VLAN-aware NICs. Alternatively, for this example, you might put four or eight non-VLAN NICs into each server, so they can be physically connected to each user LAN.

Remember to consider backup and other interserver communications. If these are substantial, you might want a separate subnet for interserver traffic.

If you use VLAN-aware servers, or put a NIC for each server into the user subnets, you do not need an additional subnet. You do, however, need to add 20 host addresses to each user subnet. If you had kept the /24 structure for the central site LANs, this would have exceeded the number of available host space on each LAN.

To increase the host space, the preferred method is to go to /23 CIDR subnets. If the hosts do not understand CIDR, you can use secondary addressing to put multiple subnets on the same shared medium, with due caution about the need to route between subnets.

Another approach is to split into 12 /25 subnets, with a lesser number of end user hosts on each subnet. It is probably impractical to put 12 NICs into the servers, so this approach requires either VLAN-aware NICs or not having all servers present on every user subnet.

Architecting an Enterprise

Let's now consider an enterprise that simply wants a coherent address plan of its own, with room to grow. It has had no Internet connectivity and has used private address space. In preparing the reverse executive summary, you have learned that the company expects to acquire several new companies in the near term.

As shown in Figure 9.7, 30 office buildings are scattered across North America and are organized into Eastern, Central, and Western regions. Each building has five floors in which users work and a central computer room. Each floor now has 50 users, but will be wired for 100 users. Each floor also has a server room for workgroup servers, and the organization plans up to eight servers per floor. Assume that each floor should form a separate broadcast domain.

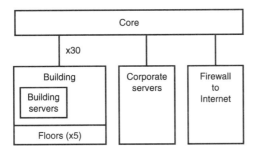

FIGURE 9.7. *A large company with subnetting and aggregation. It is sufficiently large that it could justify PI space, although private space and PA space might be better alternatives.*

Also assume that the floors are more than 100 meters distant from the server room. This distance makes it necessary to have workgroup hubs or switches to act as repeaters, regenerating the signal so it can reach the floor server room and wire closet. The central computer room is connected to each server room. There are 10 servers for the building as a whole. There also is a router with a Frame Relay interface in the server room, which connects to other sites.

End User Address Requirements

You want to start at the lowest level of the hierarchy, the floor. How many addresses do you need for clients and servers on the floor?

Clients	100
Servers	8
Total	108

One hundred eight addresses fit into a /25 prefix, which contains up to 126 hosts. As shown in Figure 9.8, this covers the floor applications, but you need additional addresses for the infrastructure.

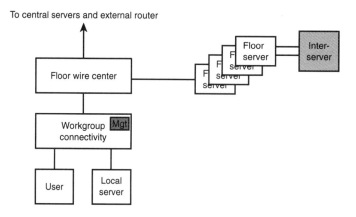

FIGURE 9.8. *This figure shows only the user hosts, not any of the connection structure.*

At the very least, you need one address for a router interface, where the floor LAN joins other LANs and the building servers.

Requirements for Additional Infrastructure

If you connect the clients and servers to managed hubs or switches, these each need an IP address for management. Some switches and hubs have external management interfaces, on which an IP address on a subnet different from that of the users can be assigned.

If you use 16-port switches, all stations are within 100 meters of the floor wire closet, and the users and servers are evenly distributed over each floor, you need eight workgroup switches. Practical wiring requires these be brought to a floor switch or router. This makes your total address requirement the following:

Clients	100
Servers	8
Floor router/switch	1
Workgroup Switches	8
Total	117

This requirement fits in a /25 prefix. Remember that these counts already reflect expected growth. There are only 50 users today, but it should help in justifying the address space that the organization has gone to the expense of prewiring for 100 users per floor.

Will there be any significant server-to-server traffic among the floor servers for backup or distributed computing? If so, as shown in Figure 9.9, you can dual port the servers and establish a server-to-server broadcast domain/subnet between them. The servers themselves handle any necessary routing between the general floor LAN and the server-only LAN, presumably acting as application gateways.

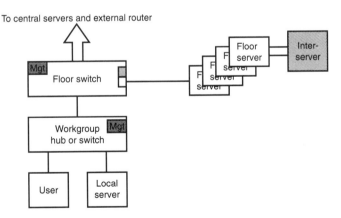

FIGURE 9.9. *The dual-ported servers with a server-only LAN can act as application gateways to the user LAN.*

You have choices in how to interconnect the building servers to the floors. One approach is to run each floor uplink switch either to a main switch port or to a small concentrating switch on the floor, which, in turn, goes via riser cable to the server room.

In the central server room, you need to connect five floor cables, or 35 switch cables, to a central relaying device. This could be a switch or router.

Several choices emerge. You could connect the floor uplinks to a central switch that contains an internal routing function and route between the floor LANs, the server LAN, and the WAN.

Routing to Central Servers

Each floor could be treated as a separate LAN and connected to a router port. Classical routers that can interconnect a significant number of 100 MBps devices are expensive.

As shown in Figure 9.10, either a switch or router can combine the floors. A switch is particularly appropriate if VLANs are used. Some routing functionality is needed for external access. It's probably cheaper to use a small external router than to use high-speed resources in the switch.

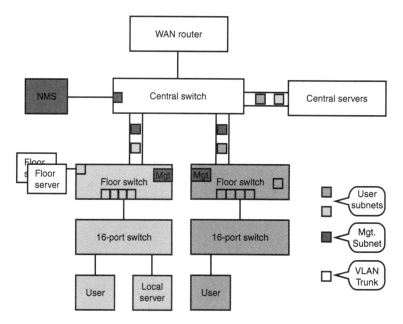

FIGURE 9.10. *Combining the floors using switch and router functions.*

With a central switch or router and a switch on each floor, the individual ports can be treated as VLANs. This gives flexibility in moving users between floors—although if the floor servers are truly standard, there is no requirement for this.

VLAN-Aware Servers

You could make each floor a VLAN and use a VLAN-aware card on each of the 10 servers. Doing so would add 10 server addresses to each floor VLAN, as follows:

Clients	100
Floor Servers	8
Router	1
Switches	7
Central Servers	10
Total	126

This *just* fits.

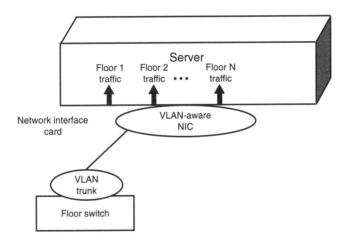

F I G U R E 9.11. *Addressing with VLAN-aware servers.*

Out-of-Band Management Without VLANs

Another approach is to split the management interfaces onto another subnet, depicted in Figure 9.12. If this is done without VLANs, it adds another riser cable from each switch.

Without VLANs, the management LAN looks like the following:

5×8 floor switches	40
Floor concentrating switches	5
Central switch	1
External router	1
Total	47

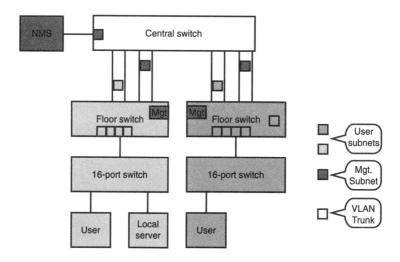

FIGURE 9.12. *Out-of-band management requires more physical media than in-band management.*

This out-of-band management subnet fits into a /26.

Out-of-Band Management with VLANs

With VLANs, the management LAN for user devices takes the same number of IP addresses, but shares the riser cable. Arguments can be made that there are availability advantages to having a separate management medium.

The following fits into a /26:

Floor switches (5×8)	35
Floor concentrating switches	5
Central switch	1
External router	1
Total	42

At this point, if we use VLAN-aware servers, we need five /25 prefixes for floors and servers and one /26 for management in each building.

Summarizing into the WAN

A simplistic approach to summarization is to round the /26 up to /25 and say we need six subnets per building. To summarize on a power of 2 boundary, we have to round this 6×/25 up to 8×/25, which means a /22 per building.

With 30 buildings, rounding up again to 32, we need a /17. A /17 can hold 32,766 hosts. Our 30 buildings, assuming VLAN-aware servers, each have 540 user hosts and 41 management hosts. We have said that each building, in the simplistic model, needs a /22, which can hold 2,046 hosts. This gives 26% building utilization.

Ignoring WAN links, we need 17,430 host addresses in the overall network, using a /17. This is 53% utilization, which is not terrible.

Can we do better? Six subnets per building wastes two subnets each. If we gave each building a /23 and then advertised a /24 from each building, we do not waste subnets. A /23 holds 510 hosts and a /24 holds 254, giving us 76% utilization.

For the 30 buildings, you need 30 /23 and 15 /24. Aggregate the 15 /24 into 8 /23, for a total of 38 /23. This has to round up to 64 /23 prefixes, again a /17. It's no better.

But what if we regionalized and got 10 /23 per region, plus 5 /24 rounded to 3 /23? This rounds up to 16 /23, or a /19 for each region. A /19 holds 8,190 hosts. (10×581)/8,190 = utilization.

Whether registries prefer to grant three /19 blocks or a single /17 depends on their current priorities. Granting three /19 blocks conserves the total number of addresses, while granting a single /17 conserves slots in the global routing table.

Preparing for Renumbering

When preparing for renumbering, you first need to take an inventory and then you need to analyze needs for additional space, or space that differs in global accessibility from your existing space. Begin by identifying the prefixes in or planned into your network, and whether they have been assigned in a systematic and hierarchical manner.

You should categorize your prefixes into those that will not be renumbered, those that will be released, and those that will be renumbered. You might find it useful to separate the ones to be renumbered into subcategories of addresses to be renumbered into public or private space.

The ideal situation is where there is a one-to-one mapping between old and new addresses. This rarely is the case. You most often see this when you are "cleaning up" an existing enterprise using private addressing, or if you are dealing with a merger where all computers are mapped into a new address space for the new company.

Ideals are rarely attainable. Not only will real-world mappings not be one-to-one, but it is likely that you will need to run certain old and new addresses in parallel. This is especially likely to be the case for addresses that are visible on the Internet because it takes time for DNS-cached addresses to expire.

It's worth looking at the mechanics of conversion. Remember that when you renumber, you are changing either the prefix, the host number, or both. You can often simplify the process by recognizing cases where only the prefix or host number has to change and then using scripts to automate the changing of configuration files.

Renumbering Scope

Especially for organizations that have collected odd pieces of classful address space over the years, renumbering is a reality if more and contiguous address space is needed. APNIC emphasizes this in its address request material:

> Although it is acknowledged that renumbering may not be a trivial task, most modern implementations of TCP/IP support or come with dynamic IP address assignment technologies such as DHCP or BOOTP. These technologies greatly simplify the tasks associated with renumbering hosts as customers will generally only need to modify the dynamic IP address server, the DNS, and the routers.

The archives of the PIER (Procedures for Internet/Enterprise Renumbering) Working Group of the IETF can be consulted for more information on renumbering and renumbering technologies; see the following URLs:

```
ftp://ftp.apnic.net/ietf/wg/pier/pier-charter.txt
ftp://ftp.isi.edu/in-notes/rfc2071.txt
ftp://ftp.isi.edu/in-notes/rfc2072.txt
```

How difficult will your renumbering be? Typically, the largest amount of work is in renumbering end hosts. DHCP can enormously simplify this task, if the changes need only to be made on DHCP servers.

In the best of circumstances, your changes need to be made on DHCP and DNS servers, and in router configurations. Where possible, running edit scripts against these machines is the easiest way to convert.

If you had an assignment of `202.222.5.0/24` from one provider, and were moved to `202.111.4.0/24` from another provider, renumbering could be very simple. Potentially, you could run scripts against configuration files to replace each occurrence of `202.222.5` with `202.111.4`.

Warning

Be careful! In this renumbering, the replacement is of the first three octets, not all four! You are changing the prefix but retaining the host structure.

This is an ideal case, in which the old and new prefixes have the same number of bits, and fall nicely on octet boundaries. If the prefixes did not fall on octet boundaries, you need to replace them after computing the new prefix. RFC 2072 gives guidance in developing scripts for recomputing prefixes and host fields.

> Prefixes partially under the control of the enterprise may change. The scope of this will vary depending on whether only the externally controlled part of the prefix changes, or if part of the internally controlled part is to be renumbered. If the length of either the high-order or low-order parts change, the process becomes more complex.

> High-order-part-only renumbering is most common when an organization changes ISPs, and needs to renumber into the new provider's space. The old prefix may have been assigned to the enterprise but will no longer be used for global routing, or the old prefix may have been assigned to the previous provider. Note that administrative procedures may be necessary to return the previous prefix, although this usually will be done by the previous provider. There often will need to be a period of coexistence between the old and new prefixes.

> Low-order-part-only renumbering can occur when an enterprise modifies its internal routing structure, and the changes only affect the internal subnet structure of the enterprise network. This is typical of efforts involved in increasing the number of available subnets (e.g., for more point-to-point media) or increasing the number of hosts on a medium (e.g., in greater use of workgroup switches).

Both the high-order and low-order parts may change. This might happen when the enterprise changes to a new ISP, who assigns address space from a CIDR block rather than a classful network previously used. With a different high-order prefix length, the enterprise might be forced to change its subnet structure.

An Example: A Consolidation

Suppose three companies merge. Each has three registered Class C addresses (that is, /24 prefixes), two used private address space in 10.0.0.0, and one used private address space in 192.168.0.0/16.

A Simple Ideal

If it is workable with the physical topology of the merged companies, the simplest method is to create a backbone to which all three companies announce their full routes, which can be on classful boundaries, and have the backbone advertise the default route back to them. All intercompany communications go through the backbone. The backbone addresses are unique, probably private, and probably on a classful boundary for compatibility.

Warning

If the enterprises have not used effective, and preferably linked, DHCP and DNS, implementing these services is an important part of the consolidation. Budget DHCP and DNS servers along with any Network Address Translation (NAT) devices used as interim solutions. NAT technology is discussed in Chapter 6.

The ideal is shown in Figure 9.13. Unfortunately, there is at least one major obstacle for this ideal: duplicate use of 10.0.0.0/8 address space in Companies A and B. Both of these two companies need to renumber or network address translation needs to be implemented between the backbone and one company network. If a new block of addresses is picked for the merged company, a NAT or address-translating firewall might be appropriate between each company and the backbone.

No Clear Backbone

In the real world, the companies, after acquisition, might be reorganized into functional rather than geographic units. Subnets are assigned to the new business units and no longer have the geographic aggregation they once did. Figure 9.14 shows an example of this realistic but messy result of reorganization.

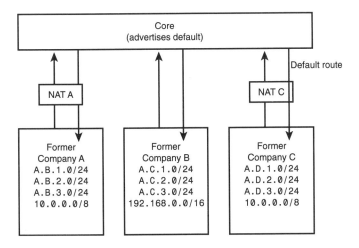

FIGURE 9.13. *NAT at the boundary of each former company domain is an alternative to renumbering, although renumbering is the preferred long-term strategy.*

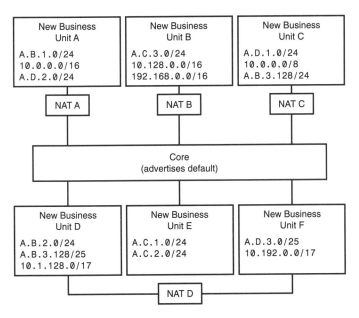

FIGURE 9.14. *If renumbering is impossible, either multiple NATs or address tunnels are necessary.*

One of the key things to remember in structuring the merged network is that address summarization need not be absolute. It certainly is desirable to summarize as much as possible, but even when two prefixes can be summarized into one, there is a gain in routing stability.

Using NAT here becomes more complex, because addressing might need to be translated at several points. There is no longer the option to have a single NAT between each separately administered block of private address space.

Numbering Conventions for an Area Structure

We won't get into the details here, but you can use OSPF design as a prototype for internal summarization and the associated numbering plan. Figure 9.15 shows an OSPF routing domain with a backbone area 0.0.0.0 and four user areas 0.0.0.1 through 0.0.0.4.

Area 0.0.0.0			
Area 0.0.0.1	Area 0.0.0.2	Area 0.0.0.3	Area 0.0.0.4

F I G U R E 9 . 1 5 . *Hierarchical address structures assign one or more contiguous address ranges to each lower-level area. These address ranges are usually summarized into the core.*

In each of the nonzero areas, there is a part of legacy address space and a part of a new address loan that is intended to lend itself to CIDR summarization and aggregation.

Do not be overly concerned that some of your existing address space does not cleanly summarize. It is not necessary that a given OSPF area only advertise a single summary prefix. Even a small amount of summarization will help stability by reducing routing table change.

When you are assigning new addresses, however, you do want them to summarize well. Again, it's important to be realistic about this.

The Basic Bit-Splitting Method for Assigning Addresses to Areas

Many industry courses and references suggest that you should decide how many areas you have and split your address space evenly among them. To split things evenly when the things are based on binary arithmetic, you need, in this model, a number of areas that is a power of two.

For a routing domain with four nonzero areas, this allocates a /20 prefix to each area, as follows:

/20 starting 00xxxx...   Area 1

Starting 01xxxx...   Area 2

Starting 10xxxx…   Area 3

Starting 11xxxx…   Area 4

An Enhanced Bit-Splitting Method for Assigning Addresses to Areas

This approach seems straightforward but suffers from several limitations. First, what about area 0? No space has been left for it. In any case, it is likely that a /20 assigned to area 0 would waste a great deal of space, because area 0 should have a small number of router interfaces in it.

One technique when using the bit-split method, and assuming registered addresses are used in the nonzero areas, is to use RFC 1918 private address space for area 0. This can be quite reasonable because it is hard to imagine legitimate reasons why an arbitrary external Internet host would need to access a backbone interface internal to an enterprise network. One possible criticism of this approach is that traceroutes that traversed the backbone might show the private address space, but it is usually apparent when this is happening.

Another and more general approach is to bit-split to a level deeper than the number of areas. In the preceding example, there were four nonzero areas and four /20 blocks. The /20 comes from it being the first power of 2 that can contain four areas.

Consider, however, going two or three powers of 2 deeper. Divide the available address space into 8, 16, or 32 blocks. These, respectively, would be /21, /22, or /23 address prefixes.

One of these blocks can be assigned to Area 0. It is a reality that the number of users in individual areas will vary, so area 1 might, for example, need three /21 blocks, area 2 might need two such blocks, and area 1 might need one. Several blocks can be reserved for growth as needed.

Non-IP Prefix Derivation

After you have developed a rational IP addressing structure, you can use it to generate rational identifiers for some of your non-IP protocols, several of which are discussed in the following sections.

Novell IPX Derivation

IPX addressing is the easiest, because it has a 32-bit network number field. Let's assume the IP prefix for a given subnet is 129.249.131.224/28. Write out the octets and convert to binary:

```
129.     249    .131.     224
10000000.11110001.10000011.11100000
```

Insert a period for readability between every four bits. Four-bit groups correspond to hexadecimal digits, when converted:

```
1000.0000.1111.0001.1000.0011.1110.0000
8    0    F    1    8    3    E    0
```

This is the perfectly valid IPX network address 80F183E0.

AppleTalk Derivation

AppleTalk's 16-bit network number does not directly map to a full 32-bit network number, but there are still useful tricks. Let's use the same IP prefix as in the Novell example and assume it is a public prefix in the classical Class B space. This means that the first 16 bits are centrally assigned and will not change inside your enterprise.

Take the low-order 16 bits of the earlier prefix:

```
1000.0011.1110.0000
```

Convert this into decimal:

```
32768+512+256+128+64+32 = 33760
```

33760 would be a perfectly valid AppleTalk network number. In practice, you assign a cable-range of contiguous network numbers to a physical medium, using the guideline of one network number for each 50 Macintoshes.

If you had 200 Macintosh computers on the medium, a reasonable cable range would thus be 33,760–33,763. You are using the host bits of the IP address to provide the additional AppleTalk network numbers needed for the cable range of four network numbers.

An Evolutionary Example

Let's return to the first enterprise we looked at in Chapter 6. It has cleaned up its addressing, but has developed some new requirements, including Internet commerce from arbitrary users and major international expansion. To get the European and Asian connectivity the enterprise wants, it has been most practical to use provider-based addressing.

An enterprise had a Class B, or /16, prefix for a number of years. After several corporate mergers and acquisitions, it found itself short on address space. Because the corporate architecture expects to use encrypted tunnels, the enterprise wants all its address space to be registered.

Originally, the enterprise used a /24 prefix. This allowed single subnets to service large numbers of Ethernet or Token Ring users on headquarters LANs. There were two major campuses, each with two links to the other campus.

Version 1 RIP was used as the routing protocol, which does not support class-less addressing and thus does not support subnet 0.

The Chapter 6 discussion focused on the actual renumbering. Here, the focus is on the address justification.

Core and Distribution Tier Address Justification

Looking at this enterprise hierarchically, there is a simple core but much more complexity at the distribution and access tiers. Two /30 links are needed for connectivity between the two major campuses.

Warning

Don't fall into the trap of assuming that every WAN link will be in the core, or the core will need large amounts of address space. Collapsed backbones, or small numbers of intercampus links, often are excellent core design.

Each of the two campuses contained distribution and access tier links as well as its end of the core link. Distribution links and associated address space ran between servers and between routers.

Note

The distribution versus access distinction isn't completely clear for the switched media to which clients are connected via hubs. Such media would have been clear at the access level if all traffic went to the local servers, and only output of local servers went beyond. Because traffic might go to the firewall or to servers at other campuses, the distinction is not precise—and is not something to worry about.

Access Tier Address Justification

The major growth in address space requirements would be at local sites, which are clearly in the access tier. Each local site needs a /29 for its LAN and a /30 for its WAN link to the campus to which it is homed. From an addressing standpoint, it will use a /30 whether this WAN link is implemented as a dedicated line or a Frame Relay PVC.

Twenty-five remote sites were linked to each campus, but this number was expected to double each six months. Fifty sites per campus were planned at the first six-month checkpoint, 100 sites at 12 months, 200 at 18 months, and 400 at the end of the 24-month planning period in the address space justification.

In this organization, remote sites actually have up to eight users, one shared printer, and one local file server. In the event of a connectivity failure, individual workstations dial up for backup to a RAS server at each campus. Workstations then use a host address associated with the RAS server subnet.

At first glance, this might suggest that 400×8, or 3,200 additional host addresses would be needed at each campus. This does not reflect reality. First, backup connectivity would be needed only if a specific remote office went down, which would mean up to eight users would need connectivity. The nature of the applications in use is not such that remote workers need continuous server connectivity to do their jobs.

> **Tip**
>
> *Reading electronic mail is a fairly obvious application that needs only occasional connectivity, as is Web access. Lotus Notes is another commercial application that only occasionally needs a database update.*

If you assume that no more than 5% of sites were down at any given time, there would be a need for 20×8, or 160 host addresses at the peak. But if only 25% of the workers at a given site actually need server connectivity at any given time, the real RAS address requirement is closer to 40. A /27 would allow 30 users. Two /27 or one /26 prefix would be reasonable.

Exterior Routing Considerations

Even though you might have received a registered allocation directly from a registry, there is no guarantee that it will be generally routable on the Internet. Rules for the routability of prefixes, unfortunately, change frequently and are not written in one place. They are affected by registry policies, but are affected even more by the operational policies of major carriers.

Although the real criteria are much more complex, the basic rule is that prefixes longer than /19 cannot be globally routable due to provider filtering. Another way to look at this is to say that /19 prefixes are portable and do not need to be renumbered when changing upstream providers. This makes them highly desirable for ISPs.

Address Allocations for ISPs

Again, policies differ from one registry to another. ARIN's requirements are typical and are based on an assumption that startup ISPs use space assigned by their upstream provider(s). As they grow and demonstrate effective utilization based on real customer usage, they can apply for a direct allocation of address space.

Historically, the threshold for a direct allocation has been justification of a /19 prefix, which theoretically could contain 8190 hosts. A practical guideline might be a 0.50 utilization ratio for this address space.

Note

ARIN is experimenting with a new procedure to help small but growing ISPs get globally routable / 19 prefixes. Assume an ISP has made efficient use, according to the published efficiency guidelines, of a / 21 assigned from an upstream provider.

The growing ISP can apply for a policy where it requests a direct allocation of a / 20. This / 20 is half of a / 19, and the other half is not allocated while the ISP is in this quick-start program. The ISP is allowed to advertise the / 19 to which its / 20 belongs.

ISPs in this program have to agree to renumber into the PI / 20 which has been allocated to them. If they cannot justify the full / 19 in a defined period of time, currently 18 months, they have to agree to release the / 20 and renumber into PA space. If their growth continues, however, they will expand into the other half of the / 19.

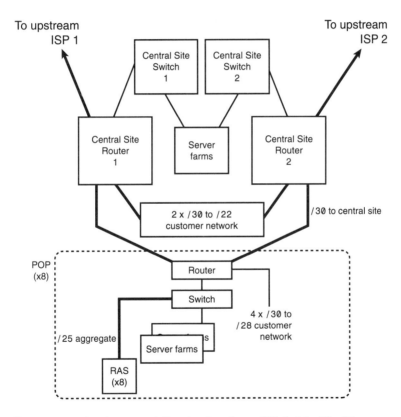

FIGURE 9.16. *A representative structure for an ISP that justifies PI space.*

What might an ISP network that justifies an allocation look like? Begin with eight points of presence (POPs), shown in Figure 9.16, each of which has 12 / 28, one / 27, and one / 25:

- Eight POPs, each with 270 host addresses, for a total of 2,160 addresses in use now.

- One hundred twelve dial-in ports on eight 14-line access servers, each with an additional aggregate interface. Each access server would fully occupy a /28 prefix.

- A local infrastructure LAN containing the aggregate ports for the eight dial servers, a cache or secondary DNS server, a Web cache engine, a TFTP server for booting servers and routers, and a local authentication server. Router interfaces to two more ISP backbone routers also appear on this LAN, as well as the interface of an access router that services dedicated customer LANs. This makes a total immediate requirement for 14 devices on this LAN, with reason to believe it will grow. A /27 prefix is certainly reasonable.

- Four small customer LANs, each a /28 with 10 machines and a router interface.

- One medium customer LAN, with 100 machines justifying a /25.

How could these be aggregated? Each four /27 prefixes aggregate into a /25. Allocating two /25s covers the existing dialup servers.

For simplicity, treat the customer LANs as /27 rather than /28. Combining the four small LANs with the medium-sized LAN calls for one /25 aggregate and one /25 non-aggregate.

So, there is an immediate requirement for four /25s, or a /23 aggregate for each POP. Eight POPs require a /20.

This ISP expects to grow by adding POPs rather than increasing the size of individual POPs:

- A main and a backup server farm for guest domains and Web pages. Each has a /27.

- A primary infrastructure LAN containing the primary DNS, mail server, news server, and so on. This reasonably would be a /27 or /28. Larger spaces might be feasible with 100 MBPS or faster media, or LAN switching.

- A secondary infrastructure LAN. Again, assume a /27.

- Two large customer networks with high speed connections. Each has 500 hosts with 25% growth planned, which requires a /22 each.

- A backbone network interconnecting the router interfaces of the 16 POPs, two server farms, and six customer networks and two infrastructure networks. This requires 26 host addresses now, so reasonable growth justifies one /26 or two /27s.

Non-POP requirements can be viewed as five /27s and two /22s. The five /27 subnets can be aggregated into two /25s. The two /22s aggregate into another /21.

The backbone, server farms, and large customer networks justify a /21, while the POPs justify a /20. Together, these make a reasonable case for a /19.

Routability of Registered Address Space

Some ISPs do not advertise long prefixes that do not belong to their customers. This is not intended as a means of creating new business. Operational policies that underlie the carriers' filters for long prefixes are based on professional assessments of the requirements to keep the provider network and the Internet stable. Unfortunately, respected routing architects disagree with one another on the extent of filtration needed. Consult the North American Network Operators' Group (NANOG) Web page at http://www.nanog.org for recent information on provider filtering policies.

Enterprises usually have a lesser need for portable address space than ISPs, because they usually do not assign address space. Portable address space is definitely not the only way to achieve effective multihoming, although multihoming is often cited as a justification for portable address space.

Connecting to Providers

Although a detailed discussion of the ways to which you connect to providers is beyond the scope of this book, you need to know something about the topic to fill out applications for address space.

The two main ways to connect to providers are at an *exchange point* or through *private peering*. In the first case, your organization runs a point-to-point line or virtual circuit to an exchange point. See the section "Exchange Points" in Chapter 6.

Private peering is simpler and often better when there is substantial traffic to exchange. Exchange points do become congested and are somewhat more unpredictable because they involve traffic from more than two parties.

Private peering involves a point-to-point line or virtual circuit run directly between routers of the customer and service provider. For especially high volume applications, this link might be at Layer 2, running over ATM or PPP-over-SONET, and connecting directly to a switch which fans traffic out to routers.

There are hybrid methods where a customer line comes into an exchange point, but connects directly to a provider router there rather than to the exchange switching fabric.

Autonomous System Numbers

Autonomous system numbers are 16-bit numbers used to identify autonomous systems. Global Internet routing with the Border Gateway Protocol version 4 (BGP-4) is based on paths composed of sequences of autonomous system numbers (ASNs). BGP refers to these sequences as *path vectors*.

Approximately 8,000 of the 65,000 possible ASNs have been issued. Only 2,000 to 3,000 actually appear in global Internet routing tables. Although there is not a current shortage, registries responsible for allocating ASNs are asking for more and more justification to be sure they are used wisely.

> **Tip**
>
> There are times when a large enterprise can make use of BGP to separate its routing domains, but have little or no connectivity to the general Internet. For such cases, a block of the autonomous system number space is reserved for private use, just as RFC 1918 sets up private address space ranges. RFC 1930 specifies that the top 1 KB, starting from 65,535 and counting down, is available for private BGP connectivity that does not propagate onto the Internet.

RFC 1930 gives key guidelines for whether a given network needs its own AS number. The detailed justification for AS number assignment is beyond the scope of this book, but in general, it requires that an organization communicate with the Internet through at least two other networks, each of which advertises its own AS number onto the general Internet.

The average end user organization probably does not need its own ASN, because it is part of its ISP's autonomous system as seen by the rest of the Internet.

An increasing number of ISPs check that the AS that initiate the advertising of address blocks have actually had that address allocated to them. A special case arises when an ISP has customer(s) that have their own, directly allocated address blocks. Such an address block might not show as allocated to the ISP, and some ISPs reject the block unless it is registered in the Routing Arbiter Database (RADB) maintained by MERIT or other routing registries.

Provider Coordination Issues

Enterprise networks and ISPs that use PA space usually do not need to worry about routing registries. Routing registries record the exterior routing policies of autonomous systems, which include the address blocks these AS advertise. If an organization uses PA address space, these addresses are part of the larger block already advertised by the upstream provider.

Problems can occur when an organization has directly allocated PI addresses, but connects to the Internet via an upstream provider. If the organization's only external connectivity is through that provider, the organization is architecturally part of the provider's AS. The policy definition of that AS needs to include the PI address blocks of its downstream customers as well as advertising its own.

When an organization changes upstream providers, it is the responsibility of the former provider to stop advertising the PI address blocks and indicate this in its routing policy. It is the responsibility of this new provider to include the PI blocks in its routing policy and its BGP routing advertisement.

Clearly, there has to be some specific time at which advertisements cut over from the old to the new provider. Because not all Internet routers receive the changed announcement simultaneously, there is a period of at least some unreachability while the global Internet reconverges.

Even if you renumber into new PA space, contained within your provider's aggregate block, it is difficult to change providers transparently. Assuming you have your own DNS name, some external DNS clients will have cached the old address that corresponds to your DNS host names and will try to send traffic to the old addresses. Avoiding this requires that you either have duplicate servers during a conversion period, half numbered in the old space and half in the new, or you have your servers respond to both addresses for the conversion period. You might be able to make creative use of NAT, establishing tunnels to the actual servers.

Looking Ahead

By following the procedures in this chapter, you should be able to obtain appropriate PA or PI address space. After you know your address values, the next step is to enter them into configurations. Configuring networking equipment is more than simply typing them in; you need to understand the specific address requirements of different types of devices.

Chapter 10, "Addressing and Name Services," discusses the ways in which you establish relationships between names and addresses. Chapter 11, "Addressing in End Hosts," discusses how to assign addresses to end hosts, both statically and dynamically. It looks at dynamic assignment from the client perspective.

Chapter 12, "Addressing in Hubs and Switches," deals primarily with Layer 2 addressing in both LAN- and WAN-oriented devices. It also considers the Layer 3 addressing needed to manage Layer 2 relays. Chapter 13, "Addressing in Routers," continues a discussion of issues in configuring interconnection devices, but at Layer 3.

Chapter 14, "Selective Forwarding Inside Routers," discusses special addressing considerations in routers, including address-based filtering, tunneling, and bandwidth management. The final chapter, 15, "Your Addressing Strategy: Integration for the Present and Planning for the Future," looks at the server perspective of address and name management. It also discusses IPv6 and other addressing issues that you will see in the future.

PART IV

Implementing Network Addressing

CHAPTER 10

Addressing and Name Services

What's in a name?

—William Shakespeare

From another place I take my name | An house of ancient fame.

—Edmund Spencer

Set down my name, sir.

—John Bunyan

The Domain Name System (DNS) is a complex subject, and the details of DNS administration fill books of their own [Albitz & Liu 1997]. Beyond administration, however, are the more subtle and leading-edge interactions of addressing mechanisms with DNS.

This chapter is not intended to make you a DNS administrator. It is, however, intended to give you the background to understand the interactions of DNS with addressing, especially between emerging DNS technologies and addressing. Chapter 3, "Application Topology: Naming Endpoints," describes the architectural aspects of naming, and this chapter discusses the details of DNS support for that architecture.

Special emphasis is given to the interaction between DNS services and addressing, and the address structure among DNS servers themselves. Increasingly, DNS is likely to have more and more of its data machine generated rather than hand administered. DNS/DHCP interaction, for example, may lead to the generation of DNS names not routinely seen by people.

Names and Their Syntax

It's worth reviewing the rules for name syntax before going into name definition. The general form of a DNS name is a sequence of label fields separated by periods. Fields go from most significant on the right to least significant on the left, the opposite of IP addresses.

There is no strict limitation to the length of a label field, but practical human readability suggests it be capped at 8–16 characters. The total length of a domain name must not exceed 255 characters [RFC 1034], although individual implementations may not support names this long. A name this long would be almost impossible for a person to use, but plausibly could be generated by an automatic name and address management system.

In principle, any eight-bit character other than a period can be used in a label field, but this leads to problems. Although technically any 8-bit character other than a period can be used, getting reliable behavior from the wide range of Internet implementations of DNS names means using only A through Z, a through z, 0 through 9, and hyphen (-).

These are the basic rules of DNS syntax. You also need to understand some of the semantics of DNS names. DNS names represent locations in the domain name space. Each level of the domain tree is represented by a field in the full DNS name. Figure 10.1 shows the basic structure of a DNS name.

Although rarely seen in practice, a domain name that ends in a period (for example, `example.com.`) is a complete domain name, called an *absolute* or a *fully qualified domain name* (FQDN). The root of the DNS name conceptually follows the rightmost period.

Relative domain names, or partially qualified domain names (PQDNs), do not end with periods. Software has to interpret a partial name, and the most common convention is to interpret it relative to the root. With this convention, you can interpret

`second-level-domain.top-level-domain`

as

`second-level-domain.top-level-domain.root`

There also might be cases in which a partial name entry is concatenated on the left of the local domain name. This is common in implementations based on

BIND, the most common DNS software, where the local domain is defined in the boot file that directs how to load zone files.

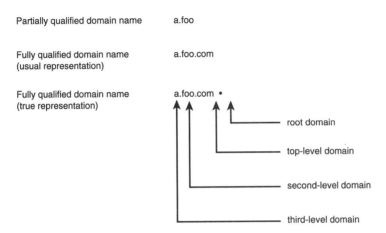

Partially qualified domain name   a.foo

Fully qualified domain name   a.foo.com
(usual representation)

Fully qualified domain name   a.foo.com •
(true representation)

root domain

top-level domain

second-level domain

third-level domain

FIGURE 10.1. *Basic DNS name structure.*

To reinforce the use of DNS names, before going into the nuances of server definition, you might want to think about some very simple applications of DNS names, without the complexity of full servers.

DNS Lookup Without Full Name Services

One of the most basic forms of name service is static definition in a router configuration. This is inflexible and does not scale, but might be a practical necessity for the router to find servers relevant to network management. Also, according to Murphy's Law, if there is a significant network problem to be diagnosed from a router, the DNS server is apt to be down or unreachable.

Routers use the DNS in several ways, not as strict parts of Layer 3 routing, but in the management of the routing process. First, the command executive can use names rather than addresses as arguments for remote logins (for example, telnet sessions) and for diagnostics such as ping and trace.

Cisco's AutoInstall feature is an interesting example of how a simple file can work in an environment without DNS. This is how it works:

1. Initially, the router to be configured has no addresses at all. Using the proprietary Serial Line Address Resolution Protocol (SLARP), the router determines its serial interface address from its upstream router.

2. In a non-DNS environment, the router then being configured issues a broadcast TFTP request for a configuration file, which actually is a list of host names and addresses.

3. After the router being configured has this list, it does an inverse lookup of its own serial interface address and retrieves the hostname of the router.

4. The router constructs a standard router-specific configuration filename and retrieves that file from the TFTP server. That file contains its full configuration.

To resolve these names when DNS service is not available, you can set up simple name-to-address translation on the router. On a Cisco router, you use the `ip host` command:

```
ip host router-1-e0   192.168.1.254
ip host router-1-any  192.168.1.254    192.168.2.33
```

In a small network, you can make this a manual configuration task, as long as people discipline themselves to do it. A better step, at the moderate level of complexity, is to build a master `ip host` table and put it on a TFTP server, where it can be merged with specific configurations using the `config net` command with the `network` option. See Chapter 15, "Your Addressing Strategy: Integration for the Present and Planning for the Future," for more discussion of integrated configuration.

Your basic router configurations should also contain the local domain name:

```
ip domain-name company.com
```

The local domain name is suffixed to any host names that are not fully qualified.

Explicit IP addresses of DNS servers also should be configured:

```
ip name-server 192.168.2.34
ip name-server 192.168.1.253
```

Tip

If DNS service will not be available—a bad idea in production but often a reality in a test lab or in pre-production checkout—turn off name lookup. If you do not do this, whenever you mistype a command name, the IOS assumes it is a host name to which you want to telnet, and you have to wait for the DNS client in the router to time out before you can type another line. To turn off DNS lookup, type

```
no ip domain-lookup
```

Flat name resolution files are common in hosts as well, such as hosts.txt in UNIX or LMHOSTS in Windows. Flat files, of course, do not scale well. They can be useful in very small networks or for initializing a router.

Zone Files and Servers

Where a domain is an administrative abstraction, a zone file is an actual database that defines the names and addresses that exist inside a zone. Zone files define parts of the domain space, one zone file per zone. The authoritative copy of a zone file lives on a primary server, and backup copies are on secondary servers. These server relationships are depicted in Figure 10.2. This is the database model, in the sense that it defines where the master copy of data lives.

Historically, the secondaries periodically retrieved complete copies of the current primary zone file using the zone transfer mechanism. This meant, of course, that secondaries did not stay completely synchronized to their primaries. Various new methods allow much closer synchronization.

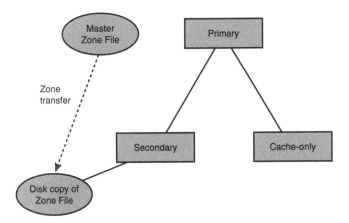

FIGURE 10.2. *The basic DNS server relationships involve primaries and secondaries, complemented by caching-only servers.*

Addressing Relationships Among Servers

The pure primary and secondary relationships also have evolved. Early on, the idea of a caching-only server was a reasonable performance improvement. Caching-only servers keep a memory-resident table of name-to-address correspondences. They query primary or secondary servers on the first occasion when they are asked about a previously unknown name and then respond to subsequent queries for the same name from the memory-resident cache. Caching-only servers also can run on UNIX boxes.

The question frequently comes up whether a router might act as a caching-only server. This is technically possible, but can place significant demands on already tight router memory. In some applications it might be useful, and there needs to be a tradeoff between putting this function into the router or a physically adjacent general-purpose host.

Primary and secondary servers typically run on UNIX hosts, although DNS implementations exist for most major operating systems. For small to medium networks, DNS and certain other support functions (such as TFTP) can run on 386- or 486-class PCs using a public domain or inexpensive UNIX such as Linux or BSDI.

BIND, rather than the basic DNS standards, introduced the idea of *forwarders*, shown in Figure 10.3. They are a different sort of cache mechanism. Think of them as application gateways for DNS. When a traditional primary or secondary server cannot answer a query for a name *outside the site*, it does not then send a request directly to the outside server, but to a forwarder.

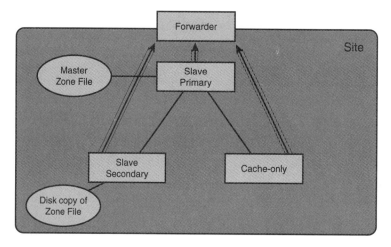

FIGURE 10.3. *Forwarders with associated master/slave relationships complement the traditional DNS relationships.*

Another type of restricted server defined by BIND is the *slave*. A slave only contacts forwarders to do name searches, although it still responds from its cache and from its authoritative data. A slave can be a primary, secondary, or caching-only server. Primary servers contain authoritative data in a zone file, but can only ask forwarders for additional information. Secondary servers transfer zone files from the primary, but can only ask forwarders for information that goes into their caches.

A subset of slaves is the *stealth server*, which is like a slave server except not listed in an NS resource record (RR) for the zone. A stealth server, unless explicitly configured to do otherwise, sets the AA bit in responses and is capable of acting as a master. A stealth server is known by other servers only if they are given static configuration data indicating its existence.

Zone Files and Resource Records

Zone files are made up of RRs. The syntax of resource records often, for historical reasons, is obscure. They are commonly referred to by strings of letters such as SOA, PTR, or CNAME, which are sometimes arbitrary rather than strict acronyms. Figure 10.4 shows the relationships among the basic record types and the general meanings of the type codes.

The first resource record in a zone file is a start of authority (SOA) record that defines the zone.

> **Note**
>
> A zone file is a set of records that begins with an SOA record. It ends either with the end of a physical file or with another SOA file. In other words, you can have multiple zone files within a single physical file.

In a zone file, you must not define information for hosts outside your zone, although you can include references to higher-level domains. Remember that DNS learns dynamically about hosts outside your domain. Be sure you distinguish between the zone file, which initializes a DNS database, and the current state of that database, which includes things that DNS learns dynamically.

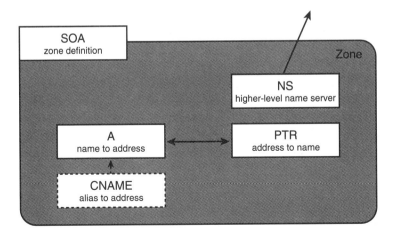

FIGURE 10.4. *RRs can resolve information only about names and addresses in your zone. The NS RR links your zone to other zones and allows requests to progress through the DNS naming hierarchy.*

Especially in secure DNS, it can be meaningful to speak of a set of resource records within a zone. These are called *RRsets*. In general, DNS does not guarantee that resource records will be used in a certain order, but when an RRset is defined, and a digital signature created for it, that signature reflects an ordering.

Not putting information about other domain hosts into your zone files does not mean that your DNS software cannot have information about them. Commonly used external information is cached.

RR Syntax

Although case is ignored in DNS lookups, it is preserved in fields loaded into a name server. It's probably best to limit field names to lowercase.

A comment starts with a semicolon . Everything on a line after a semicolon is ignored. Parentheses create groups of data that can span multiple lines. Asterisks define wildcards. The @ sign indicates the current default domain name that should be substituted for the @.

Resource records have the following basic format:

```
<name>    [<ttl>]    [<class>]    <type>    <data>
```

Fields of the RR are separated by whitespace. The *<name>* field is optional on a given RR, but if the name is left blank, it defaults to the name on the first previous RR that does have a nonblank name.

Time to live (TTL) values appear in most resource records. If you do not set the TTL on some specific record, it inherits the value on the SOA record. See the much more detailed discussion of TTL in the section "DNS Database Aging and Updating."

The *<type>* field defines what type of data is in the rest of the RR. There are many DNS record types, some of which are obsolete or experimental and some of which are not relevant to this discussion. The following discussion deals only with those RRs that routinely are manually coded.

Tip

RR syntax can be obscure. An increasing number of software packages, or built-in features in operating systems such as BSDI UNIX, provide a front end to RR definition. Make use of such tools when they are available.

Records That Are Often Manually Configured

Although there are an increasing number of menu or graphic front ends for configuring DNS zone files, a key set of resource records is often manually coded. You should be aware of the content of these records because you might need to examine them in the response to a DNS query.

Some DNS record types are obsolete, or are intended for specialized applications beyond the scope of this discussion. We are concerned with the SOA, NS, A, CNAME, and PTR records because they are often manually configured. Some additional record types are machine generated, so their function but not their syntax is discussed.

The SOA RR

Zone files start with an SOA record and end just before the next SOA record, if multiple zones are defined in the same server. There is no explicit end of authority record. The format of the SOA record is

```
<name>  [<ttl>]  [<class>]  SOA   <origin>  <person>  (
                           <serial>
                           <refresh>
                           <retry>
                           <expire>
                           <minimum>  )
```

The first field of the SOA record defines the zone it is describing. Other administrative information on the record includes the *<origin>*, which is the name of the primary name server host, and the *<person>*, the administrative contact for the zone.

Although the *<person>* field defines a mailbox, it does not use the usual *person@domain* form. Instead, the notation is *person.domain*.

Several fields of the SOA record relate to change control and zone file backup. The *<serial>* field is a locally defined version number of the file and should be incremented whenever the zone file is changed. Good operational practice suggests that at least one, and preferably two or three, earlier copies of the zone file should be kept.

Secondary servers periodically query the primary to see whether it has been updated, meaning that a zone transfer to the secondary is needed. The *<refresh>* field is the interval, in seconds, between secondary checks of the primary. A value of 3,600 seconds (1 hour) is typical.

<retry> is the time, in seconds, a secondary should wait to query the primary again, after a failure. 600 seconds, or 10 minutes, is a generally used value. *<expire>* is the time that data on a secondary server should be assumed to be current. A common value is 3,600,000 seconds, or approximately 42 days.

<minimum> is the shortest time value to be used for a TTL in *any* RR. The usual value is one day or more, or at least 86,400 seconds. This, however, is a very long interval if active changes are in progress.

BIND historically has imposed a minimum of 300 seconds, regardless of the setting of *<minimum>*. New versions might remove this restriction. Long *<minimum>* values are the bane of dynamic DNS tools such as DistributedDirector.

The class field is historical, with the value IN denoting the Internet. There are no practical alternative values, but too much existing software expects it to be present.

The NS RR

NS records point to the name of a name server that provides name service for a domain, typically other than your own domain. Referencing a server outside your domain does not break the rule of not keeping information about other domains in your zone file. It does not break the rule because you are not hard-coding information about the other domain, but simply pointing to an authoritative server for that domain. The format of the RR record is

```
<domain>   [<ttl>] [<class>]   NS      <server>
```

Let's say MY.DOMAIN receives name service from two servers, one in the MY domain and one not in it. The RR records would be

```
MY.DOMAIN       NS      NS1.BIGCARRIER.NET
                NS      NS2.BIGCAMPUS.EDU
MY.DOMAIN       NS      NS1.MY.DOMAIN
```

There must be complementary NS records in each subdomain, and in the domain that delegated it. A special case applies when name servers are inside the same domain as the NS record. In that case, you need to configure a *glue record*, which is an RR that specifies the address of the higher-level name server. For the domain COMPANY.DOMAIN, you would need

```
COMPANY.DOMAIN.                                      NS
SUB.COMPANY.DOMAIN.   SUB.COMPANY.DOMAIN.   A        10.1.0.5.
```

Why is there a need for a glue record? Remember that the DNS structure consists of zones and subzones. Any subzone, in turn, can be the parent of a lower level of subzones. A parent zone is assumed to have the address of name servers in its parent. Its child, however, simply has the name of a name server and is expected to refer to its parent zone to determine the address of the name server.

Because the name server address is normally in the parent, and the child contains only a name of a name server that is part of the parent zone, the normal case has no conflict. If the name server is part of the subzone, however, then the subzone is in the impossible position of having to refer to itself to resolve an address. Remember that name resolving implies traversing the hierarchical tree of DNS names. If you simply create a name server within a zone, you have a loop of names, not a tree.

Glue records solve this problem by making an explicit name server address available to the subzone. With an explicit address, there is no need to traverse the name tree to find the name server.

The A RR

You need an Address record for every IP host. In this context, a host can be an end system, a router interface, or an address in a dynamically assigned pool. The format of the A record is

```
<host>    [<ttl>] [<class>]    A    <address>
```

The data for an A record is an Internet address in dotted-decimal form. A sample A record looks like the following:

```
MY.DOMAIN.            A        10.0.0.42
```

The CNAME RR

Canonical name (CNAME) RRs define what are called *nicknames* in the DNS documentation, but are often referred to as *aliases*. In a CNAME record, <nickname> is the alias you are defining, and the data part is the official name. CNAME records have the format

```
<nickname>    [<ttl>] [<class>]    CNAME    <host>
```

```
            NEW.COM.        CNAME    OLD.COM.
```

Renaming hosts is a very common application for CNAMEs.

The PTR RR

A records map names to addresses. PTR records complement A records by mapping addresses back to names. You define PTR records for official names, not CNAMEs. The PTR record format is

```
<special-name>    [<ttl>] [<class>]    PTR    <name>
```

The major application for PTR records is *inverse mapping*, or participating in the IN-ARPA.ADDR distributed database that allows registered IP addresses to be traced back to their owning domains. The special names used for PTR records are not obvious; see the detailed discussion in the section "Reverse Mapping."

Machine-Generated Records

Primarily involved with secure DNS are several records that normally are software generated. Because they may contain cryptographic signatures, it is not possible to generate them without at least some computer assistance. These types include SIG (signature), KEY (public key), and NXT (Next).

SIG resource records contain a digital signature that covers a set of records with the same owner name, class, and type. It is a signature that includes the signer's identity, the time of signing, and the expiration date of the digital signature. This signature is encrypted either with a verified zone key or another key traceable to the zone key.

KEY resource records, reasonably enough, store public keys. Any given key entry must be able to be authenticated by a digital signature in a SIG record. KEY RRs for any given zone need to be stored both in the higher-level domain zone file, as well as in the zone files of subdomains, so a verifiable sequence of verified signatures exists from the highest to the lowest level of the DNS-naming hierarchy.

The NXT RR is automatically generated by secure DNS. It terminates a set of a given type of RR, which allows a digital signature to be applied to the set as a whole. It is an example of *sequential integrity* in secure processing, which protects against addition, deletion, or duplication of a sequence of records. Sequential integrity is distinct from *unitary integrity*, which protects against alteration of a specific record.

DNS Database Aging and Updating

Viewed from the overall Internet standpoint, DNS is a distributed database. Traditionally, each zone had a primary server, and secondary servers replicated its contents when TTLs expired, using a zone transfer. Newer methods go beyond simple expiration timers. These new methods include forced notification of zone changes when a master server knows a change has occurred, incremental updates of only parts of zone files, and dynamic updating.

Classical Zone Transfer

The DNS application protocol has two contexts for its use: Queries and responses run over UDP port 53, while the zone transfer mechanism for synchronizing the servers runs over TCP port 53. Because queries and responses usually involve exchanging only a pair of records, the overhead of setting up a TCP connection is not justified. TCP, however, is more efficient for the large volumes of a zone transfer.

In retrospect, it probably would have been better if the query/response and zone transfer services had been assigned different port numbers. Zone transfer should only be initiated by authorized hosts, because it can change the database. When DNS was designed, however, security was less of a concern than it is today.

Many modern applications cannot wait for multiday expirations. As zone files grew in size, the overhead of a complete zone transfer became excessive.

TTLs, in theory, can be as low as 1 second. In practice, many BIND-derived servers do not recognize values less than 300 seconds (that is, five minutes). The tradeoff is between accuracy and performance. Low TTL values allow DNS caches to accurately reflect the contents of the authoritative server, but cause more frequent DNS requests and responses to flow over the network. High TTL values decrease workload but also reduce accuracy.

Low TTL values are essential for load-sharing schemes based on DNS. With high TTL values, a remote cache might point all traffic for a given DNS name at a single IP address, whereas the load-sharing algorithm expects to spread workload over several addresses.

In the absence of load sharing, typical TTL values are between one day (86,400 seconds) and one week (604,800 seconds). All resource records of the same name, type, and class should have a consistent TTL value. You really need to consider how often you change DNS records. A small enterprise would do so very infrequently and as a manual operation. An ISP or a large enterprise might do so several times per day, possibly generating changes through automatic scripts.

It is perfectly reasonable to lower the TTL value while you are doing database maintenance, then reset it to a higher value. When there is a dynamic linkage between DNS and DHCP, the TTL on dynamic records should reflect the DNS lease time and have a relatively small value.

Simple aging might not be sufficient to maintain a reasonable level of accuracy across the global Internet. Emerging technologies to deal with this problem include forced notification of zone changes, initially deployed only to force changes within a domain.

Forced Notification of Zone Changes

A new transaction type, DNS NOTIFY, permits a master server to tell its subordinate zones that the authoritative file has changed, and the slaves must retrieve a new zone file. Remember, informing all the slaves at one time that they need to retrieve updates causes a burst of workload. With increasing numbers of slave devices, this bursty behavior does not scale indefinitely.

It is certainly reasonable that forced notification could be scaled within an enterprise by having the master send forced notifications selectively, spreading them out over a reasonable period of time. Spreading them out, of course, results in some servers having newer information.

The major part of the workload in a traditional zone file update is doing a complete file transfer, even though many of the records may not have changed. Another scaling technique that should alleviate much of the workload and be more scalable to the general Internet is incremental zone change.

Incremental DNS Update

Although it is not widely deployed at the time of this writing, a reasonable approach that balances update overhead against absolute database synchronization is incremental DNS update [RFC 1995]. This method builds on the NOTIFY mechanism, but produces less overhead in transferring the updates.

The efficiency of this method varies with the specific implementation. In particular, an incremental transfer primary server does not have the storage to hold an infinite number of prior versions. A simple rule applies: If the length of a prior version, counting deletions and additions, would be greater than the length of the current zone file, the prior zone file can be deleted. In addition, when the SOA expire period of the prior version expires, the prior version can be deleted.

Incremental DNS update is still driven by timers or other mechanisms in the master servers. It does not necessarily reflect new assignments, which is done by dynamic DNS update.

Dynamic DNS Update

A variety of applications cannot live with the slow TTL cache mechanism of traditional DNS. They need a mechanism that can dynamically update DNS.

DNS was originally designed to support queries of a statically configured database. Although the data was expected to change, the frequency of those changes was expected to be fairly low, and all updates were made as external edits to a zone's master file.

Dynamic update with the UPDATE DNS command allows resource records, or sets of resource records, to be added or deleted by the DNS server that is authoritative for those records. The details of such updating is beyond the scope of this text, because it may involve prerequisites for adding or deleting. You cannot add a.b.company.com, for example, if b.company.com is not already defined. UPDATE does not take place unless all prerequisites are met [RFC 2136].

Dynamic updating, even more than zone transfer, can be a security vulnerability. Supplemental security mechanisms have been defined for dynamic DNS [RFC 2137].

Secure DNS Update

Just as dynamic update introduces the UPDATE, secure DNS update introduces several new functions. The central function is the SIG RR, which authenticates other DNS entries using cryptographic digital signatures. Other secure DNS RRs include the KEY record, which contains public keys, and the NXT record, which defines the end of an RRset that is signed with a signature covering the entire RRset.

There are both transaction SIGs and request SIGs. *Transaction* SIGs end a response, linking it to the corresponding request and authenticating the request-response pair. *Request* SIGs end a request and authenticate the identity of the sender of the request.

Reverse Mapping

The original approach to reverse mapping—translating addresses back to names—assumed classful IP addresses, where all allocations were on octet boundaries. A special domain, IN-ADDR.ARPA, was defined for reverse mapping information.

Given an IP address in the format W.X.Y.Z, if W is in the Class A space (1–126), there is a corresponding subdomain W.IN-ADDR.ARPA. In this subdomain is a PTR record Z.Y.X.W.IN-ADDR.ARPA that points to the host W.X.Y.Z. For example, the reverse mapping for 1.2.3.4 is 4.3.2.1.IN-ADDR.ARPA.

Look at this carefully. Remember that the most significant part of an IP address is on the left, or the W octet in this example. In using reverse mapping with IN-ADDR.ARPA, you need to put the most significant part of the IP address in the most significant part of the DNS name.

Figure 10.5 shows the relationships between A and PTR records in a classful zone file.

```
SRI-NIC.ARPA.  A 26.0.0.73  ──────►  73.0.0.26.IN-ADDR.ARPA.PTR  SRI-NIC.ARPA.
               A 10.0.0.51  ──────►  51.0.0.10.IN-ADDR.ARPA.PTR  SRI-NIC.ARPA.


ACC.ARPA.      A 26.6.0.65  ──────►  65.0.6.26.IN-ADDR.ARPA.PTR  ACC.ARPA.
```

FIGURE 10.5. *This example, from RFC 1034, shows basic reverse mapping for classful addresses.*

Classless Reverse Mapping

Reverse mapping with PTR records was originally defined for classful addresses, where each octet of an IP address, written in dotted decimal, could map to a domain level of a reverse mapping name. With classless interdomain routing (CIDR), it is no longer valid to assume that all the addresses associated with a given octet of an IP address belong to the same organization. RFC 2317 defines a workaround to this problem. Figure 10.6 shows a first approach to reverse mapping for CIDR blocks. This first approach does not solve the problem of classless reverse mapping, but it is a conceptual step along the path to the eventual solution.

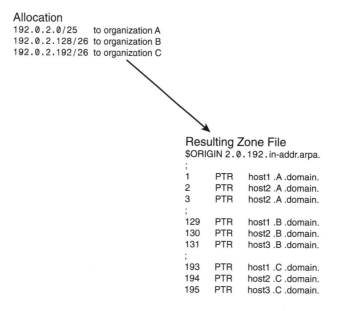

```
Allocation
192.0.2.0/25     to organization A
192.0.2.128/26 to organization B
192.0.2.192/26 to organization C
```

```
Resulting Zone File
$ORIGIN 2.0.192.in-addr.arpa.
;
1       PTR     host1 .A .domain.
2       PTR     host2 .A .domain.
3       PTR     host2 .A .domain.
;
129     PTR     host1 .B .domain.
130     PTR     host2 .B .domain.
131     PTR     host3 .B .domain.
;
193     PTR     host1 .C .domain.
194     PTR     host2 .C .domain.
195     PTR     host3 .C .domain.
```

FIGURE 10.6. *The basic approach to classless IN-ADDR.ARPA addressing uses the traditional mechanisms, but does not really work well because only one zone can contain these reverse mappings.*

With the basic approach, only one organization can maintain the reverse mappings. This is not operationally practical because there might be no business relationships among the several organizations.

Figure 10.7 shows the RFC 2317 method, which provides the "hooks" to let multiple organizations control different mappings inside a CIDR block.

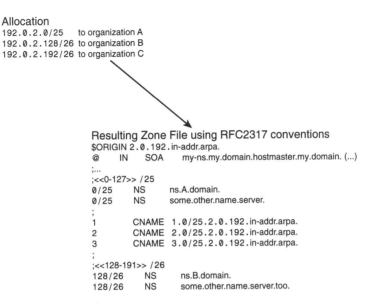

Allocation
192.0.2.0/25   to organization A
192.0.2.128/26 to organization B
192.0.2.192/26 to organization C

Resulting Zone File using RFC2317 conventions
$ORIGIN 2.0.192.in-addr.arpa.
@   IN   SOA   my-ns.my.domain.hostmaster.my.domain. (...)
;...
;<<0-127>> /25
0/25   NS   ns.A.domain.
0/25   NS   some.other.name.server.
;
1   CNAME   1.0/25.2.0.192.in-addr.arpa.
2   CNAME   2.0/25.2.0.192.in-addr.arpa.
3   CNAME   3.0/25.2.0.192.in-addr.arpa.
;
;<<128-191>> /26
128/26   NS   ns.B.domain.
128/26   NS   some.other.name.server.too.

FIGURE 10.7. *By introducing a convention in which the CIDR length block notation, such as /26, can be introduced into zone files, separate zone files can be defined for each separately administered block.*

The authors of this approach assume that CNAME records will be automatically generated, so a large number of entries will not create great inconvenience. Do be aware that a / character in a DNS name is not understood by some DNS implementations.

Domain Administration

Operational techniques change over time. The basic reference is RFC 1033, but it is a good idea to check the DNS FAQ at www.users.pfmc.net/ ~cdp/cptd-faq/. The Usenet group comp.protocols.tcp-ip.domains is also a good and current source of information.

DNS/DHCP Interaction

DHCP-based, server-assigned addressing is highly friendly to renumbering. Unfortunately, many network management tools such as ping, traceroute, and snmp have IP addresses as their arguments. It is rather difficult to ping to an unknown address!

In the basic design of DHCP, the information exchange is between the DHCP client and server. DHCP does not make the assignment known to network management. Individual DHCP server implementations might have log files or other means for the network operator to find out which address has been assigned to a specific DHCP client, but, at best, this is vendor specific and not designed to work with other management tools.

A partial solution to this problem is to allow DHCP to update DNS [Rekhter, 1998]. Network management tools then use the DNS name to refer to hosts and allow the DNS server to resolve the actual address. Existing DHCP has the capability to assign addresses to hosts as well as pass parameters to the host. DHCP, however, does not have any inherent capability to let any network management infrastructure know what addresses it has assigned. Some specific DHCP server implementations might keep the assignments in a log file, but there really is no generally accepted mechanism for tracking assignments.

The IETF consensus has been that the most reasonable way to track DNS assignment is to establish a linkage between DHCP and DNS, using DNS dynamic updating. Both A and PTR records would need to be updated for each assignment, and removed when the address is released (as, for example, by DHCP lease expiration). Each assignment or release, therefore, would generate two DNS update transactions, one for A and one for PTR.

Either the DHCP client or server could update the DNS server. In practice, the operationally reasonable methods would be as follows:

- After receiving an assignment, the DHCP client generates a new A record, and the DHCP server updates the PTR record.

- The DHCP server updates both the A and PTR records.

DNS/Routing Interaction

DNS responses also can vary if the name server is programmed to consider routing information. You saw an architectural reference to this in Chapter 6, "Internet Failing: Details at 11," in the discussion of the load-sharing network address/port translator [RFC 2391]. Cisco's DistributedDirector is a commercial product that implements routing-aware DNS name service.

DistributedDirector uses a Cisco-proprietary protocol called the Director Response Protocol (DRP) to retrieve routing information from agents on routers. These routers must have access to full IGP and BGP information relevant to the client and server path.

DistributedDirector works as follows:

1. An application client makes DNS request.

2. The local DNS server sends a DNS query, which eventually reaches the DNS server for the destination domain. This DNS server then refers the query to DistributedDirector, which is treated as a subdomain.

3. DistributedDirector accepts the original client query, looks up the server agents (that is, routers) that service the application server name being requested, and sends DRP queries to these agents.

4. DRP agents collect the metrics defined in DistributedDirector: external, internal, and server. These are returned to DistributedDirector.

5. DistributedDirector selects the best server among the responses returned by the agents and returns an A RR to the original local DNS server. This RR points to the best server. TTL on this RR defaults to zero but is configurable.

6. The local DNS server returns the best server address to the client.

The load sharing efficiency of DistributedDirector varies significantly with the degree to which requestors cache the DNS responses of DistributedDirector. The more the requestor caches name-to-address bindings, the more that all application client requests from that DNS requestor will use the same application server.

Ideally, responses would have a zero TTL, so they would not be cached at all. The zero TTL would force the DNS requester to resolve each query independently, so DistributedDirector would have a new opportunity to respond with the best server address applicable at that moment.

A zero TTL increases traffic due to requests, but that might be an acceptable tradeoff. A more important limitation is that many DNS resolvers, such as most versions of BIND, do not accept a zero TTL but substitute 300 seconds—5 minutes.

Looking Ahead

Names provide the bridge between application and internetwork topologies. Names define the endpoints of the application structure, while addresses define both the end and intermediate points through which data flows.

End hosts need both names and addresses. Mechanisms by which addresses are assigned to them are detailed Chapter 11, "Addressing in End Hosts."

Subsequent chapters deal with address assignment to intermediate points on hubs, routers, and switches. It can be convenient for network management to assign DNS names to these intermediate points.

CHAPTER 11

Addressing in End Hosts

What is there more of in the world than anything else? Ends.

—Carl Sandburg

When I find the road narrow, and can see no other way of teaching a well-established truth except by pleasing one intelligent man and displeasing ten thousand fools, I prefer to address myself to the one man.

—Moses Mainmonedes

A guest never forgets the host that has treated him kindly.

—Homer

Given an addressing structure, it is necessary to get addressing information into end systems and routers. This chapter deals with the issues of getting IP addresses and related information into end hosts, both application clients and servers. Renumbering-friendly DHCP (Dynamic Host Configuration Protocol)—which focuses on the DHCP client side of the DHCP interaction—is emphasized in this discussion. Chapter 15, "Your Addressing Strategy: Integration for the Present and Planning for the Future," deals with server aspects of DHCP. Chapter 9, "The Address Plan," establishes the structure of IP subnet prefixes into which the host addresses will fit.

Let's first discuss the problem you are trying to solve: categorizing hosts.

Categorizing Hosts

You first want to think about the requirements on individual hosts, or classes of hosts. You began this process with the address plan you created in Chapter 9, but that process was oriented toward subnets rather than hosts.

Endpoint Addresses

If your site does not let random computers connect to its LANs, it needs to have some sort of endpoint identifier for them. Such an identifier is the basic granule of control. It can be a MAC address or a DNS name. You need both, but you will tend to build one or the other as your primary key for assigning IP addresses. In addition, if users will be reading electronic mail or using Internet services, they are apt to need a user name, even on single-user machines.

The IP address is the goal, not the starting point. The IP address is more likely to be assigned after the endpoint identifier is defined. The assigned address might be chosen automatically. For practical troubleshooting, there must be a means to associate the machine friendly Layer 3 address with the endpoint identifier, whether that endpoint identifier is a DNS name or a MAC address.

User Classes

DHCP does not always return the same information to every requesting host. It can differentiate its response based on the specific user identifier, the vendor type code in the request, or user class information. A good rule of thumb, if the responses to these identifiers differ, is always to take the most specific match.

A proposed addition to DHCP can help enormously in managing different user requirements: the user class identifier. This is an additional option the client sends to the DHCP server, which gives site-specific information about the DHCP client. The user field would contain a single network virtual terminal (NVT) definition, but the designers of this feature assume that NVT strings actually understood by the DHCP server would be configured to meet the needs of a user that belongs to several administrative or technical categories.

For example, there might be requirements to identify users, such as the following:

- Mobile access is authorized.

- Needs the name of an NTP server.

The class might be `mobile-time`, and other users that do not need mobile access are members of the class `time`. The DHCP server would have a block of addresses and parameters to assign to any client that includes mobile-time in its DHCP request, and a different block for those clients that include time as their user class.

What a Host Needs to Know

Although many discussions speak of needing to give a host its own IP address, many other parameters are required for any effective operation. If your host has multiple interfaces to ensure that each make DHCP requests, you need to be careful that you know how to handle the situation when the differing interfaces return different global parameters.

For example, a host operating system might only be able to use a single DNS server address. If this host had two interfaces, it would submit a DHCP request on each of its interfaces. The two requests are necessary because each interface needs its own address.

But a DHCP response can return parameters beyond the simple address. What if the response for interface 1 included a DNS address of 10.1.0.50, but the response for interface 2 included a DNS address of 10.2.0.47? Which one should the host use?

In all probability, either one will work, but you need to have a clear understanding which one your host will use. It might use the first one learned or the last one learned. Unless you understand how hosts with more than one interface behave when faced with such a conflict, it will be very difficult to troubleshoot how the host interacts with DNS.

Solaris UNIX, for example, designates one interface as primary for the purpose of obtaining global parameters, but there is no standard method for choosing the definitive source.

Note

Remember that this discussion speaks of modern hosts. It is unfortunately far too common to find hosts that cannot even be configured with a subnet mask, but simply assume the default mask for classful addressing.

The Scope of IP Addresses

IP addresses are necessary for the host to work as part of an active internet. But additional information is necessary for a host to participate as part of an addressing structure, such as the address mask and the default gateway router address.

Chapter 9 describes criteria by which you decide what sort of address—private or registered—is needed by a given host. Before you do the final address assignments, consider the guidance of two documents, RFC 1918 and RFC 1775, which define various functional requirements for Internet connectivity.

RFC 1918 discusses classes of applications that can use private address space. RFC 1775 discusses user-oriented perspectives as to what it means to be on the Internet. The first RFC emphasizes address requirements, and the second is consciously aimed at a higher level of abstraction, dealing with applications rather than addressing.

RFC 1918 focuses on hosts that need IP addresses that are not connected to the Internet, and RFC 1775 deals in part with determining if an IP address is needed at all.

Building on the RFC 1775 and RFC 1918 categories, Table 11.1 shows a set of IP usage categories that might be used for a user inventory.

TABLE 11.1. HOST ADDRESS REQUIREMENTS.

Class	IP Address Needed	Address Source	On the Internet Category	Typical Usage
1	Public	Local or LAN server	Full	Public
2	Temp public	Local or LAN server	Client	Client of public apps
3	Temp public	Local or dial server	Client	Client for public applications (telecommuter)
4	Private	Firewall	Client	IP application via firewall
5	No	—	Mediated	Non-IP terminal
6	No	—	Messaging	Non-IP terminal
7	Private	Local	Not on fixed or temporary	Private LAN IP client
8	Private	Local	Not on fixed or temporary	Private dial IP client
9	Private	Local fixed	Not on fixed or temporary	Embedded system
10	Private	Local	Not on fixed or temporary	Private router

Hostwide

Hosts need to know a variety of parameters to operate. These include actual values such as the host's IP address, subnet mask, and DNS host name. The host needs to know its own place in the DNS naming structure, so it can use DNS to find other servers by name rather than address. Minimizing references to server addresses makes renumbering much easier.

For a host to know its place in the DNS, it needs to be able to find a DNS server. Although some hosts can broadcast a DNS query, it is far more desirable to obtain the DNS server address through DHCP.

If DHCP does not return DNS information, you need to make sure that broadcast DNS queries can reach a DNS server, if there is no DNS server on the local medium. Arbitrary DNS queries often are sent as UDP/IP broadcasts, which do not propagate beyond the local router interface.

DHCP has an optional capability of providing a DNS server address or preferably a list of them arranged in order of decreasing preference. It is hard to imagine why DHCP should not provide DNS information, or at the very least a server address. Note that not all clients understand that a DNS server list can have more than one entry. Windows did not know how to walk a list of servers until Windows NT 4.0 Service Pak 2. *Walking a list* means that the client first tries the first server address in the list. If that server does not respond, the client then tries the next server in the list.

DHCP also can return the DNS name and local domain for the host.

Management Server Information

DCHP can return names of other management servers. After the names are known to the hosts, their addresses should be obtained through DNS resolution. Local broadcasts to find servers should be discouraged, because broadcasts often do not scale well. Servers whose names can be returned include the following:

- SMTP trap server

- Network Time Protocol (NTP)

Diskless workstations were once fairly popular. They had no local disk and used Trivial File Transfer Protocol (TFTP) to obtain their initial executable image. After they were running, they needed to know the address of a swap server. DHCP returns the IP address of a swap server.

Fashions come and go in computing, and it remains to be seen whether the network computers advocated by some will have many of the attributes of a diskless workstation.

General Application Services

DHCP might inform its client of the names of some well-known application servers, such as the lpr print service. Legacy clients might have hard-coded server addresses, which is undesirable if renumbering is a possibility. The preferred approach is to have clients request the current address of a server from an appropriate directory service, typically DNS. For some high-performance transaction processing, the directory might be the portmapper service.

Per-Interface

Hosts need to be able to configure various parameters on a per-interface basis. The most obvious parameters needed are the IP address and subnet mask.

Remember that each interface is connected to a medium. In almost every case, hosts have only one interface on a given medium. Most commercial routers, in fact, do not permit having more than one interface on a given medium.

On each of these media, there are one or more routers. Hosts need to be able to find a default gateway router to let them send traffic destined to destinations not on their local subnet.

Perhaps the most common, if not the best, practice is to have a hard-coded default gateway address. This is undesirable because the host must be reconfigured if the default gateway address changes. DHCP can return a list of one or more default gateway routers to be used in order of preference.

If the requesting host intends to act as a router, DHCP defines the capability to provide certain routing-related information, beginning with the decision whether or not to provide routing services on a given interface. This capability is not used on commercial routers with dedicated or LAN interfaces. Some routers intended for dialup applications might obtain addresses dynamically, but they use PPP dynamic assignment to do this, not DHCP.

It is not unreasonable for a generic host to obtain static routes to special servers from DHCP, and DHCP has that capability. This capability is not widely used, but could pass the following information to the host:

- Destination

- Destination mask

- Type of service

- First-hop router address for this route

- Ignore redirects

- Maximum transmission unit (MTU)

- Perform MTU discovery

Alternatives to receiving a list of routes, of default gateways, or both is for the host to run the Routing Information Protocol (RIP) in passive mode. In passive mode, RIP listens for routers but does not generate route advertisements. A passive RIP interface does generate RIP query messages so other RIP routers are aware of its existence. Passive does not mean completely silent.

On media where hosts run passive RIP for router discovery, in other than very special cases, the real routers—the default gateway—should only advertise the default route `0.0.0.0/0`. For security reasons, these routers should not accept route advertisements from stub networks, as shown in Figure 11.1.

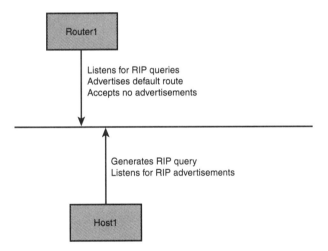

FIGURE 11.1 *Default gateway routers connected to a stub network should not accept route advertisements from the stub network. Passive hosts on the stub network do need to send minimum protocol messages to the default gateways.*

> **Note**
>
> A stub network *is one that is connected to one or more default gateways, but has no router on it that accepts traffic from one router and forwards it to another router.*
> *Many RIP implementations do not advertise any routes onto a stub network until they hear a RIP query message on that network.*

Remember that the default gateway address given by DHCP to a host can be a virtual interface address, as seen in the "Fault Tolerance and Addressing" section of Chapter 13, "Addressing in Routers." A virtual interface address can be shared over a group of redundant routers.

Yet another way for a host to be able to send traffic off its local network is to be sure the host always sends an Address Resolution Protocol (ARP) packet for every destination and to enable the proxy ARP mechanism on all router interfaces on the medium. If the true destination is on that medium, it responds directly to the ARP requester. If the destination is not on the medium, but a connected router knows how to reach the medium containing the Layer 3 destination address, that router interface responds to the ARP request.

Generating an ARP for each request is not ideal, because it produces twice as many frames as a TCP/IP stack that knows the default router address. Unfortunately, some stacks are not as intelligent as others in learning that router address. Proxy ARP works in some situations when there is no other way to find the router.

Samuel Johnson said that the important thing about a dog walking on its hind legs is "not how well he does it, but that he does it at all." Sometimes, your only alternative for achieving any connectivity is accepting an inefficient means of doing so.

Finding Configuration Information

Configuration information is either preconfigured on the end host or obtained from an address server.

There can be special problems in finding a configuration server, because, by definition, a host trying to get an IP address doesn't know how to send requests that it wants to be returned. If it doesn't know its own IP address, it certainly doesn't know server addresses.

At hardware initialization time, the only thing a host knows is its MAC address on a LAN. On dialup links, it might not know even that. Dialup hosts might have a preassigned IP address they propose to the remote access server, but the preferred practice is for them to request address assignment from the remote access server.

How Does a Host Learn?

The simplest and least operationally convenient way for a host to learn relevant addresses and parameters is to retrieve them from a configuration file in a local disk. The problem in doing so is that if any of these addresses and parameters change, there is a requirement to physically go to the remote host and update them. Slightly more appealing alternatives are to use `telnet` or other remote logins, but still to reconfigure on a host-by-host basis.

In an organization of any appreciable size, host-by-host configuration is too labor-intensive to be scalable. Some type of server-based update process is preferred.

Most server-based mechanisms involve DHCP [RFC 2131]. DHCP, a superset [RFC 2132] of the Bootstrap Protocol (BOOTP) [RFC 0951], is intended for operation over broadcast-capable LANs and needs additional software when it is used for hosts connected via dedicated, demand, or nonbroadcast multiaccess (NBMA) media. Access services for such media might use a relaying service that lets their hosts access LAN-attached DHCP servers. Alternatively, access control services such as RADIUS can maintain a database of the necessary parameters. Most remote access servers can do minimal parameter exchange, such as address assignment.

DHCP has been extensively discussed in earlier chapters, but from the standpoint of its architectural function. It is now time to look at its implementation in actual host clients. DHCP and its predecessor BOOTP are effective means for providing LAN-attached hosts with this information. Point-to-Point Protocol (PPP), used with RADIUS or TACACS, and the IP Control Protocol (IPCP) can provide addressing information to dialup hosts.

DHCP has the following three modes of operation:

- *Manual*—A host presents a 48-bit identifier to the server and is given a predefined IP address and other parameters. The 48-bit identifier is usually a MAC address from the host.

- *Automatic*—A host requests an address and other parameters and is given the next one in a pool available to the DHCP server.

- *Dynamic*—A host requests an address and other parameters and is given the next one in a pool available to the DHCP server. There is a *lease time* associated with the address provided by the server that specifies how long the host can use the address.

Client Address Sources

Several sources of addressing are available to hosts. Applicable sources differ on whether an IP host needs its own address or needs some other host's address.

Conflicts can ensue if, for example, a workstation attempts to retain a connection with a server that has relinquished its address.

Hosts in Table 11.1 Classes 1 and 2 should obtain IP addresses from BOOTP/DHCP hosts with a block of public addresses. Typically, Class 1 hosts obtain a fixed address at initialization time, or obtain an address from a pool only if the Class 1 host can register the acquired address in DNS. Class 1 hosts are likely to have locally configured IP addresses.

Class 3 hosts are similar to Class 2, although the source of the address is more likely to be PPP negotiation than Class 2. Many current accesses of this type use a fixed address defined by their provider.

This might be fairly transparent if the provider registers the provider-furnished addresses in a provider-operated DNS database that is publicly available.

Let's look at some of the ways various clients can be statically configured with IP information.

PPP/IPCP

IP addresses can be assigned to network dial-in users using the IPCP of PPP. The calling client can propose an IP address it wants to use, or the client can accept a dynamically assigned address. If the client-proposed address is acceptable to the server, the client address need not be on the same subnet as the associated server port address.

> **Note**
>
> Although statically assigned addresses for dial-in clients make administration simpler, RFC 2050, the guidelines for address registries, prohibits justifying address space based on static addresses for individual dial-in hosts. Static assignments are acceptable for dial-in routers.

Dynamic assignments can come from a pool of addresses on the remote access server, from an authentication server such as RADIUS, or from DHCP via a proxy in the remote access server. As an example of pool assignment on the remote access server, the following is the command to set a starting address for a pool of dynamically assigned addresses on a Livingston Portmaster:

```
set assigned_address ip address
```

The PortMaster defaults to making the pool size equal to the number of ports found at system initialization. If you want to have a smaller number of addresses in the pool, add the following command:

```
set pool Number
```

UNIX

`ifconfig`, whose basic function is shown in Figure 11.2, is the usual UNIX command to assign IP addresses to interfaces:

```
ifconfig
interface name}
 ip address netmask mask value
 broadcast {directed broadcast address}
```

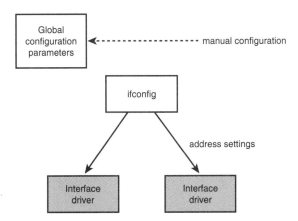

FIGURE 11.2 ifconfig *is the main interface for statically configuring UNIX addresses.*

Although implementations vary among vendors, Sun's DHCP builds on the basic `ifconfig` structure shown in Figure 11.2. Sun's has two processes—called *daemons,* following UNIX conventions—that deal with the two functions of DHCP. These are shown in Figure 11.3.

Sun views DHCP as performing the basic function of address assignment, and the second function of acquiring system- and application-level parameters. A daemon called `dhcpagent` manages the first function. One of the special requirements met by this daemon is handling the periodic expiration of address leases. It interacts on a continuing basis when addresses do have lease times.

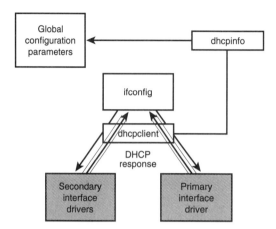

FIGURE 11.3 *In Sun's HCP, two daemons build on the basic ifconfig structure.*

When it starts, dhcpagent does not know which interfaces are active. Its activities are triggered by internal service requests from ifconfig, which has been extended to interface with DHCP. ifconfig remains the central point of Solaris address management.

A second daemon, dhcpinfo, manages the function of obtaining non-address parameters from DHCP. A major reason for having this daemon is to resolve differences in parameters received on different DHCP interfaces. As part of Solaris configuration, one interface is designated as the primary for DHCP, while others are secondary. When any system process asks dhcpinfo for information, that daemon returns the parameter values learned on the primary interface. The primary interface is designated on ifconfig. After a primary interface is designated, the host cannot complete its boot process until DHCP interaction is complete on the primary interface. If there are multiple servers on the primary interface's medium, any server can complete the interaction.

The following sections describe the procedures you use to configure IP addresses on specific platforms Windows and Macintosh.

Windows

In Windows NT, go to the Control Panel | Network | Protocols menu. Add TCP/IP if it is not configured. Answer the question about DHCP and install software if required.

Close the box, and the TCP/IP Properties box appears. The IP address, subnet mask, and default gateway fields are in this box. You choose whether to configure them here, or check the button that tells your machine to obtain these from DHCP.

If you click Advanced, you get a supplementary window that allows you to do the following:

- Assign secondary addresses to interfaces (up to five each)

- Add additional default gateways

- Enable PPTP tunneling on interfaces

- Set simple packet screening by IP protocol ID, TCP port number, and UDP port number

Returning to the main window, you then set up DNS.

Macintosh
Configure the client IP addressing mechanism in the MacTCP control panel or use the Internet Assistant if you are using the newer Open Transport software.

Locally Administered MAC Addresses

As mentioned in Chapter 8, "The Existing IP and Non-IP Address Structure: Preparing for Remodeling," some architectures modify the MAC address based on considerations such as logical address.

Selecting the MAC address is quite specific to device driver software and the operating system. You need to read your specific software documentation to see how to do it on your specific platform.

Operational Client Issues

It can be incredibly frustrating and embarrassing for the network administrator, who wisely insists on deploying DHCP, to find that a previously working host stops working when you change it from manual to DHCP configuration. A common reason for such failures is that you only set address assignment information in the DHCP server, but fail to set global options such as DNS and router addresses.

IP Interactions

Some DHCP client or server implementations do not properly handle broadcast or secondary addresses. Even though Microsoft now deploys excellent DHCP software, there were some problems in early versions.

Another problem of early DHCP clients is that they could only receive up to 576-byte IP packets. As more and more information comes from DHCP, the packets become larger. There is a newer DHCP option that allows clients to negotiate the maximum DHCP message size. Again, correcting this problem generally requires an upgrade to recent software.

Issues of Overloaded IP Addresses

Up to this point, we have talked about assigning addresses to hosts on traditional IP subnets, which are associated with single physical media. The same principles apply on VLANs. Most VLANs assign a host to a specific VLAN based on the physical port or the MAC address. These schemes work well with DHCP. A VLAN that assigns devices to a VLAN on their IP address, however, can become confused by machines that do not yet have assigned MAC addresses. IP-based VLAN selection is fundamentally incompatible with dynamic IP address assignment.

Another range of problems with dynamically assigned IP addresses occurs with firewalls, or other security mechanisms such as host-based access lists, that expect a fixed IP address associated with a given host. You can sometimes work around such a limitation by specifying a range of acceptable addresses in the filter, rather than a specific address.

Unless your DHCP system dynamically updates your DNS, double DNS lookup schemes usually do not work. In such a scheme, a server that receives a request from a host does a reverse DNS lookup on the requester's source address. The server attempting to validate your request then does a forward DNS lookup of the name returned by reverse lookup. If the IP address in the request packet does not match the address returned by the forward lookup, the server discards the request. In such a scheme, if there is no DNS PTR record for the specific host, the reverse lookup fails.

Looking Ahead

We have now defined the endpoints of the network, from the perspectives of naming and addressing. It is now time to look inward to the network infrastructure. Chapter 12, "Addressing in Hubs and Switches," and Chapter 13, "Addressing in Routers," deal with addressing on the primary types of components in that infrastructure.

CHAPTER 12

Addressing in Hubs and Switches

Who will stand at either hand/And guard the bridge with me?

—William Macaulay

In skating over thin ice our safety is in our speed.

—Ralph Waldo Emerson

We must select the illusion which appeals to our temperament, and embrace it with passion, if we want to be happy.

—Cyril Conolly

Hub and *switch* are not really technical terms, but marketing buzzwords. The term hub is most commonly used to mean a Layer 1 multiport repeater, but this usage varies among vendors, especially Bay, which uses the term *hub* to refer to a chassis that can include Layer 1 repeaters, LAN switch, and router functions. The term *switch* is somewhat more consistently used to refer to a Layer 2 relay, either as a high-performance bridge for LANs or a frame, cell, or packet-forwarding device for WANs. Various vendors and journalists confuse the Layer 2 emphasis with a variety of terms, such as Layer 3 switching, IP switching, and so on. The term *switch* here is a Layer 2 device.

Note

This chapter takes a somewhat unusual approach to switching in that it includes both LAN and WAN switches as well as ATM switches that do not fit neatly into either the LAN or WAN category. I put these topics in the same chapter because I learned the concepts much better when I thought of switches as Layer 2 devices rather than artificially distinguishing the protocols they used. My thinking here was accelerated by ATM technology spreading across both LANs and WANs.

It's quite common to have Layer 1, Layer 2, and Layer 3 functions in the same physical container. This chapter focuses on Layers 1 and 2. Chapter 13, "Addressing in Routers," focuses on Layer 3.

> **Note**
>
> Layer 1, 2, and 3 devices all participate in realizing network hierarchy. Hubs and switches generally are limited to enforcing hierarchy through the way devices are physically connected to them, while routers add the capability to enforce hierarchy through the use of hierarchical addressing as well as physical connectivity.

Regardless of what devices are called, you need to begin with a clear mental picture of what chassis you are dealing with and how they interconnect. You also need to consider how you will configure and control them before you get into actual configuration commands.

LAN bridges and switches generally organize their traffic from patterns dynamically learned from a spanning tree protocol. WAN switches are most likely to be manually configured, although there are dynamic protocols that can set up paths among ATM switches. ATM is also involved in WAN switching, and the lower-speed feed to ATM usually is Frame Relay. There are some proprietary dynamic setup mechanisms for Frame Relay switches.

Some Terminology

Some of the functions of switches and hubs are discussed in Chapter 4, "Transmission System Identifiers and Logical Address Mapping: A View from the Bottom," and Chapter 7, "Addressing, Security, and Network Management." This chapter extends those concepts, illustrating them with examples of commercial implementations.

Key ideas include virtual LANs (VLANs) and the set of domains used to scope the extent of control over management functions and types of traffic.

Bridging Review

As shown in Figure 12.1, Layer 2 topologies are divided into various sorts of domains. The highest level, the management domain, does not deal directly with devices that forward frames, but defines the scope of configuring those devices. Broadcast domains define the scope of Layer 2 broadcasts and correspond to Layer 3 prefixes (for example, IP subnets). Bandwidth domains define the scope of devices sharing a common medium.

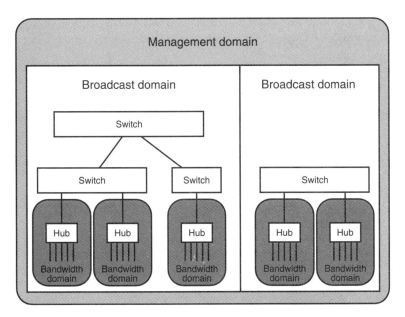

FIGURE 12.1. *Management, broadcast, and bandwidth domains.*

Several types of domains characterize the scope of switch operation. The management domain is most general and consists of one or more broadcast domains. Management domains are especially important when VLANs are in use, because the management domain defines the assignment of end system addresses to VLANs.

Broadcast Domains

The broadcast domain has the greatest addressing significance. Remember the local versus remote assumption in Chapter 4? IP assumes that a host on the same subnet is reachable through the data link protocol, so the medium underlying a subnet is assumed to be point-to-point or broadcast capable.

A broadcast domain is generally equivalent to an IP subnet, IPX network, AppleTalk cable range, or other network layer prefix. It can be composed of a set of interconnected switches, of which all port-level broadcasts are sent to all other ports. It can be composed of a VLAN.

A broadcast domain is a broadcast multiaccess medium. It can be contained in one or more physical chassis linked by trunk cabling. Broadcast domains terminate at router interfaces.

Chapter 4 discussed address resolution mechanism for mapping a Layer 2 address to a Layer 3 address. Most such mechanisms depend on an underlying broadcast medium, which is why the scope of an IP subnet needs to match a broadcast domain.

Consider a single chassis switch. You could configure it as a single broadcast domain or as separate broadcast domains that do not communicate with another. For the moment, assume that all ports under discussion are in the same broadcast domain.

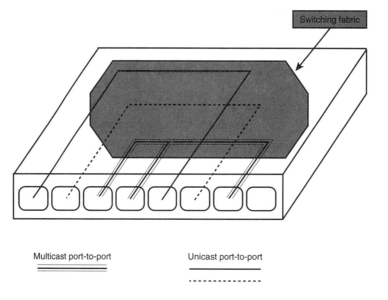

Multicast port-to-port

Unicast port-to-port

FIGURE 12.2. *Edge-port-to-edge-port flow must be within the same broadcast domain unless routing or cut-through switching is used.*

Within each broadcast domain/subnet, the end systems connected to the ports can communicate with one another as unicasts or multicasts. If source and destination are on the same chassis, they will communicate with one another via the switch's internal fabric.

Bandwidth Domains

Regardless of whether the MAC mechanism of a LAN is token passing or CSMA/CD, the underlying idea is that a station will not transmit until the medium is available to it. The set of stations contending for the shared medium is a bandwidth domain. Bandwidth domains are sometimes called collision domains, but this is Ethernet-specific terminology and does not cover token-based schemes. Bandwidth domains do not have special significance in addressing, but are a part of establishing the topology of the overall hierarchical network.

In a Layer 1 hub, hosts connect to the hub, which is a shared medium in a single chassis or set of interconnected hub chassis. Hosts plug into the hub at a port. At Layer 1, there is little difference between the edge ports into which hosts plug and trunk ports that interconnect hubs. The distinction is mostly one of wiring.

In traditional bridging, bandwidth domains terminate at a bridge interface. In general Layer 2 bridging, the term segmentation is used to indicate that bridges separate shared media, hiding the contention on one medium from the other media in the bridged system. These interfaces, or ports, can accept the output of a hub, or a host can plug directly into them.

The most straightforward way to connect devices to a switch is to connect one host to each edge switch port. When only one device is connected to each port, that device does not see the unicast traffic of other hosts on the virtual medium and is not subject to delay while contending for the medium. This direct mode of communication is called *microsegmentation*. Microsegmentation extends the idea of hiding contention to the lowest possible level, the individual host. It extends the idea of segmenting shared media to the level of a specific host on a nonshared medium.

Note

If a port is configured to be half duplex, the default for most LANs, it still might see one form of contention even if microsegmented. A host connected to a half-duplex port still has to wait for access to transmit onto the virtual medium, while it receives unicasts intended for it and while it receives broadcasts. Many switch ports can be configured to be full-duplex so transmitting and receiving can be simultaneous, free from waiting to receive data.

The term *feeder port* is used by some vendors to denote an edge (that is, non-VLAN) port to which end hosts do not connect directly, but are "fed" to the VLAN-capable port via an external Layer 1 shared-medium hub. Other vendors have internal shared-medium hub functions, so slower or less critical hosts can connect to a less expensive shared-medium port.

Although the price difference between intelligent hubs and switches continues to reduce, there are still perfectly valid reasons to use inexpensive "dumb" hubs to extend the capabilities of switches. One common use is simply to connect devices more than 100 meters of cable distance from the switch.

VLANs

A LAN is a single, multiaccess, broadcast-capable physical medium. VLANs are used for multiplexing traffic from several different LANs so that they can share common trunk media used to interconnect switches and occasionally servers.

If you define multiple broadcast domains on multiple switches and you want to interconnect those switches, you either must have separate interbox links between chassis, one for each broadcast domain, or use VLANs to share trunks.

Frames enter the VLAN on edge ports of VLAN-capable switches. The internal logic of the switch copies these frames to any ports of the same VLAN and forwards frames for nonlocal destination onto the appropriate trunk port.

Note

In most products, an edge port belongs to one and only one VLAN. 3Com and other vendors have extended the concept of port assignment to let a port belong simultaneously to more than one VLAN.

Although this is a violation of the traditional VLAN architectural model, it does offer some configuration convenience. A printer, for example, could be shared among multiple workgroup VLANs without the need for a routing function to reach it.

I would approach this technique with caution, although it can be appropriate in carefully selected circumstances. The danger of the technique is that it defeats the broadcast isolation provided by VLANs, unless additional broadcast control features are implemented. If the device connected to the multiple VLANs produced large numbers of broadcasts due to a software error, all the connected VLANs would be affected. In like manner, the device connected to the multiple VLANs will receive all broadcast traffic from all the VLANs.

After traffic enters a VLAN-capable edge or feeder port, the frames are assigned to a VLAN. As detailed in Chapter 4, there are several types of VLAN trunking. They can be connectionless, IEEE 802.1Q and various proprietary techniques including Cisco Inter-Switch Link (ISL), or connection oriented, including ATM Forum LAN Emulation (LANE) and proprietary techniques such as Cabletron SecureFast.

In the connectionless techniques, a VLAN trunk header is prepended to the LAN frame entering the box and forwarded onto a trunk. The trunk is multiplexed, serving multiple VLANs. The header allows hosts receiving the VLAN-tagged frame to recognize the VLAN to which the frame belongs and to deliver it to edge ports associated with that VLAN.

In the connection-oriented techniques, the switch does not put a header on the frame, but forwards it over one or more virtual circuits to the switch(es) serving the edge ports of the VLAN.

Product Architecture

First think of the product space that LAN switches and hubs occupy functionally. The simplest hub is a dumb one that has no remote management capability. More powerful hubs and switches do have a management function.

This management function is controlled by a local or remote terminal or through SNMP, HTTP, or other IP-based protocols. For remote management, it is necessary to assign one or more IP addresses to the chassis itself, simply to access it for management. The chassis also needs to know one or more IP addresses of network management servers.

> **Note**
>
> *Commercial hub and switch products come in a bewildering variety of physical packaging. They can be fixed configuration, requiring a total replacement of the chassis to change interface cards. They can be modular chassis, with slots in which all electronics can be added or removed.*
>
> *The particularly confusing case is the* stack. *Among different vendors, a stack can be no more than a pile of similarly shaped chassis, with physical proximity their only real relationship. The true stack is a set of tightly coupled* chassis, *where one chassis provides the management function for the entire set of components.*
>
> *In this book,* chassis *denotes a set of hardware components under a single management function. Stack products can include several physical chassis, but these components are cabled together to produce a single virtual chassis.*
>
> *Consistently describing complex relationships among physical components is a challenging task, given the diversity of commercial implementations. The IETF's Entity Management Information Base (MIB) working group is developing standardized methods for doing this, but has not finished what turns out to be quite difficult.*

From the perspective of management, any chassis more complex than a dumb hub is an IP host. As such, it needs to know the things any IP host does—its address, the address of a DNS server, the address of its SNMP trap server, the address of a `syslog` server, and so on. It must learn a default gateway address or participate, at least passively, in routing.

A chassis always has some number of edge ports to which user devices connect. In the Optivity network management system used to control Bay LAN devices, a cluster is a group of edge LAN interfaces that are grouped together. On the 48-port Cisco 5000 Group Ethernet Module, groups of 12 edge ports can be configured as 4, 3, 2, or 1 broadcast domains. Each broadcast domain can be part of a separate VLAN.

Alternatively, there can be a single edge port per bandwidth domain, but the edge port shares a common broadcast domain with other ports. Even the term *chassis* can differ from one commercial switching product to another. Larger switches tend to be modular chassis into which a management processor and medium-dependent port cards are plugged. Some of these modular chassis allow redundant management processors for fault tolerance.

Conceptually, stacks of chassis have physically separate chassis, but are tightly coupled to a single management processor. Stacks can be implemented as pairs of switches or as a larger number of chassis interconnected through a matrix unit. Different vendors interpret the term *stack* in different ways, and some stacks are no more than a pile of equipment, with multiple (or no) management functions.

Ports

As shown in Figure 12.3, chassis have an assortment of port types. All ports (other than ATM or WAN) have associated MAC addresses for the port. They learn the MAC addresses of devices connected to them.

The most basic type of port is the edge port, to which hosts connect directly. The next most basic type is the trunk port, used to interconnect switches. Remember that a trunk can link multiple switches in a single non-VLAN broadcast domain. When the trunk runs a VLAN protocol, it can carry multiple broadcast domains, each a VLAN.

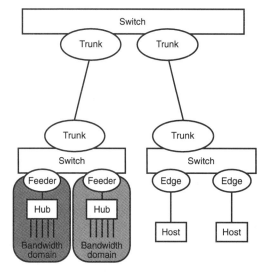

FIGURE 12.3. *A chassis can have edge and trunk ports.*

Edge ports can be grouped into a common bandwidth domain, which effectively is a shared medium in a single chassis. In the Optivity network management system used to control Bay LAN devices, a cluster is a group of edge LAN interfaces that are grouped together. On the Cisco 5000 Group Ethernet Module, groups of 12 edge ports can be joined or connected directly to a broadcast domain.

Alternatively, there can be a single edge port per bandwidth domain, but the edge port shares a common broadcast domain with other ports.

Chassis Usage

Depending on where and how the switch is used in your network, it might need to keep track of additional addressing. It's worth spending a moment to characterize types of switches:

- *Campus/data center*—Modular and might include full ATM cell switching.

- *Wiring closet*—Often modular or stack.

- *Workgroup*—Usually fixed configuration. Ethernet/Token Ring or perhaps 10/100 speed-sensing Ethernet edge ports. Usually single-fixed trunk port. If this is ATM, it is a LAN emulation client.

Chassis Types

Switches come in a variety of physical configurations, typically trading off cost for flexibility.

Fixed-Configuration Chassis

Chassis with a fixed number of ports are probably most common, as they are the simplest, cheapest design. The way in which their ports are numbered really varies with the specific product. If the chassis is especially intended as a workgroup concentrator into a system of chassis, a distinction can be made between trunk and edge ports.

Figure 12.3 was carefully selected to show low-end chassis. Consider carefully your needs in selecting a chassis, and don't get capabilities you do not need now or in the plausible near term. Remember that the price of chassis tends to drop as performance and functionality increase, and you might do well to defer obtaining a capability you don't need now.

Examples of fixed-configuration chassis include Baystack 50 series hubs, which are fixed-configuration, nonmanaged devices aimed at the desktop. A 3Com SuperStack II Switch 320 switch is a low-end device with a fixed port configuration and no SNMP management. The Cabletron ELS10-26TX has SNMP management and modular uplink interfaces; the boundary between fixed and modular configurations can be very blurry at times.

Fixed-configuration chassis differ in their mechanical structure. Small devices, such as the Baystack 50 series hubs, can be in small chassis designed to sit on a desktop. Larger devices can be designed for rack mounting or for shelf or wall mounting in a wiring closet.

Fixed-configuration chassis can include SNMP management. SNMP-manageable switches and hubs are increasingly comparable in cost, but non-managed fixed-configuration hubs are much cheaper than switches. A fixed-configuration chassis has a single management processor. Although dumb hubs are significantly less expensive than switches, the cost difference between managed hubs and switches is becoming so small that it usually makes sense to purchase switches rather than managed hubs.

When 10/100 MBps Ethernet ports are used and the trunking technology is Fast Ethernet, there is little reason to distinguish between edge and trunk in the physical cabling system. There is a functional difference between edge and trunk cabling, because the edge ports do not use the VLAN trunk tagging technique while tagging is present on the trunk cable. Trunk cables most frequently run among switches, but can also connect to VLAN-aware servers.

Switch chassis of this sort include the Baystack 300 series and Cisco/Catalyst 1200 and 2900. These are often called desktop or workgroup switches. The Catalyst 2820 has fixed edge ports, but has modular trunk cards.

Tightly Coupled Chassis

Tightly coupled, or stack, chassis systems interconnect multiple chassis into a single system with a single management processor. They are an intermediate alternative between fixed-configuration chassis, which essentially are not upgradable, and the highly flexible but more expensive modular chassis discussed in the next section.

Depending on the product, there are several ways to interconnect the chassis:

- Pairs of chassis interconnected with a back-to-back cable

- Arbitrary numbers of chassis interconnected through a daisy chain of chassis-to-chassis cables

- Connection of switching chassis to a common matrix chassis

Most, but certainly not all, freestanding Layer 1 multiport repeaters are fixed configuration. Some chassis, such as the Cisco 1500 series, can interconnect several chassis into a stack. Such stacks can be SNMP managed and meet the requirements of tightly coupled chassis in the next section, or the stacking can be done simply to provide more ports in a dumb, non-managed hub. The virtue of common management is that it simplifies SNMP management of all ports.

3Com SuperStack II and Cisco/Catalyst 3000 series products are examples of stacked, tightly coupled systems.

You need to understand how your chassis assign port and chassis numbers in a stack. This varies among vendor implementations.

Modular Chassis

Modular chassis structure is common among higher-capacity switching products. There are a fixed number of slots, typically 3 to 15, with one or more slots used for processors and the rest for plug-in port cards. The processor boards often have trunk ports on them. Processor boards, which might be redundant for high availability, often are called CPUs or management processors. The port cards have various vendor-specific names, often interface processors.

Catalyst 5000 and 5500 series switches, for example have plug-in separate management processor and port module cards.

Modules are numbered relative to the top slot, and ports on modules are numbered left to right. If there is a redundant management (that is, "Supervisor") module, it goes into slot 2. The syntax to refer to a port is:

`module-number/port-number`

You can refer to contiguous and noncontiguous ranges of ports as well, with a hyphen to show a continuous range or commas to show elements in a noncontiguous series. For example, `3/1, 4/2` would indicate module 3 slot 1 and module 4 slot 2.

VLANs are referred to by single numbers or using the following range conventions:

- `1` indicates VLAN 1

- `100-103` indicates VLANs 100, 101, 102, and 103

- `103-105, 108` indicates VLANs 103, 104, 105, and 108

MAC addresses are in the form of six two-digit hexadecimal fields, separated by hyphens, as in the following:

`00-00-0C-12-34-56`

Some modular switches, such as the Catalyst 5000, allow hot swapping—replacing electronic modules while the chassis is operating. This is more than a matter of protecting the hardware from electronic surges. Remember that the spanning tree algorithm is aware of MAC addresses on bridge ports as well as host ports. If bridge MAC addresses were burned into port modules, how could they be changed nonintrusively? The answer, on a Catalyst 5000, is that MAC addresses are not actually burned into boards, but are kept in a non-volatile memory in the supervisor card. MAC addresses are associated with the slot in the chassis, not with the module plugged into the slots.

Static Relationships Among Chassis

Full multichassis topologies are loosely coupled, in the sense that each chassis has an independent management processor. The simplest multichassis topologies form a broadcast domain. More complex topologies include VLANs, each a broadcast domain.

Figure 12.4 illustrates a cascaded chassis topology. The trunks either all belong to a single broadcast domain or carry VLANs. Observe that the switch at the top of the hierarchy does not have any edge ports. A switch without edge ports is called a backbone switch.

Cascaded-chassis, non-VLAN systems can be highly appropriate if you need to deal with switches from multiple vendors. The IEEE 802.1D protocol used to maintain single spanning trees is likely to interoperate among multivendor chassis.

VLAN control protocols often are proprietary (for example, Cisco Inter-Switch Link [ISL], Bay LattisSpan, Cabletron SecureFast, and Cisco Virtual Trunk Protocol [VTP]). Although the IEEE 802.1Q spanning tree protocol comes from a standards body, it has not been finalized at the time of this writing. There are sufficient choices in 802.1Q that multiple implementations have a significant chance of not interoperating.

The inter-chassis links use the same type of MAC frames as the clients and servers. Spanning tree management protocol data units do flow on the inter-chassis links.

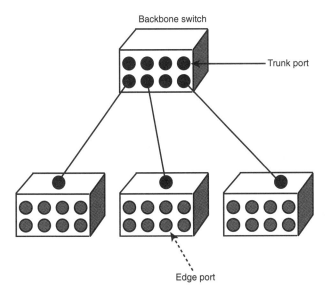

FIGURE 12.4. *Physical interconnections among cascaded chassis.*

Although some modular chassis have the capability for mixing Ethernet and Token Ring interfaces, this should generally be seen as a method for maintaining several distinct broadcast domains, rather than trying to interconnect them at Layer 2. Some switches offer translation between Ethernet and Token Ring, or between Ethernet and FDDI, but Layer 2 translation between such dissimilar MAC protocols has a great many problems. If the protocol carried in the frames is routable, it is preferable to route, not bridge, between the two media types. Routing avoids problems such as failing to reorder the bits of MAC addresses carried in the data fields of frames.

More complex VLAN-based topologies involve multiple broadcast domains with trunk protocols between chassis. Bay uses the term switch community to refer to a system of 28xxx and 58000 switches that intercommunicate with LattisSpan, Bay's proprietary trunking protocol. A Bay switch community can contain up to 64 VLANs.

Bandwidth Domains: Imposing Topology

In Ethernet-style CSMA/CD, the medium is available only if no transmissions are sensed to be in progress and no stations have entered the collision state. In token-based technologies, such as 802.5 Token Ring or FDDI, the station waits for a token to be released from its upstream neighbor.

Pure addressing has little to do with the characteristics of a bandwidth domain. Mechanisms to manage bandwidth are physical-level collision detection, simple receipt of a token, and so on.

Topology, however, is significant. All parts of a hub, or Layer 1 repeater, are part of the same bandwidth domain.

Regardless of the methods used to mediate access, the more active devices sharing a medium, the less effective bandwidth is available to a given device in a unit time.

Switches, as evolved bridges, help but do not solve the problem of end station delay as they wait for available bandwidth. Think of the problem of serial versus parallel processing. If there is a single resource, the shared medium, a device potentially must wait for all other devices to transmit. Remember that the network is not always the problem. Servers are shared and may be the real bottleneck.

Switches speed transmission by removing the bandwidth access delay seen by every station waiting to transmit and, through internal very-high-speed media, deliver it quickly to the destination. Several real-world factors make this work very well in some common situations, but not so well in others.

Minimizing delay to access the medium is fairly straightforward after the frame is inside the switch, where it is on a switching fabric one to three orders of magnitude faster than the switch ports. The switching fabric may be a fast medium or active electronics. There is no appreciable delay delivering it to the destination, if all goes well.

This traffic assumption is quite valid in true peer-to-peer applications, but begins to break down in client/server applications when there are many flows terminating in a small number of destinations. It breaks down almost completely in many-to-one applications.

If all ports are the same speed and ten devices transmit simultaneously to a single server, the clients indeed might not be delayed in transmission. When the server is on a port of the same speed as the clients, however, it may be overloaded by a factor of 10.

Collapsed Backbone/Backbone-in-a-Box

On most switches, you can configure groups of ports to act as separate broadcast domains, equivalent to IP prefixes/subnets. This would be perfectly reasonable in a data center or server farm. If the ports of the group each are assigned to a single host, then you have a "VLAN in a box." VLANs do not necessarily have trunks.

Alternatively, some ports might be in the same bandwidth domain. The rationale for sharing bandwidth is simply to allow all devices, fast or slow, to cable to a common box, simplifying wiring. It is most often, however, wise to microsegment all server ports.

Collapsed backbones, or "backbones in a box," at their simplest consist of a chassis containing a switching fabric to which all hosts connect. Hosts can connect directly to the fabric or possibly through hubs. This is shown in Figure 12.5.

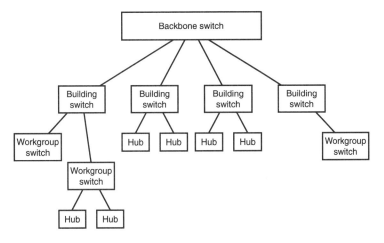

FIGURE 12.5. *A single chassis is a trivial example of a collapsed backbone.*

Backbone switches, which do not connect directly to any end hosts, are quite common in large building and campus switching systems. In Figure 12.5, an ATM switch is the collapsed backbone chassis to which building-level LAN switches connect. A high-capacity LAN switch is an equally plausible backbone chassis. Indeed, with the advent of Gigabit Ethernet, a backbone chassis with single or inverse multiplexed Gigabit Ethernet links might be more cost effective in selected circumstances than an ATM backbone.

Interconnecting multiple chassis requires that the chassis understand the topology. The topology is constrained by the spanning tree algorithm. Spanning tree topologies are simpler than can be achieved with Layer 3 routing, but are fast and simple to implement in hardware. Spanning tree algorithms also are less flexible than routing in terms of load sharing and alternate path selection. Extensions of spanning tree to improve functionality in these two areas are discussed in the following section.

Dynamic Relationships Among Hubs and Switches

LAN switches—and high-speed bridges—do Layer 2 path determination and frame forwarding. Layer 3 path determination mechanisms can add to the Layer 2 forwarding table, but that is outside our present scope, as is ATM cell switching.

Modern bridges and switches dynamically learn about MAC addresses, so your addressing concern is usually more with making sure that these devices have appropriate storage for address tables at Layer 2. In basic operation, you should be more concerned with the topological relationships among switch ports and chassis than with explicit addresses.

You need to set one or more IP addresses for management functions. After management controls are established, you can choose to set up filters that are aware of MAC addresses. MAC addresses certainly are significant in organizing data from remote monitoring (RMON) probes and other management devices. RMON is discussed in Chapter 7.

Commercial bridges preceded routers and, for many years, offered cost and performance advantages over bridges. As routers evolved, their speed met or exceeded that of older bridges, while offering more features, such as broadcast control, mixed media conversion, and more flexible topologies. Routers are more scalable, but switches nicely complement them to provide cheaper bandwidth in well-defined parts of the network.

Bridge developers did not stand still and introduced their own improvements, generally called switching. The term *switch* became an industry buzzword, often seeming to mean everything and nothing. Some vendors attacked routers as slow, but routers and switches can be of comparable speed. The former Wellfleet, now Bay Networks, used the slogan "Switch if you can, route if you must." Cisco, the predominant router manufacturer, acquired a number of "switching" companies and now has an assortment of products called switches and routers, as do most major vendors. Most major vendors also have router modules that can be inserted into products called switches, and vice versa.

Complicating things even further is the use of ATM. LAN switches might have ATM trunks to a pure ATM switch, but might not do true cell switching. Other high-end switches do include cell switching.

A bridge or basic LAN switch represents a single broadcast domain, or broadcast multiaccess (BMA) medium. Value added features include Layer 2 filtering, network management, and medium translation. More complex switches add VLAN/ELAN functions. Each one of these features adds address complexity.

MAC Address Learning

The bridge is connected to LAN media and learns the MAC addresses present on, or reachable by, each medium. It does so by monitoring the source address in frames it sees on each of its ports. Bridge ports operate in promiscuous mode in the MAC protocol, decoding every frame on the medium. In promiscuous mode, the interface responds to any destination address, not just its own.

By listening promiscuously to every frame on the medium, the bridge collects the source addresses and learns which MAC addresses are local. Figure 12.6 shows that the bridge stores this information in two conceptual places: a per-interface filtering table and a chassiswide MAC address to port table. The per-interface table is used to block further propagation of frames whose destination address is on the same medium as the source address. The chassis-wide table is used to direct unicast frames to destinations known to be directly connected to the bridge.

When the bridge does not know the specific location of a unicast destination, the bridge forwards the frame towards the root. When that frame reaches the root and the root does not know a specific location, the root bridge forwards the frame away from it, down appropriate branches of the spanning tree.

Frames with multicast and broadcast destinations are flooded out all interfaces of a bridge. This can be affected by implementation-specific filtering.

IP Addressing for Switch Management

Although switches operate at Layer 2, devices attached to them—and the switches themselves—need IP addresses so network management can be applied to them. Figure 12.7 shows representative relationships of the switch's management entity to various management servers.

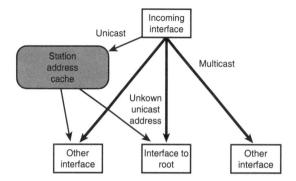

FIGURE 12.6. *Bridges learn MAC addresses both to filter local-to-local transfers and to learn the interface to which to forward to known unicast destinations.*

The switch usually is preconfigured with an IP address, although it conceivably might request one through DHCP. If the server addresses are not on the same subnet, the switch needs, at a minimum, the address of a default gateway router to reach them. A default gateway address can be preconfigured or learned from DHCP. Alternatively, the bridge might participate in routing and dynamically learn the location of a default gateway router.

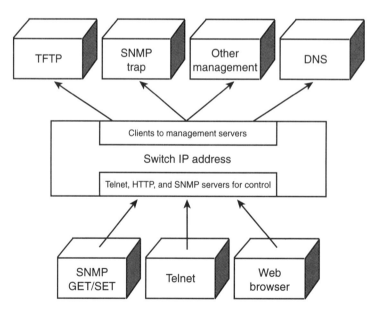

FIGURE 12.7. *A switch needs an IP address for an assortment of management functions.*

When the switch initializes, it is likely to need to find certain management servers, such as DNS. It needs to be programmed with their addresses, reach them on the local subnet via broadcasts, or communicate with the servers through a local router that will forward broadcasts as unicasts or directed broadcasts.

In LANs, the actual forwarding of traffic is based on MAC addresses. Much of the time, the "burnt-in" MAC addresses on devices are perfectly adequate. There are occasions where they need to be locally administered, as discussed in Chapter 11, "Addressing in End Hosts." In general, however, the switch does not need explicit programming with MAC addresses, either for user devices or its own interface. The nature of modern bridges is that they learn relevant MAC addresses.

Locally administered MAC addresses might be necessary for Token Ring bridging or where MAC address filtering is used for security elsewhere in the network.

Spanning Tree

When Layer 2 relays involve more than a single chassis, bridging needs to be defined among the chassis. Remember that bridging is controlled by a spanning tree algorithm, so there can only be one active path between bridges.

In Figure 12.8, although there is physical connectivity between bridge B1 and bridge B5, and between B2 and B4, these paths can only act in hot standby. B2 and B4 will forward frames destined to known unicast address directly to their local Ethernets, but will send other unicasts to the root.

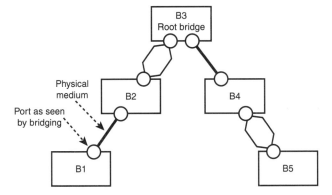

FIGURE 12.8. *The spanning tree algorithm allows only one active path between two bridges, shown as solid lines. Inactive potential paths, currently blocked by the spanning tree algorithm, are shown as dashed lines.*

Variants on Parallel Path Topology

Figure 12.9 shows some vendor-specific exceptions to the single path rule, but these effectively are inverse multiplexing techniques that combine several parallel physical paths into one virtual one seen by the bridging system. Fast Etherchannel is one example introduced by Grand Junction; it is now part of the Cisco product line. Inverse multiplexed links can be used for reliability, bandwidth, or both. Fast EtherChannel can group two or four full-duplex Fast Ethernet ports into 400 or 800 MBps aggregate channels.

Cabletron's inverse multiplexing is called port trunking. Regardless of the name, you must remember that the inter-chassis trunks need to comply with spanning tree rules.

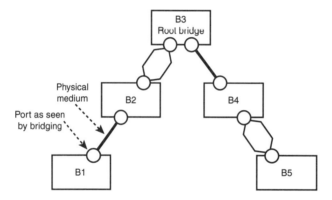

FIGURE 12.9. *A limited exception to spanning tree really doesn't violate the algorithm, because the multiple physical paths are hidden from the algorithm.*

You have to configure explicitly the relationship between physical and spanning-tree-visible paths, through the interconnection of cards, software commands, or both.

In the example in Figure 12.9, the two physical paths between B2 and B3, and the three between B4 and B5, are treated as a single path from the perspective of spanning tree.

Inverse multiplexing has been common in the past on WAN links between two half-bridges. The term *half-bridge* originated in IBM Token Ring networking and referred to a pair of bridges linked by a point-to-point WAN circuit. Each bridge has a LAN interface and a WAN interface.

Other terms for bridges linked by a medium other than the basic LAN include encapsulated bridges and remote bridges. To get more bandwidth, some of these WAN-oriented bridges used parallel point-to-point circuits. Frames received on the various physical interfaces were recombined into a single stream before the bridging software saw them.

Use of high-speed inverse multiplexing in a LAN context is relatively new. Increased bandwidth requirements led to using parallel Fast Ethernet media.

IEEE 802.1D and Addressing in the Spanning Tree

As soon as more than two chassis enter the configuration, spanning tree becomes important. If you cascade chassis within the same broadcast domain, the basic means of communication is a spanning tree. Two spanning tree algorithms are in use: the IEEE 802.1D and the DEC proprietary algorithm. Unless there is a specific need to use chassis that cannot speak other than the DEC spanning tree algorithm, such as the DECbridge 100 or the Vitalink Translan, the IEEE algorithm should be used everywhere.

Spanning tree rules require that interconnected bridges form a tree that grows from a root bridge. Forwarding must always be in the direction of the root, or through the root.

The structure of the spanning tree is determined by:

- Bridge priority fields, part of the bridge identifier, which affect the likelihood of a bridge being elected root

- Path costs associated with individual ports

- Port identifier, which uses the port MAC address as final tie-breaker

Trunk ports, as well as edge ports to which servers are connected, might be of higher speed than general edge ports. Switches are a convenient mechanism for obtaining faster access to servers without upgrading the entire network. It is quite common to have 10 MBps edge ports and 100 MBps trunk and server edge ports. Some chassis designate certain of their ports as edge or trunk only. On others, any port can be configured as edge or trunk, with the caveat that VLAN trunks generally assume 100 MBps or faster media.

There can be only one active path between two bridges. A partial exception to this is if there are multiple parallel physical links between a pair of bridges, and these parallel paths are treated as a single, inversely multiplexed, path for the purpose of bridge topology.

These topological rules are enforced by a dynamic management mechanism, the spanning tree algorithm.

Bridges transmit management information using Bridge Protocol Data Units (BPDUs) defined in IEEE 802.1D, which is also ISO/IEC 15802-3. BPDUs have a scope of one physical medium, in that they are not relayed to the next bridge, but used by a bridge to compute new BDPUs that are sent to its neighbors. Effectively, BPDUs are hello messages among bridges.

BPDUs describe the interconnections of a bridge to other bridges. Logically, this means there must be a unique identifier, or address, for the bridge itself rather than any of its interfaces. The bridge describes its interfaces in the BPDUs, but it has to identify itself.

The bridge identifier is a combination of a priority field with a unique 48-bit globally unique MAC address. The lower the value of the priority field, the more likely the bridge is to be elected root.

After root bridge election, each bridge designates one of its interfaces as topologically closest to the root. This has a port identifier based on the interface MAC address.

Note

Keep in mind that spanning tree constraints apply to each VLAN.

Inter-Subnet Communications

If you define more than one subnet on a switch, or set of switches, you must enable some form of routing between the subnets if you want them to intercommunicate. Routing, in this context, includes both classical dynamic routing and cut-through switching.

Note

Don't assume that you necessarily want different VLANs to communicate! Remember that VLANs were developed not as means of easing configuration, but as security methods hiding the traffic of one VLAN from another on shared trunk media.

You might connect a physical router to one of the switch ports or, if the "switch chassis" permits, run routing on the switch.

Catalyst switches use the term route group to refer to the set of ports that forms one IP subnet. These need not be contiguous on the chassis. Ports are assigned to route groups during edge port configuration. In reality, you are configuring at Layer 3 when you configure route groups for edge ports, or using route groups to establish a subnet prefix in which you will define management interfaces.

Chassis Configuration Management

To make a chassis act as part of more than the most trivial network, you have to enable some form of network management interface that allows you to set configuration parameters. Typically, there is both a local console port and some remote configuration software such as a vendor-dependent SNMP MIB. SNMP is also used for other forms of network management.

> ### Note
>
> *You see less consistency among the command languages of switches than you do for routers from what might seem to be the same vendor. Major internetworking vendors, such as Bay and Cisco, have gone through a variety of mergers and acquisitions of companies with strong switching technologies, and the vendor-specific control interfaces have not been immediately integrated into the command language of the main vendor.*
>
> *Inconsistencies within a single vendor's offerings are not restricted to human interfaces. Many products have private extensions to the generic MIB used by SNMP. The private extensions, however, can differ within a given vendor product line. These extensions might have been defined by the original implementer of a product, before the product was acquired by the larger vendor. Subsequent to the acquisition, MIB extensions might again be modified to make them consistent with the larger vendor's overall private MIB conventions.*

Vendor Configuration Strategies

Most chassis offer a choice of in-band or out-of-band management. In-band management means that an IP address for switch management is defined as part of a broadcast domain that includes user edge ports or possibly trunk ports. Out-of-band management does not share space with user traffic.

The advantage of in-band management is that it does not need separate wiring for a management path. A first advantage of out-of-band management is that user traffic cannot interfere with the flow of management information. Medium congestion might interfere with management information reaching its destination.

An additional reason to use out-of-band management is that the management port of a switch often has a higher internal priority than user ports. This is reasonable, because it might be utterly critical to run diagnostics or issue commands to clear a problem on user ports. Under stress, if both management and user traffic appear on the same port, the user workload may "leak in" and overwhelm the management processor. Management processor load is a different problem than medium congestion.

> ### Note
>
> Configuration command examples in this chapter are just that—examples. They were selected to help you understand the general process by which specific implementations are told to implement various software-defined functions. Material in this book might not agree with the specific version of vendor software on your platform, and you should consult current vendor reference manuals for exhaustive and specific command formats.

Bay Switches

Bay switches tend to be controlled primarily through SNMP rather than a local console interface. Bay products might differ in specific commands, but the basic process is to set up connectivity for SNMP communications as the main management interface. There are additional screens for setting port characteristics, characteristics of the spanning tree, and so on. Originally, all were menu oriented rather than command line, but Bay now has alternatives for both modes of entry.

Cisco Switches

Cisco switches, in many cases, come from acquisitions of companies such as Catalyst, Grand Junction, Kalpana, and so on. The early versions of these switches did not run Cisco's internetwork operating system (IOS), so their command languages vary. Cisco historically emphasized command languages, although some acquired products began with menu interfaces.

Cisco's larger strategy is to provide various graphic interface tools to a management platform that includes SNMP and TFTP.

For management purposes, the Catalyst itself has an IP address set for in-band management using the set routegroup command:

```
set routegroup
    {routegroup number}
    {port list}
    {ip address} {subnet mask}
```

The Catalyst 1200 has a SUM port (sc0) that is used purely for out-of-band management. If an IP address is assigned to this port, out-of-band management with the SUM port is mandatory. You set the out-of-band management address with the command

```
set interface sc0 {ip address} {subnet mask}
set interface sc0 up
```

Catalyst 1900 switches have their in-band management addresses set with the `network management->ip configuration` menu.

Catalyst 5000 switches use IP addresses associated with the console (`sc0`) interface or SLIP console (`sl0`) interface for management. These addresses can be assigned manually, or obtained dynamically with BOOTP. The IP address is configured to `0.0.0.0.` to invoke BOOTP.

`sc0` defaults to being part of VLAN 1 on the switch, but it can be configured in a separate prefix. If it is not in one of the VLAN prefixes, a `set ip route` command needs to be entered to establish a static route to it.

> **Note**
>
> *In general, if a switch is not running a dynamic routing protocol, it needs at least a default route to reach management addresses, even management addresses in the same switch. You typically use explicit static routes to reach other prefixes in the same switch and a static route to the 0.0.0.0/0 prefix to reach management servers.*

The Humble Console Function

Most switches have some type of command-line or simple menu interface that can be accessed with a plain text terminal function. The following are some examples of parameters you need to know to set up the console function:

- *Local console*—If you consider DTE and DCE status as primitive addressing, then there very well may be some addressing associated even with the local port. Vendors are not consistent on making console and auxiliary ports electrical DTEs or DCEs. Cisco's general convention is to have the console port as a DCE and the auxiliary port as a DTE. On the Bay Accelar switch, both are DTE. It's not unheard of that the vendor changes the convention during production of a specific model, and it is always worth checking the documentation received with your chassis.

- *Telnet access*—To be able to telnet to a chassis, the chassis needs an IP address.

- *Remote access with auxiliary ports*—On Catalyst switches, you can use the `set interface` command to enable a Serial Line Interface Protocol (SLIP) connection on the console interface (`sl0`).

- *Web control*—Some chassis act as HTML servers, so the control interface to them requires TCP port 80.

Addressing for Trivial File Transfer Protocol

Your switch is likely to need to know the address of one or more Trivial File Transfer Protocol (TFTP) servers, from which it downloads its executable software images and possibly its configuration.

Several name and address relationships must exist before configurations or executables can be loaded using TFTP. The switch must know its own IP address to put into the TFTP request.

If the switch does not know the IP address or DNS name of the TFTP server, it needs to broadcast its request, and a router connected to the switch's subnet must convert the local broadcast into a routable unicast or directed broadcast.

If the switch knows the DNS name of the TFTP server, but not its IP address, it must know how to reach a DNS server that can resolve that name. To reach DNS, the switch must know the IP address of one or more DNS servers or a suitable broadcast forwarding mechanism must have been predefined.

On a Catalyst 5000 with recent software, loading the flash memory from a TFTP server is a manual operation using the `copy tftp flash` command. Actual rebooting is from the local flash memory.

Addressing for SNMP and Related Network Management

Your switch needs to know the address of a trap server and might need assorted security settings for management. At the very least, the SNMP manager should use community string passwords to access the SNMP client on the switch.

System-level information needs to be set in the MIB. There is an increasing need to set system ID, because this persists beyond IP address. On the Catalyst 5000, use the `set system name` command to set system ID.

Monitoring Ports

Especially for applying RMON, many switches have a special port or equivalent function that can be configured to copy frames from specific user data ports. Such special ports can also be used for out-of-band management, as opposed to in-band management, to switch on one of the main data ports.

Explicit commands are needed to put the monitor on specific user or trunk ports. Depending on the switch, more than one port can be monitored simultaneously.

Monitoring ports receive copies of all or selected—if the switch supports selection—traffic passing through one or more monitored ports.

Catalyst 1900 and 2820 switches allow you to define a capture list of ports whose traffic can be copied to a monitor port.

On the Catalyst 1200, the switched port analyzer (SPAN) feature copies traffic to a specific monitoring port. You can use any port except sc0 with this command, subject to the real-world extension that you cannot monitor a greater volume of traffic from a given management port than the bandwidth of the management port. For example, you cannot monitor the FDDI port from an Ethernet port.

On Bay 28000 switches, the conversation steering mechanism allows traffic from one or more edge ports to be copied to a monitoring port.

RMON

Switches vary as to whether they have an internal RMON capability or an external RMON probe needs to be attached to a switch port. A protocol analyzer such as the Network General Sniffer also can be assigned to a monitoring port.

Depending on the RMON capability in use, the RMON probe might store only summaries of traffic statistics and/or send alarms when preprogrammed thresholds are reached. See Chapter 7 for more details of the data collected by RMON.

Edge Port Configuration

Remember that a switch, as opposed to a classical bridge, is intended as a performance-enhancing device. Whereas bridges improve performance by segmenting media, allowing some filtering of unicasts, switches microsegment or give apparently dedicated bandwidth to each connected device.

This fine-grained device connectivity can give more control and also is more work to configure. Individual devices can be configured with full-duplex connectivity to many switches.

Your switch might offer the capability to name ports. This is usually a way to make displays more meaningful. It should not be confused with DNS naming, because that is at the IP level that is transparent to the switch ports. IP addresses assigned to management functions on the switch can, of course, be given DNS definitions.

Ethernet ports default, on most switches, to operate in half duplex. You can configure them to be full duplex.

As shown in Figure 12.10, there can be a mixture of connection types in a switched system. Edge ports connect directly to end hosts or to Layer 1 hubs that connect to end hosts. Trunk ports are part of a single broadcast domain (that is, a single instance of the spanning tree algorithm) or have multiple spanning trees multiplexed on to them using VLAN protocols.

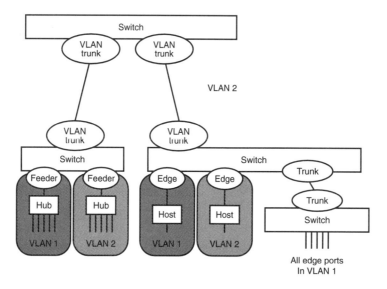

FIGURE 12.10. *VLAN and non-VLAN ports can coexist in a network.*

Checklist for Basic Edge Port Configuration

☐Should the port be enabled or disabled?

☐Is there a port-specific name used in management?

☐If the port supports different speeds, such as 10/100 MBps Ethernet, for what speed should the port be configured, or can it be put into an auto-configuration mode? Will the port reliably autosense the speed?

☐Should the port run in half or full duplex?

☐If the LAN protocol, or switch extensions, support different priorities, what priority is associated with this port?

☐Are port-level filters needed? For specific MAC addresses? For multicasts or broadcasts?

This checklist for basic edge port configuration does not consider additional requirements for VLANs in general or technology-specific VLAN information. Specific details vary with the particular switch product.

General Checklist for Edge Port Configuration When VLANs Are in Use

☐ If VLAN assignment is based on physical ports, to which VLAN is this port assigned?

☐ If VLAN assignment is based on MAC address, protocol type, or Layer 3 address, are the rules for such assignment defined?

Additional configuration decisions with VLANs are technology-specific. LANE and 802.1Q, for example, need additional information, as discussed later in this chapter.

Trunk Port Configuration

Trunk configuration is fairly simple when VLANs are not in use and usually is self-configuring. In the absence of VLANs, the IEEE 802.1D spanning tree protocol usually takes care of most configuration quite automatically.

You can influence the probability of a given bridge/switch chassis becoming the root of a spanning tree. The 802.1D protocol includes the idea of a bridge priority, which all major vendors allow you to alter from the default value. 802.1D also has a notion of link cost, which, after root bridge election, helps select the particular paths taken between bridges. Vendor-dependent differences in the realization of spanning tree are seen when inverse multiplexing is used. Cisco's Fast Etherchannel is one example of inverse multiplexing. On a Catalyst 5000, it is enabled with `set port channel {port-list} on`.

When VLANs are used, more configuration is required on trunks to specify which VLANs traverse which trunks.

Checklist for Trunk Port Configuration

☐ Inverse multiplex links configured if used?

☐ Spanning trees enabled?

☐ VLANs assigned to trunks?

VLANs

You will find that setting up multiple VLANs is much like setting up several independent, multichassis switched LANs. The major differences are that you have a wider range of choices in assigning hosts to broadcast domains, and you have to configure trunk protocols. Each physical port on a switch needs to be defined as an edge or trunk port with respect to VLANs.

An area of caution is the number of slots available in MAC address port tables. Different vendors might have a pool of addresses they partition or allocate blocks of address memory in some hardware-dependent way. This usually is not a practical limitation, as you should be cautious in making VLANs, or any broadcast domain, larger than 1 KB addresses.

Bay, for example, allows 1024 addresses per VLAN, and the number of VLANs on a single switch is up to the number of physical ports on that switch. Catalyst switches, at the time of this writing, have up to 16 KB address table slots that are partitioned among the various VLANs. None of these, of course, approach the 4094 VLAN limit of the 802.1Q protocol.

VLAN Assignment by Physical Port

The most common way to assign ports to VLANs is by manual configuration. The following sections describe the manual configurations for several VLANs.

The Bay 28xxx VLAN

A physical switch can have up to the number of VLANs that it has ports. There can be a total of 8192 MAC addresses per switch community, but only 1024 per switch community using VLANs across trunk links. In other words, after the VLANs cross a trunk link, the sum of MAC addresses in the various VLANs across the trunk cannot exceed 1024.

Actual assignment of ports to VLANs is done through the Optivity network management system via SNMP commands. The local chassis configuration interface does not support assignment of ports to other than the default VLAN.

The Bay Accelar 1000 Routing Switch

Accelar 1000 routing switches manage their VLANs using the idea that ports are assigned to VLANs. A graphical user interface is used with the Bay Accelar VLAN for assigning ports and protocols to VLANs. Each VLAN belongs to a spanning tree group (STG).

Accelar routing switches support up to 125 VLANs plus the default VLAN. The number of VLANs is reduced by 1 for each STG. A VLAN cannot span multiple STGs; all ports in a VLAN must be in the same STG. Trunk ports can belong to multiple VLANs and multiple STGs. The STG structure generally defines the Layer 2 topology.

Traffic can be assigned to a VLAN by port or by protocol type. An access port can only belong to one and only one port-based VLAN. A port in a port-based VLAN can belong to other policy-based VLANs. An edge port can belong to only one port-, policy-, or protocol-based VLAN. Protocol membership wins over port when there is a conflict on VLAN assignment.

The Catalyst (5000) Switch

Using Catalyst switches, VLANs are created first in the management domain, and then ports are mapped to VLANs or designated as trunks. To assign ports to VLANs, use

```
set vlan {vlan-number} {port-list}
```

To assign switch ports to work as trunks, use

```
set trunk {module/port} {on | off | desirable | auto} [allowed-vlans]
```

on sets permanent ISL mode. off is the default mode for FDDI trunks. desirable negotiates becoming a trunk and is not allowed on FDDI or ATM. Auto indicates the port is willing to be a trunk if a peer wants it to be. auto is the default for Fast Ethernet and is not allowed for FDDI or ATM.

VLAN Assignment by MAC Address

Assigning devices to VLANs based on MAC addresses is often cited as a way to manage VLANs, but a moment's reflection reveals that it requires an explicit knowledge of MAC address assignments. This might be desirable under specific security policies where no one is allowed to install a host without the awareness of network operations. It also might be perfectly reasonable when network drivers routinely require fixed, locally administered addresses, such as SNA and some Novell environments. It also makes sense for DECnet, where the MAC addresses of hosts are set dynamically to reflect the DECnet logical address.

Cisco defines a VLAN Membership Policy Server (VMPS), which contains an ASCII file of MAC-address-to-VLAN mappings. This file is downloaded to switches.

When a given MAC address arrives at an edge port, the MAC address is sent to the VMPS server over UDP. VMPS looks up the MAC address and returns the VLAN ID if the MAC address is found. Optionally, the VMPS server might check the MAC address to see that it is coming in on a predefined range of ports. In other words, MAC address 1234.5678.9ABC might be associated with the Payroll VLAN, but only if it comes in from a port on the third or fourth floors.

Fault-Tolerant Trunking

Bridge topologies are limited by the spanning tree algorithm, and a single VLAN can be present only on one trunk between two bridges. One of the advantages of VLANs, however, is they can be distributed over trunks among switches. Such distribution provides both load sharing and fault tolerance.

In Figure 12.11, the gray VLAN traffic normally goes over Port 1, and black over Port 2. In the event of a failure of either port, all traffic moves to the other logical port. Trunk ports could be implemented over multiple physical interfaces using inverse multiplexing.

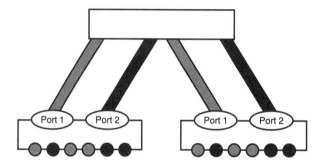

FIGURE 12.11. *Parallel trunks with fault tolerance.*

Spanning tree constraints still hold. Traffic of a given color does not go over more than one port at any given time. Both paths are known to each per-VLAN spanning tree. 802.1D path cost values need to be manipulated to make the gray trunk preferred for the gray VLAN and the black trunk for the black VLAN.

VLAN-Aware Servers

A VLAN-aware server card essentially is an access multiplexer for VLANs, with a physical trunk interface and a set of virtual port addresses seen by the server software as separate network interfaces. These effectively place a VLAN switch on each card, as shown in Figure 12.12.

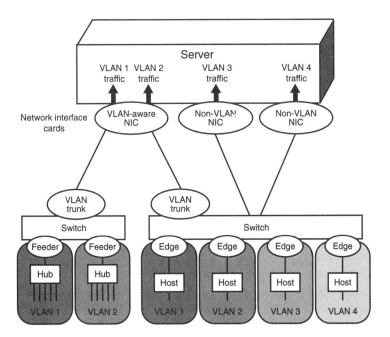

FIGURE 12.12. *A server can use both VLAN-aware and regular, non-VLAN aware network interface cards (NICs).*

In Figure 12.12, contrast the way VLANs 3 and 4 enter the server on separate NICs to the way VLANs 1 through 2 enter through the VLAN-aware card. This is a perfectly reasonable approach when VLANs 1 and 2 need much more bandwidth to the server.

Observe that there is inter-VLAN communication at an application level here. No router function is required; each VLAN appears to the server as a separate interface. Application gateway software in the server might transfer records from port to port, but the server is not acting as a Layer 3 router.

VLAN-aware servers are especially attractive when there is relatively light traffic to the server from a significant number of LANs, too many to justify separate NICs for each. When there is major traffic from a given LAN, give that LAN its own port.

Under license from Cisco, Intel makes network interface cards that understand the ISL protocol. There are several manufacturers of LANE-aware NICs.

Filtering

Filtering based on fields of the MAC header is common. Typical fields on which decisions are made include

- MAC layer address
- Vendor code and protocol type in Ethernet frames
- Vendor code and type in LLC headers

Additional filtering rules and actions can be defined by specific vendors for additional security and broadcast control.

Port Blocking for MAC Addresses

Some switches go beyond the enforcement of permitting or denying specified source MAC addresses to pass through the port. They provide the capability to shut down the port and/or generate an SNMP trap if other than a specific source MAC address sends traffic across the port. This can become a maintenance nightmare unless the device connected to the port has a locally administered MAC address, as discussed in Chapter 11. Otherwise, the MAC address changes whenever the network interface card on the host is changed, and the port blocking function then triggers.

On the Catalyst 5000, you enable this function with

```
set port security mod_num/port_num enable [mac_addr]
```

An application for this could be in a data over cable TV application, where each set-top chassis/cable modem is configured with a MAC address that identifies the customer.

If the user cannot pass packets through the switch, the user's DHCP request packets cannot get an IP address, and an unauthorized user thus cannot get Internet access.

Handling Layer 2 Broadcasts and Multicasts

One of the major scaling limitations of bridged systems is their poor recovery from broadcast storms. Although the most common means of limiting broadcast propagation is to separate broadcast domains with routers or application gateways, many switches have additional broadcast control mechanisms that complement routers and gateways.

Broadcast Storm Control on Switches

On some switches, such as the Catalyst, you can prevent broadcast storms by setting a threshold value on a per-edge-port basis. When this threshold is reached, no more broadcast packets are forwarded from the port.

On a Catalyst 1900 or 2820, go to the `main menu->system configuration->` `broadcast storm control` menu. Broadcast storm control is disabled by default.

By default, after broadcast storm control is enabled, it begins blocking at a level of 500 frames per second at a port. A second threshold value lets a broadcast-blocked port begin to forward broadcasts again, after the broadcast count drops below the threshold. By default, this second threshold is 250 frames per second. The values for both of these thresholds can be changed in this menu.

On the Catalyst 5000, broadcast suppression is set differently, with the command

```
set port broadcast {module/port} {threshold} [%]
```

Layer 2 Multicast Control

Although the usual practice in generalized multicasting is to multicast at Layer 3, Layer 3 addresses certainly do map into Layer 2 multicast addresses. The Catalyst 5000 has a Cisco-proprietary feature called Cisco Group Management Protocol (CGMP), which is a mixture of Layer 3 and Layer 2 technologies.

Membership in a multicast group can be statically configured on the switch or learned dynamically from a router connected to the switch. The router learns IP multicast group normally with the Layer 3 IGMP protocol and sends CGMP Layer 2 information to the switch. From the CGMP information, the switch copies frames among ports of the multicast group.

You set static multicast groups with the `set cam` command:

```
set cam
    {permanent|static}
    {multicast-mac-address}
    {port-list}
```

Permanent definitions are kept in nonvolatile read-only memory (NVRAM); static definitions are not subject to aging but are cleared when the chassis reboots.

Addressing in Configuring LAN Emulation

When you set up a LAN emulation system, as shown in Figure 12.13, you need to enter configuration information into one or more LAN Emulation Clients (LECs), a LAN Emulation Server (LES) per ELAN/VLAN, and a LAN Emulation Configuration Server (LECS) for each LANE environment.

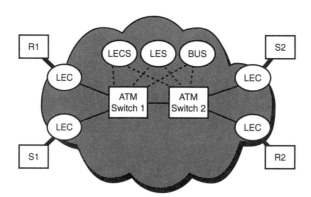

    ━━━━━━ Emulated LAN (outside LANE cloud)

    ────── Data VC (inside LANE cloud)

    ------- Control VC (inside LANE cloud)

FIGURE 12.13. *Even nonredundant LAN emulation involves complex relationships between LECs, LECS, LES, and BUS infrastructure servers, and ATM switches.*

Next Hop Resolution Protocol

Recall that NHRP gives the addressing information used to make route- versus cut-through switch decisions for virtual circuit–capable transmission systems. Beyond basic systems as shown in Figure 12.14, NHRP is an essential part of extensions to LANE such as MPOA, which were introduced in Chapter 4.

If your environment uses the newer fault tolerance mechanisms, you also need to set up backup relationships among the servers.

Setting Up the LANE Servers

You need to decide how many emulated LANs (ELANs)—that is, VLANs using ATM trunking—you will have. Each ELAN needs:

- A name.

- One or more LAN Emulation Servers. Servers after the first are backups.

- One or more Broadcast and Unknown Servers (BUS). Again, additional servers are backups. In many implementations, the BUS is colocated with the LES and is created when the LES is created.

- Rules for including LAN Emulation Clients (LEC) in the ELAN. The ELAN can have restricted or unrestricted membership.

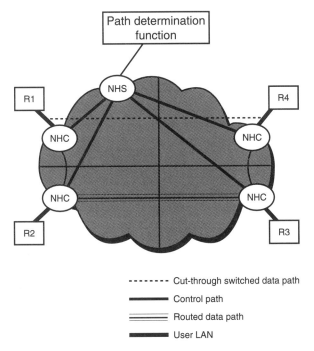

FIGURE 12.14. *NHRP clients, typically in edge devices such as switches, query NHRP servers to determine whether to open a virtual circuit to the destination or to route to it. MPOA is not used in this figure.*

Each ELAN/VLAN represents a separate broadcast domain. Its size is limited by general experience with the capability of bridged systems to handle broadcasts. In addition, because broadcasts are actually generated by the BUS function in an ELAN, the processing power of the BUS is a significant factor in sizing.

On a Lightstream 1010 ATM switch, the LECS address is set up with the command

```
atm lecs-address {atm-address}
```

On a router or switch, first establish the local ELAN on the first subinterface and then enable the LES/BUS function:

```
interface atm0.{subinterface-number}
lane server-bus ethernet {elan-name}
```

Next, LECS databases need to be set up. Commands differ for the default ELAN, for unrestricted-membership ELANs, and restricted membership ELANs. All begin with the command

```
lane database {database-name}
```

The default ELAN is selected with the command

```
default-name {elan-name}
```

For a pure default LANE environment, the default ELAN needs to be bound to a server address:

```
name {elan-name} server-atm-address {atm-address}
```

Unrestricted databases can also have a default specified for addresses not explicitly bound to an ELAN. Explicit ELAN membership is specified with the following command format, one line per ELAN:

```
name {elan-name-1} server-atm-address {atm-address}
name {elan-name-2} server-atm-address {atm-address}
...
default-name {elan-name}
```

For restricted databases, the command differs slightly:

```
name {elan-name-1} server-atm-address {atm-address} restricted
name {elan-name-2} server-atm-address {atm-address} restricted
```

Checklist for LANE Server Setup

☐ LECS defined?

☐ Definition for each ELAN configured into the LECS?

☐ LES and BUS functions defined for each ELAN?

☐ If server redundancy is used, are the multiple servers defined? Is a redundancy protocol such as SSRP or SCSP enabled? Figure 12.15 illustrates the positioning of redundant servers and interserver protocols.

Setting Up the LAN Emulation Clients

On a Catalyst 5000, LECs are defined on a per-subinterface basis:

```
interface atm0.{subinterface-number}
LANE client ethernet {vlan_num} {elan_name}
```

Checklist for LANE Server Setup

☐ LEC on each device interface?

☐ If server redundancy is used, are the multiple servers defined? Is a redundancy protocol such as SSRP or SCSP enabled?

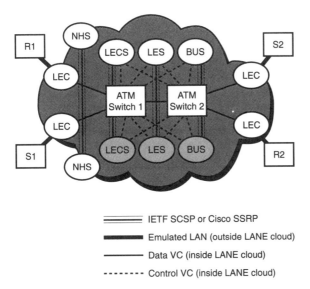

IETF SCSP or Cisco SSRP

Emulated LAN (outside LANE cloud)

Data VC (inside LANE cloud)

Control VC (inside LANE cloud)

FIGURE 12.15. *Additional components are needed for server redundancy.*

ATM Switching

When used with appropriate network management tools, the configuration process for a single ATM switch acting as a collapsed backbone can be relatively straightforward. The configuration of a system of ATM switches, however, can be much more complex.

As with other types of switches discussed in this chapter, a management IP address needs to be established to remotely manage an ATM switch. The most basic function in configuring the switch proper is to establish ATM NSAP addresses on the switch interfaces. Management and ATM routing protocols then can be used to build virtual circuits traversing these interfaces.

Checklist for ATM Switch Addressing

☐Interfaces default to NSAP address or are manually configured with appropriate addresses

☐Manual switching tables defined or ATM routing enabled

☐Switch has IP address for management

☐Switch knows the names or addresses of its management servers

ATM to Frame Relay Interworking

Frame Relay is primarily intended as a customer-to-provider access protocol, while ATM was designed as an internal carrier and intercarrier protocol. There is an obvious requirement to map between them.

Frame Relay Switching

Frame Relay is intended to provide a simple user interface, the simplest consistent with multiplexing. Its internal implementation inside a Frame Relay cloud is less simple.

Frame Relay switching makes hop-by-hop switching decisions based on the DLCI field in incoming frames, which is functionally similar to a destination MAC address. It differs from a MAC address in that its significance is normally local to a single medium and can change on successive Frame Relay hops.

Internally, a Frame Relay service can encapsulate the frame's data field in LAP-F or in some other frame, packet, or cell protocol. Frame Relay, X.25, and SMDS are all interface specifications, defining what is seen at the customer interface. The internals of the underlying carrier service are hidden from the customer.

Edge or access switches provide DCE or NNI LAP-F interfaces. Trunk switches do not interface directly to end users or other networks. Connectivity between edge and trunk switches might or might not use Frame Relay.

In commercial frame services, edge switches might also need to access accounting hosts as well as network management hosts.

Frame Relay on Bay

Large Frame Relay services based on Bay equipment use IP tunnels between trunk switches and between edge and trunk switches. You set up permanent virtual circuit routes in the Configuration Manager from the `circuits->edit circuits->edit->add` menu. Parameters set here include:

- Calling DLCI

- Called DLCI

- IP address associated with the called DLCI

- VC input throughput

Bay also provides ATM connectivity between frame switches. Parameters here are set with a menu specific to the Frame Relay–to–ATM-interworking module installed in the switch.

Frame Relay on Cisco Routers

In what Cisco calls local switching, Frame Relay interfaces can be DTE, DCE, or NNI. Frame Relay can run over GRE tunnels over a general IP network; this is called remote switching. In either mode, frame switching needs to be explicitly enabled with the command

```
frame-relay switching
```

After the Frame Relay switching service is enabled, you can configure individual interfaces as DTE, DCE, or NNI:

```
frame-relay intf-type [dce | dte | nni]
```

For local switching, you then configure Frame Relay routing, a term for enabling the next-hop decision. Specific routes are defined with the command

```
frame-relay route in-dlci out-interface out-dlci
```

Checklist for Frame Relay Switch Addressing

☐ DLCIs defined for all user-visible circuits? These must map to some internal identifier for the transit network and eventually to a destination DLCI.

☐ Management mode selected on interfaces, and the proper management DLCI agreed to?

☐ Inverse ARP support set up if this is a requirement?

☐ Switching/routing tables set up to cover all destinations?

☐ Frame-over-IP tunneling or Frame-ATM Interworking defined if this is a requirement?

X.25 Switching

Like Frame Relay, X.25 switching involves chassis-by-chassis tables that define the outgoing ports for particular persistent identifiers, in this case X.121 addresses. Unlike Frame Relay, the forwarding tables are usually defined for the entire chassis rather than per interface.

The most common type of X.25 virtual circuit is the *switched virtual circuit* (SVC), which is set up dynamically between pairs of endpoints with X.121 interfaces. Permanent virtual circuits (PVCs) are set up over a specific route of interfaces.

Traditionally, X.25 packets are encapsulated in LAP-B. Cisco calls switching from one LAP-B to another LAP-B interface local switching. X.25 can be encapsulated in TCP using Cisco XOT [RFC 1613]. XOT switching is called remote switching. Whether the X.25 packets are carried in TCP or some other link-level protocol, the backbone of an X.25 provider network usually runs something other than X.25. Pure packet switching is more usually seen at the edge of networks, either collapsed networks or interfaces between user and public networks.

In Cisco routers, both local and remote switching are explicitly enabled with the command

```
x25 routing
```

The handling of incoming calls is based on the destination X.121 address and CUD values in the incoming packet. On a Cisco router, the forwarding rules are defined in x25 route commands. See the "Tunneling" section of Chapter 14, "Selective Forwarding Inside Routers," for a discussion of the remote switching format. For local switching, the command format is:

```
x25 route
  [#position]
  x121-address
  [cud pattern]
  interface type  number
```

X.25 PVCs

You can create PVCs on X.25 switches. This is unusual, however, because in modern cases, Frame Relay provides a PVC function with much lower overhead. You might need it for compatibility with very old legacy systems. A more common reason to do it today is when there is a requirement to run over a very poor quality slow link where the link retransmission of LAP-B can combine with X.25 packet fragmentation and optimize throughput.

As a result, DTEs that require permanent circuits can be connected to a router acting as an X.25 switch and have a properly functioning connection. X.25 resets are sent to indicate when the circuit comes up or goes down. Both interfaces must define complementary locally switched PVCs in this way:

```
x25 pvc number1 interface type number pvc number2 [option]
```

X.25 Address Manipulation

There are a number of situations where you might need to change the source or destination address in an X.25 packet you are switching. One example might be where you are converting from a public X.25 network to a private network, but do not want to change the called X.121 addresses in the DTE.

Many carriers have a security policy of not trusting user-originated source X.121 addresses. The source address field of packets entering the network is automatically replaced, in such policies, with the address of the first provider-controlled X.25 interface the user traffic encounters.

Checklist for X.25 Switch Addressing

☐All interfaces assigned X.121 addresses?

☐Logical channel sequence number ranges set on each interface, with appropriate consideration of PVC, one-way incoming, one-way outgoing, and two-way usages discussed in Chapter 4?

☐Address substitution mechanisms set up if this is a requirement?

☐Switching/routing tables set up to cover all destinations, either with a default outgoing interface or an explicit policy to drop packets destined to a non-matched X.121 address?

☐X.25 tunneling defined if this is a requirement? Are there clear mappings between X.121 and IP addresses?

Looking Ahead

This chapter shows how to arrange the address-significant topology within the bandwidth and broadcast domains of hubs and switches. In LAN devices, most MAC address activity is learned dynamically, but this chapter considers how those addresses are learned and filtered.

Layer 2 address assignment is more explicit in Frame Relay, X.25, and ATM switching than in LANs.

This chapter shows the management relationships among various chassis types, and how to make these chassis operate with Layer 3 addressable management devices. Actual Layer 3 data flow between different subnets (realized as broadcast domains) remains a routing function, which is discussed in Chapter 13.

CHAPTER 13

Addressing in Routers

Have you heard of the wonderful one-hoss shay/
That was built in such a logical way/
It ran a hundred years to the day?

—*Oliver Wendell Holmes*

Speaking, he addressed her winged words.

—*Homer*

The paths of glory lead but to the grave.

—*Thomas Gray*

Routers are computers. They might have special-purpose processors, but all have a general-purpose processor that contains configuration information. This special-purpose computer needs to be configured before any useful routing can be done. Configuration operations involve management and control functions of the router platform, as well as the interface addresses that need to be configured to allow the router to act as a forwarding device.

IPv4's basic model of a router is as a collection of host addresses on different prefixes. Originally, there was no thought of an identifier for the "box" itself, but needs for such identifiers have evolved.

Note

Real-world implementations might combine pure router functions with switches, hubs, or servers, all in the same physical chassis.

> **Note**
>
> This chapter deals with a router as a Layer 3 forwarding device. Various industry references use the term routing *rather broadly to encompass path determination for ATM and other essentially Layer 2 systems. Unless specified otherwise, that is not the usage you will find in this chapter.*

See Figure 13.1 to get an idea of the kinds of interfaces and related constructs found on routers. You assign addresses to some of them, but not all of them.

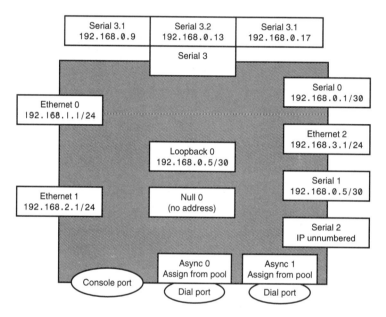

F IGURE 13.1. *Pure routers do not have a single address, but are identified by a set of at least two logical addresses.*

Router implementers tend to distinguish between *router interfaces* and *router ports*. An interface is assumed to receive traffic that will be sent out one or more other interfaces, depending on the contents of the routing table. Ports are often asynchronous and used to access internal processes inside the router. The most common port function is for connecting the console terminal to the router.

When the router provides dialup services, the asynchronous interfaces into which a user dials are usually called ports. They are ports, not interfaces; they provide access to internal software processes that modify packets received on ports to be suitable for routing through interfaces.

Interfaces usually, but not always, have assigned Layer 3 addresses. Some exceptions include unnumbered and null (also called blackhole) interfaces, the details of which are discussed later in this chapter.

Most interfaces have physical existence, external to the router box. Some software-defined interfaces are internal to the box but appear in the routing table as if they truly are external.

Interfaces can be placeholders or superinterfaces for groups of software-defined interfaces of which routing is aware. In Figure 13.1, Serial 3 is a Frame Relay interface with three virtual circuits mapped to it. Each virtual circuit is mapped, in turn, to a software-defined *subinterface.* Subinterfaces and superinterfaces are discussed later in this chapter. The term *superinterface* is not a standard one, but there is no generally accepted term that refers to a group of interfaces. Superinterface is a nice contrast to the more generally used subinterface.

The primary configuration techniques differ significantly among routers from different manufacturers.

Note

It is not the intention of this chapter to provide a complete configuration language reference for each implementation. Rather, the intention is to present various general functions in router address configuration and then illustrate these functions with implementation-specific examples.

Some of the differences are for historical reasons. For example, Cisco and then-Wellfleet (now Bay, which is now being acquired by Nortel) made some early hardware design choices for their platforms. Cisco decided that a floppy disk drive was too unreliable as an operating system storage device and put its initial system software in ROM. ROM storage imposed significant size restrictions, so a command language was the only feasible method of configuration, given no separate management station.

Wellfleet used a floppy drive, trading off hardware reliability for what was perceived as greater user convenience. Given the additional storage available on a floppy, it was feasible to have a menu-oriented interface.

With the availability of flash memory to both vendors, the original constraints disappeared. Each vendor had a user base familiar with one style or the other, so the original techniques remained dominant for that product line. Over time, each vendor has developed techniques that draw from the methods preferred by the other: HTML browser style menus for Cisco and the Wellfleet/Bay technician interface.

Other vendors use either command-line or menu interfaces. Livingston, now a part of Lucent, emphasizes command lines, as does 3Com. Ascom Timeplex uses menus.

GateD is the basis for a number of router implementations. Because GateD is portable software that runs on an assortment of platforms, platforms that usually run some form of UNIX, it is much harder to generalize the configuration methods. In general, GateD systems use a text-based configuration language, edited with standard UNIX text-handling tools.

Note

GateD differs from the other implementations discussed here; it is not vendor-specific but the product of a not-for-profit consortium. GateD was originally developed at Cornell University in 1987, and its code was used as the base for the pioneering NSFnet. The original research project evolved into the GateD project in 1992 and is now based at Merit, which is affiliated with the University of Michigan [GateD].

GateD code is the base for a significant number of commercial router implementations, and it is widely used in academic and research contexts.

There are other sources from which routing code is licensed. The former Proteon is now OpenROUTE Networks, which licensed code to clients including IBM and Digital (now part of Cabletron). Cisco also licensed internetwork operating system (IOS) code to Digital. Bay acquired a company from which it had licensed code, Phase2 Networks [McClimans 1998].

Remember that many of the major internetworking vendors are the product of multiple mergers and acquisitions. This has meant that the product designers are faced with the problem of integrating command interfaces from several different vendors. Cisco, for example, acquired LAN switches from Catalyst and Kalpana, WAN switches from Stratacom, and NAT technology from Network Translation. Bay Networks was formed from a merger of Synoptics and Wellfleet, and the merged Bay, in turn, is being acquired by Nortel, the former Northern Telecom. Livingston was acquired by Lucent, which split off from the former AT&T.

As a consequence of these changed corporate relationships, you might see differences in the command interfaces of specific products from the same vendor examples given here. Figure 13.2 depicts the basic architectures of command interfaces.

The configuration process also might involve the router acting as a client to a configuration server, using TFTP or SNMP. We will discuss these and other router platform relationships to servers at the end of this chapter.

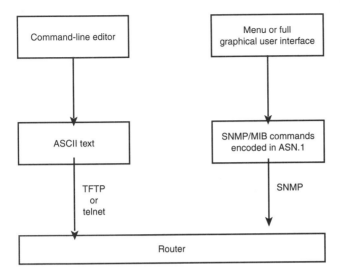

FIGURE 13.2. *Vendor configuration strategies began with either command or menu approaches. Most major vendors now support both, but internal configuration storage formats reflect the vendors' original designs.*

What Is Interface Configuration?

An interface configuration command assigns a specific network layer to an interface. But it can do much more than that:

- By providing a subnet mask or prefix length on the interface, it tells the router the prefix associated with the specific address. By the local versus remote assumption, the router now can assume it can reach any address in the prefix.

- Supplemental commands tell the router how to map the logical address to a transmission system address. These commands can include directions on working around local versus remote problems on partial mesh nonbroadcast multiaccess (NBMA) or demand media.

Interface Configuration Methods

Cisco, Livingston, GateD, and Wellfleet/Bay, as well as virtually all other commercial router implementations, all have a major configuration function associated with interfaces. At its most basic, this function binds together an address, a subnet mask, and a specific interface of a specific type. Vendor implementations vary as to whether address and mask specifications are configured on a single command or multiple command lines are needed. As an alternative to commands, several implementations use sequences of menus or fields in menus or a full graphic user interface.

> **Note**
>
> *The continuing battle between advocates of command-line versus graphical user interfaces is no less common in internetworking devices than in general purpose computing. I find it most useful to think in terms of expert-friendly versus novice-friendly interfaces and am of the opinion that there is no one best type.*
>
> *My experience shows that menu or graphical user interfaces are faster for novices to learn and allow those novices to start doing basic work in a shorter period of time. Menu or graphical user interfaces, however, are slower to use on large configurations or by thoroughly experienced administrators.*
>
> *My personal preference is for command lines, but that has to be considered in the context of my background as a programmer on IBM mainframes and UNIX. Many of today's new administrators do not have experience in algorithmic programming languages or in scriptable command languages and simply are more comfortable with a graphical metaphor.*

Details of interface configuration also vary with the interface type but are worth considering:

- Real interfaces

  Broadcast multiaccess (for example, LANs)

  Point-to-point dedicated

  - With IP addresses

  - Unnumbered

  NBMA

  Demand

- Virtual interfaces

  Loopback/circuitless; an address associated with the router box rather any of its interfaces

  Group or superinterfaces

  Subinterfaces

  Tunnels

  Null interfaces

Cisco IOS

`interface` is a major command in the IOS configuration language. Major commands establish contexts in which subcommands can be entered; they have no direct effect themselves.

The general form of an `interface` command is:

`interface {type} [number]`

Type parameters include both physical and software-only interfaces. Interface types include:

- Real

  ATM

  BRI

  Ethernet

  FDDI

  High-speed serial

  Serial

  Token Ring

- Virtual

  Asynchronous

  Dialer

  Loopback

  Null

  Tunnel

Numbering schemes vary with specific router and physical interface types. On fixed-configuration boxes such as the Cisco 2500, the interface numbers are marked on the back panel. 7xxx series router interface designations are relative numbers in the form *port/slot*, based on the slot into which the interface processor is inserted. Slot numbering conventions vary with the interface type and are marked on the boards.

4xxx series routers are modular but do not use the rational convention of the 7xxx series. Starting from the rightmost slot, interfaces are numbered cumulatively by interface type. An example helps here. Assume you have a 4000 router with a dual Ethernet module in each slot. The module-specific convention for this module is the top port is port 1 and the bottom port is port 0:

- Port 0 of the right module is `interface ethernet 0`.

- Port 1 of the right module is `interface ethernet 1`.

- Port 0 of the middle module is `interface ethernet 2`.

- Port 1 of the middle module is `interface ethernet 3`.

- Port 0 of the left module is `interface ethernet 4`.

- Port 1 of the left module is `interface ethernet 5`.

Now, substitute a four-port serial module for the middle Ethernet board:

- Port 0 of the right module is `interface ethernet 0`.

- Port 1 of the right module is `interface ethernet 1`.

- Port 0 of the middle module is `interface serial 0`.

- Port 1 of the middle module is `interface serial 1`.

- Port 1 of the middle module is `interface serial 2`.

- Port 1 of the middle module is `interface serial 3`.

- Port 0 of the left module is `interface ethernet 2`.

- Port 1 of the left module is `interface ethernet 3`.

Livingston

Livingston's best-known product is the Portmaster remote access server. Best known as an access device, this machine is a full-featured router.

Synchronous WAN ports need to be selected before they can be configured. The set command starts the port configuration process:

```
set <port-id> network    [dialin | dialout | twoway | hardwired]
```

Depending on the specific hardware platform, `<port-id>` can be S1 through S4, W1, or W1 through W59. Check your hardware reference manual to find the specific convention for the box you are configuring.

After the port is selected, you enter a variety of commands to set physical, data link, and network attributes.

GateD

GateD's configuration language also has a major command `interfaces`. The following is a simplified version of the command:

```
interfaces {
    interface interface_list
        [ passive ]
        [ simplex ]
        [ reject ]
        [ blackhole ]
        ;
    define address
        [ broadcast address ] | [ pointtopoint address ]
        [ netmask mask ]
        [ multicast ]
        ;
} ;
```

Interface specification is more general in GateD than in most proprietary router implementations. Whereas most other routing implementations specifically name interfaces by their physical or virtual type, GateD allows interfaces to be named several ways:

- Physical type and number

- IP address

- Domain name

- Unnumbered

GateD also supports various kinds of interface lists, which can be used to specify multiple interfaces. One reason to specify multiple interfaces is to allow some property, such as the broadcast address, to be inherited by multiple interfaces. Another reason is to aggregate interfaces into groups, or superinterfaces. The most general interface list uses the keyword `all` to indicate all interfaces on the router.

Interface lists can be defined at four increasingly specific levels:

- `all` refers to all interfaces on the router.

- `interface name wildcard` refers to all interfaces that share a character string in their name. This character string indicates a common software driver. For example, `ie` usually indicates Interlan. A wildcard reference `ie` would match `ie0`, `ie1`, and so on.

- `interface` *name* indicates a single specific interface such as `ie1`. This is a commonly used form, although it can become complex when there is more than one address assigned to an interface, and an interface needs to be matched to each address.

- `interface` *address* matches only a single address; it is impractical for secondary addresses. At this level of specificity, you can specify either a dotted-decimal IP address or a DNS name. In both cases, you need to be cautious. If an address changes, you need to reconfigure the router.

  If you use a DNS name, before the interface is usable, you have to ensure that the DNS name can be resolved to an IP address. If name resolution relies on a DNS server external to the router, you need to be sure that router is reachable. That might be an acceptable assumption if you can reach the DNS server with a local broadcast, but it is a much more questionable assumption if routing needs to be operative to reach a nonlocal DNS server. Static name-to-address translation tables configured inside the router might be a viable alternative to using a DNS server.

- `interface` *interface-list* sets interface options on the specified interfaces. Options available on this statement are:

  `define` *address*: Defines the broadcast characteristics of an interface. If the interface is not specified as broadcast or point-to-point, it is assumed to be NBMA.

  `broadcast` *address*: Defines the interface as broadcast capable, which usually means a LAN physical interface—and specifies the broadcast address.

  `pointtopoint` *address*: Defines the interface as running a serial-oriented data link, such as SLIP or PPP. The first address specifies the local address for this interface.

  The address specified on the `pointtopoint` keyword defines the remote address that will complete a dialed session. There can be multiple `pointtoppoint` addresses, but each must be unique from the perspective of the local router. Think of this need for uniqueness as requiring a different phone number to dial for each remote destination.

- `netmask` *mask* is ignored on point-to-point interfaces, but is used to indicate the prefix length on broadcast and NBMA interfaces.

- `multicast` means the interface is multicast capable, in addition to broadcast capable.

Wellfleet/Bay

Bay began with a menu-oriented local interface to its routers and has evolved to include a style very different from Cisco's. SNMP and Management Information Base (MIB) concepts are deeply integrated into Bay's control mechanisms.

At a Site Manager workstation, the operator goes from menu to menu. Bay's notation for this is `higher-level-menu->lower-level-menu`. The Bay Command Console (BCC) provides a command-line alternative to Site Manager. BCC is comparable to Cisco's command lines.

Bay also supports the Technician Interface, an alternative to the menu system, which requires intimate knowledge of SNMP MIBs and the object-oriented methodology used to design MIBs. Individual commands under this structure look something like Cisco's but are more structured; yet simultaneously, they are less human friendly. They are excellent for writing scripts.

Basic Interface Configuration Functions

In general, any router interface has one or more IP addresses. Because IP is at a logical level, the underlying interfaces can either be physical or software defined. There also might be relationships where several physical interfaces can be treated as a group, or a single physical interface can have multiple logical addresses associated with it.

Configuration commands generally deal at the level of an interface, with subcommands that are specific to the real or virtual address type.

Real Physical Interfaces

Real interfaces represent real media. In IP and most architectures—the notable exceptions being VINES and DECnet—the address assigned to the interface reflects the prefix associated with the medium.

Although classless inter-domain routing (CIDR) is the standard of the Internet, many router configuration commands limit you to classful data entry—including preventing you from configuring the all ones and all zeroes subnets—until you enter an "I really mean this" command. (Examples of such enabling commands are under the specific implementations in this chapter.)

Tip

Although IP standards specify that the local broadcast address is all ones, written in dotted decimal as 255.255.255.255, some old, primarily UNIX, implementations might assume the broadcast address is 0.0.0.0. Most vendors allow you to configure an all-zeroes broadcast when needed for compatibility. Cisco does it on a box-wide basis, whereas other implementations allow the broadcast address value to be set on a per-interface basis.

Cisco

In a Cisco configuration, IP addresses and subnets are entered for specific router interfaces using the `ip address` subcommand of `interface`:

```
ip address 192.168.1.33 255.255.255.240
```

Two commands are needed for Cisco routers to accept full CIDR conventions:

```
ip classless
ip subnet-zero
```

Livingston

After the port is selected, enter the IP address with a

```
set <port-id> address <address>
```

The subnet mask is set with a separate command:

```
set <port-id> netmask <mask>
```

GateD

The equivalent GateD commands would be:

```
interfaces {
    interface e0
        ;
    define broadcast 192.168.1.33
        netmask 255.255.255.240
        ;
} ;
```

Wellfleet/Bay

Using Site Manager on a Wellfleet/Bay router, select the Protocols->Interfaces->IP Configuration menu and follow the appropriate prompts. To code an interface address with the BCC, type

```
ip address ip_address mask address_mask
```

To allow full CIDR address data entry, type the following with the BCC:

```
all-subnets-enabled
```

Or, set this on the Site Manager Edit IP Global Parameters menu.

Multiple Prefixes per Medium

When a router uses secondary addressing, it has one or more interfaces that have more than one IP address each. These IP addresses are in different prefixes. The idea of having complex mappings between logical and physical media has a variety of applications, and these mappings are especially powerful when used with VLANs, as shown in Figure 13.3.

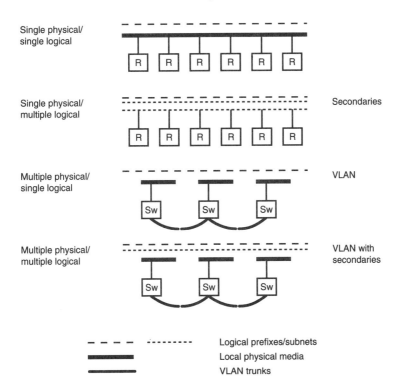

FIGURE 13.3. *Although the basic concept of IP maps a single logical prefix to a single physical medium, there are legitimate applications for many permutations of such mappings. Other mappings can include multiple logical to single physical, single logical across multiple physical—the basic VLAN case—and multiple logical across multiple physical.*

Secondary addressing is an interface-centric way of defining multiple prefixes on the same medium. A different method is to use subinterfaces, one virtual interface per medium prefix. The latter approach works best with OSPF and other dynamic routing, but the secondary address approach is more widely implemented.

Cisco and Wellfleet both support secondary addressing but GateD can only do so if the underlying UNIX implementation supports more than one IP address per interface.

Secondary addresses are most often needed when the addressing environment is classful, as workarounds to various limits of classful addressing introduced in Chapter 5, "Classical IP Addressing: An Evolution." Applications of secondary addresses include:

- Bridge to router transition

- Providing more host address space on a single medium or VLAN

- Healing discontiguous networks

Note

Routing protocols with a hello mechanism, such as OSPF and EIGRP, often only route between the primary, not secondary, interfaces on a common medium.

On a Cisco router, the basic configuration command involves placing the keyword `secondary` on an `ip address` statement. Bay routers call this function *multinet interfaces*. By whatever name, they are a way of associating multiple logical addresses with one or more transmission systems. The transmission system can be a physical medium or a VLAN.

Secondary Addresses in Bridge-Router Transition

Two media are now connected by a bridge. The media form a single broadcast domain, which maps to an IP subnet. The goal is to split the two media into two subnets by replacing bridge B1 with a router.

Before the bridge is replaced, the hosts on the segment now on the far side of B1 (with respect to R1) are being renumbered into `192.168.2.0/24`. After B1 is replaced with a router, there is no problem in having R1 reach `192.168.2.0`. Before the router is replaced but after the hosts are renumbered, how will R1 know about the second subnet being introduced into the bridged system? A secondary address on R1's Ethernet interface lets it reach both subnets (see Figure 13.4).

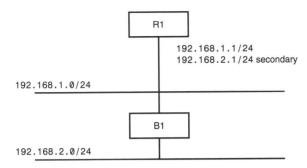

FIGURE 13.4. *Two physical media operate now as a single broadcast domain. The addressing plan shown here means that the bridge can be replaced with a router without renumbering.*

Secondary Addresses for Discontiguous Networks

One of the means to heal a discontiguous subnet is to place secondary addresses on the medium that break the contiguous relationship. This configuration problem is shown in Figure 13.5. When networks are discontiguous, two or more parts of a classful network are partitioned by parts of a different classful network number. Using secondary addresses makes the partitioned network number visible to the partitioning router.

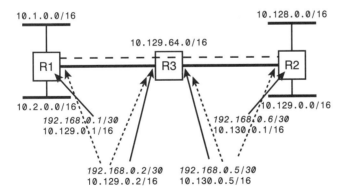

FIGURE 13.5. *Using secondary addresses to heal a discontiguous network: the dashed line shows the healed partition. Addresses in italic belong to the partitioning network.*

A Cisco configuration for healing this topology is:

```
! router 1
interface serial 0
ip address 192.168.0.5  255.255.255.252
ip address 172.16.1.1   255.255.255.0    secondary

! router 2
interface serial 0
ip address 192.168.0.5  255.255.255.252
ip address 172.16.1.2   255.255.255.0    secondary
interface serial 1
ip address 192.168.0.9  255.255.255.252
ip address 172.16.2.1   255.255.255.0    secondary


! router 3
interface serial 0
ip address 192.168.0.10 255.255.255.252
ip address 172.16.2.2   255.255.255.0    secondary
```

Secondary Addresses for Greater Host Space

Assume that a typical branch office LAN has up to 14 hosts, but the headquarters LAN has 200 hosts. For a Class C network number, you can define two subnets of 254 hosts each with the mask `255.255.254.0`. You can assign space for 510 hosts (including router interfaces) to the headquarters LANs by assigning a primary and two secondary subnets to the router.

If the hosts and the routers understand classless addressing, the secondary address commands are not needed. Simply configure the subnet masks in all devices as /23, or `255.255.254.0` in traditional dotted decimal. For the topology in Figure 13.6, the Cisco configuration for this would be:

```
interface ethernet 0
ip address 192.168.1.33 255.255.255.0
ip address 192.168.1.65 255.255.255.0 secondary
```

If multiple subnets are on a LAN, performance problems can arise between clients on one subnet and servers on another subnet. Even though both are on the same medium and should be able to communicate directly at the data link layer, their software might simply decide that traffic should go through the router, because by definition the router interconnects different subnets. Even though going through the router works, going through the router increases delay and overall router workload. Generally, the best way around the problem is to force end user hosts to ARP rather than rely on a default gateway. This is done with the proxy ARP mechanism, also called the *ARP hack*.

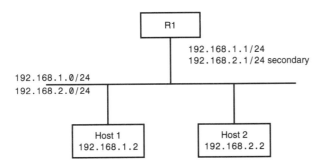

FIGURE 13.6. *Secondary addresses allow the LAN to be treated as a /23 subnet. Increasing subnet size in this manner is very common in LAN switch applications.*

If the client and server hosts simply will not ARP to one another, performance through a single Cisco router interface can be improved by a subcommand under that interface:

```
ip route-cache same-interface
```

Failing to set this option forces packets through the slowest path on the router—process switching.

```
ip unnumbered
```

Most router implementations have the capability to manage router-to-router connections over serial lines without assigning explicit IP addresses to the interface. The major reason to do this is to conserve address space, although it has a limited utility in avoiding discontiguous subnets.

There is no question that using such a technique makes network troubleshooting more difficult. Ping and traceroute need IP addresses as arguments. SNMP interface functions also need an IP address. The IP Route Recording option requires that the interface address be recorded, but what should be done if there is no address?

Routing tables can be confused when there is no address to put into the usual next hop entry.

Cisco uses an approach that creates a virtual router composed of two routers linked by a serial line, shown in Figure 13.7.

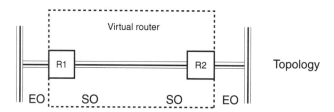

- R1 and R2 form a virtual router
- The serial has no IP address
  - All packets arriving at SO of either router immediately go to its EO
  - All packets generated at EO go onto serial link
- Conserves addresses but makes management harder

FIGURE 13.7. *The serial line is treated as an internal bus inside the virtual router.*

Using the `ip unnumbered` option, traffic on the serial interface is directed to a LAN interface that does have an IP address:

```
interface ethernet 0
ip address <address> <mask>
interface serial 0
ip unnumbered ethernet 0
```

RFC 1812 points out limitations of this method, such as the fact that it does not scale well to multilink topologies. Further, there is no standardization of the interaction between the two virtual half-routers, making it vendor dependent.

Software-Defined Interface Functions

Certain useful interface functions are not associated with any hardware:

- Circuitless/loopback

- Null

- Tunnel

Tunnel interfaces are discussed in Chapter 14, "Selective Forwarding Inside Routers." Different implementations define differently the function of loopback interfaces. Cisco defines them as separate interface types, whereas GateD groups the functions of both under its loopback interface type.

Loopback/Internal Functions

In the IP architecture, a router does not have an identity of its own, but exists as a collection of medium interface addresses. There are a substantial number of non-administrative reasons why a router might need a unique identifier (or identifiers) not associated with a specific medium interface, and most major implementations have a way of defining such identifiers.

Typical functions for which a box-level interface are used include:

- OSPF router identifier

- Tunnel endpoint for TCP, used with BGP, remote source route bridging, and so on

- A general place to `ping` to test connectivity

Wellfleet/Bay probably has the clearest term for this: a *circuitless interface*. Cisco calls it, for historical reasons, a *loopback interface*. Cisco has at least three distinct usages of the word *loopback*, which are completely unrelated. On Cisco platforms, the *loopback interface* is a software-only interface. The *loopback subcommand* is available on certain physical interfaces that support a hardware loopback mode, where transmit signals are connected directly to receive lines. Finally, the *loopback address* is the special one associated with the null address function. RFC 1812 defines the loopback address as `127.0.0.1`.

Some Addresses Are More Interesting Than Others

A ritual recurs every August at many colleges, as the freshmen arrive and begin to enjoy uncensored Internet access. Somewhere, a rumor begins that, shall we say, there is a server with very interesting visual content at IP address `127.0.0.1`?

After a few days of not being able to reach it, a certain number of freshmen seek assistance from the academic help desk. The help desk people, of course, are quite familiar with the problem. "Oh," says the help desk consultant, "you can't get to `127.0.0.1`? Mmmm...Joe is our specialist in that, and he's at lunch."

The student waits for Joe, who asks, "Oh, what are you trying to do with `127.0.0.1`?"

"Ummmm...research. Yeah, that's right. Research."

Joe, with a straight face, says, "Well, I used to be the specialist in that. But I'm not up to date. You'll have to see Sally, but she's off today."

A really good help desk can keep the student wandering for several days. Eventually, many of the beginners learn enough about the Internet to know they have been hoaxed.

Cisco allows the creation of multiple loopback interfaces. When this is done, the OSPF/BGP router ID is taken from the numerically highest IP address on any loopback interface, when loopback interfaces are defined. If there are no loopback interfaces, the router ID is the highest active IP address on an active interface when the OSPF or BGP process initializes.

Having different loopback interfaces allows using different addresses for different functions. For example, one loopback interface might be used to set an OSPF router ID, another to serve as an endpoint of a tunnel in IBM networking, and yet another as a source of Novell/IPX statically defined Service Advertisement Protocol advertisements.

GateD has a very contrasting approach, with a loopback interface definition that includes the function of the Cisco null interface; there is no explicit null interface in GateD. The primary address on this interface *must* be 127.0.0.1, although secondary addresses can be assigned.

Following the definition of the loopback address, the loopback interface is first intended to behave as a blackhole. A secondary purpose allows the OSPF and/or BGP router IDs to be set by setting an additional IP address on the loopback address; this secondary address is used as the router ID.

On 3Com routers, there appears to be less of a tendency to assign a general internal interface, but rather to create specific box-level identifiers for specific functions.

Null/Blackhole Functions

With Cisco, there is an explicit software-defined null interface. GateD uses the loopback interface for blackholing. An additional address can be assigned to the GateD loopback interface to set the OSPF or BGP router IDs.

Applications for null interfaces vary considerably. The most common application is probably using the null interface as an "anchor" for a summary route, as shown in Figure 13.8. A router using this technique advertises that it can reach the summary, but has more specific, more preferred internal routes that are used for actual forwarding of packets that arrive at the router.

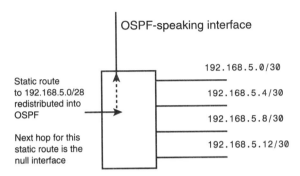

OSPF-speaking interface

192.168.5.0/30

Static route
to 192.168.5.0/28
redistributed into
OSPF

192.168.5.4/30

192.168.5.8/30

Next hop for this
static route is the
null interface

192.168.5.12/30

FIGURE 13.8. *The less-specific summary route is advertised into the routing system, but the more-specific static routes over dial interfaces are visible only inside the router.*

Another technique is an alternative for the specific packet filtering requirement of discarding certain packets based solely on their destination address. The subtle rationale for this technique is that routers are optimized to forward traffic rather than to filter it. Routers might have caches or other hardware assistance for forwarding, but might need to do filtering in a slower general-purpose CPU.

To illustrate this principle, the following Cisco static route commands are the fastest way to discard packets destined to private address space. (See Chapter 14 for the specific format of Cisco static route and access list commands.) Setting up routes that discard traffic destined to the private address space would be a very reasonable thing to do on a router acting as the default gateway to the Internet:

```
ip route   10.0.0.0     0.255.255.255   null0
ip route  172.16.0.0    0.15.255.255    null0
ip route  192.168.0.0   0.0.255.255     null0
```

Group Interfaces

Increasingly, there has been a trend to have software-defined interfaces that either describe address spaces associated with a physical interface as distinct software-defined interfaces or that group together multiple real interfaces in some meaningful aggregate.

Use of such software-defined interfaces usually involves some inheritance of properties. Figure 13.9 shows how a set of IP-address-to-dialed-number mappings can be defined on a superinterface, and have this table inherited by the various physical lines in a pool of dial-out interfaces.

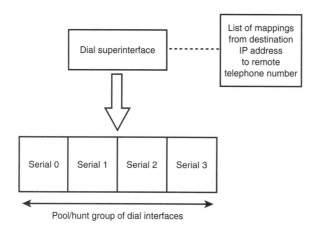

FIGURE 13.9. *Configuration commands can be much less verbose if you can put certain commands on a superinterface and let subordinate interfaces inherit their properties.*

Subinterfaces of Real Interfaces

One of the first examples of group interfaces was a solution to various problems associated with NBMA Frame Relay for OSPF networks, described in RFC 1586 and adopted in the OSPF standard. The suggestion was that routing worked better if OSPF saw individual PVCs as interfaces.

NBMA Media

Cisco supports subinterfaces for all types of NBMA media, such as Frame Relay, X.25, and ATM. The convention for configuring them is to define physical and minimal data link attributes on the real interface and then define a subinterface for the virtual circuits:

```
interface serial 0
encapsulation frame-relay ietf
interface serial 0.40 point-to-point
frame-relay interface-dlci 40
ip address 192.168.1.1 255.255.255.252
    ! assign logical address
interface serial 0.41 point-to-point
    ! provide transmission system address
frame-relay interface-dlci 41
ip address 192.168.1.5 255.255.255.252
ip address 192.168.1.1 255.255.255.252
interface serial 0.42 point-to-point
frame-relay interface-dlci 42
ip address 192.168.1.9 255.255.255.252
```

Defining a single subinterface for each point-to-point virtual circuit certainly is the most clear. An increasingly common documentation is to make the fractional part of the subinterface number—the .42 in 0.42—the same as the local data-link connection identifier (DLCI) assigned by the Frame Relay service provider.

In the Cisco IOS, each interface that you define takes up system resources, such as an interface descriptor block (IDB) data structure and interface buffers. There has long been a limit of 256 real and virtual interfaces that can be configured on a Cisco router, a limit that has been raised slightly in recent releases in the 11.x family.

Large numbers of subinterfaces can exhaust these resources, so using point-to-multipoint subinterfaces can reduce the total number of interfaces. Using point-to-multipoint subinterfaces is usually not an operational restriction when large numbers of PVCs are used. Most of the restrictions on NBMA topology, such as the local versus remote assumption discussed in Chapter 4, "Transmission System Identifiers and Logical Address Mapping: A View from the Bottom," the split horizon rule, and the need for pseudobroadcasting in a partially meshed subnet, are concerns with dynamic routing.

Note

Split horizon is a rule of routing architecture requiring a router to remember the interface (or subinterface) on which it first learned about a destination. Under split horizon, when the router generates routing updates, it must never announce that it can reach a given destination over the interface in which it first learned about the destination.

For further details, see Enterprise Routing and Switching *from Macmillan Technical Publishing or RFC 1058.*

Large numbers of PVCs, however, are most commonly associated with static routing in a hub-and-spoke topology. You might, for example, have many PVCs if you were replacing a multidrop analog IBM network with Frame Relay. In such networks, the communication is strictly to the central point, without alternate paths that need dynamic routing.

InterVLAN Routing

Vendors including Bay and Cisco use a subinterface mechanism to identify VLANs present on a LAN trunk interface. After the VLANs are identified, routing among them can be defined.

Using Bay's Accelar management tool, you select a physical port select VLAN->VLAN from the device management menu bar, and click on routing. Then type in the appropriate IP address and mask.

With Cisco, VLANs with identifiers 100 and 101 appear as subinterfaces of real router interfaces:

```
interface fastethernet 0.100
encapsulation isl 100
interface fastethernet 0.101
encapsulation isl 101
```

Physically Multiplexed Interfaces

Fractional T1 and T3 services enter the router with a single physical interface, through which come one or more multiplexed data streams. Each data stream is treated as a separate interface. Cisco uses a different convention to represent physical layer multiplexing than it does to identify Layer 2 multiplexing such as VLANs or Frame Relay.

Regardless of the router type, if the interface type supports multiplexing, the multiplexed channels are indicated with a colon following the interface number. On a 7xxx series, ports on the primary rate ISDN/channelized T1 MIP card are denoted like this:

```
interface pri {slot} {/port} {:channel}
```

On a 4xxx series, the equivalent would be

```
interface pri {port} {:channel}.
```

Primary/Secondary Pairs

An assortment of fault tolerance and bandwidth-on-demand techniques establishes a relationship between pairs of interfaces. This is a primitive form of addressing.

A more complex relationship can exist in router fault tolerance mechanisms. In its simplest form, Router 1 might become the primary router for some address Group A, and Router 2 remains the backup router. More complex mutual backup schemes exist where the address group is partitioned into Groups A and B; Router 1 becomes the primary for Group A and the secondary for Group B, whereas Router 2 is the secondary for Group A and the primary for Group B. Details of these schemes are discussed in the section "Fault Tolerance and Addressing."

Superinterfaces

One common application for superinterfaces is familiar from telephony: the use of rotaries or hunt groups, where a single telephone number maps to a set of physical lines. Incoming calls are directed by the telephone switching to the first line not in use.

There can be an assortment of reasons for using superinterfaces. Both incoming and outgoing hunting on ISDN or POTS are common. Superinterfaces also can reduce the configuration size by serving as macros.

Both Cisco and Bay use superinterfaces in configuring dial services. Bay calls them *line pools*, and Cisco calls them *dialer groups*. Both aggregate multiple real interfaces into one logical pool. This pool is the router's way of identifying the telephony concepts of hunt groups or rotaries.

Although GateD, Cisco, and Bay use different methods to establish the list of address prefixes to be advertised by a router's dynamic routing processes, there is again a concept of creating an instance of a superior class, the routing process, which has subordinate prefix elements.

Dial Interface Aggregation

With Cisco, a superinterface such as a dialer is an object. The subordinate objects are included in the superior object with xxx-group commands, where xxx is an identifier of the superior object. Note that the xxx can have its own suffix that identifies the configuration statement as a superior object. The following is an example of creating a dialer superinterface:

```
interface dialer 0
[dialer-level statements]

interface serial 0
dialer-group 0
[serial interface statements]

interface serial 1
dialer-group 0
[serial interface statements]

interface serial 2
dialer-group 0
[serial interface statements]
```

Bay calls its superinterfaces *demand pools*. Each pool has a demand pool ID, to which lines can be assigned. Asynchronous, ISDN, and synchronous interfaces can mix in a single demand group.

Lines in the group do not have a permanently assigned address; the address is established on circuit establishment.

Defining Media for Which Prefixes Are to Be Advertised

Cisco routing processes are specified with box-level router commands; the addresses specified to them are with network statements:

```
router rip
network 192.168.1.0
network 192.168.2.0
```

In this example, the Cisco software tests the address of each interface to see if it falls into one of the address ranges defined by an address subcommand of the router rip statement.

In GateD, interface lists can serve a similar purpose. The following example illustrates how the Routing Information Protocol (RIP) is advertised or accepted on certain interface groups:

```
rip yes {
        interface all noripin noripout ;
        interface le ripin ;
        interface le1 ripout ;
} ;
```

Each group of interfaces (for example, le0 and le1) is associated with specific addresses. RIP packets would only be accepted from interfaces le0 and le1, but not from du0. RIP packets would be advertised on interface le1 only. These constructs use the GateD interface list, which is a recursive list of references to interfaces or interface groups.

Physical Layer Interface Issues

Relatively little physical layer information enters the router configuration and even less tends to affect addressing. There are a few issues on LANs, such as Token Ring speeds and Ethernet connection type. If the router emulates a WAN DCE, clocking must be set.

Because GateD runs on multiple platforms, with different variants of the UNIX operating system, physical layer specifications vary with the platform. This section concentrates on Bay and Cisco platforms, each with a standard operating system.

Simplex Interfaces

When dealing with half-duplex transmission systems such as Ethernet or FDDI, it might be a practical way of increasing bandwidth to establish pairs of interfaces that effectively are full-duplex.

This technique shares a single IP address across both interfaces.

There are several applications for simplex interfaces. Figure 13.10 allows you to have a theoretical 20 MBps of throughput between a router that only supports standard half-duplex Ethernet and a switch that does support full-duplex Ethernet.

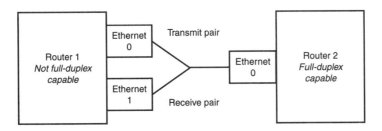

FIGURE 13.10. *An adapter cable makes two half-duplex interfaces on the router appear as one interface to the switch.*

Another application, commonly seen in transoceanic applications, involves a one-way satellite path for bulk transfers, coupled with a slower, one-way terrestrial path for requests and acknowledgments.

Demand Interfaces

In the next section, we will speak of several ways in which dialing can be initiated on circuit-switched interfaces. Both Bay and Cisco's simplest method for doing this is to raise the Data Terminal Ready signal on a DTE (Data Terminal Equipment) interface, which is connected to a DCE (as Data Circuit Terminating Equipment) device that responds with some circuit-switched action. This action is typically initiating a telephone call on a modem or ISDN TA, but it can be any action that can be triggered by a voltage change on an interface. It has been used, for example, to cause a RS-232 two-way switch to change to an alternate position.

Other actions that can be taken are physical layer from the perspective of higher-layer communications, but can involve higher-level C-plane protocols. These include sending character strings on synchronous or asynchronous interfaces or sending Q.931 commands over an ISDN D channel.

The term *demand interface* has come into use to describe interfaces that connect to media that require a circuit setup process to be usable.

Transmission System Interface Commands

Most configuration complexity is associated with WAN interfaces, due to the need for cooperation between the user equipment and the carrier's end switch. There can be a long and painful process of assuring that all the configuration options match between end equipment and switch.

Less frequently, there can be LAN-specific configuration. This is often related to the coexistence of IP and non-IP protocols on the same router, because XNS, Novell IPX, DECnet, and Banyan VINES all can manipulate MAC addresses.

Dedicated Services

In Layer 2–oriented services, there is a need to insert a data link level address. This can be simple and automatic, as with PPP and HDLC, or can reflect multiplexing as with Frame Relay.

For routing to work, there is often a need to configure pseudobroadcasting on virtual circuit, NBMA media.

Multiple protocols can run over the same virtual circuit. Adding protocol families, however, can increase overhead because queues are needed for each family.

Frame Relay

The most basic question in configuring an interface for Frame Relay or other NBMA protocols is whether routing will see the single physical interface for the access interface or each virtual circuit as a separate virtual interface. The latter is preferable in almost every case.

A major configuration option is selecting the appropriate Local Management Interface from the three choices of Annex D, Annex A, or Gang of 4. Cisco can autodetect this in releases beginning with IOS 11.2.

When configuring virtual interfaces, they are either point-to-point or point-to-multipoint. It is necessary to associate local DLCIs with these interfaces.

If Inverse ARP is used, it either must be explicitly configured or be the default. Otherwise, explicit statements are necessary to map logical addresses to remote DLCIs. If the router is to broadcast over DLCIs, that also must be specified.

SMDS

In setting up Switched Multimegabit Data Service (SMDS), you need, at a minimum, to set the local transmission system address, which is an E.164 value. You then need either to define an ARP mechanism or statically map remote logical addresses to remote SMDS addresses.

Configuration becomes somewhat more complex if you have multiple Logical Independent Subnets (LISs) mapped onto the SMDS transmission system. Each of these conceptually is a broadcast domain, so, if you use ARP, you need to set different multicast addresses for each LIS.

If you will use multicast addresses, these need to be configured. SMDS can support closed user groups, but these usually need to be set up through administrative requests to the service provider.

ATM PVCs

When you set up ATM PVCs from end to end, you need to set up mapping tables in each switch along the path. Supplementary things that might need to be set are traffic shaping rules, which go back to the aggregate flows you expect to traverse the interface, and traverse downstream paths.

Locally Administered MAC Addresses

Most modern routers allow at least one MAC address to be configured manually on real interfaces. More commonly, the MAC address can be changed automatically by non-IP protocols coexisting on the same router, as discussed in Chapter 8, "The Existing IP and Non-IP Address Structure: Preparing for Remodeling."

Several vendor-dependent fault tolerance schemes manipulate MAC addresses. Typically, a MAC address is assigned to a group of interfaces, but is active in only one place at a time. This is seen both on routers and on fault-tolerant hosts such as redundant IBM front-end processors.

Dial/Demand Services

In all types of demand service, you have to specify the local transmission system persistent address (that is, the endpoint address associated with your interface). In all types of demand service except ATM, you have to map a called address, the endpoint address of the remote interface, to the logical address you want to reach.

POTS

POTS dialups vary with the type of dialing to be done. Three forms are common at the calling end:

- V.25, usually on synchronous interfaces, with the called number stored in the router.

- Hayes command set, usually on asynchronous interfaces, with the called number stored in the router. In this type of dialing, you can define interactive *chat scripts* to interact with the modem and *system scripts* to log you in to the computer.

- Data Terminal Ready control, either on synchronous or asynchronous interfaces, with the number to be dialed stored in an external device.

There might be additional parameters to be set, especially for security. You have a choice of using caller ID, callbacks, or PPP with CHAP (preferred) or PAP authentication. PPP/CHAP is usually the most flexible.

X.25 SVCs

When setting up IP over X.25, you need to set:

- X.121 address

- Mapping between X.121 and IP addresses

Depending on the implementation, the mapping statement might automatically set the Call User Data (CUD) field, or you might have to configure CUD. CUD is not necessary on PVCs. You might also need to define parameters including:

- Maximum number of logical channels permitted on the LAP-B access link.

- X.25 facility parameters (for example, reverse charging).

- Pseudobroadcasting.

- Passenger protocol identifier. RFC 1356 defines a standard for identifying protocols in X.25 packets, but Cisco also has a proprietary method. The identifying codes differ between the IETF and Cisco methods. Datagrams can be identified with a 1-byte identification (0xCC) or a 6-byte identification (0x80 followed by the 5-byte SNAP encoding).

ISDN

As with Frame Relay, the most important part of configuration is matching the provider's switch options. This usually begins by defining the switch itself.

There is a series of switch-dependent questions, the most important of which tend to be if the switch needs a Service Profile ID (SPID) and, if so, the format of the SPID. Switch types that tend to require this include the Nortel DMS-100, the National ISDN-1 profile, and some AT&T ESS#5 switches.

Calling parameters need to be set, or if the service is B-nailed or a semi-permanent virtual circuit, that must be configured. The specifics required for your specific implementation vary greatly depending on your ISDN provider's implementation. Nevertheless, there are some general guidelines. If you are configuring a Basic Rate Interface (BRI), request that both lines be called by one number. If a router is the only device to be connected to the BRI, request data-only service configured as point-to-point. If you are sharing the BRI with nondata devices, such as ISDN telephones or facsimile machines, request voice-and-date configured as point-to-multipoint. Point-to-multipoint ISDN addresses require subaddresses on the basic telephone number.

When trying to turn up an initial ISDN service with a carrier, it is often necessary to respond to carrier ordering and installation personnel with a pleasant, but firm and repetitive, incantation of "That's nice. I know you don't know. Please refer me to a technical support person who can give me the Cisco/Motorola/Ascend/etc. configuration options to work with your switch." Keep repeating this. All too often, the telephone company's response is, "What kind of computer do you have? You should call your ISP." This is not terribly useful when you *are* the ISP. Regardless of what the telephone company people might say, there is certain information, such as the switch type, that they know and need to convey to the person doing configuration.

Fault Tolerance and Addressing

Various vendor-specific mechanisms protect against failures of interfaces, media, and routers. Addressing becomes involved here in several ways. In general, you want the addressing in the fault tolerance mechanisms to be as transparent as possible to end hosts. Complexity should be kept in the router.

A general Virtual Router Redundancy Protocol (VRRP) is being defined by the IETF, with participation from Ascend, Digital, IBM, Ipsilon, and Microsoft [RFC 2338]. Bay and Cisco have mechanisms, generally proprietary, to detect connectivity failures. VRRP is described as quite similar to *Hot Standby Router Protocol* (HSRP), but is not Cisco proprietary. Cisco does offer licenses for HSRP.

Interface Redundancy

Both Bay and Cisco have features to protect routing against the failure of specific interfaces and specific routers. The idea is to have a primary interface backed up by a secondary interface. The secondary interface is inactive unless some failure or load condition occurs on the primary.

Each interface has its own address, but the address on the secondary interface becomes active only if triggered by the designated condition on the primary.

Although Bay and Cisco both have a concept of a primary and one or more backup interfaces, the two vendors tend to use the concept in quite different ways when speaking of interface redundancy. Bay's method emphasizes loss of connectivity on LAN interfaces. You define a group of interfaces that share a common virtual MAC address—that is, only active on one router interface at a time. This MAC address is:

2y-yy-A2-xx-xx-xx

where 2 indicates that this is a locally administered address. y-yy indicates the circuit number, which maps to a VLAN identifier. A2 is the organizationally unique identifier (OUI) assigned to Bay. xx-xx-xx is the unique router identification number.

Cisco's *dial backup* features emphasize backing up serial interfaces after detecting a physical layer failure, a data link failure, or a data link load level on the primary. Cisco does have a method that provides a dynamic MAC address that moves among router interfaces connected to a common LAN, but this is called the *Hot Standby Router Protocol* (HSRP) rather than being referred to in an interface-oriented way.

Router Redundancy

HSRP operates both at Layer 2 and Layer 3 [RFC 2281]. It is a reliability feature quite effective in dealing with the specific cases it was designed for, but often is assumed to do things it was not intended to. Fully fault tolerant applications need to use HSRP for protecting against certain routing failures and quasi-static or dynamic routing to deal with remote router failures.

As in Bay's interface redundancy, a MAC address moves from router to router in the event of failure. In addition, an IP address moves from active interface to active interface. In contrast to Bay, the backup interface can operate when not acting as the primary for a group. The main restriction is that more than one interface cannot have the group IP address active at any one time.

Cisco's HSRP MAC addresses are:

00-00-0C-07-AC-xx

where

00-00-0C is Cisco's IEEE-assigned vendor code, 07-AC is a Cisco prefix for HSRP, and xx is the HSRP group number.

In basic HSRP, shown in Figure 13.11, a primary router sends HSRP keepalives to a backup router in the same group. If the backup router does not hear the keepalives within a specified period, it activates the virtual MAC address and IP address.

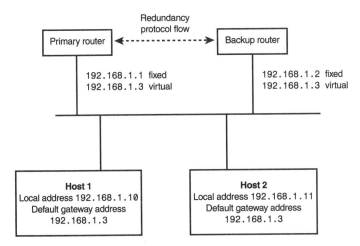

FIGURE 13.11.   *A basic router redundancy topology has a single group of routers or interfaces that participate in the redundancy mechanism.*

Some very real hardware-dependent features govern implementation of HSRP on different platforms. HSRP can load share among several routers by defining overlapping HSRP groups, as shown in Figure 13.12.

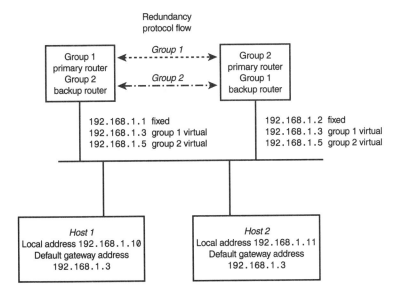

FIGURE 13.12.   *This configuration has overlapping redundancy groups, with one router the primary for each group. Hosts are split into two sets, one of which has the virtual address of the first redundancy group as the default gateway address, and the other set has the second group virtual address as its default gateway address.*

Routers that participate in overlapping HSRP must have the capability to store several MAC addresses in each interface:

- The interface-specific MAC address

- The virtual MAC address for the first group

- The virtual MAC address for the second and additional groups

Not all Cisco Ethernet interface chips can hold more than one address. The chips that can handle multiple addresses are on high-end routers such as the 7200 and 7500 series.

Bay's router redundancy mechanism defines groups of routers, all of which start in a secondary state. They bid for primary status, and one router wins.

When a router is in a secondary status, it can carry traffic for other than the primary group. If that router takes on primary status, however, it only handles primary group traffic. For this reason, Bay recommends that secondary routers be dedicated to backup and not be used when the primary is active.

Server References in Routers

Retrieving configurations from configuration servers is only one of the many client/server relationships of a modern router. Routers can be clients for any of a number of network management functions. To reduce traffic, they can act as full-capability, cacheing, or hard-coded servers. They can also act as proxies for real servers, passing host requests transparently.

In general, configuration is most flexible when servers are referred to by name rather than address, letting DNS resolve the name based on the addressing in place at the time of the request. Maximizing the use of names simplifies renumbering of routers just as it simplifies renumbering of hosts. DNS name server references are a significant exception to referring to servers by name.

Router as Client

Routers need to know the actual addresses of DNS name servers. There might be special cases where the name server can be found by UDP broadcasts of DNS requests, but this is significantly inefficient for general use.

In general, the IP addresses of one or more name servers needs to be hard-coded in the configuration.

In a Cisco configuration, up to six name server addresses can be specified in the `ip name-server` command. These are addresses that the router uses as the destination of DNS queries that it generates.

After the router can reach a DNS server, it can resolve the names of other servers such as Network Time Protocol (NTP), Simple Network Management Protocol (SNMP), logging services (`syslog`), and so on. Although you can hard-code the IP addresses of non-DNS servers, that is generally not a good idea because those addresses might change if you renumber.

Tip

To be renumbering-friendly and minimize the effort you need to go through when you renumber, absolutely minimize the number of hard-coded server addresses in your router configurations. In general, you only need the hard-coded addresses of DNS servers.

Because DNS servers are so important in resolving other addresses, be sure to have redundant DNS servers defined.

Router as Server

Routers, and remote access servers acting as routers, can provide various network management server functions. Because purpose-built routers rarely include mass storage, server functions on the router have to be services that can keep the relevant tables in RAM. For services that need significant databases, the router is likely to act as a proxy, passing requests to a dedicated server.

One common function where the router acts as a server is to do dynamic address assignment for dialup users. To do this, the router acts as a server for the IP Control Protocol (IPCP) function of the Point-to-Point Protocol (PPP). In typical configurations, the router has a pool of addresses that are assigned to dialup connections for the duration of a dialup session.

This might be a single pool for all dial-in capable addresses on the router, or there might be a fixed address assignment for each interface. Regardless of the method of assignment, the router still fulfills the expectations of IPCP in acting as a server.

Router as Proxy

Routers often act as proxies that pass requests seen on their direct interfaces to the real server that fulfills the request. Proxy services are especially common when the request is sent to the local broadcast address, 255.255.255.255. The proxy is needed because local broadcasts do not propagate beyond the local interface, yet clients might not know the specific server address and have to broadcast their request.

In most routed protocols, there is a stringent rule that local broadcasts do not propagate beyond a local interface. If this were allowed, all the broadcast-limiting value of routers would be lost, and you would essentially have a bridged environment. Broadcasting often limits the scalability of bridged networks. There are several ways to deal with broadcasts.

BOOTP/DHCP Relay Agent Operation

BOOTP specifically defined a *relay agent* mode for forwarding [RFC 1542]. BOOTP requests to a server not reachable by local broadcasts. This relay agent capability has been preserved in DHCP and is illustrated in Figure 13.13.

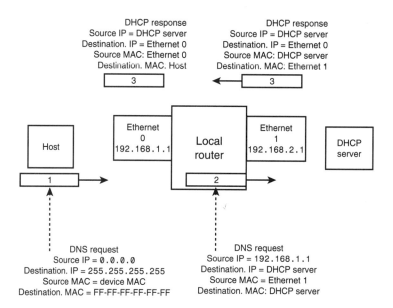

FIGURE 13.13. *DHCP relay agents need to change both source and destination addresses.*

BOOTP and DHCP broadcast handling is especially complex. In dealing with most local broadcasts, such as DNS or TFTP requests, the need is to translate the destination address from 255.255.255.255 to a specific address. In BOOTP/DHCP relaying, there is an additional request to return a response to a host that does not yet have an IP address. The source IP address in a BOOTP/DHCP request is not yet meaningful.

When a router interface receives a DHCP request that has the source address set to 0.0.0.0, it replaces the zero value with its own address and forwards the request to a defined DHCP server. Having the router interface address in the request allows the receiving DHCP server to reverse the send and receive fields and return the response packet to the router interface that forwarded it.

After the DHCP response has arrived at the relay agent interface, the DHCP agent code can examine the internals of the DHCP packet and find the MAC address of the client that originated the request. That MAC address can be used as a new destination address to return the response to the originating host.

Broadcast Address Translation

When the source address is defined, local broadcast translation becomes much easier. Only the destination address needs to be translated to a routable unicast or directed broadcast address. Directed broadcasts have all ones in the host field, but only generate a broadcast on their destination subnet, not everywhere in the network (see Figure 13.14). This sort of translation is common for DNS or TFTP requests.

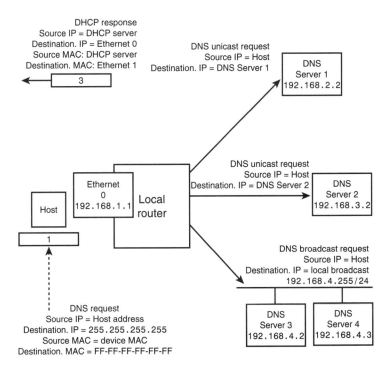

FIGURE 13.14. *Cisco's IP helper mechanism lets local broadcasts be translated to one or more unicasts and/or one or more directed broadcasts.*

One packet is generated for each `ip helper` statement in the command sequence:

```
interface e0
ip helper 192.168.2.2
ip helper 192.168.3.2
ip helper 192.168.4.255
```

Warning

Turn off directed broadcasts on subnets where they are not specifically needed, and do not accept direct-ed broadcasts that have a source address that is not inside your network. These measures help protect against a malicious hacking attack called smurfing, *in which the attacker repeatedly pings the directed broadcast addresses of multiple subnets and creates a broadcast storm.*

Proxy ARP

Another case in which the router acts as a server is *proxy ARP*. When proxy ARP is enabled on a router interface, the router responds to ARP requests for a specific device, as long as the router has a route to the prefix of the destination in the active routing table of the router.

On a Cisco router, the interface subcommand `ip proxy-arp` needs to be entered. On a Bay router, use the `proxy` option of the `IP interface` menu.

Proxy ARP does have potential problems. A router responds to a proxy ARP whenever the prefix to which the host address belongs is in the routing table. The router, however, might not know if the real prefix is reachable due to aggregation. As a consequence, traffic might be sent to a blackhole.

Looking Ahead

This chapter shows you the basic address configuration practices for routers. Such practices assume that a packet entering the router will leave the router on another interface, following first-in-first-out (FIFO) rules.

Chapter 14 examines the addressing implications of changing this assumption. Some alternative assumptions include filtering out some outgoing packets, changing the output policy to non-FIFO, or tunneling one packet inside another before forwarding it.

Selective Forwarding Inside Routers

Life being all inclusion and confusion, and art being all discrimination and selection.

—Henry James

We don't see the end of the tunnel, but I must say I don't think it is darker than it was a year ago, and in some ways lighter.

—John F. Kennedy

It is quality rather than quantity that matters.

—Seneca

Selective forwarding is at least a two-step process. First, traffic has to be recognized as belonging, or not belonging, to a category of interest. When recognized, the traffic optionally can be modified. Finally, it is permitted to flow into an interface or internal process or it is discarded.

Figure 14.1 shows basic placement of selective forwarding mechanisms in a router. Selective forwarding mechanisms are called *inbound* when they apply to packets immediately after being received on a router interface. The mechanisms are called *outbound* when the filtering is applied after the packets have been through the output forwarding code—the routing table—and are moving to one or more output interfaces.

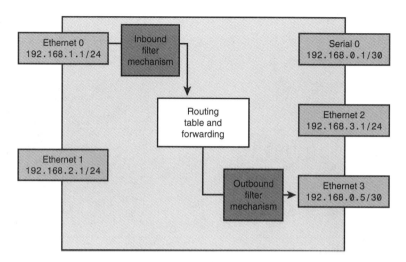

FIGURE 14.1.   *In this basic routing flow from a single input interface to a single outbound interface, inbound filtering precedes the forwarding decision, whereas outbound filtering follows the forwarding decision.*

Filtering is not restricted to basic routing, from inbound interface to outbound interface. As shown in Figure 14.2, it can apply to network infrastructure such as dynamic routing protocols.

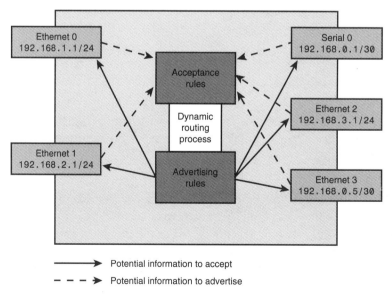

FIGURE 14.2.   *Filtering can govern the flow of route acceptance and route advertising.*

Whatever function selective forwarding carries out, it consists of two basic parts: pattern matching to recognize the traffic to which selective flow rules are to be applied and actions to take after a particular pattern is recognized. The most common actions are to pass it on (accept it) or discard it (deny it). Other actions include triggering actions, such as creating a dialup connection or altering fields in the packet.

Pattern Matching for Traffic Recognition

There are two basic ways to recognize traffic: Its destination address can be matched against a route in the routing table, or arbitrary fields of a packet can be matched against some type of pattern recognition rule.

Bay calls pattern recognition rules *templates*. Cisco is less consistent, but most commonly calls them *access lists*.

Real-World Experience with Terminology

When I started working with Cisco routers, I found it confusing that the term *access list* referred both to individual pattern recognition rules and to sets of rules. I needed to recognize that the singular and plural were the same here.

To remember this, it helps me to think of an old Hollywood story of the making of the movie *Rikki-Tikki-Tavi*, starring a heroic mongoose. The producer began to write a letter to the exotic animal supplier: "Dear sir: please send me a mongoose."

The producer stopped and reflected that making movies was expensive. He had understudies for the human actors…but what if the mongoose got sick? Or, even worse, escaped, given the speed and agility of the creature?

He restarted the letter: "Dear sir: please send me two mongeese." Again he stopped. Mongeese? That didn't sound right. Again he restarted: "Dear sir: please send me two mongooses." Still, there was something wrong with that.

He brightened, and his pen moved swiftly: "Dear sir. Please send me a mongoose. While you are at it, send me another."

And so it is with Cisco. With any vendor, you create rules for recognizing traffic and specify actions to take when a particular address pattern is recognized.

With Cisco, the specification of recognition involves writing individual `access list` rules. While you are at it, you create rule sets, all with the same access list number.

Several commands activate the application of access lists on a specific interface or process. The most common is `access group`.

The principle of recognizing traffic of interest is common among vendors, but the syntax of the recognition rules varies widely. There is no one best way to write rules, and you will, in all probability, prefer the style you use most often.

Whatever style your router uses, there are several common elements. Generally, there are one or more recognition rules. These rules are evaluated in some sequence, either top-to-bottom order or a rule number.

Individual rules match on one or more fields of packets. Fields are tested against a single value or a range of values. Some action is defined if the pattern is matched. After a pattern is matched, no more rules are applied.

Actions normally include a decision whether to forward the packet through the filtering point or to discard it. An action might be to log the decision. Other actions can involve changing fields of the packet.

Bay

Inbound filters are protocol specific; the particular protocol family is indicated by the menu path you take to reach the filter definition screen. Bit patterns are specified relative to reference points in the header:

- HEADER_START—The first byte of the IP header.

- HEADER_END—The first byte after the IP header. This is the first byte of the higher-level protocol, such as TCP, UDP, ICMP, OSPF, and so on.

- IP_WAN_HEADER_START—The first byte of a PPP or Frame Relay header. This is the data link header.

- IP_WAN_HEADER_END—The first byte after DLCI in Frame Relay, or after protocol identifier in PPP.

Unlike Cisco practice, with Bay you can filter on both the data link and network layer headers of the same packet. Some fields can reflect the position of a field while a packet or frame is being tunneled:

- IP_SR_START—The beginning of the source routing packet, or the high-order byte of the destination MAC address.

- IP_SR_DATA_LINK—The first byte after the RIF field. This is the first byte of the LLC header when that header is present.

Bay provides a wide range of mnemonics for common field values, and it allows you to set match values in hexadecimal.

The following is the general process of creating a Bay template:

1. Go to the Filters window for the selected circuit and click on Template; then click on Create.

2. Name the template and type the name into the Filter Name block.

3. Go to `criteria->add` and select the criterion this template will use. There can be only one criterion per template; create additional templates if you need more criteria.

4. The exact criteria and ranges specified are protocol specific. In general, you select a field from the `criteria` menu, which brings up a protocol-specific add range screen. If you are checking against a single value, put that value into the minimum and maximum fields. Values are interpreted as decimal unless preceded with `0x`.

5. Click on OK.

6. Add additional ranges if desired. This does not violate step 3. You can have only one criterion per template, but that template can have up to 100 ranges.

7. Select `action->add` and then specify the actions to be taken when the template is matched. Click OK to finish.

Criteria and filters can be edited with appropriate menus once created.

Deferring for the moment to the techniques of applying the filters, consider how the patterns to be matched are specified. To specify filtering out the private address space, you create three Bay template rules that specify complete ranges:

- `10.0.0.0` to `10.255.255.255`

- `172.16.0.0` to `172.31.255.255`

- `192.168.0.0` to `192.168.255.255`

In the next section, you will see the Cisco method for describing the same prefixes.

Cisco

Cisco router recognition rules are written in the textual Cisco configuration language, a more compact but probably more complex notation than Bay's. You need to be familiar with binary arithmetic to write the rules.

Rules are generally specified in `access-list` statements. Access lists have the general format:

```
access-list <number> permit|deny {match-condition}
```

where `<number>`

- Identifies the general type of the access list. The 1–99 range specifies rules that match source IP addresses, 100–199 specifies complex IP access lists, 1000–1099 specifies Novell IPX SAP filters, and so on.

- Groups together rules in a specific rule set. All access list rules with the number 1 are treated as one set within the source IP access list family, whereas the number 2 identifies a different rule set.

- Gives the filtered interfaces a way to refer back to the rules to be applied.

Permit or deny rules specify actions to be taken on a match condition. In general, a deny causes the packet to be dropped, whereas a permit allows it to be forwarded to the next process.

At the end of every access list is an implied, yet invisible, rule to drop every packet that did not match a prior condition. This is called the *implicit deny all* and realizes a fundamental assumption of security, the principle of least privilege. This principle states that no privilege should be assumed without explicit authorization.

Note

Prior to Cisco IOS release 10.3, if filtering were invoked on an interface by pointing to an access list, and no explicit rules had been defined in that list, the default behavior was to assume the list consisted only of an implicit deny all and to block all traffic on that interface. In subsequent releases, pointing to an undefined access list has no effect on traffic.

match-condition specifies a starting pattern and a *wildcard mask* that indicates which bit positions in the traffic being examined must be matched exactly and which bit positions in which either a one or zero are matched. A zero in a wildcard mask means to match exactly, whereas a one means that either a one or zero bit in the traffic passes the match rule.

A mask to match every possible pattern, therefore, is all ones, written 255.255.255.255. A wildcard mask to match only one 32-bit pattern, such as a specific host ID, would be 0.0.0.0.

Wildcard mask patterns were chosen for historical reasons related to hardware design and were used before subnetting. The meaning of a one bit in a subnet mask and a wildcard mask is completely the opposite: In a subnet mask, a one bit means you care about the corresponding traffic value in making a routing decision, whereas in a wildcard mask, a one bit means you do not care.

So to match every host address in the private address space, you would create rules with a starting point and a wildcard mask:

```
10.0.0.0        0.255.255.255
172.16.0.0      0.15.255.255
192.168.0.0     0.0.255.255
```

It is easy to make mistakes with this syntax. If you specify 0.0.0.0 as the mask for 10.0.0.0, you would match only packets with a source address of exactly 10.0.0.0. But 10.0.0.0 is an impossible source address, because it would represent the prefix rather than any host in it.

Filter Positioning

Most routers began their filtering capabilities with filtering on output only, and this still is often a good idea. Routers, as their name should convey, are optimized to forward packets rather than filter them.

One reason to filter on output is that the routing process might discard some packets and avoid the need to scan them for filtering. Another reason is that a filtering rule might only be applicable, for example, for packets destined for WAN interfaces. In Figure 14.3, if only 10% of the packets go to the serial interface, only 10% of the packets need to go through the filtering code.

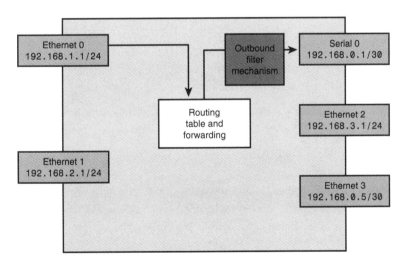

FIGURE 14.3. *If filtering is CPU intensive and only 10% of the packets need to have the filter applied, by placing filtering only where needed, you lower the CPU demand.*

Depending on the complexity of matching rules, filtering can take substantial CPU power. In simple cases, such as filtering on source or destination address only, the filtering possibly can be done in a high-speed forwarding processor rather than the main processor.

Actions on Matching

The term *access control* is used extensively in the literature on security. There are usages of *mandatory access control* and *discretionary access control*, which might or might not apply to the access control done in routers. Mandatory access control requires that every unit of information be marked with a sensitivity label, and when the information is being transferred, the label is checked to see if the receiver is entitled to receive material of that sensitivity level. There are many other refinements, such as checking that the sender is authorized to create material of the indicated sensitivity level.

Discretionary access control provides user-enforced tests, rather than system-enforced tests. A given file, for example, might or might not be assigned a password; but if one is assigned, it must be checked.

Mandatory and discretionary access control are more likely to be relevant to the process of logging into a remote access server than in general routing. The Internet Protocol Security Option, discussed in Chapter 7, "Addressing, Security, and Network Management," can implement the label requirement of mandatory access control—it can be set to discard unlabeled packets or force a label into packets.

Mandatory and discretionary access control have much more of a sense of maintaining state—of knowing some relationship between a protected object and a user—than is common in router filtering. Router filtering is most often stateless, with independent decisions being made on each packet.

Router access control is not limited to security. Filtering using access control mechanisms is used extensively for tuning performance by restricting unnecessary flow.

Permitting or Denying Flow

In a router, the most common action taken on matching is to permit or deny a packet to flow from one process to another. As shown in Figure 14.4, one process might be the routing table and forwarding logic, whereas the second process might be the code of the outgoing interface.

The source of the packet could be an incoming interface, the packet forwarding process (that is, the routing table), or the acceptance part of dynamic routing protocol (that is, a path determination process). The destination could be an interface, the routing table, or the part of a dynamic routing process that advertises to other routers.

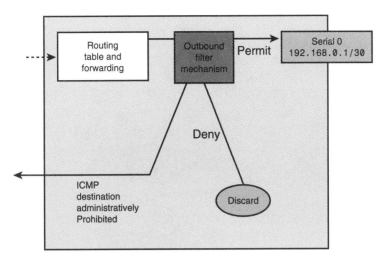

FIGURE 14.4. *Filters either allow or block flows.*

One or both processes can be internal to the router. For example, there might be controls on the processes that can be accessed by certain operator consoles, especially remote ones.

There are many examples where filters apply to network infrastructure rather than user traffic. In an IP network, perhaps the most important application of infrastructure traffic filters is the use of filters to control the acceptance or advertising of routing updates.

In networks using desktop protocols, such as Novell IPX, NetBIOS, or AppleTalk, infrastructure traffic filtering is a fundamental way to reduce overhead. For example, a common practice is to use filtering to control Novell Service Advertisement Protocol (SAP) announcements of printers and other servers that only need to be seen on a local network.

Logging

Logging is appropriate, especially when a packet is denied flow, as shown in Figure 14.5. If the router has internal mass storage, it might log to a local disk. For important alarms, the event might be logged to a console.

Most routers do not have mass storage, so they need to send logging traffic to a remote logging server. UNIX `syslog` server conventions are commonly used for this communication.

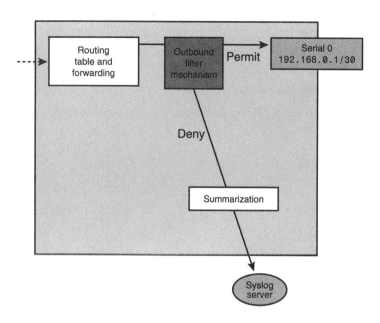

FIGURE 14.5. *Every filtering event can be logged, only some types can be logged, or only summaries of specific types can be logged.*

There are subtle security implications to logging violations. Although keeping an audit trail—a log file—is the basis of any serious security program, logging can contain the seeds of its own destruction.

Consider a malicious hacker who invades your router and knows that you are likely to log violations of access lists. A log server has finite storage. If the hacker wants to cover his actions, he might do a system penetration and then deliberately cause trivial errors intended to fill all log space. When a log file fills, the logging server has two choices: stop recording or wrap to the beginning of the file and overwrite the oldest entries. Either of these methods can conceal hacker activities.

Some router implementations help protect against attacks such as this by putting a limit on the number of events of a given type that can be logged. For example, the first violation of an access list might be logged explicitly, but subsequent violations between the same source and destination are summarized. The router might only record, after the first, the number of violations per five-minute period.

Categorizing Traffic

Access lists are a key part of mechanisms that characterize traffic by outbound priority. The action on a match might be to assign a packet to a particular outbound queue, as shown in Figure 14.6.

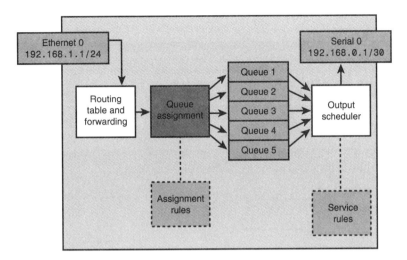

FIGURE 14.6. *Rules for queue assignment can be manually written or automatic.*

Categorizing traffic often means looking at source and destination IP addresses, source and destination TCP or UDP port numbers, and possibly other fields of the packet. Most modern categorization methods are attempting to categorize packets as belonging to end-to-end flows, which are discussed in Chapter 3, "Application Topology: Naming Endpoints."

Categorizing traffic, the process shown in Figure 14.6, does not always require manually configuring recognition rules. Some traffic management methods, such as weighted fair queueing, have built-in categorization algorithms. See the section "Weighted Fair Queueing," later in this chapter.

Triggering Events

Matching a given access list criterion can trigger processing in the router. A frequent application of this is *dial on demand routing* (DDR), where recognizing that an outgoing address must be dialed to be reached triggers an autodialing process. See the discussion in the later section "On-Demand Connectivity."

Modifying Packets

Especially for exterior routing with the Border Gateway Protocol, Version 4 (BGP-4), it can become useful to modify the contents of routing updates. This also can be useful in exchanging routing information between different dynamic routing protocols.

> ### Warning
>
> Changing the contents of routing protocol packets can be extremely dangerous. You need a thorough understanding of the routing protocol itself and the routing design in which it is used. Cisco's route map mechanism is effectively a programming language with more powerful constructs for matching than offered by access lists. Route maps have match commands and set commands, the latter changing packet contents. Get expert advise before trying these the first time.

Although the details of changing fields in routing updates is beyond the scope of this text, the idea certainly is a complex example of selective forwarding. One example, shown in Figure 14.7, illustrates the use.

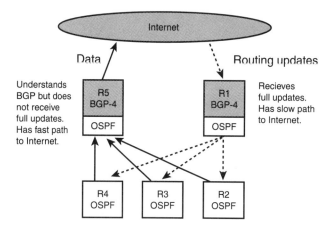

FIGURE 14.7. *A route map running on R1, which receives the routing update, changes the next-hop address for a given destination. This forces other routers, such as R2-R4, to use the faster external connection on R5.*

Planning Filtering

Figure 14.8 shows what I have found to be the best way to plan the placement of selective forwarding decisions.

Many people think of selective mechanisms in terms of physical interfaces, which leads to the misleading assumption that such mechanisms work the same way in both directions. Using directional drawings helps greatly in staying on the right conceptual path.

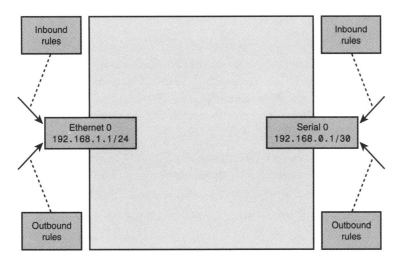

FIGURE 14.8. *Write separate rules at each interface for recognizing inbound and outbound packets.*

Tip

It's hard to overemphasize the importance of filters being one directional. This is emphatically a feature, not a bug. Some beginners think it would be easier to have filtering rules set up for sessions, which are inherently bidirectional. Setting filtering up by sessions, however, would take away your ability to have different policies in different directions. The world is full of asymmetrical power relationships—should networks be different?

Filtering has long been one directional, but for practical and not theoretical reasons. The advent of flow specification reinforces the idea of one-directional filtering, because flows, the basis of many new networking services, are one directional. At least two flows are needed to describe an interactive session.

In networking technology, the basic principles of filters have evolved not just to permit or deny transfer, but as a means of recognizing flows.

The question often arises, "How can I prevent traffic for a certain Internet application from flowing in one direction but not another?" This is often fairly easy to answer as long as your access lists can examine TCP or UDP port numbers.

Remember that Internet applications flow from client port to server port. Denying traffic from Port 23, for example, blocks flow from the client to the server. TCP Port 23 is the well-known port for the Telnet server; the client ports in a Telnet session have values above 1023 (and preferably 2047).

If you deny traffic to Port 23 of address Host 2 by placing a filter at Interface 2, you have blocked Host 1's capability to Telnet to Host 2, but not Host 2's capability to Telnet to Host 1. Host 1's second filter at interface Host 1 would be needed to block Telnet in both directions.

Assume that you only have the filter at Interface 2. Telnets to Host 1 from Host 2 are not affected because the filter at 2 does not check incoming traffic.

Remember that in the absence of cryptographic authentication, you cannot trust the source address field in a packet. It is much more reasonable to trust the destination and, to a lesser extent, TCP or UDP port fields. Even if a packet is coming from a hacker, if he tries to reach the Telnet server on something other than Port 23, the attempt fails.

You will find that filters—access lists—can be strong in traffic categorization but easy to defeat for security. Security mechanisms need to be multilayered, with authentication and bastion hosts as well as packet filtering.

Access lists are critical *parts* of firewalls. For a detailed discussion of the sorts of traffic that should be filtered in a firewall, refer to this chapter's section in Appendix A for a listing of documents by Chapman and Zwicky and Cheswick and Bellovin.

Guidelines for Packet Filtering

The following are rules of thumb in defining access lists:

- Define what you want to do and in which directions. If you are defining security filters, you need to have a security policy in hand. Something to consider in a policy is what to do with traffic types that are not explicitly authorized. Some types, such as BOOTP, might be necessary for operation even if they do not appear to have user functions. In general, UDP-based services are more dangerous than TCP-based services.

- Draw the selective filtering logic. As opposed to the usual connectivity drawings among routers, it's often convenient to draw unidirectional links between routers.

- Informally write out your filtering rules. From the standpoint of understandability, it is best to go from most specific to least specific.

- From the standpoint of performance, you want to go from most likely to match to least likely to match.

- Next, determine which rules need to be on which routers. Explicitly consider the direction of flow and the possible existence of additional paths that could inadvertently bypass a filter. There is often a tradeoff between placing the filters as close as possible to the source, which minimizes traffic downstream of the sources, and placing a smaller number of filters more centrally, which simplifies maintenance.

- Review the lists to see if there are any rules that deny traffic by destination address only. Such filtering can be done much more efficiently using static routes that direct traffic to the null interface.

- Consider maintenance of the lists. Access lists with more than a very

continues

continued

few rules should be written and edited on a text editor, then downloaded to the router. It is impractical to edit most access lists on the router.

- A good practice is starting each stored list with a command that deletes the entire list, so that the statements following start from a known state.

Selective Outbound Traffic Management

Traffic management generally is based on categorizing traffic into flows and then setting different classes of service for the different flows. The more recent a traffic management technique, the more likely is it to be described in terms of flows. You can find an excellent review of quality of service mechanisms in Ferguson and Huston's *Quality of Service: Delivering QoS on the Internet and in Corporate Networks*. The state of the art in congestion control is discussed in RFC 2309.

There are two broad classes of traffic (or congestion) control mechanisms: *reactive* and *proactive*. Reactive mechanisms come into play after congestion has been detected. They act much like a traffic police officer at the parking lot following a large sporting event. The traffic officer points at various groups of cars and allows them access to a single exit. The officer's underlying assumptions are usually to equalize the flow of cars from the multiple parking lanes to the single exit.

Reactive mechanisms try to clear the "traffic jam" at a congested network link by selecting which traffic next has access to the exit and which traffic must wait. Going beyond the vehicle traffic metaphor, reactive congestion control mechanisms can drop certain packets rather than try to transmit them at all. Because many protocols retransmit dropped packets, this effectively defers the load created by certain flows until, hopefully, congestion moderates.

Proactive mechanisms are intended to prevent the overloading conditions by which congestion is created. Returning to the vehicle metaphor, a proactive congestion control mechanism would not allow more cars to park than can leave through the exit at a steady rate. The method recognizes that car arrival is spread over time, so more cars can enter over the pregame period than the postgame exit would allow to leave at a decent rate.

Reactive Methods

The first congestion management mechanisms implemented on routers dealt with congestion after it had occurred. In a congestion condition, the way to relieve it is to defer some traffic over others. Selective mechanisms, often, but not always, based on access lists, select the traffic to be given priority.

First-in-first-out (FIFO) buffering is not a selective technique, but should be kept in mind because effective solutions do not always need to be complex. If all traffic is of equal priority, but there are occasional bursts of traffic at a rate too fast for the output medium, you simply might need to increase the number of buffers at the output interface.

Current implementations of reactive congestion management usually come into play only when an output interface is congested. As long as the output interface can keep up with the traffic rate, packets go directly to output rather than entering the traffic management queues.

Preemptive/Drastic Queueing

Most major router vendors implement a scheme that categorizes traffic into a small, fixed number of output queues, as shown in Figure 14.6. Conceptually, the router sends a packet out the designated output interface, and then decides what packet to send next. It always begins its decision making by checking the highest-priority queue. If packets are waiting in the highest-priority queue, they are transmitted in the order in which they arrived in that queue. As long as packets are queued in the highest-priority queue, they are transmitted without regard to the waiting period of packets in lower-priority queues. This method is variously called *preemptive, drastic,* or *priority queueing.*

There are both political and technical reasons to use drastic queueing. This queueing discipline guarantees that a high-priority service always has its packets sent. In the real world, you might be faced with a management decision to merge IBM and IP networks in the interest of lowering overall costs. IBM protocols can be very sensitive to congestion; they assume they have sufficient dedicated bandwidth.

The IBM networking staff might very well point this out and say they will be responsible for their services working only if they have guaranteed bandwidth equal to what they had on their dedicated network. As you will see in the discussion of guaranteed minimum bandwidth, there are indeed mechanisms to do this, if you have reasonably good information on the characteristics of the traffic—packet lengths and quantitative estimates of the required bandwidth for each service. If you do not have good statistics, or if the IBM workload in this example changed frequently, the only realistic alternative might be to say, simply, "If IBM traffic arrives at the outgoing interface, it will always be sent before any other traffic."

Drastic queueing also is easier to implement in a router and easier to configure than other methods. Next to changing FIFO buffer allocations, it is the simplest method.

As shown in Figure 14.9, the router establishes a set of access lists that assign traffic to queues. Implementations usually have three or four predefined queues.

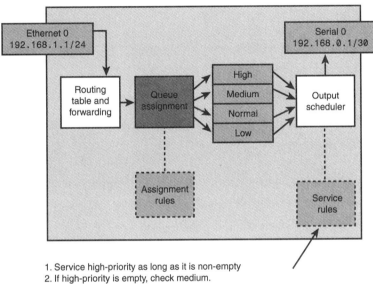

1. Service high-priority as long as it is non-empty
2. If high-priority is empty, check medium.
   if medium traffic waiting, send 1 medium packet and go to rule 1.
3. If medium is empty, check normal.
   if normal traffic waiting, send 1 normal packet and go to rule 1.
4. If normal is empty, check low.
   if low traffic waiting, send 1 low packet and go to rule 1.

FIGURE 14.9. *A drastic queueing system has three major components: a set of queues, the mechanism that assigns traffic to queues, and a mechanism that selects the queue to be serviced for outgoing traffic.*

Tip

You often will find that application traffic splits conveniently into two or three classes, such as time-sensitive interactive, general interactive, and non-interactive, as in printing and file transfer.

Remember that these are application-oriented classes, and you generally want to assure that network management traffic goes in the highest priority class. If you lower the priority of network management, you might not be able to send critical reset messages or diagnostics when congestion is taking place.

Most network management queries are low volume. Software reloads are of high volume but utterly critical. Routine monitoring and autodiscovery of new network elements can be placed in a lower priority.

The selective forwarding aspect of drastic queueing is in the filters that assign traffic to queues.

Bay router commands to invoke drastic prioritization are quite intuitive. Cisco's command language for the equivalent prioritization mechanism is more obscure, but gives additional functions.

On a Cisco router, you assign traffic to queues with `priority-list` commands. There are a great many criteria by which you can assign traffic with such a list, including:

- Protocol family (IP, AppleTalk, Novell, and so on)
- Source and/or destination network layer address
- Source and/or destination TCP or UDP port
- Incoming interface
- Packet length

You invoke priority queueing on specific outgoing interfaces using `priority-group` subcommands of `interface`.

Time-Sharing/Guaranteed Minimum Bandwidth

Also called *class-based queueing* in formal networking literature, this prioritization method gives a minimum bandwidth to each of a set of queues. Cisco calls this *custom queueing*. The queues, often called *classes*, are shown in Figure 14.10. If there is no traffic for a particular queue, its bandwidth allocation is shared equally over other queues.

Setting the appropriate bandwidths for each queue requires an accurate knowledge of typical packet lengths. Although the detailed response to inaccurate length information is implementation specific and potentially complex, the effect of inaccurate specification is either to make the traffic more bursty or to give an unfair bandwidth allocation to classes of traffic whose packet length statistics were inaccurately specified.

Weighted Fair Queueing

I must confess that when I first saw a description of weighted fair queueing (WFQ), it seemed rather implausible. Its implausibility was that it is so simple. With experience, I have learned it works quite well, as long as its assumptions fit your traffic-handling policy.

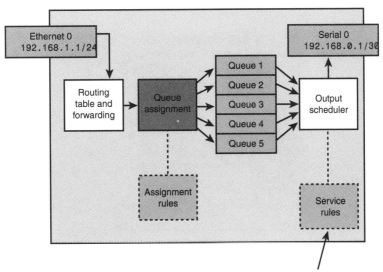

1. Service queue 1 as long as it has traffic, AND the number of bytes sent does
   not exceed the quota for the cycle.
2. Check next queue. If it is non-empty, send up to the quota number of bytes.
3. Move to the next queue. Sevice if non-empty. Go to rule 3, jumping back to queue 1
   if this is the last queue.

FIGURE 14.10. *Your responsibility in setting up selective forwarding is to define the rules that assign traffic to queues.*

WFQ automatically identifies flows and keeps track of the traffic in each flow. It assumes that interactive applications have low volumes and that non-interactive, bulk transfer applications have high volumes. Such assumptions are quite accurate for traditional Internet applications such as Telnet and FTP. The assumptions do not work well for tunneled SNA traffic, and they can be of marginal value when Web applications are transferring large files.

The basic model of WFQ, shown in Figure 14.11, is to start with flow identification on incoming packets.

After packets are assigned to a flow, the flow monitor keeps track of the volume associated with individual flows. Based on their volume, the flows are assigned to high or low volume queues.

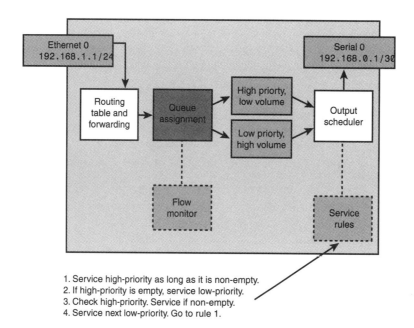

1. Service high-priority as long as it is non-empty.
2. If high-priority is empty, service low-priority.
3. Check high-priority. Service if non-empty.
4. Service next low-priority. Go to rule 1.

FIGURE 14.11. *WFQ does not need configuration but does categorize traffic into flows, using internal algorithms.*

Proactive Methods

Proactive traffic management methods attempt to prevent congestion from happening, rather than react to congestion after it has happened. They do so by limiting traffic flow before the medium becomes seriously congested, using either fixed traffic allocations or dynamic congestion monitoring.

Guaranteed Maximum Bandwidth

You need to specify rules for categorizing traffic into classes of service, and how much bandwidth to give to each class. As shown in Figure 14.12, each class of service is only allowed to send a steady average rate, with an opportunity to send bursts when there is capacity to do so.

There are multiple applications for this sort of selective forwarding. You might have customers with access to a high-speed medium such as a 100 MBps Ethernet, but these customers might be billed based on access bandwidth. Guaranteed maximum bandwidth can restrict them from using more bandwidth than they have paid for.

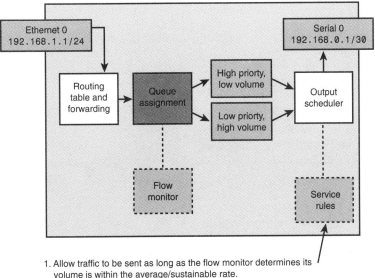

1. Allow traffic to be sent as long as the flow monitor determines its volume is within the average/sustainable rate.
2. If traffic is within the burst size, send it but mark it eligible for drop.
3. Drop traffic over the burst size.

FIGURE 14.12. *When configuring this service, you need to specify the rules for recognizing classes of service and how much bandwidth to give to each class.*

Another application is to protect downstream sites with low-bandwidth access links from being overrun by upstream links that otherwise might send large bursts. A data center might, for example, have a DS1 access line with Frame Relay virtual circuits. Although a given virtual circuit might have a Committed Information Rate (CIR) of only 64 KBps, the data center might be able to dump bursts into the Frame Relay provider network at the DS1 speed of the access link. Guaranteed maximum bandwidth can restrict, in the router or switch before the access link, that traffic does not go out faster than the receiver can accept.

Random Early Detect

Random Early Detect (RED) always reminds me of a dramatic movie focused on survivors in an overcrowded lifeboat. In the movie, the only way that anyone will live is that someone will die, and the boat officer must make tough decisions.

RED is a bit more cheerful than the movie, because the packets that must die for the many are resurrected by TCP retransmission. Because the largest traffic source on the global Internet is the Hypertext Transfer Protocol (HTTP) used for Web browsing, and HTTP runs over TCP, RED offers significant potential for managing global Internet congestion.

As shown in Figure 14.13, RED requires a means of identifying traffic and a criterion for selecting the priority of flows on which traffic is dropped.

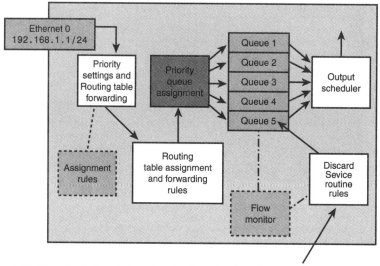

1. Mark incoming traffic as to type of service if not already marked, or specified by RSVP.
2. Assign traffic to queue based on type of service.
3. Monitor congestion in queue. If the flow monitor detects severe congestion, the discard routine selects random TCP packets to discard, starting with lowest priority, until congestion stops.

FIGURE 14.13. *Traffic can be identified as destined for a certain queue either with the Resource Reservation Protocol (RSVP) or by settings of the precedence bits in the IP header.*

Because hosts are rarely capable of setting precedence bits, Cisco implemented some access lists that, when matched, trigger the action of modifying the precedence bits of the IP header.

Selective Forwarding Based on Dialup Information

Filtering need not be applied only to logical addresses. There are very useful applications driven by the telephone number, which is a transmission system address. Other applications create an outgoing phone call, either analog or ISDN, after they know a specific logical address needs to be reached.

Caller Identification

In dial applications with analog lines or ISDN, the calling phone number might be available from the telephone company and used to validate the user identity. This sort of identification, of course, relies on a capability to associate users with specific telephone numbers. Such associations are rarely practical for traveling users, but can be perfectly reasonable for fixed sites that use dial access for:

- Backup connectivity from routers

- Telecommuting

- Hosts with only periodic update needs, such as reading email or sending inventory updates

The exact commands for verifying calling number identification vary both with the telephone switch type that services you and the type of router you use.

On-Demand Connectivity

Dial-on-demand routing (DDR) depends on defining associations between destination logical addresses and destination telephone numbers needed to reach them. The telephone number can be ISDN or analog, and, indeed, the principles of on-demand connectivity extend to any circuit-oriented transmission technology such as X.25, switched Frame Relay, or ATM.

You use access lists to select traffic eligible for creating dialup links. This is the first part of address-oriented on-demand connectivity. Although it is possible to set up DDR for all traffic of a given protocol type, you will do so much more often on a more selective basis, picking specific logical addresses known to be reachable only by dialing.

After the requirement to dial is known, you have to specify which interface is to be used for the dialing. This is a simple decision when there is only one dial-capable interface, but becomes more complex when there is a pool of interfaces with dialing capability. Interface pools normally are identified as a super-interface, and mappings of logical addresses to dialed numbers are done at the superinterface level.

Selecting the next available line in a group of lines subordinate to a dialer interface usually is a simple configuration matter. The addressing complexity comes in:

- Establishing the number to call for a given Layer 3 address.

- When modems are used for the dialing, selecting the appropriate modem command script and sending these commands to the modem to force it to dial. Command scripts are cryptic, most often using the Hayes command language. They also can be complex, including actions to take, for example, if the dialed number is busy.

- After the connection is made, a command script might be necessary to create a PPP or other Layer 2 connection. Depending on the authentication modes used by the destination—and in the ISP world, there are many local variations—you might have to configure one or more password challenge-response sequences, user identfication challenge-response sequences, and so on.

Do not think of dial applications as maintenance free. Especially when they are from a customer to an ISP, the ISP can change login sequences, age out passwords, or do other things that require you to change your configuration. Unfortunately, many ISPs are not good about informing their customers that they are changing access procedures. Many customers are equally guilty of not maintaining a current email or telephone contact for their ISP to notify them of changes.

Tunneling

Think of the way a corporate mailroom sends out large quantities of postal mail or express shipments. Each individual envelope has an envelope and label of its own, giving source and destination.

The mailroom, however, bundles the multiple envelopes together in a mail bag or tray, which is used to transfer the aggregate of envelopes to the post office or express carrier. Effectively, there is the bag label with a set of envelope labels inside.

This analogy holds well for tunneling. The tunnel is analogous to the service relationship between the mailroom and the post office.

In tunneling, the role of selective filtering is to resolve the need to put payload packets, with their individual headers, into delivery or mailbag packets that traverse the tunnel. See Figure 14.14 for the relationships between payload and delivery information.

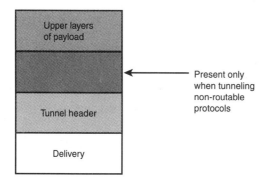

F IGURE 1 4.1 4 . *The relationship between payload and delivery information.*

In routers, tunneling depends on a mechanism called *recursive route lookup* (see Figure 14.15). In normal, nontunneled routing, when the destination of an outgoing packet is found in the routing table, the routing table points to an outgoing interface. When the packet is forwarded to the code associated with the outgoing interface, that code wraps the Layer 3 packet in an appropriate Layer 2 frame, containing the Layer 2 addresses of the outgoing interface and the next-hop destination.

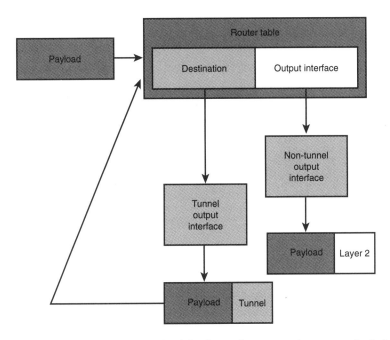

FIGURE 14.15. *The left side of this figure shows normal, nonrecursive lookup. The right side shows the additional step in recursive lookup associated with tunnel processing.*

In tunneling, the destination is still found in the routing table, but when the packet arrives at an output *tunnel interface*, processing is different. The tunnel interface code wraps the outgoing payload packet in a Layer 3 or Layer 4 packet and puts the tunnel destination address into the destination address field of the delivery packet containing the payload packet. A tunneling protocol header goes into the delivery packet, immediately following the delivery packet header and before the payload packet header.

The tunnel interface code then sends the delivery packet back to the main routing process. This triggers the recursive lookup, where the delivery destination address is now looked up, and an output interface is again selected. The output interface selected is normally a real interface, the code for which wraps the delivery packet in a Layer 2 frame and sends it out the interface to the next hop. It is possible, however, to have multiple levels of tunneling, where the output interface selected by the first tunnel interface lookup is itself a tunnel.

Note

Cisco uses the terms local *and* remote *switching to describe carrying Layer 2, respectively, over Layer 2 or Layer 3 delivery protocols. Remote switching is another name for tunneling. Frame Relay connectivity among routers, using DCE or NNI interfaces on the router, is local. Frame Relay over IP and X.25 over TCP are remote. X.25 DTE and DCE connectivity among a set of router interfaces is local.*

Generic Route Encapsulation

Generic Route Encapsulation (GRE) was developed by Cisco, but has been licensed by multiple vendors and is a *de facto* standard for sending traffic that does not need guaranteed delivery with retransmission [RFC 1701]. It is generic in the sense that it does not have specific requirements as to the payload or delivery protocol type.

A completed GRE packet has a delivery header, a GRE header, and the original IP header. The general structure of a GRE packet is shown in Figure 14.16.

FIGURE 14.16. *A payload header. This three-part structure is characteristic of most tunneling mechanisms.*

Most commonly, GRE runs over IP [RFC 1702]. An IP protocol identifier number of 47 identifies GRE-containing packets.

On Cisco routers, you specify GRE as the mode on a tunnel interface:

```
interface tunnel 0
tunnel mode gre
tunnel source serial 0
tunnel destination 172.16.1.2
ip address 192.168.1.1 255.255.255.0
ipx network 2000
```

Frame Relay Tunneling

Frame Relay services can be provisioned over IP. IP and other protocol families routinely operate over Frame Relay.

Frame-over-IP has been a special strength of Bay Networks, which has products that use OSPF dynamic routing to find alternate paths between Frame Relay switches at the edges of a Frame Relay carrier network. Cisco also offers frame-over-IP services.

Remember that Frame Relay is a connection-oriented multiplexing service. Logically, Frame Relay provides end-to-end service using Layer 2 mechanisms. There is a tunneling process involved, where packets or frames from various payload protocols, to be sent over Frame Relay, are put into an RFC 2427 tunnel analogous to that of GRE. Both GRE and RFC 2427 encapsulation have payload, tunneling, and delivery headers. ATM networks use RFC 1483 encapsulation in a manner very similar to that of RFC 2427. RFC 2427 is a new version of what was previously RFC 1490.

XOT X.25 Routing

Cisco developed the X.25-over-TCP (XOT) tunneling protocol and described it in informational RFC 1613. Various terms have been used for this mechanism, including *remote X.25 routes*. Remote routes run over TCP/IP delivery protocols, with TCP required to give the retransmission that the X.25 packet layer protocol expects from the underlying protocol layer. In regular X.25, this underlying layer is LAP-B, which provides link-level retransmission.

Carrying SNA Traffic

After the SNA information is packaged for transmission, you need to decide among the several different ways to carry it through the network. For general network transport, the trend certainly is to TCP encapsulation. This is the only means supported by Data Link Switching Plus (DLSw+) and is an option for Remote Source Route Bridging (RSRB) and Serial Tunneling (STUN).

TCP imposes greater overhead on the end routers and also increases the packet size. Nevertheless, it gives much greater flexibility and indeed might give the appearance of improving end user response time.

For RSRB, there are lower-overhead alternatives, direct and Fast Sequenced Transport (FST) encapsulation. Direct encapsulation also is available for STUN. RFC 2427 Frame Relay is yet another alternative.

Reducing cost, by combining separate IBM and non-IBM networks, is usually the first motivation for integrating SNA into a general routing network. The second motivation, however, usually is increasing availability by letting IP routing select alternate paths in the event of failure. Given IBM defaults, the magic number for Token Ring sessions is 14 seconds. If an alternate path can be found in this time, a session does not break. However, 14-second convergence is quite a short time for basic routing to reconverge on alternate paths.

Before going to extreme measures to assure convergence time, assess the effect on your network of a timeout caused by slow convergence. Do you have a single point of failure? All the world's redundant routers won't help if a single mainframe fails.

Convergence strategies include:

- Do nothing to the network. Accept the cost of occasional session loss

- Spoof the endpoints (that is, tell the SNA end devices to trust the network to deliver traffic)

- Change the end equipment timers

- Decrease convergence time

- Simple failure protection

- Dead router protection

Spoofing requires reliable transfer across the network, which in turn requires the SNA frames to be encapsulated in TCP. Cisco can carry SNA traffic in three encapsulations, plus local Token Ring and native encapsulation in Frame Relay. These options, as well as the next generation DLSw+, are compared in Figure 14.17.

DLSw does not preserve the end-to-end Layer 2 information and always uses TCP encapsulation.

Note

The original implementation of DLSw was IBM proprietary, but documented in RFC 1434. A multivendor consortium, including IBM, developed a new open specification published as RFC 1795. This multivendor specification is the state of the art for carrying IBM traffic over IP networks and is used by many vendors.

The lower-overhead encapsulations, direct and FST, are incompatible with spoofing. Direct encapsulation has the lowest overhead, but is not routable. It is useful when two routers are linked by a single, reliable medium.

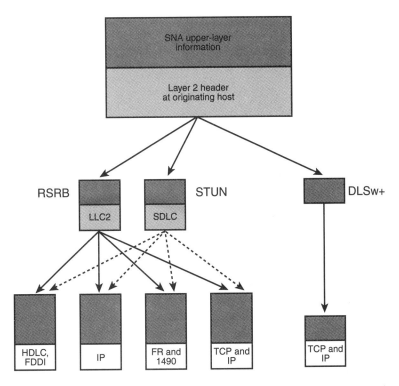

FIGURE 14.17. *RSRB and STUN preserve data link headers and are vendor specific. DLSw+ is multivendor, with vendor-specific extensions that can be negotiated away between different vendor implementations.*

FST is routable, but is no more robust than direct encapsulation. Router networks supporting FST must be configured with special care to avoid out-of-sequence problems. FST is most useful when only one path exists between two sites, but that path contains multiple router hops running over fairly fast lines. If multiple potential paths do exist, it is important that load balancing between them be on a per-destination basis. If per-packet load balancing is appropriate, FST is not appropriate. FST also does not work between media with different MTU sizes, if fragmentation is needed. TCP encapsulation with spoofing at the endpoints probably is better.

Network Address Translation

You need to consider several factors in configuring basic, non-load-shared network address translation (NAT):

- Will the mappings be one-to-one (that is, pure NAT) or many-to-few (that is, network address and port translation, also called port address translation)?

- Is there any overlap between the inside and outside address ranges?

The key thing to understand in NAT is that separate translation mechanisms exist on both sides of the NAT. This lets you do different mappings of 10.0.0.1, for example, when going from local-to-global and global-to-local.

On Bay routers, static NAT is configured through Site Manager through the menu sequence Protocols->IP->NAT->Static. Dynamic NAT—network address and port translation—is invoked through Protocols->IP->NAT->Dynamic->Local/Global.

As shown in Figure 14.18, you specify ranges of addresses to be translated from the local side and the global side. The same destination address might have different mappings, depending on whether it is first seen by the local or global interface of the NAT.

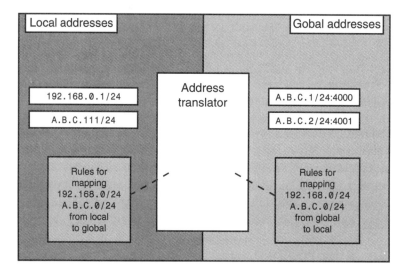

FIGURE 14.18. *By specifying different mapping rules on the local and global sides, the same address could appear on both sides but be translated differently depending on the interface on which it arrived.*

Being able to define different mappings is especially useful when connecting two enterprises that have used the same private address space. Both enterprises could continue to use 10.0.0.0 internally.

Looking Ahead

This chapter shows the basic structure that implements Layer 3 addressing in the network infrastructure. It also refines Layer 3 addressing techniques, adding selective flow and Layer 4 tunneling. Chapter 15, "Your Addressing Strategy: Integration for the Present and Planning for the Future," presents the big picture involved in tying together the various address implementation techniques and looks at emerging networking technologies.

PART **V**

Integration and the Future

CHAPTER **15**

Your Addressing Strategy: Integration for the Present and Planning for the Future

This chapter focuses on the servers and operational procedures involved in a smooth configuration control strategy, primarily DHCP and DNS. It complements Chapter 11, "Addressing in End Hosts," which deals with the client side of autoconfiguration.

In the days when most servers used UNIX or mainframe operating systems, it was reasonable to assume that most sites had people who could write programs to do administration. This is no longer the case. Nevertheless, the benefits of relatively simple, installation-specific administration scripts can be immense. It can be very worthwhile to develop Perl programming skills in system administrators or use consultants for this important integration task.

> **Note**
>
> *My most fundamental rule in developing a good operational system for managing addresses:* Never manually enter an address more than once. *This is often a goal rather than an immediately attainable objective, but it should guide your philosophy.*
>
> *When you add user and server hosts, you should do so with scripts—programs—that update all relevant servers. Relevant servers include DNS, DHCP, firewalls and access servers, SNMP, and so on. The script should request or assign names.*

The role of IP version 6 (IPv6) remains controversial. Many Internet experts consider it a solution in search of a problem, because there are IP version 4 (IPv4) extensions that provide almost every function proposed for IPv6. There is a good deal of agreement that IPv6 packages these functions more logically, and in a more efficient manner for hardware processing, than IPv4. Many people argue that this packaging, however, is not worth the cost of migration.

A Review of Operational Requirements

Consistency in address management requires that you reconcile the different views of the various things that use address information, as illustrated in Figure 15.1. There are consistency aspects of different scope. You certainly need to be consistent within your own enterprise. If you do not connect to the global Internet, the responsibility for consistency stops.

If you do connect to the global Internet, you need to ensure that the parts of your naming and addressing that are visible from the outside are consistent. Remember that services such as split DNS, network address translation, and so on can quite reasonably hide parts of your network from the Internet.

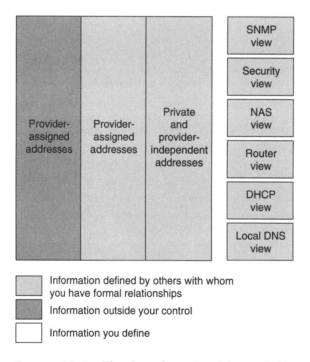

FIGURE 15.1. *There is an abstraction of the set of address and name information in your organization, and there are many views of this abstraction, both internal and external.*

Local Point of Reference

You need to have some way of uniquely identifying devices that acquire addresses. The traditional way, of course, is to have a central group responsible for manually configuring devices with addresses. Such a practice tends not to scale well in large and/or geographically distributed organizations.

Some of the ways you can establish a key for LAN-attached devices include:

- Strictly record the MAC address assigned to each device, with appropriate administrative practices to record changes caused by changing network interface cards with new burnt-in addresses.

- Capture the MAC addresses of devices plugged into LAN switch ports.

- Locally administer the MAC address on each device.

- Assign a unique DNS name to each device permitted on the network, storing this name on a local disk.

Dynamic Host Configuration Protocol (DHCP) has a somewhat more flexible client identifier concept than does BOOTP. BOOTP specifically uses a MAC address as the client identifier. DHCP, however, can use almost any identifier, such as a DNS name, as a client identifier. The main restriction on identifiers is they must be unique within the medium on which DHCP requests and responses are broadcast.

Dialup users using PPP also need to have unique identifiers. These can be validated locally on a remote access server that assigns address, by a RADIUS or TACACS server, or by a DHCP server to which the RAS acts as a proxy.

Global Scope

Figure 15.2 offers numerous reminders of ways in which your naming and addressing might need to be globally visible. One of the advantages of using provider assigned (PA) address space is that you might be able to let your provider manage some aspects of global administration.

Address assignments and allocations come from address registries for *provider independent* (PI) space and from ISPs for *provider assigned* (PA) space. Reverse DNS mappings are normally done by the owner of the space, so they are the responsibility of your provider when you use PA space.

Prefixes are part of your addressing plan. When they are aggregated, they become route objects advertised by your autonomous system (AS). If you have your own AS, you need to register route objects in the appropriate routing registry. If you do not have your own AS but have PI space, you need to coor-dinate their registration with your service provider and possibly with a reg-istry. Even though you have had PI space allocated to you, the AS maintainer is responsible for the announcement of this space.

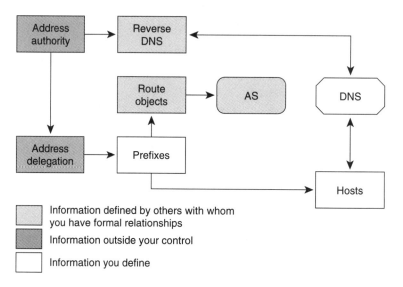

FIGURE 15.2. *When you look at addressing and naming information, consider who controls it.*

Some Case Studies

When you look at creating or reengineering the address structure of an organi-zation, it's often wise to think of implementing that new structure primarily as a database problem and only secondly as a networking problem. As a database problem, you begin with the inventory described in Chapter 8, "The Existing IP and Non-IP Address Structure: Preparing for Remodeling," and move to a planning level superset of the inventory as described in Chapter 9, "The Address Plan."

Wherever possible, think of your deployment problem as getting information out of the database and into the network infrastructure servers that can use it. That usually centers around getting information into DNS and DHCP servers in a consistent way. If you have dynamic updating between DHCP and DNS, your focus is more apt to be getting the names into DNS and establishing address ranges in DHCP.

Don't underestimate the human part of administration. Your database can be used to generate paper or electronic mail informing users of upcoming changes.

The following sections illustrate three examples of different organizations that need to design and implement addressing plans.

A Small Firm

Chapter 9 describes a small firm that has a single location with 20 workstations that want occasional Internet access. These workstations connect to three local servers. The firm intends to establish a public Web presence.

The small address requirement of the firm precluded it from using provider independent space. It really had two alternatives when it established its Internet connectivity, depending on its security methods. It could use registered PA space, or it could use private address space and go through a firewall that did network and port address translation. Due to the small size of the firm, it would probably be wise to let the ISP run the firewall, rather than develop specialized firewall administration experience in-house.

Let's assume the firm is ready to create that Web presence. The firm has obtained the domain name smallfirm.com, but relies on its ISP to run the DNS servers. The ISP might put the firm's workstations and local servers in private address space, reachable through an ISP firewall. Split DNS, as discussed in Chapter 7, "Addressing, Security, and Network Management," would manage the process by which internal machines reach external destinations. There is no requirement for the local servers to be visible on the Internet, only that the local workstations be able to reach arbitrary Internet destinations. From the security standpoint, in fact, it is highly desirable that the local servers *not* be visible on the Internet, and the firewall enforces this access control.

One of the simplest ways to realize the Web presence is to put www.smallfirm.com not at the customer site at all, but at a Web farm at the ISP's site. Such a guest server farm can very well have uninterruptable power and air conditioning, 24-hour technical support, multiple connections to upstream ISPs, and other reliability-increasing services that would not be feasible for the firm itself to provide.

If the public server were to be located at the ISP site, there really is no complexity to the addressing and naming. The ISP would have a DNS entry for www.smallfirm.com, and global Internet requests for that name would return the address in the server farm. This address would be likely to be registered and provider assigned, even if the workstations and local servers would be in private address space.

It would be wise for the firm to install DHCP and secondary DNS on one or more of its local servers. If the local network grew, either in private address space or PA space, there very well might be a need to renumber in order to have a larger host field in the prefix. From a network administration stand-point, the simplest way to do this would be to define a new range in the DHCP server and disable assignments from the old range. As leases expired, assuming all DHCP assignments were dynamic, new addresses would be assigned from the new range.

If the DNS and DHCP servers were dynamically linked, little more configuration would be needed for these services. If there were no dynamic linkage, additional administration would be needed.

If the firm uses address translation on a pure NAT or a firewall, the address mapping tables would need to change to translate properly from the local to global space. If network management is set up to access hosts by DNS name, there should be no problem there.

Introducing Hierarchy into a Flat Network

A large European research center, one of the pioneers of networking, went through several major changes that demanded it change its address structure. First, it moved from a large, flat, bridged network to a routed network. Second, it changed its ISP and needed to renumber hosts currently in the old provider's PA space into the new provider's space, keeping Internet reachability for its Internet-connected clients and servers. There were also a substantial quantity of hosts in the private address space, which needed to continue operating through the change.

This center had long run a bridged network because early routers lacked the performance to handle the huge volumes of data generated by experiments. As the center's network approached 20,000 devices, however, broadcast storms were becoming hard limits to the size of their bridged network. It was necessary to use routers to split their networks into separate broadcast domains. Reliable VLAN technology was not available at the time they needed to find an alternative to their nonsubnetted bridged network.

Not all addresses—including servers—were managed by a central administrator. The organization could not simply reconfigure DNS, because not all servers were in DNS, and a certain number of DNS servers were not accessible to the central networking group.

The challenge was converting host addresses in the DNS, allowing reachability during the transition period. The networking group met this challenge by creating a database of users, addresses, and names, from which the DNS and DHCP server configurations would be built. This database also allowed the central networking group to send administrative notifications to users and servers, telling them when they would need to change addresses and flagging those that did not respond. Incidentally, the notifications were deliberately sent by interoffice postal mail, not email. The organization's culture was such that the network administrators believed there was a higher probability that users would pay attention to paper mail than email.

It was estimated that servers' addresses would be cached in global DNS up to one week. Most of this organization's servers supported multiple addresses.

With significant external coordination, this organization arranged an overlap between the new and old PA address spaces. Their DNS returned the new addresses as well as the old during the transition period. Although not all clients would "walk the list" of the multiple DNS responses, a substantial number did so and automatically learned the new addresses. In the DNS responses, the new addresses came in first in the list of responses, which is in order of preference.

A Merger

Three companies, each with PI space, merged. Their sales groups reorganized on a geographic basis, although manufacturing and research remained in divisions corresponding to the previous companies. A new corporate headquarters was defined.

The various companies had used classful routing and now faced huge problems with discontiguous networks. They had been able to make the configuration work, but sometimes needed as many as 10 secondary addresses per medium to heal the discontiguous networks. Thus, many secondary addresses became a maintenance nightmare for the router administrators. It was all too easy to forget to add one secondary address on a given interface and lose connectivity to a significant part of the merged interface network.

Classful addressing also wasted a great many addresses on point-to-point media. This was a concern if the merged company wanted greater Internet connectivity.

Prior to the merger, the networking groups of each company assigned all addresses. After the merger, the combined network group was responsible for assigning subnet addresses and router interface addresses, but no longer was responsible for assigning client and server addresses. The user host address assignment function was transferred to local network administrators, who frequently had, at best, minimal training in addressing.

To fix these problems, one of the most urgent needs was to move to classless routing. By doing so, the discontiguous network problem disappeared, and the enterprise could start adding appropriate subnets of appropriate length for point-to-point media. Although the enterprise network engineers recognized that they needed to move toward summarized hierarchical addresses as part of their long-term performance and reliability improvement, they gained immediate improvement in network reliability by moving to classless routing.

During the move to classless routing, a parallel effort was launched to find hard-coded addresses in user hosts and convert these to DNS names. Eventually, the plan was to be sure all hosts had DNS names, and the DNS was linked to DHCP for address assignment. Addresses in router configurations were also tied to scripts driven from the DNS database.

DHCP

DHCP and DNS are the foundations of an integrated address management strategy. To minimize the number of places you need to reconfigure in the event of renumbering, even servers should obtain their IP addresses from a DHCP server. When servers obtain addresses using DHCP, they should not use an option that gives them addresses with a lease time.

Yes, it is certainly plausible to say that setting up a separate DHCP server is not worth the effort in a very small network. If you had four workstations, a server, and a router, it would not be terribly difficult to renumber manually were you to change ISPs and use a new set of PA addresses.

If you doubled the size of your network and had eight workstations, two servers, and a router or two, it still might be convenient to go to 10 devices and change their addresses. Including time for moving from one machine to the next, it might take you 10 minutes to renumber each machine. Where it took an hour before, it now takes two hours. At some point, however, the time to travel to different machines, and even to log into each machine to reconfigure them, becomes significant.

You should look at DHCP first as a means of reducing your administrative workload and second as a means of reducing your need for IP addresses. In fact, it is perfectly reasonable never to use address leasing, if your clients and servers normally need Internet connectivity, either directly or through an address-translating gateway. In the former case, they need unique addresses to be reachable on the Internet, and in the latter, you can use abundant private address space on the inside and have no real reason to use dynamically leased addresses to conserve address space.

Think also of the skill level of the people who assign addresses to machines. A qualified network administrator is apt to maintain a DHCP server, but as less and less experienced people maintain workstations, there is more and more chance for error.

All too often, I have seen a novice administrator manage to configure his workstation and then copy his configuration—including his static IP address—and innocently give that configuration to a coworker, innocently saying, "Hey, this worked for me—you can try it." This practice, of course, introduces a duplicate address.

DHCP, and related services for dialup users, is the key to making address assignment relatively automatic. Chapter 11 deals with the client aspects of DHCP, and the focus now is on DHCP servers and their administration.

Evaluating DHCP Servers

Evaluating DHCP servers might be a slightly misleading phrase here because an ideal DHCP server product might be tightly coupled with other services such as DNS, SNMP, remote access services, firewalls, and so on. Nevertheless, let us look at features that might differentiate one DHCP server product from another:

- Backward compatibility with BOOTP

- Address configuration:

    - Manual specification based on MAC address, with or without lease times. If lease times are supported, can you configure them? At what level of granularity?

      Do you have to manually configure each address, or can you import a file of MAC and the associated IP addresses (and parameters)? Can you update the DHCP with interprocess communication from a script?

    - Automatic allocation from a range, without setting lease values.

      Dynamic allocation from a range, with support for leases. Can you manually set lease times, at the granularity of MAC addresses, MAC vendor codes, user classes, and so on?

- Interaction with name/directory services:

    - Dynamic DNS update, with or without security. Does the DNS server need to be on the same machine as DHCP?

- Is there an audit trail of assignments? Can this be sent to `syslog`?

- Interaction with name resolution services other than, or in addition to, DNS, including NETBios, NIS, and so on?

- Support for addressing variants:

  - Multiple subnets per medium or VLAN

  - Manual allocation of more than one IP address to a single MAC address

- Fault tolerance with multiple DHCP servers

DHCP servers must assure that only one client can use a given IP address at a given time.

When manual or automatic allocation is done, a client with a given identifier should get the same address assignment after each client reboot. Parameters other than addresses preferably should remain consistent over reboots, although it clearly makes no sense to keep giving the client the address of a router or DNS server known to be out of service.

DHCP Manual Allocation

Manually configuring the DHCP server to return a specific IP address and parameters based on a known MAC address gives the greatest possible control. The challenge in using this method is knowing the MAC address the client will use.

If the client supports local configuration of a MAC address, and the network administrator has the infrastructure in place to assign MAC addresses to specific devices, it is a good situation.

Local techniques can be developed to learn the MAC address on a switch port and make it available for network management.

DHCP Dynamic Allocation

The first challenge in using dynamic allocation is to decide on the appropriate lease time. If fault tolerance is needed, the next challenge is coordinating the activities of redundant servers so the same address is not assigned by more than one DHCP server.

First, consider if you have more users than you will have active IP addresses. This involves several factors:

- How many subnets do you have, either true LAN subnets or multiaccess subnets simulated by remote access servers? Is it plausible that all devices connected to a given LAN will be active at all times?

- Is it realistic that some devices can do useful work without IP addresses, because they use addresses in some other protocol family? Is this assumption reasonable on a long-term basis, with the general industry trend being migration to IP?

If you have more users than a requirement for active IP addresses, dynamic allocation with short lease times is reasonable. Times as low as 15 minutes have been suggested in the DHCP FAQ. Remember that a station starts trying to acquire a new address halfway through its lease time, so short lease times mean increasingly high workloads on the DHCP server. There has been a consensus on DHCP mailing lists that a two-hour lease adequately levels DHCP server load in plausible networks.

Do you have a reasonably good estimate of the duration of a typical user session? It's reasonable to set the lease time to slightly more than that session length.

Lease Considerations Related to Availability

What if the DHCP server is remote from a site, and the WAN link to that site fails? What is an acceptable time for a station to be down because it cannot acquire a new address after its lease expires, but it cannot reach the DHCP server? Of course, if the WAN link to the DHCP server is also the link for application server access, the point of not being able to acquire a client address becomes moot.

If the DHCP server itself fails, how long do you estimate it will take to restore it? Users might not notice a DHCP server failure if the lease time is sufficiently long that a DHCP server failure is corrected before they need to acquire or renew a leased address. Lease times for such situations typically are a small number of days.

Lease times of at least six days are necessary to avoid outages if a DHCP server, or connectivity to it, fails over a weekend and can be repaired on the first business day of the next week. To cover long holiday weekends, seven- to eight-day leases might be more appropriate.

Lease Considerations Related to Pseudo-Multicasting

There is no question that hard-coded IP addresses for servers are inflexible. Hard-coded IP addresses for workstations are even more inflexible. But there might be requirements, typically of old software, for stations informing one another of IP addresses. One area where this occurs is in collaborative applications or multiplayer interactive games, where multicast routing is not available. Participants in such collaborations often exchange IP addresses and explicitly set up group relationships among them, using multiple unicasts rather than true multicasts.

If you have such applications, and you use dynamic assignment, your lease times should be sufficiently long that, after one station learns the IP address of another, the IP address persists throughout the relationship among the stations. This sort of relationship really is undesirable and should be migrated to use multicasting.

When you do need such persistent assignments, lease times of weeks are reasonable requirements.

Server Leasing

It is generally undesirable to use dynamic assignment for servers, but there are cases when this practice might make sense. If you are assigning server addresses and do not use dynamic DNS update, it is reasonable to have long lease times.

If you use DHCP primarily to centralize address administration, there are cases where you might want to assign addresses for a long, but not indefinite, period. Think of the networks at a week-long trade show, or of setting up departmental servers for a semester at an educational institution. For a trade show, considering setup time, a lease of six to eight days is sensible. For educational use, a four-month lease would cover summer or trimester break outages.

DHCP Servers

Sun's Solaris typifies UNIX pure DHCP servers as distinct from integrated DHCP/DNS. Major components of the Sun DHCP server are shown in Figure 15.3. UNIX provides a reasonable infrastructure for scripts that link DHCP and DNS.

Remember that the DHCP server(s) must be reachable. If you do not have a server on each medium, you need to design DHCP relay agents in routers connected to those media in a manner that lets DHCP requests reach the servers.

Basic DHCP service has no redundancy mechanism. Achieving some fault tolerance with standard DHCP requires that you use one of the following:

- *Manual configuration*—If a host always gets the same IP address when it sends a DHCP request containing its unique client ID (usually a MAC address), there is no ambiguity if more than one server responds. Each server responds with the same IP address, as long as care has been taken to ensure that the IP address assignment tables are identical in both hosts.

- *Automatic configuration*—If automatic configuration is used, ensure that each server's assignable address range is unique.

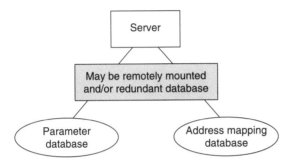

F I G U R E 1 5 . 3 . *The two parts of the DHCP database, one for addresses and one for parameters, complement the two daemons in the DHCP client.*

Protocols to synchronize multiple DHCP servers are in development, but are not yet widely accepted in products. Sun's DHCP/BOOTP server, shown in Figure 15.3, is built on two databases, one for parameter information and the other for address information. Parameters are defined in the dhcptab database. They are internally stored in a textual representation similar to that used by UNIX termcap terminal definitions.

The dhcp network database contains the mappings of client identifier to IP addresses. Using UNIX file-sharing protocols such as NFS, it is possible to share this database among several physical servers, potentially with backup copies of the database.

It is more general to have an explicit synchronization mechanism among DHCP databases rather than rely on UNIX mechanisms. The IETF is working on mechanisms for redundancy among DHCP servers.

Multicast Addressing

Multicast addresses have long been defined in the IPv4 address space as the Class D block, but their use has been limited. There is a great deal of interest in multicast applications, but there are also a great number of challenges in realizing multicasting. Among these challenges are interdomain multicast routing and reliable multicast.

Class D multicast addresses are 32-bit IP addresses like any other, and there is no reason that DNS cannot return a Class D address. Treating multicast addresses as completely general, however, is a significant operational risk. The need to replicate multicast packets can become a severe performance load on routers, and uncontrolled use of multicasting in the Internet can result in overloaded or failing routers and media.

The *administratively scoped IPv4 multicast space*—effectively the private address space for multicast routing—is defined as the range 239.0.0.0 through 239.255.255.255 [RFC 2365]. General Internet routers with multicast capability should not accept these addresses.

Generalized multicast routing among multiple AS remains a research problem, although there are a sufficient number of real-world applications for multicasting where the technology is being developed aggressively. At present, however, there is no production-quality solution. Mission-critical multicast applications should run over virtual private networks engineered for multicasting.

IPv6

IPv6 is a proposed replacement for the current IPv4 [RFC 1883]. It is controversial, and some respected networking experts consider it a solution in search of a problem. I think it will come into widespread use, but it will take a long period of time.

This section does not purport to be a complete discussion of IPv6, but focuses on the addressing issues. In particular, it describes the problems that IPv6 addressing innovations were meant to solve and the alternative IPv4 mechanisms that have evolved in response.

IPv6 has an overall objective of rationalizing the separately developed protocol mechanisms supporting IPv4. As discussed in the next section, the layout of the IPv6 header was optimized for hardware processing.

Another area of rationalization concerns the IPv6 equivalent of ARP. ARP for IPv4 runs directly over the data link layer and is not routable. In IPv6, the function equivalent to ARP, plus additional functions for router discovery, dead node detection, and so on, have been made part of ICMPv6. ICMP, with either IPv4 or IPv6, runs over IP and is routable. The ARP equivalents in IPv6 are called *neighbor discovery*.

Header and Options

When you compare an IPv4 packet header with an IPv6 packet header, you find their first four bits, the version number, are the only fields in common.

This lack of commonality in structure emphasizes the idea that IPv6 really is a completely new protocol, although it still provides most of the functions of IPv4.

As shown in Figure 15.4, IPv6 has a relatively small, fixed header followed by zero or more fixed-length optional headers. In contrast, IPv4 has a variable-length options field that follows the fixed header. The IPv6 assumption that there either will or will not be a header following each header, and, if present, each header will be of known length, is extremely efficient for hardware processing and is one of the arguments that IPv6 is superior at both ends of the transmission speed spectrum. At the low end, it puts minimum workload on the limited processing power of such devices as cellular phones. At the high end, it offers benefits for special-purpose forwarding processors that can operate at gigabit rates.

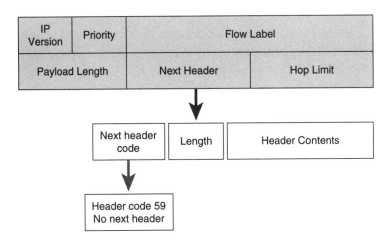

FIGURE 15.4. *The dark fields of the IPv6 header are fixed. Header extensions form a chain from the Next Header field of the fixed header, a chain which ends when the next header code is 59.*

IPv6 has three, not IPv4's two, basic address types:

- Unicast addresses have a meaning similar to that in IPv4. Each unicast address is associated with a single physical interface, although multiple unicast addresses can map to the same physical interface.

  A unicast address can map to multiple physical interfaces when that set of interfaces is treated as a single network layer point. This usage, for example, would be appropriate for multilink PPP, sharing the bandwidth of several media.

- Multicast addresses are also similar to the IPv4 usage. They identify a set of interfaces. When a packet is sent to a multicast address, it should be delivered to all interfaces in that set.

- Anycast addresses are a new idea in IPv6. Like multicast addresses, anycast addresses identify a set of interfaces. When a packet is sent to an anycast address, the routing system delivers one and only one packet to the nearest interface. *Nearest* is defined by criteria specific to the routing mechanisms in use.

The Basic IPv6 Address

IPv6 has 128-bit addresses. Contrary to urban legend, this is not primarily intended to add huge numbers of addresses to the global address space. Indeed, even with IPv6, there still needs to be restrictions on the size and update frequency of global routing tables.

Think about the increasingly finicky need to use the 32-bit IPv4 address space efficiently. Think of the complexity of renumbering if, during a provider change, you went from a /16 to a /20 prefix.

The length of the IPv6 space was intended to avoid the complexity of IPv4 practice. During the discussions on the final format of IPv6, there was considerable debate as to whether it should be 64 or 128 bits long. The consensus to go with 128 bits was not reached because 128 bits gave more host space. The consensus was reached because a larger address space gave more flexibility in autoconfiguration and routing.

Three ways to write IPv6 addresses in human-readable form have been defined:

- Preferred form: *x:x:x:x:x:x:x:x*, where *x* is a hexadecimal value of the corresponding 16 bits of the IPv6 address. Leading zeros are not required, but there must be a zero in each field.

- Alternate, *compressed*, form for addresses with many zeros: *x:x::x:x:x:x*, where the :: denotes several 16-bit groups of zeroes. Only one :: pattern is permitted in an address.

- Alternate form for IPv4 carried in IPv6: *x:x:x:x:x:x:d.d.d.d*, where the *x* values are hexadecimal equivalents of 16-bit values, and the *d* values are dotted-decimal octets.

IPv6 prefixes are written in a form based on IPv4 classless inter-domain routing (CIDR) conventions: `ipv6address/prefix-length`.

Addresses contain their own format identification, which is shown in Table 15.1. The complexity of the format identification convention is somewhere between the bit values that define IPv4 address classes and the Authority and Format Identifier in NSAP addresses.

TABLE 15.1. IPv6 FORMAT IDENTIFIERS.

Allocation	Prefix (Binary)	Fraction of Address Space
Reserved	0000 0000	1/256
Unassigned	0000 0001	1/256
Reserved for NSAP allocation	0000 001	1/128
Reserved for IPX allocation	0000 010	1/128
Unassigned	0000 011	1/128
Unassigned	0000 1	1/32
Unassigned	0001	1/16
Aggregatable global unicast addresses	001	1/8
Unassigned	010	1/8
Unassigned	011	1/8
Unassigned	100	1/8
Unassigned	101	1/8
Unassigned	110	1/8
Unassigned	1110	1/16
Unassigned	1111 0	1/32
Unassigned	1111 10	1/64
Unassigned	1111 110	1/128
Unassigned	1111 1110 0	1/512
Link-local unicast addresses	1111 1110 10	1/1024
Site-local unicast addresses	1111 1110 11	1/1024
Multicast addresses	1111 1111	1/256

Motivations for Using 128-Bit Addresses

The structure of IPv6 addresses and the associated address allocation administrative machinery have not been fully defined. All one can say definitively about an IPv6 address is that it is 128 bits long.

**IP and Star Trek—Coincidence?
You Decide**

Prior to the selection of the specific IPv6 proposal, the overall project was called IP, the Next Generation, or IPng, in conscious imitation of the *Star Trek* universe. I attended the Toronto IETF meeting where the final decision was made, and the consensus reached to have 128- rather than 64-bit addresses.

From this meeting, I do cherish some byplay in the audience. Someone on the podium had been speaking of how IPv4 had served us well for many years, and it was time for the Next Generation. A voice from the audience cried out, "But what

are we going to call the version that comes after IPv6?"

With lightning speed, another voice called out, "IP Deep Space 9!" The next available version number, incidentally, would in fact be IPv9.

Adding to the humor of the moment, someone else observed that at least one major internetworking company planned to support IPds9, because television's *Deep Space 9* is commanded by Benjamin Sisko. It was felt that a name change from Cisco to Sisko wasn't implausible in several centuries!

There certainly are proposals for structuring these addresses. IPv6 addresses, in one proposal [Hinden 1998b], are split into three parts, corresponding to the elements shown in Figure 15.5:

- *Public topology*, or the set of service providers and exchange points who provide public Internet connectivity services

- *Site topology*, or the internal connectivity among the various media of an enterprise

- *Interface identifier*, or the identifier of an interface that is local to a medium

In this model, exchanges have a quite different role than today's function as intercarrier *meet points*. In the new model, the role of an exchange is much more like a local telephone company. It assigns addresses to subscribers and provides connectivity to long-haul providers.

The long-haul provider part of the address is assigned at the exchange, so no renumbering is necessary when changing providers. Multihomed routing through multiple providers is also fairly simple, because the long-haul provider prefix is prepended by the exchange router.

Fields in the IPv6 address, shown in Figure 15.6, map to each level of the hierarchy.

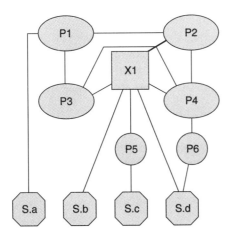

FIGURE 15.5. *The hierarchy includes top-level providers (P1 through P3), exchanges (X1 and X2), regional and local providers (P4 and P6), and subscribers (S.x).*

3	13	8	24	16	64	bits
FP	TLA	RES	NLA	SLA	Interface ID	

FP		Format prefix (001)
TLA	ID	Top-level aggregation identifier
RES		Reserved for future use
NLA	ID	Next-level aggregation identifier
SLA	ID	Site-level aggregation identifier
Interface ID		Interface identifier

FIGURE 15.6. *Hierarchical addressing lets a given router be concerned only with one or more fields starting at the left of the IPv6 address.*

Increased Host Space

In Chapter 6, "Internet Failing: Details at 11," you saw that the doomsayers who predict the end of the Internet, if they are technically knowledgeable, are really more concerned with the collapse of the routing system than exhaustion of the host address space.

When IPv4 addressing was classful, there was indeed concern over the shortage of host addresses. This was alleviated by two factors. CIDR helped make address allocation more efficient, simply wasting less. Another factor that alleviated demands on the registered address space was widespread use of address-translating firewalls, with the bulk of inside addresses in the private address space. This sort of address translation greatly limited the requirements for outside addresses.

From an architectural standpoint, address translation does break the IP assumption that addresses have end-to-end significance. Nowhere was this architectural violation more apparent than in the conflict with end-to-end security using IPsec. Although some IPsec modes run from user computer to security gateway, and then from security gateway to security gateway, many security experts believe the best security is end-to-end. End-to-end security requires end-to-end address significance.

Widespread use of end-to-end security mechanisms might reverse the easing of demand on registered addresses enabled by address-translating firewalls. In general, end-to-end IPsec is incompatible with firewalls. If end-to-end IPsec becomes widespread, I believe this will result in an address shortage and accelerate migration to IPv6.

Acquiring IPv6 Addresses

Remember that IPv6 can be considered an architecture as much as a specific protocol. It considerably extends the IPv4 addressing capabilities based on DHCP, with two methods for host configuration and a proposed protocol for router renumbering.

The first method of acquiring IPv6 addresses is based on DHCP, with changes to handle the differing IPv6 address structure. Operation of DHCPv6 is not significantly different from existing DHCP.

The second method, stateless autoconfiguration, offers considerable potential in reducing administration [RFC 1971]. It is reminiscent of self-configuration schemes used in OSI network addressing and, to a lesser extent, of AppleTalk network addressing.

Stateless Autoconfiguration

Stateless IPv6 autoconfiguration requires the underlying medium be multicast-capable. To understand its general principles of operation, you need to understand several IPv6 addressing terms:

- *Link-layer address*—An identifier at the data link layer that identifies an interface, such as an IEEE 802 MAC address, an E.164 address for ISDN, or an ATM NSAP address

- *Link-local address*—An interface address that is unique within the scope of a single medium and can be used to reach any other interface on the same medium

- *Site-local address*—An interface address that is unique within the site or enterprise, but not within global Internet address space

The first step in stateless autoconfiguration is for the node configuring itself to create a tentative link-local address and verify that no other device on the link is using this address. The node does so by sending an ICMPv6 Neighbor Solicitation message, soliciting a response from any device that is using the tentative address. A positive response that another device is using the address stops the autoconfiguration process. Alternate addressing can be defined, but is not part of the specification.

If the link-local address is unique, the host now has IP connectivity to other hosts on the same medium. To communicate with them, it prefixes a link-only prefix to its interface address.

To configure an address of site or global scope, the node needs to hear or solicit a Router Advertisement ICMPv6 message and learn the site- or globally-unique prefix from that message. After the node hears such a message, it puts the high-order bits of the advertised prefix into its own address.

Router Renumbering

Stateless autoconfiguration, especially when dynamically linked to DNS, obviously simplifies address administration within a site or enterprise. But how can administration of changing ISPs be simplified? What if the organization merges with another one and the site prefix changes?

A proposed router renumbering protocol for IPv6 routers complements the host-oriented function of stateless autoconfiguration [Crawford 1998]. This protocol has operations to add, change, or delete prefixes in use on the router.

Because routers are critical elements in network reliability, the router renumbering protocol has extra error-checking when compared with host protocols. A renumbering message contains the existing prefix to be altered. If the old prefix in the protocol message does not match the currently configured protocol, there is no effect. The protocol also has message sequencing and supplemental authentication.

IPv6/IPv4 Interaction

The main transition strategy proposed for moving from IPv4 to IPv6 is to tunnel the less prevalent protocol over the more prevalent one. In today's environment, IPv6 is rare, whereas IPv4 is common; so IPv6 experimentation in the global Internet involves the *6bone*, a set of IPv6 tunnels running over the general IPv4 Internet.

At such time as IPv6 becomes the dominant protocol in the Internet, the intention would be to tunnel IPv4 over IPv6. The address structures are already in place to do this, by prefixing IPv4 addresses with an IPv6 prefix that allows the IPv4 address to be reached via IPv6 routing.

Tunneling does impose additional overhead, and various approaches have been proposed to do network address translation between IPv6 and IPv4. These approaches are being explored in the IETF.

Bibliographic References

Chapter 1

ISO 7498. "Open Systems Interconnection Reference Model." International Organization for Standardization, 1984.

RFC 1518. Rekhter, Y. and T. Li. "An Architecture for IP Address Allocation with CIDR." 1993.

Chapter 2

ISO 7498. "Open Systems Interconnection Reference Model." International Organization for Standardization, 1984.

ISO 8646. "Internal Organization of the Network Layer." International Organization for Standardization, 1988.

ISO 9575. "OSI Routeing Framework." International Organization for Standardization, 1989.

ISO 10000. ISO Technical Report 10000. "Framework and Taxonomy of International Standardized Profiles (Part 1 and Part 2)." International Organization for Standardization, 1990.

RFC 822. Crocker, D. "Standard for the format of ARPA Internet text messages." 1982.

RFC 1700. Postel, J. and J. Reynolds. "Assigned Numbers." 1994.

RFC 1812. Baker, F. "Requirements for IP Version 4 Routers." 1995.

Chapter 3

gTLD-MoU. Generic Top Level Domain Memorandum of Understanding. www.gtld-mou.org/.

ISC. "DNS, BIND and load balancing." Internet Software Consortium. www.isc.org/bind-lb.html.

ISO 3166. "Codes for the representation of names of countries and their subdivisions—Part 1: Country codes." 1997.

NLANR. "Squid Internet Object Cache." National Laboratory for Applied Network Research (NLANR). http://squid.nlanr.net/Squid/.

RFC 1034. Mockapetris, P. "Domain Name System Concepts & Facilities." 1987.

RFC 1178. Libes, D. "Choosing a name for your computer." 1990.

RFC 1579. Bellovin, S. "Firewall-Friendly FTP." 1994.

RFC 2391. Srisuresh, P. and D. Gan. "Load Sharing Using IP Network Address Translation (LSNAT)." 1998.

Chapter 4

ATMForum AF-LANE-0084-000. ATM Forum Technical Committee. LAN Emulation over ATM, Version 2: LUNI Specification. 1997.

Cisco 1996 Cisco Systems. ISL Functional Specification. www.cisco.com/warp/public/741/4.html.

RFC 1209. Piscitello, D.M. and J. Lawrence. "Transmission of IP Datagrams over the SMDS Service." 1991.

RFC 1356. Malis, A., D. Robinson, and R. Ullmann. "Multiprotocol Interconnect on X.25 and ISDN in the Packet Mode." 1992.

RFC 1483. Heinanen, J. "Multiprotocol Encapsulation over ATM Adaptation Layer 5." 1993.

RFC 1490. Bradley, T., C. Brown, and A. Malis. "Multiprotocol Interconnect over Frame Relay." 1993.

RFC 1577. Laubach, M. "Classical IP and ARP over ATM." 1994.

RFC 2225. Laubach, M. and J. Halpern. "Classical IP and ARP over ATM." 1998.

RFC 2334. Luciani, J., G. Armitage, J. Halpern, and N. Doraswamy. "Server Cache Synchronization Protocol (SCSP)." 1998.

RFC 2390. Bradley, T., C. Brown, and A. Malis. "Inverse Address Resolution Protocol." 1998.

Chapter 5

RFC 760. Postel, J. DoD standard Internet Protocol. 1980.

RFC 791. Postel, J. Internet Protocol. 1981.

RFC 950. Mogul, J.C. and J. Postel. "Internet Standard Subnetting Procedure." 1985.

RFC 1332. McGregor, G. "The PPP Internet Protocol Control Protocol (IPCP)." 1992.

RFC 1701. Hanks, S., T. Li, D. Farinacci, and P. Traina. "Generic Routing Encapsulation (GRE)." 1994.

RFC 1702. Hanks, S., T. Li, D. Farinacci, and P. Traina. "Generic Routing Encapsulation over IPv4 Networks." 1994.

RFC 1812. Baker, F. "Requirements for IP Version 4 Routers." 1995.

RFC 1878. Pummill, T. and B. Manning. "Variable Length Subnet Table For IPv4." 1995.

RFC 1897. Hinden, R. and J. Postel. "IPv6 Testing Address Allocation." 1996.

RFC 1918. Rekhter, Y., B. Moskowitz, D. Karrenberg, G.J. de Groot, and E. Lear. "Address Allocation for Private Internets." Internet Engineering Task Force, 1996.

RFC 2050. Hubbard, K., M. Kosters, D. Conrad, D. Karrenberg, and J. Postel. "Internet Registry IP Allocation Guidelines." Internet Engineering Task Force, 1996.

Chapter 6

Huitema 1995. Huitema, C. *Routing in the Internet*. Englewood Cliffs, NJ: Prentice Hall, 1995.

O'Dell 1996. O'Dell, M. Posting to Internet Engineering Task Force Multiprotocol Label Switching (MPLS) Working Group Mailing List. "A Connection Based Internet?" December 17, 1996.

Partan 1995. Partan, A.S. October 1995 private communication cited in RFC 2008.

RFC 1338. Fuller, V., T. Li, J. Yu, and K. Varadhan. "Supernetting: An Address Assignment and Aggregation Strategy." 1992.

RFC 1517. Hinden, R. "Applicability Statement for the Implementation of Classless Inter-Domain Routing (CIDR)." 1993.

RFC 1518. Rekhter, Y. and T. Li. "An Architecture for IP Address Allocation with CIDR." 1993.

RFC 1519. Fuller, V., T. Li, J. Yu, and K. Varadhan. "Classless Inter-Domain Routing (CIDR): An Address Assignment and Aggregation Strategy." 1993.

RFC 1520. Rekhter, Y. and C. Topolcic. "Exchanging Routing Information Across Provider Boundaries in the CIDR Environment." 1993.

RFC 1631. Egevang, K. and P. Francis. "The IP Network Address Translator (NAT)." 1994.

RFC 1918. Rekhter, Y., B. Moskowitz, D. Karrenberg, G.J. de Groot, and E. Lear. "Address Allocation for Private Internets." Internet Engineering Task Force, 1996.

RFC 1930. Hawkinson, J. and T. Bates. "Guidelines for Creation, Selection, and Registration of an Autonomous System (AS)." 1996.

RFC 2050. Hubbard, K., M. Kosters, D. Conrad, K. Karrenberg, and J. Postel. "Internet Registry IP Allocation Guidelines." Internet Engineering Task Force, 1996.

RFC 2072. Berkowitz, H. "Router Renumbering Guide." Internet Engineering Task Force, 1997.

RFC 2391. Srisuresh, Pyda and Kjeld Egevang. "The IP Network Address Translator (NAT)." 1998.

Chapter 7

Chapman 1996. Chapman, B. and E. Zwick. *Building Internet Firewalls.* O'Reilly, 1996.

Cheswick 1994. Cheswick, W. and S. Bellovin. *Firewalls and Internet Security: Foiling the Wily Hacker.* Reading, MA: Addison-Wesley, 1994.

L2TP. Rubens, A., W. Palter, T. Kolar, G. Pall, M. Littlewood, A. Valencia, K. Hamzeh, W. Verthein, J. Taarud, and W. Townsley. "Layer Two Tunneling Protocol 'L2TP.'" Internet Engineering Task Force, Work in Progress.

Libicki 1995. Libicki, M. "What is Information Warfare?" National Defense University, ACIS Paper 3, August 1995. www.ndu.edu/ndu/inss/actpubs/act003/a003.html.

RFC 1108. Kent, S. "U.S. Department of Defense Security Options for the Internet Protocol." November 1991.

RFC 1492. Finseth, C. "An Access Control Protocol, Sometimes Called TACACS." Internet Engineering Task Force, 1993.

RFC 1775. Crocker, D. "To be 'on' the Internet." 1995.

RFC 1812. Baker, F. "Requirements for IP Version 4 Routers." 1995.

RFC 1825. Atkinson, R. "Security Architecture for the Internet Protocol." Internet Engineering Task Force, 1995.

RFC 2138. Rigney, C., A. Rubens, W. Simpson, and S. Willens. "Remote Authentication Dial In User Service (RADIUS)." Internet Engineering Task Force, 1997.

RFC 2233. McCloghrie, K. and F. Kastenholz. "The Interfaces Group MIB using SMIv2." 1997.

RFC 2271. Harrington, D., R. Presuhn, and B. Wijnen. "An Architecture for Describing SNMP Management Frameworks."

Waldbusser, S. "Remote Network Monitoring Management Information Base." 1991.

Chapter 8

Berkowitz. Berkowitz, H. "Will the Real X.25 Please Stand Up?" Corporation for Open Systems OSI Interoperability Symposium, 1988.

Chappell. Chappell, L. *A Guide to NetWare LAN Analysis.* Alameda, CA: Novell Press, 1993.

Ranade. Ranade, Jay and George Sackett. *Introduction to Sna Networking: A Professional's Guide to Vtam/Ncp.* McGraw-Hill Series on Computer Communications, 1995.

RFC 1001. "Protocol Standard for a NetBIOS Service on a TCP/UDP Transport: Concepts and Methods." NetBIOS Working Group, 1987.

RFC 1002. "Protocol Standard for a NetBIOS Service on a TCP/UDP Transport: Detailed Specifications." NetBIOS Working Group, 1987.

RFC 1234. D. Provan. "Tunneling IPX traffic through IP networks," 1991.

RFC 1434. Dixon, R. and D. Kushi. "Data Link Switching: Switch-to-Switch Protocol." 1993.

RFC 1490. Bradley, T., C. Brown, and A. Malis. "Multiprotocol Interconnect over Frame Relay." 1993.

RFC 1795. Wells, L. and A. Bartky. "Data Link Switching: Switch-to-Switch Protocol AIW DLSw RIG: DLSw Closed Pages, DLSw Standard Version 1." 1995.

RFC 2114. Chiang, S., J. Lee, and H. Yasuda. "Data Link Switching Client Access Protocol." 1997.

Chapter 9

Berkowitz 1998a. Berkowitz, H. "To Be Multihomed: Requirements and Definitions." Internet Engineering Task Force, Work in progress, 1998.

RFC 1918. Rekhter, Y., B. Moskowitz, D. Karrenberg, G.J. de Groot, and E. Lear. "Address Allocation for Private Internets." Internet Engineering Task Force, February 1996.

RFC 1930. Hawkinson, J. and T. Bates. "Guidelines for Creation, Selection, and Registration of an Autonomous System (AS)." Internet Engineering Task Force, March 1996.

RFC 2050. Hubbard, K., M. Kosters, D. Conrad, D. Karrenberg, and J. Postel. "Internet Registry IP Allocation Guidelines." Internet Engineering Task Force, November 1996.

RFC 2071. Ferguson, P. and H. Berkowitz. "Network Renumbering Overview: Why Would I Want It and What Is It Anyway?" January 1997.

RFC 2072. Berkowitz, H. Request for Comments (RFC) RFC 1930. "Router Renumbering Guide." Internet Engineering Task Force, January 1997.

Chapter 10

Albitz & Liu. Albitz, P. and C. Liu. *Managing DNS and BIND, 2nd Edition.* Sebastopol, CA: O'Reilly, 1997.

Rekhter 1998. Rekhter, Y. "Interaction Between DHCP and DNS." IETF DHCP Working Group, Work in Progress.

RFC 1033. Lottor, M. "Domain Administrators Operations Guide." 1987.

RFC 1034. Mockapetris, P. "Domain Name System Concepts & Facilities." 1987.

RFC 1995. Ohta, M. "Incremental Zone Transfer in DNS." 1996.

RFC 2136. Vixie, P., Y. Rekhter, S. Thomson, and J. Bound. "Dynamic Updates in the Domain Name System (DNS Update)." 1997.

RFC 2137. Eastlake, D. "Secure Domain Name System Update." 1997.

RFC 2317. Eidnes, H., G.J. de Groot, and P. Vixie. "Classless IN-ADDR.ARPA Delegation." 1998.

RFC 2391. Srisuresh, P. and D. Gan. "Load Sharing using IP Network Address Translation (LSNAT)." 1998.

Chapter 11

RFC 0951. Croft, W.J. and J. Gilmore. "Bootstrap Protocol." 1985.

RFC 1775. Crocker, D. "To be 'on' the Internet." 1995.

RFC 1918. Rekhter, Y., B. Moskowitz, D. Karrenberg, G.J. de Groot, and E. Lear. "Address Allocation for Private Internets." Internet Engineering Task Force, February 1996.

RFC 2050. Hubbard, K., M. Kosters, D. Conrad, D. Karrenberg, and J. Postel. "Internet Registry IP Allocation Guidelines." Internet Engineering Task Force, 1996.

RFC 2131. Droms, R. "Dynamic Host Configuration Protocol." 1997.

RFC 2132. Alexander, S. and R. Droms. "DHCP Options and BOOTP Vendor Extensions." 1997.

Chapter 12

RFC 1613. Forster, J., G. Satz, G. Glick, and R. Day. "Cisco Systems X.25 over TCP (XOT)." 1994.

Chapter 13

GateD. GateD Consortium home page. www.gated.org/.

McClimans 1998. McClimans, F. "Bay Tries New Route Around Cisco." *Network World Fusion*. www.nwfusion.com/forum/0706current.html.

RFC 1058. Hedrick, C.L. "Routing Information Protocol." 1988

RFC 1356. Malis, A., D. Robinson, and R. Ullmann. "Multiprotocol Interconnect on X.25 and ISDN in the Packet Mode." 1992.

RFC 1542. Wimer, W. "Clarifications and Extensions for the Bootstrap Protocol." 1993.

RFC 1586. deSouza, O. and M. Rodrigues. "Guidelines for Running OSPF over Frame Relay Networks." 1994.

RFC 1812. Baker, F. "Requirements for IP Version 4 Routers." 1995.

RFC 2281. Li, T., B. Cole, P. Morton, and D. Li. "Cisco Hot Standby Router Protocol (HSRP)." 1998.

RFC 2338. Knight, S., D. Weaver, D. Whipple, R. Hinden, D. Mitzel, P. Hunt, P. Higginson, M. Shand, and A. Lindem. "Virtual Router Redundancy Protocol." 1998.

Chapter 14

Chapman & Zwicky. Chapman, D.B. and E.D. Zwicky. *Building Internet Firewalls*. Reading, MA: O'Reilly, 1996.

Cheswick & Bellovin. Cheswick, W. and S. Bellovin. *Firewalls and Internet Security: Foiling the Wily Hacker*. Reading, MA: Addison-Wesley, 1994.

Ferguson & Huston. Ferguson, P. and G. Huston. *Quality of Service: Delivering QoS on the Internet and in Corporate Networks*. New York, NY: John Wiley & Sons, 1998.

RFC 1434. Dixon, R. and D. Kushi. "Data Link Switching: Switch-to-Switch Protocol." 1993.

RFC 1483. Heinanen, J. "Multiprotocol Encapsulation over ATM Adaptation Layer 5." 1993.

RFC 1613. Forster, J., G. Satz, G. Glick, and R. Day. "Cisco Systems X.25 over TCP (XOT)." 1994.

RFC 1701. Hanks, S., T. Li, D. Farinacci, and P. Traina. "Generic Routing Encapsulation (GRE)." 1994.

RFC 1702. Hanks, S., T. Li, D. Farinacci, and P. Traina. "Generic Routing Encapsulation over IPv4 networks." 1994.

RFC 1795. Wells, L., Chair, and A. Bartky, Editor. "Data Link Switching: Switch-to-Switch Protocol AIW DLSw RIG: DLSw Closed Pages, DLSw Standard Version 1." 1995.

RFC 2309. Braden, B., D. Clark, J. Crowcroft, B. Davie, S. Deering, D. Estrin, S. Floyd, V. Jacobson, G. Minshall, C. Partridge, L. Peterson, K. Ramakrishnan, S. Shenker, J. Wroclawski, and L. Zhang. "Recommendations on Queue Management and Congestion Avoidance in the Internet." 1998.

RFC 2427. Brown, C. and A. Malis. "Multiprotocol Interconnect Over Frame Relay." 1998.

Chapter 15

Crawford. Crawford, M. and B. Hinden. "Router Renumbering for IPv6." Internet Engineering Task Force, Work in Progress, 1998.

Hinden 1998b. Hinden, R., M. O'Dell, and S. Deering. "An IPv6 Aggregatable Global Unicast Address Format." Internet Engineering Task Force, Work in Progress, 1998.

RFC 1883. Deering, S. and R. Hinden. "Internet Protocol, Version 6 (IPv6) Specification." 1995.

RFC 1971. Thomson, S. and T. Narten. "IPv6 Stateless Address Autoconfiguration." 1996.

RFC 2365. Meyer, D. "Administratively Scoped IP Multicast." 1998.

Index